Scripture as Logos

DIVINATIONS: REREADING LATE ANCIENT RELIGION

Series Editors

Daniel Boyarin
Virgina Burrus
Charlotte Fonrobert
Robert Gregg

A complete list of books in the series is available from the publisher.

Scripture as Logos

Rabbi Ishmael and the
Origins of Midrash

AZZAN YADIN

PENN

University of Pennsylvania Press

Philadelphia

10 9 8 7 6 5 4 3 2 1

Published by
University of Pennsylvania Press
Philadelphia, Pennsylvania 19104-4011

Library of Congress Cataloguing-in-Publication Data

Yadin, Azzan.
    Scripture as logos : Rabbi Ishmael and the origins of midrash / Azzan Yadin.
        p. cm.—(Divinations)
    Includes bibliographical references and index.
    ISBN 0-8122-3791-9 (cloth : alk. paper)
    1. Mekhilta of Rabbi Ishmael—Hermeneutics. 2. Sifrei. Numbers—Hermeneutics.
3. Bible. O.T. Exodus—Criticism, interpretation, etc., Jewish. 4. Bible. O.T. Numbers—
Criticism, interpretation, etc., Jewish. 5. Halakhic Midrashim—History and criticism—
Theory, etc. I. Title. II. Series.

BM517.M43Y33 2004
296.1′41—dc22   2003070539

νοῦς; beautiful; the most beautiful of all . . .

Plotinus, *Enneads* iii.8.11 (MacKenna, p. 250)

אשתו כגופו אחר לאו כגופו

ברכות כד ע״ב

Contents

Legal Midrash

In the introduction to his book *Midrash and Theory*, David Stern reflects on the study of midrash and the dramatic changes it has seen over the course of the last two decades. Observing a process in which he has played a central role, Stern argues, "Under the impact of theory, midrash has gone through a veritable sea change. The focus of the field, its methods, and its conceptual premises, have all experienced a fundamental, radical transformation."[1] He then goes on to cite "a few of the most important books,"[2] among them *Midrash and Literature*, Daniel Boyarin's *Carnal Israel* and *Intertextuality and the Reading of Midrash*, James Kugel's *In Potiphar's House*, José Faur's *Golden Doves with Silver Dots*, Steven Fraade's *From Tradition to Commentary*, Michael Fishbane's *The Garments of Torah*, and Stern's own *Parables in Midrash*.[3]

The list is striking for its heterogeneity. The authors employ a wide array of literary and theoretical approaches, applying them to a great number of midrashic texts. But these works also have something in common—they all deal primarily with aggadic midrash, the homiletic or nonlegal midrash. The focus on the aggadic material is particularly evident in Boyarin's *Intertextuality and the Reading of Midrash* and Fraade's *From Tradition to Commentary*, since both are studies of works that are mostly halakhic—the Mekhilta of Rabbi Ishmael and the Sifre Deuteronomy, respectively—but concentrate on the aggadic pericopes. Menahem Kahana's comparison of the Mekhilta of Rabbi Ishmael and the Mekhilta of Rabbi Shimon bar Yohai also deals with an aggadic tractate, while Jay Harris's *How Do We Know This?: Midrash and the Fragmentation of Modern Judaism* studies legal midrash largely as interpreted by later generations, not in and of itself. The exception that proves this rule is Moshe Halbertal's *Interpretive Revolutions in the Making*, a study of axiology in the interpretive process, but his remains a solitary voice in the study of midrash.[4]

Midrash Halakhah

The current study is devoted to the Mekhilta of Rabbi Ishmael and the Sifre Numbers, two of the *midreshei halakhah*, or halakhic midrashim.

Unlike the Mishnah and the Tosefta, the halakhic midrashim present tannaitic legal discussion in the form of a running commentary to the Torah. They deal mostly with legal matters but contain sizable aggadic sections, in keeping with the structure of the biblical book expounded. There is no halakhic midrash to Genesis, owing to the paucity of legal material in that book. The following halakhic midrashim survive as relatively complete texts: Mekhilta of Rabbi Ishmael to Exodus,[5] Sifra to Leviticus,[6] Sifre Numbers,[7] and Sifre Deuteronomy.[8] In addition, modern scholars have produced editions of halakhic midrashim using medieval citations, material embedded in other collections, and fragments from the Cairo Genizah: Mekhilta of Rabbi Shimon bar Yohai, Sifre Zuta, Midrash Tannaim, and Sifre Zuta Deuteronomy, published by Menahem Kahana.[9] The Cairo Genizah continues to yield important findings regarding the textual traditions of the halakhic midrashim.[10] I accept the consensus view that the legal midrashim contain mostly tannaitic material, that underwent a redactional process that probably began in the second century B.C.E. (for the earliest redactional stratum of the Mekhilta) and concluded in the fourth century, though many additions were undoubtedly made after that point.[11]

Rabbi Ishmael and Rabbi Aqiva

In 1888, David Hoffmann published *Zur Einleitung in die halachischen Midraschim*, in which he showed that the halakhic midrashim form two groups, each with its own terminology, interpretive methods, and rabbinic figures cited.[12] The Mekhilta and the Sifre Numbers form one group, and the Sifra and the Sifre Deuteronomy form another. Hoffman explained this discrepancy in source-critical terms: the Mekhilta and the Sifre Numbers originate in the school of Rabbi Ishmael, and the Sifra and the Sifre Deuteronomy in the school of Rabbi Aqiva. Hoffmann's hypothesis has met with widespread approval, particularly among Israeli scholars, largely due to the enduring influence of J. N. Epstein's *Prolegomena to Tannaitic Literature*, the third section of which is an analysis of the halakhic midrashim and their school affiliation.[13]

Another scholar who took over Hoffmann's interpretation of the halakhic midrashim, but developed it in a very different direction, is Abraham Joshua Heschel in his *Theology of Ancient Judaism* (*Torah min hashamayim*).[14] In this work, Heschel analyzes a series of rabbinic disputes (sometimes extending into medieval texts) that he attributes to theological differences between the schools of Rabbi Ishmael and Rabbi Aqiva. Heschel makes sweeping claims about the two schools, often at the expense of more nuanced readings and a fuller consideration of the historical setting of the various corpora that make up rabbinic literature.[15]

Nonetheless, *Theology of Ancient Judaism* is a work of lasting value, particularly for its insistence that interpretive differences in midrash halakhah embody meaningful conceptual and theological differences—an aspect of these texts often neglected by those scholars whose interest is purely philological.

Despite their differences, Heschel and the philological scholars share a belief in the basic reliability of halakhic midrashim (and rabbinic literature in general) as historical witnesses—that is, the notion that the midrashim provide a relatively unmediated vista to the historical figures whose sayings they purport to preserve.[16] This view is no longer tenable. A great deal of scholarship has been done on the problematic historical status of rabbinic literature in general and rabbinic biography in particular, and it is clear that the historical information contained in rabbinic literature cannot be lifted directly from the text—if at all.[17] Dealing specifically with the attribution of the tannaitic midrashim to the schools of Rabbi Aqiva and Rabbi Ishmael, Jay Harris has argued that the references to "Rabbi Aqiva" and "Rabbi Ishmael" as markers of distinctive interpretive traditions in the Babylonian and Jerusalem Talmuds are largely a product of amoraic (or later) rabbinic redactors.[18] The force of Harris's claim is not completely clear, as he does not systematically analyze the halakhic midrashim as such, since his focus is the reception of midrash in later Jewish writings, but the argument can be understood as denying the division as such. If that is Harris's claim, two responses are possible and, with them, two corresponding ways to maintain the Rabbi Aqiva–Rabbi Ishmael distinction as a useful tool. First, Harris does not speak to the findings of Hoffmann, Epstein, and their followers, especially Menahem Kahana, who have identified distinctive patterns of terminology, rabbinic authorities cited, and hermeneutical methods typical to each school, and these remain significant even if the source-critical association with Rabbi Aqiva and Rabbi Ishmael is challenged. On such a reading, the phrases "Rabbi Ishmael" and "Rabbi Ishmael midrashim" are not making claims about the authorship of the midrashim; rather, they function as a shorthand for a set of distinct and recognizable interpretive practices, assumptions, and terms that appear in the halakhic sections of the Mekhilta of Rabbi Ishmael and Sifre Numbers.[19] Second, Harris does not address the most obvious question that arises from his findings: What caused the two Talmuds—each in its distinct fashion and independently of each other—to construct disputes around the names of Rabbi Aqiva and Rabbi Ishmael? Absent an explanation, it is most probable that the Talmuds are extending and elaborating a distinction that each received from tannaitic literature regarding the two interpretive schools. Harris may be right regarding the forced and artificial nature of some of the derashot that employ the Rabbi Aqiva–Rabbi

Ishmael distinction.[20] But on a deeper cultural level, the drive of the Palestinian and the Babylonian Talmuds to maintain these constructs argues that both are grappling with a tannaitic identification of Rabbi Aqiva and Rabbi Ishmael as representatives of distinct midrashic schools. The tannaitic division likely reflected in the amoraic constructs need not be historically accurate, but it would represent a culturally consistent representation of the tannaim in question as interpreters. So while it is historically naïve to accept the dominant role of Rabbi Ishmael and his students in the Mekhilta and the Sifre Numbers as proof of authorship or school affiliation, it may be culturally illuminating at certain junctures to compare the midrashim with the representation of Rabbi Ishmael elsewhere in rabbinic literature.

The minimalist understanding of "Rabbi Ishmael midrashim" as containing particular interpretive techniques, sages, terminology, and the like limits the scope of investigation to the halakhic sections of the midrashim. For whatever reason, the aggadic sections do not fit the criteria of a Rabbi Ishmael text. For example, one characteristic used to identify a text as "Ishmaelian" is the names of the sages cited therein. Epstein noted that different sages are mentioned in the various tractates of the Mekhilta:[21] thus in the first tractate, Pisha, Rabbi Ishmael is mentioned twenty-nine times; his students Rabbi Yonathan and Rabbi Yoshaiah eighteen and fifteen times, respectively; and Rabbi Aqiva, his chief disputant, fourteen times. Yet in the next four tractates—be-Shalah, Shirata', va-Yesa', and 'Amaleq—his name is mentioned once in each of the first three and never in the fourth. The references to his students are likewise few. He then returns to a position of prominence in Bahodesh, Neziqin, Kaspa', and Shabta'. The four tractates that contain the fewest references to Rabbi Ishmael deal, not coincidentally, with the aggadic sections of Exodus. A similar situation holds in the Sifre Numbers, where §78–§106, §131, and §134–§141 contain almost no references to Rabbi Ishmael or to his students.[22] These sections will be used as little as possible. It should also be noted that there are sections identified with the Rabbi Ishmael school in the Sifra, especially parts of the tractate Qedoshim.[23] So, while my decision to concentrate on legal midrash is motivated primarily by literary and philosophical concerns, it also is consistent with the findings of philological scholarship regarding the "Ishmaelian" elements in the midrashim.

Though this study is not a full-fledged comparison between the Rabbi Ishmael and Rabbi Aqiva midrashim, there will be throughout references to the Rabbi Aqiva midrash par excellence, the Sifra. These brief comments are intended to show that the Mekhilta and the Sifre Numbers present a distinct hermeneutical approach to Scripture.[24]

Manuscripts and Translations

Though the primary focus of this study is hermeneutic, not philological, I quote the rabbinic sources according to the best manuscripts for each: MS Oxford 151 for the Mekhilta, MS Vatican 32 for the Sifre Numbers and Sifre Deuteronomy, MS Vatican 66 for the Sifra, and MS Kaufmann for the Mishnah. I have reproduced the rabbinic Hebrew in these manuscripts, completing standard abbreviations where necessary and with occasional linguistic comments, especially concerning MS Vatican 32, which some scholars consider the finest full manuscript in all of rabbinic literature.[25] When faced with unsustainable readings I have departed from the manuscripts and quote according to the critical editions: Horovitz's edition of the Sifre Numbers, the Horovitz-Rabin edition of the Mekhilta, and the Finkelstein edition of the Sifre Deuteronomy.[26] The Sifre Numbers is cited by section number and page number in Horovitz's edition, while the Mekhilta (throughout this study, "Mekhilta" refers to the Mekhilta of Rabbi Ishmael) is cited by tractate, section, and page number in Horovitz-Rabin. I have used Jacob Lauterbach's elegant translation of the Mekhilta, reworking it as necessary to clarify points critical to the discussion, and cite Lauterbach (by volume and page number) as well.[27] There is currently no full English translation of the Sifre Numbers. Jacob Neusner has translated §§1–115, but the work is not yet complete, so I have translated the passages from the Sifre Numbers myself. The Mishnah translation is based on Herbert Danby's, with occasional changes.[28] An important resource for the study of Rabbi Ishmael is Gary Porton's survey of all the sayings attributed to Rabbi Ishmael in the major tannaitic and amoraic sources.[29] For biblical citations, I use the new Jewish Publication Society translation as a base, modifying it as needed in light of the ensuing midrashic discussion.[30] I transliterate Hebrew words and short phrases, but cite the original in Hebrew for longer citations. The transliteration is standard, but is not used for names or words that are commonplace in English, thus שומע אני is transliterated shome'a 'ani, but רבי ישמעאל is "Rabbi Ishmael" and not "Rabbi Ishma' 'el."

Finally, I cite the Rabbi Ishmael midrashim frequently and, at times, at some length. This is necessary for two reasons. First, my conclusions do not always agree with current scholarly consensus, and I wish to replicate for the reader, as far as possible, the process that led me to these conclusions. Second, though I am well aware of the role of the reader in any interpretive act, on a very basic level I feel that my role is to clarify and organize the Rabbi Ishmael midrashim such that they—impossibly—speak for themselves.

Introduction

On the Hermeneutic Dimension of Midrash Halakhah

The present study is concerned with the legal hermeneutics of the Rabbi Ishmael midrashim, not with their legal conclusions. The study asks how the Mekhilta and the Sifre Numbers interpret Torah and what assumptions regarding Torah, language, and interpretation inform and determine this process. This approach is controversial among many scholars of legal midrash, and I would like to address a number of arguments that have been made against a hermeneutical approach to legal midrash.[1] The first is historical: that legal midrashim served only to justify existing halakhic traditions and are thus hermeneutically vacuous. This argument is tied to a long-standing debate concerning the relationship between legal midrash and the non-midrashic, apodictic presentation of rabbinic law, without recourse to scriptural authority (the Mishnah and the Tosefta). Opinion has shifted over the past century as to which of these forms, midrashic or apodictic, is the original. According to some scholars, rabbinic law was from the earliest times an interpretive enterprise that only later came to be formulated in nonexegetic legal codices (the various "mishnahs," of which one, Rabbi Yehudah ha-Nasi's, came to be *the* Mishnah). Others argue that legal midrash is a late attempt to buttress existing legal traditions by grounding them in Scripture.[2] The most influential advocate of the latter position is J. N. Epstein, who claimed that halakhic exegesis aims to support existing legal decisions.[3] On this interpretation, legal midrash is essentially derivative and should be read in light of its halakhic orientation and not as an independent hermeneutical activity.

These objections are spurious. Even if it could be established that the authors of the midrashim saw themselves as handmaidens to existing legal decisions (and, for the Rabbi Ishmael midrashim, it cannot), they nonetheless undertook a sustained literary and cultural project that is irreducibly hermeneutical. Indeed, even if the Rabbis had voiced vehement opposition to midrashic interpretation (and they did not), reading a text against the aims of its author is not an act of methodological daring; it is standard procedure in the humanities and has been for decades.

But this is all hypothetical—there is no need to read the legal midrashim against the grain, since they openly and explicitly engage in interpretive discourse. Particularly pertinent in this regard are the derashot that record differences of interpretation even though the disputants reach the same legal conclusion. The Mekhilta teaches:

"[אל תאכל ממנו נא] ובשל מבושל במים" (שמות יב ט): אין לי אלא מים שאר כל המשקין מנין. היה רבי ישמעאל אומר אמרת קל וחומר היא ומה אם מים שאינן מפנין את טעמן מנין הרי הן אסורין בבישול שאר המשקין שהן מפנין את טעמן דין   הוא שיהיו אסורין בבישול. ר' עקיבה אומר אין לי אלא מים שאר כל המשקין מנין   תלמוד לומר "ובשל מבושל" להביא שאר המשקין.

"[Do not eat any of it raw] or cooked [*bashel mevushal*] in any way with water" (Exod 12:9): From this I know only that it is forbidden to boil it in water. From where do I learn regarding boiling it in other liquids? Rabbi Ishmael used to say: You can reason by *qol va-ḥomer*[4] [inference from minor to major premises]. If it is forbidden to boil it in water, which has no taste to impart, it follows that it should be forbidden to boil it in other liquids that have a taste of their own to impart. Rabbi Aqiva says: From this I only know that it is forbidden to boil it in water. From where do I learn regarding boiling it in other liquids? The scriptural expression *bashel mevushal* includes all other liquids in the prohibition. (Mekhilta Pisḥa 6, pp. 20–21; Lauterbach 1.49)

Exodus 12:9 describes the preparation of the paschal offering, specifying that it is not to be eaten raw or cooked in water. The question raised by both Rabbi Aqiva and Rabbi Ishmael is whether this prohibition applies to cooking in water or, more broadly, to cooking in any liquid. Rabbi Ishmael reasons by *qol va-ḥomer*, inference from minor to major premises, that since it is prohibited to cook in the most neutral liquid, how much more so for other liquids. Rabbi Aqiva argues that the repetition of the root *b-sh-l* (cook) in the phrase *bashel mevushal* (a hyperliteral translation that reflects the doubling: "in cooking cooked") indicates that it applies to other liquids as well. The two reach the same legal conclusion: cooking paschal offerings in liquids other than water is prohibited. The debate is of no halakhic consequence—indeed the conclusion may be preordained, recognized by both sides as current practice, or otherwise uncontroversial. Nonetheless, the speakers debate the various interpretive approaches by which this legal conclusion is reached, and the debate is preserved in the Mekhilta as culturally (if not halakhically) important. Derashot of this type demonstrate that even if the interpretations support established legal traditions, the *midreshei halakhah* consider the interpretive path by which a decision is reached a significant topic in its own right. Numerous derashot record interpretive disputes that lead to the same conclusion.[5]

It might be objected that Rabbi Aqiva and Rabbi Ishmael were not, in fact, debating the matter; rather, the redactor of the Mekhilta juxtaposed independent arguments. This objection is beside the point, since the jux-taposition of interpretive disputes that have no halakhic import is cul-turally significant even if it is done by the redactor. The Mekhilta is concerned with hermeneutics, irrespective of the context of the derashot prior to their inclusion in the Mekhilta. Moreover, in other derashot, disputants explicitly address the hermeneutical shortcomings of their interlocutors:

"[כי יתן איש אל רעהו כסף או כלים לשמר וגנב מבית האיש אם ימצא האיש הגנב ישלם שנים. אם לא ימצא הגנב] ונקרב בעל הבית אל האלהים [אם לא שלח ידו במלאכת רעהו . . . על כל אבדה אשר יאמר כי הוא זה עד האלהים יבא דבר שניהם אשר ירשיען אלהים ישלים שנים לרעהו]" (שמות כב ו-ח): הרי אחד, "עד האלהים יבא דבר שניהם," הרי שנים, "אשר ירשיעון אלהים" הרי שלשה,6 מכאן אמרו דיני ממונות בשלשה, דברי ר' יאשיה. ר' יונתן אומר, הראשון תחלה נאמר ואין דורשין תחלות. "עד האלהים יבא דבר שניהם," הרי אחד, "אשר ירשיעון אלהים," הרי שנים, ואין בית דין שקול, מוסיפין עליהם עוד אחד, הרי שלשה.

"[When a man gives money or goods to another for safekeeping, and they are stolen from the man's house—if the thief is caught, he shall pay double; if the thief is not caught] the owner of the house shall depose before *ha-'elohim* [that he had not laid hands on the other's property . . . or any other loss, whereof one party alleges 'This is it'—the case of both parties shall come before *ha-'elohim*: he whom *'elohim* declares guilty shall pay double to the other]" (Exod 22:6–8): Behold this is one. "Both parties shall come before God," this makes two. "He whom God declares guilty," behold this makes three. Hence the sages said: Civil cases [*mammonot*] must be tried by a tribunal of three. These are the words of Rabbi Yoshaiah. Rabbi Yonathan says: As regards the first of these passages—that is the very statement of the subject. And the first statements cannot be employed for any special interpretation. "Both parties shall come before God," this is one. "He whom God declares guilty," this makes two. And since the tribunal must not be evenly balanced, we add one more, thus making three. (Mekhilta Neziqin 15, p. 302; Lauterbach 3.119)

Exodus 22:6–8 states that under certain conditions, people involved in a dispute should depose before *ha-'elohim*, a term that is interpreted in the school of Rabbi Ishmael, perhaps rightly, as meaning "judges." Rabbi Yoshaiah argues that *'elohim* appears three times, and this indicates that there must be three judges sitting on a civil case. Rabbi Yonathan rejects this argument, as it violates the hermeneutical rule that "first statements cannot be employed for any special interpretation"; only the second and third occurrences of *'elohim* count as evidence. He then adds a third judge, since "the tribunal must not be evenly balanced." I will discuss this derashah at length below,[7] but for now note that it records a dispute with-out a halakhic disagreement, whose interpretive nature is explicit: Is it legitimate to interpret the first instance of *'elohim*, or can interpretation begin only with the second? Whatever the historical origins and func-tion of legal midrash, the midrashim in their current form ineluctably address questions of interpretation.

A more sophisticated challenge to the legitimacy of a hermeneutical analysis of legal midrash is presented by David Weiss Halivni in his book *Peshat and Derash*.[8] Though, elsewhere, Halivni argues that scriptural interpretation is older than most scholars allow and thus less likely to function as mere support for existing legal decisions, he rejects the hermeneutical study of legal midrash. In a brief appendix, "Midrash and Modern Literary Theories,"[9] Halivni minimizes the hermeneutical dimension in halakhic midrash, arguing for its essential difference from aggadic interpretation. Of aggadah, he writes: "Its loose connection with the prooftext is well established, its extraneous nature generally assumed, so that the reader's imagination may well be deemed one of its many sources." But legal midrash is an altogether different matter:

> Legal comments in general are closer and more tightly bound to the text, more grounded in it than in nonlegal midrash. . . . Midrash Halakhah's cues overwhelmingly come from within the text. The text is the principal guide in determining what constitutes proper halakhah, the mode of behavior. The reader's (the interpreter's) role is much more limited. He interacts with the text, but what he brings to bear on it is much more impoverished. . . . The halakhist confronts the text; the aggadist joins the text. The halakhist submits to the text; the aggadist plays with it, as it were. The aggadist cooperates with the text (actively); the halakhist listens to the text (often passively)—except when reading into the text. Then, he is a determiner, a sharer in the making of the law; a co-author. . . . [Then] he is not a passive recipient but an active begetter—a creator.[10]

Halivni admits that midrash halakhah may involve active interpretation of the biblical text on the part of the rabbinic reader, but characterizes such interpretations as numerically and normatively the exception. As a rule, legal midrash requires a passive engagement of the biblical text and thus limits the role of the reader. It is well and good, Halivni suggests, to apply literary theory to aggadic material, but midrash halakhah is a different matter altogether. It is not altogether surprising to find this view articulated in the context of legal hermeneutics, an area of interpretation endowed with significant institutional power, at times resulting in life-and-death decisions. The attempt to suppress the hermeneutical element in legal midrash is, as Natalie Dohrmann argues, typical of a broader resistance to viewing law and its interpretation as modes of discourse that "can and ought be approached using the tools of literary criticism."[11]

As we shall see, Halivni's description of halakhic interpretation is a concise and accurate description of how the Rabbi Ishmael midrashim *present* their own interpretive practices. The Mekhilta and the Sifre Numbers create a complex set of hermeneutical practices aimed at minimizing the role of the reader and establishing Scripture itself as the chief interpretive agent. But rhetorical self-justification is not the same as actual interpretive practices, and the suggestion that a passive interpreter takes self-evident "cues" from Scripture is untenable because cues are never self-evident (more on this below), and, more generally, the underlying notion of an interpreter who enjoys unmediated access to the meaning of a text has been found wanting in much of the philosophical and literary thinking of the past two centuries.[12] Halivni is willing to concede that aggadic midrash is fair game for literary theory, but applies to legal midrash a notion of interpretation that was already contested two centuries ago. Beginning with Friedrich Schleiermacher, in the early nineteenth century, hermeneutics underwent a profound transformation. Up to that point, the discipline of hermeneutics matched various rules or canons of interpretation to particular textual genres: theological, legal, philological, and the like. More importantly, these rules were only employed when the reader encountered a difficult or obscure passage. Hermeneutics was anomalous; textual understanding was natural, given, with the reader resorting to hermeneutical rules only in difficult cases.

Schleiermacher's contribution was twofold. He recognized hermeneutics as a universal discipline, as the art of understanding as such. So while different types of texts pose different challenges to the interpreter, hermeneutics as such is not fragmented into subdisciplines but remains universal, "whether the text be a legal document, a religious Scripture, or a work of literature."[13] Moreover, as a universal discipline, hermeneutics is not limited to difficult, potentially misunderstood passages; rather, it is part of reading as such. It is in this context that Jean Grondin speaks of Schleiermacher's "universalization of misunderstanding."[14]

There are numerous surveys of the evolution of hermeneutical thought, and there is no need to rehearse their findings here.[15] For our purposes, the most important discussion of hermeneutics after Schleiermacher is Martin Heidegger's *Being and Time*, which effects a second transformation in the concept of hermeneutics.[16] Heidegger's terminology is notoriously idiosyncratic, so I will present his arguments in my own words and usually confine quotationss from *Being and Time* to the notes.[17] Hermeneutics plays an important role in *Being and Time*; indeed, Heidegger characterizes the philosophic project of *Being and Time* as hermeneutical in nature.[18] But the hermeneutics of which Heidegger speaks does not involve a subject interpreting a given object; it is much more fundamental and embedded in the radical holism of Heidegger's early thought. For Heidegger, *human being* (*Dasein*) itself cannot be separated from the broader context in which it is encountered.[19] Heidegger calls this broader context the world, and the basic state of *human being* is Being-in-the-World. This phrase does not refer to the spatial situatedness of an individual within the physical world, but to the impossibility of a subject, an "I," divorced from the world. *Human being* is always in-the-World because we encounter all things, including ourselves, as already existing in-the-World. In making this claim, Heidegger rejects the notion that human consciousness comes upon the world as an unknown object and proceeds to examine it by philosophical analysis—a view found most prominently in the writings of Descartes and Husserl. There is no external subject, and engagement with the world cannot be taken up and set aside; it is constitutive of human being.

The idea that *human being* is always already engaged with the world has important ramifications for Heidegger's discussion of interpretation and understanding. Though "understanding" traditionally refers to intellectually grasping a particular matter, for Heidegger it signifies a way in which *human being* engages the world.[20] This definition is significant in that it makes understanding the starting point rather than the end point. For if understanding is an *existentiale* or (in the language of earlier philosophers) a category of Being-in-the-World, and if Being-in-the-World is an always already present engagement with the world, then the world is always already—on some basic, implicit level—understood. From the very first, we engage the world—and ourselves as part of the world—with a primordial understanding. Clearly, Heidegger is not concerned with intellectual understanding but with a more fundamental understanding that manifests itself in the "automatic" or "natural" way people comport themselves. We open the door to enter the house, commute to and from work, shake hands with a new acquaintance but hug a friend —all interactions with our inanimate and animate environment that embody an implicit understanding of the function of the door, transportation, and proper physical contact, respectively. These actions are experienced as natural or self-evident, but in fact they are part of a web of contexts in which *human being* encounters its world and its self.[21] The self-evidence of these actions is, however, undermined when something goes "wrong": keys are locked in the house and the door becomes a barrier rather than an entrance; an energy crisis forces drivers to reconsider their mode of transportation; a foreign colleague meets our outstretched hand with a hug. In each case, the encounter with the unexpected lays bare previously unquestioned assumptions. The thematization of understanding, the process by which the implicit understanding of an entity is made explicit—this is what Heidegger calls "interpretation."[22] Heidegger reverses the traditional division of labor between interpretation and understanding. Interpretation does not lead to an understanding of something that was previously unknown; it grows out of an already present (though implicit) understanding. In a way that recalls the pre-Schleiermacher idea that interpretation is applied to difficult verses, Heideggerian understanding rises to the surface and becomes fully conscious—that is, becomes interpretation—when the anticipated mode of engagement with an entity is frustrated: the broken door, the unexpected hug, and so forth.

For our purposes, the key issue is this: interpretation of a familiar object is never ex nihilo, but rather reveals an understanding that is prior to it and in which it—the interpretation—is grounded.[23] This preconceptual, implicit understanding is called "fore-understanding." Interpretation, then, the conscious and explicit engagement of an entity, is always determined by implicit and preconscious engagements with the world; every explicit encounter builds on the fore-understanding of the being in question.

Though Heidegger is concerned with interpretation in the widest sense of the word, the dynamic delineated above holds for textual interpretation as well: "If, when one is engaged in a particular concrete kind of interpretation, in the sense of exact textual Interpretation,[24] one likes to appeal to what 'stands there', then one finds that what 'stands there' in the first instance is nothing other than the obvious undiscussed assumption of the person who does the interpreting."[25]

Indeed, it was the textual relevance of Heidegger's insights that became the central impetus for the philosophical work of Hans-Georg Gadamer.[26] The point is critical for the present study and merits a separate example. Consider the phrase, "Politics Dressed Up as Law," the headline of an op-ed essay that appeared in the *New York Times* on August 24, 1998. The informed reader recognizes this phrase as an op-ed headline because it appears in a large font on the recto of the last page of the first section of the newspaper, the page that carries the "op-ed" banner. There are other indications as well: the brief statement of the author's occupation and qualifications at the bottom of the column (absent from articles written by reporters), the more personal tone of the essay, perhaps an adjacent essay arguing the opposite view, and so forth. The op-ed essay is a journalistic genre—it obeys a set of conventions that distinguish it from other texts in the newspaper (news stories, stock quotes, obituaries, advertisements, and so on), each of which has its own conventions. The competent newspaper reader recognizes these conventions, identifies the text as an op-ed piece, and interprets its headline accordingly. Recognizing this phrase as an op-ed headline still allows for different interpretive responses: one reader may wonder which political events are "dressed up as law," another might surmise the events in question but wonder about the author's views, while a third reader may question how the position expressed in the headline compares with an op-ed piece in, say, the *Washington Post*. But while different, these interpretations are all determined by the reader's implicit understanding of the institution of the journalistic op-ed piece.

If the same phrase, "Politics Dressed Up as Law," were encountered at the center of an otherwise empty page in a poetry journal, the reader would reasonably assume it is a poem and subject to very different types of interpretation. For example, "Politics Dressed Up as Law" contains no verb—a meaningless trait in an op-ed headline but potentially significant in a poem. The same is true of the brevity of the phrase and of its unusual (for a poem) capitalization. Different interpretations of this (hypothetical) poem are possible (is it ars poetic? a statement about language as such?), but each interpretation is anchored in the prior, implicit recognition that the phrase in question is a poem—recognition that is not derived from the phrase itself but from the context in which the phrase is encountered. The institutions of reading that frame "Politics Dressed Up as Law," the specific fore-structures of understanding, precede and determine all possible interpretations of this text—indeed, of all texts.

The significance of this insight for the study of explicitly interpretive texts (such as commentaries) has gone largely unnoticed. In the "Politics Dressed Up as Law" example, an identical text is encountered in two different literary contexts, such that anyone familiar with op-ed pages and poetry journals would recognize that each opens before the reader various horizons of interpretation, even though the text is identical in both cases. Now, suppose there surfaced a treatise devoted to the phrase "Politics Dressed Up as Law" and this interpretation was being studied by a scholar. It is clear that part of the task of this scholar would be to determine—at least in broad strokes—whether the author of the treatise was writing on, for instance, "Politics Dressed Up as Law" the op-ed headline or on "Politics Dressed Up as Law" the poem. Even though—absent direct access to the author—such analysis must proceed from the text of the treatise itself, the scholar must be aware of the need to determine as fully as possible the implicit, prior understanding of the phrase and the concomitant interpretive horizons open to the author of the treatise. This is a particularly difficult task when dealing with an interpretive work composed in another time or culture, and whose underlying reading institutions are not intuitively familiar.[27]

For example, Proclus wrote a commentary on Plato's *Timaeus* in the fifth century C.E. Thirteen centuries later, in 1794, Friedrich Schelling wrote another. Interpretation (in the conventional sense of the word) of these commentaries requires, of course, an examination of the explicit philosophical readings that Proclus and Schelling propose for various elements of the *Timaeus*: the creation myth, the role of the demiurge, the creation of the senses, and so forth. But this analysis can properly proceed only after establishing (at least in a preliminary fashion) how each thinker engages the Platonic corpus as a whole, an engagement that precedes and determines the specific interpretations offered in the commentaries. Was Plato a divine prophet? Or a philosophic genius? Should the *Timaeus* be read as a poem, a religious revelation, or a scientific treatise? The answer is not found in the text of each commentary but rather in the broader cultural and intellectual context in which Proclus and Schelling encountered the dialogue.

Returning to Jewish interpretation, consider two descriptions of the Torah qua object of interpretation. The first is by Philo, writing in first century Alexandria, and the second by Yosef Gikatilla, in thirteenth century Castile. In *Questions and Answers on Genesis* III, 3, Philo writes: "Accordingly, the Legislation [i.e. Torah] is in some sense a unified creature, which one should view from all sides in its entirety with open eyes and examine the intention of the entire writing exactly, truly and clearly, not cutting up its harmony or dividing its unity."[28]

Gikatilla describes the Torah as follows:

ספר תורה אין לו גוון ידוע לפסוקים, אלא פעמים נדרש כן ופעמים נדרש כן, כלומר בעולם
המלאכים קוראין לו בעניין אחד ובעולם הגלגלים קוראין לו בעניין אחר ובעולם השפל
בעניין אחר, וכל שאר אלף אלפי עולמות הנכללים באלו השלש עולמות כל אחד מהם כפי
כחו והשגתו כך הוא קריאתו בספר תורה. ולפי כך אין ספר תורה מנוקד ואין בו טעמים
ולא סוף פסוק . . . שאילו הושם לו ניקוד לפסוק היה היגע לצורתו וגבולו ואין מי שיוכל לציירו
בצורה אחרת.

The Torah has no fixed meaning for its verses, rather sometimes it is interpreted in one manner and other times in another, that is, in the world of the angels they read it a certain way and in the world of the celestial spheres they read it another way and in the base world still another way, and with each of the thousands upon thousands of worlds that are included in these three worlds, each reads the Torah scroll according to its [the world's] ability and understanding . . . [and i]t is on account of this that the Torah scroll is written with neither vocalization nor trope marks nor punctuation at the end of a verse . . . for were the Torah scroll definitively vocalized it would have reached its form and its limit, and no one could have imagined it differently.[29]

These two statements express very different presuppositions concerning Torah and, when applied to specific verses, will yield very different readings. This hermeneutical holism[30]—the impossibility of fully grasping the parts (interpretation of verses) divorced from the whole (the underlying notion of Torah)—radically qualifies Halivni's claim that the Rabbis are guided by textual cues. The claim is true, but only if we recognize that the fore-understanding of Torah determines what constitutes a cue and that, as a result, cues will vary from one interpreter to another. Stylistic variance, orthographic irregularity, the numerological value of a word: Are they cues? Can an interpreter legitimately use these phenomena to interpret a biblical verse? There is no single answer: any textual characteristic may or may not be a cue, depending on the interpreter's understanding of the Torah, the Hebrew language, the nature of divine speech, and so forth.

Explicit statements as to the nature of Torah are, alas, rare. In their absence, modern interpreters of ancient interpretation must make a conscious effort to reconstruct the implicit fore-understanding of Torah that determines the ancient readings. As Lieve Teugels has written, "[R]abbinic ideas about Scripture—which substantiate themselves in rabbinic hermeneutics, methods and interpretation techniques—are certainly as determining for the midrash as its form."[31] The first part of this study tries to further our understanding of these "rabbinic ideas about Scripture" by examining the concept of Scripture that underlies the legal sections of the Mekhilta and the Sifre Numbers. This approach is not without precedent. Arnold Goldberg outlined a similar approach, Alexander Samely has devoted several studies to the background assumptions of midrash, and David Instone Brewer has devoted a study to the assumptions that underlie early midrash.[32] My own analysis and conclusions are different in ways that will, I hope, become clear in the course of this study.

Chapter 1
Torah and Ha-Katuv

In attempting to uncover the understanding of Scripture that underlies
the Rabbi Ishmael midrashim, particularly as it constitutes particular
modes of interpretation, I begin by examining the terminology employed by the Rabbi Ishmael midrashim to refer to Scripture. A helpful
starting point for this examination is Wilhelm Bacher's *Die bibelexegetische
Terminologie der Tannaiten*, which surveys the exegetic terminology of tannaitic literature as a whole, and whose conclusions are relevant to the
Rabbi Ishmael midrashim.[1] *Sub verbo* תורה (*torah*), Bacher discusses the
different meanings of the term and the various contexts and formulas in
which the word occurs, noting, "Just like כתוב [*katuv*] so too תורה [*torah*]
is employed as a personification [*Personificirung*] of Scripture."[2] In support of this claim, Bacher cites the phrase *'amrah torah*, "Torah stated"
and refers to other entries in the book that discuss actions attributed
to *torah*. Bacher's statement contains a number of claims, all of them
important for our purposes: that the Hebrew word *torah* may appear as a
"personification" of Scripture; that *torah* is one of two such personifications—the other being *ha-katuv* (literally, "that which is written" or "the
written"); and that *torah* and *ha-katuv* are synonyms.

Bacher does not define "personification" and wisely so, since the term
is notoriously slippery. It is clear that the Rabbi Ishmael midrashim do
not conceive of *torah* and *ha-katuv* as manifesting themselves in human
form, so we are not dealing with full-fledged personifications. On the
other hand, both *torah* and *ha-katuv* speak and perform other activities
(more on this presently) and in that respect are personified. Rather than
try to pinpoint the precise sense of "personification" that is adequate to
the description of Scripture found in the Rabbi Ishmael midrashim, I
propose a minimum criterion rooted in the grammatical form of a given
clause: the Hebrew words *torah* and *ha-katuv* are counted as personifications when they appear as grammatical subjects that take finite verbs
(which in rabbinic Hebrew may include the participle).[3] This criterion
covers all the occurrences of *ha-katuv* but not of *torah*, which appears, for
instance, as the object of rabbinic study, as the teaching given at Sinai,
and in other "inactive" contexts. This criterion does not adequately

define the personification to be discussed, but rather than attempt a full and adequate definition, I hope the following discussions of "personifying" passages will provide a sense for the type of personification that these texts employ.

Before turning to the relevant passages, two methodological issues require attention. First, Bacher's assertion that *torah* and *ha-katuv* are synonyms is intuitively appealing as both terms refer to—and are personifications of—Scripture. But intuition is not always the best guide in such matters, and it is worth recalling what the late Israeli linguist Haiim Rosén calls the "basic assumption in analytical procedure, namely, that functional difference must be presumed of any pair of formally different features unless and until the contrary (that is, synonymity, stylistic variation) is established by conclusive evidence."[4] In this case, the different features whose synonymity cannot be assumed are the two names of Scripture: *torah* and *ha-katuv*. And why should there be two terms used to describe Scripture? The word *torah* is biblical. Its primary meaning is "instruction" and it can also signify "divine teaching" and "corpus containing divine teaching," the latter being its basic meaning in rabbinic Hebrew. *Ha-katuv*, however, does not occur in biblical Hebrew as a nominal form (only as the passive participle of *k-t-v* 'write') and the meaning "Scripture" is unattested in biblical literature. Though I do not know its precise provenance, it is clear that *ha-katuv* came to mean Scripture when the word *torah* (in the sense of Scripture) already enjoyed wide circulation. Would Hebrew introduce a new word for Scripture for no reason? If *torah* and *ha-katuv* are fully synonymous, what purpose is served by adopting *ha-katuv* alongside *torah*? As Rosén indicates, historical linguistics suggests that languages do not generally behave in this way and that we ought to expect some difference between the apparent synonyms.[5]

The second methodological issue involves the status of words such as *torah* and *ha-katuv*. They are, the argument goes, mere figures of speech that cannot reveal much of interest regarding rabbinic thought in general and hermeneutics in particular. This view is based on the assumption that language reflects—with varying degrees of accuracy—a given external reality, and that figurative or metaphoric speech teaches us something about the stylistic preferences of the speaker or author, but nothing more. But this view is wanting. There is a substantial body of scholarship to the effect that metaphoric speech is not merely figurative but rather one of the modes of linguistic categorization. George Lakoff in particular has discussed the cognitive and cultural significance of metaphors.[6] A young man might recount a date in the following terms: "I was really doing well, *I had my game on* that night and I was sure I was going to *score*, but then nothing—I just *struck out*. I mean, I didn't even make it to *first base*. A total *shut out*. I felt like a *loser*."[7] There is no question that the italicized words are all metaphors, terms taken from the field of sports and applied figuratively to the date. But they are revealing and significant metaphors that tell us much about the way a particular group conceptualizes dating. The language of competitive sports could not be used this way in societies where, for example, young men pay dowries to their brides' families and meet their brides-to-be at the wedding. In the same way, even though *torah* and *ha-katuv* do not actually perform actions, the (metaphorical) attribution of actions to Scripture is culturally significant.

It is also significant that the Rabbi Ishmael midrashim distinguish between the two terms. Working from a sociological perspective, Eviatar Zerubavel has studied the significance of distinctions in social reality and has shown how powerfully real social and linguistic distinctions are.[8] One obvious example is a political border that divides a physically undifferentiated landscape. Though the distinction between political entities is a social construct, border disputes are often experienced by their participants as utterly objective even to the point of war. The same holds true for the social distinction between the value of gold and tin, and many other examples could be cited. This is not to say that the distinction between *torah* and *ha-katuv* is necessarily significant—the proof will be in the pudding of close textual analysis—but that the distinction should not be dismissed a priori as meaningless because it is metaphoric.

One technical note. To distinguish personified *torah* from other meanings of *torah*, I adopt the following graphic convention: Torah (in plain font) is an English word meaning Pentateuch or Hebrew Bible; *torah* (italicized) is the transliteration of the Hebrew תורה; and TORAH (in small caps) designates the term used as personified Scripture, that is, *torah* as grammatical subject whose predicate is a finite verb. Similarly, *ha-katuv* (italics) transliterates the Hebrew הכתוב, but HA-KATUV designates the term as personified Scripture.

Torah

TORAH SAID (*'amrah torah*)

The most common characterization of TORAH is as speaker, and the most common phrase to characterize TORAH as speaker is *'amrah torah*, "TORAH said,"[9] which introduces a quotation from Scripture. The Mekhilta to Exodus 12:2 is typical:

"ראשון הוא לכם לחדשי השנה" (שמות יב ב): . . . למה נאמר לפי שהוא אומר "שמור את חדש האביב [ועשית פסח]" (דברים טז א) שמור את הפסח לאביב ואביב לפסח שיבוא אביב

בזמנו, הא כיצד, עיבר את אדר שיבוא אביב בזמנו הרי שעיברו בזמנו [ולא בא אביב בזמנו],¹⁰
שומע אני יעברו את ניסן. היה ר' ישמעאל אומר הא אם אמרת כן נמצאת עושה ניסן שיני
ואמרה תורה "ראשון הוא לכם".

[This month shall mark for you the beginning of the months;] it shall be the first
of the months of the year for you (Exod 12:2): Why is this said? Because of the
following. It says: "Observe the month of *Aviv* (spring) and offer a Passover sacrifice to the Lord your God" (Deut 16:1), meaning: Keep the Passover near the
spring and the spring near the Passover; i.e., see that the spring comes in its
[Passover's] time. How so? Add, if necessary, the intercalary Adar so that the
spring should come in its [Passover's] time. Now, I might understand that if they
added the intercalary Adar and spring has not yet come in its time, they may add
an intercalary Nisan. Against this Rabbi Ishmael used to say: Behold, if you say
so, you actually make Nisan the second month of the year whereas TORAH said:
"[This month shall be] the first of the months for you." (Mekhilta Pisḥa 2, p. 8;
Lauterbach 1.19–20)

The Hebrew *'aviv* refers to the time of growth of the young barley shoots,
spring, and is also the first month of the Canaanite and preexilic Israelite
calendar, corresponding to Nisan.¹¹ The difficulty addressed by this derashah is how to coordinate the Passover sacrifice, which has a fixed date,
with the agricultural conditions of *'aviv*, which can vary from year to
year. If at the end of Adar, the month that precedes Nisan, it becomes
clear that the *'aviv* is not imminent, intercalary Adar (*'adar bet*) can be
added between Adar and Nisan, postponing the Passover. The hypothesis is then put forward that if at the end of the intercalary Adar *'aviv* is
still distant, an intercalary Nisan is to be added, pushing Passover into
a second Nisan and allowing still more time for *'aviv* to arrive. Rabbi Ishmael rejects this hypothesis as contradicting Scripture.

For the present analysis, the key issue is the role of TORAH and the
manner in which it "speaks." The context of TORAH's speech is clear:
"TORAH said" introduces a verse, Exodus 12:2. The verse is stated without
commentary or explication; the Mekhilta understands the meaning of
the verse and its bearing on the hypothetical intercalary Nisan as self-
evident, requiring no midrashic elaboration. The (assumed) self-evidence
of Exodus 12:2 explains the brevity of Rabbi Ishmael's argument. Prior
to Rabbi Ishmael's statement, the derashah cites Deuteronomy 16:1, interprets it as commanding the juxtaposition of Passover and *'aviv*, suggests
that this may be achieved through the intercalation of Adar, and proceeds to question whether such a procedure might also apply to Nisan.
This elaborate argument is pithily refuted: the proposed scenario would
make Nisan the second month whereas TORAH said, "This month shall be
the first of the months for you." The statement introduced by *'amrah
torah*, Exodus 12:2, decides the matter. It requires no proof or midrashic
elaboration, but itself provides support for the correct legal position.

All this is typical of *'amrah torah*. The formula regularly introduces uninterpreted biblical verses that decide a midrashic dispute by refuting an erroneous hypothesis. The only significant variation occurs in a number of derashot in which *'amrah torah* introduces a paraphrase of a biblical verse and not a citation:

"והיה לך לאות על ידך [ולזכרון בין עיניך]" (שמות יג ט): כרך אחד של ארבע פרשיות והדין
נותן הואיל <u>ואמרה תורה</u> תן תפילין בראש תן תפילין ביד, מה בראש ארבע טוטפות
אף ביד ארבע טוטפות, תלמוד לומר "והיה לך לאות על ידך" כרך אחד של ארבע פרשות.

"And it shall serve you as a sign on your hand [and a reminder on your forehead]" (Exod 13:9): One roll containing all four scriptural sections. Since TORAH said: "Put phylacteries upon your head," "Put phylacteries upon your hand," just as the one put on the head contains the four sections on four separate rolls of parchment, so the one put on the hand should also contain four separate rolls of parchment. [Scripture] teaches, saying [*talmud lomar*], "And this shall serve as a sign on your head"—one roll containing all the four scriptural sections. (Mekhilta Pisḥa 17, p. 66; Lauterbach 1.150)

According to this derashah, Scripture commands that phylacteries be laid both on the head and on the hand. As a result, one might draw an analogy between the two and conclude that just as in the head phylacteries there are four separate rolls of parchment, so, too, in the hand phylacteries there are four rolls, when in fact the hand phylactery contains a single roll of parchment. To deny the legitimacy of this analogy, Exodus 13:9 states, "And it shall serve as a sign on your hand and a reminder on your forehead." This verse mentions two distinct mnemonics, the sign (*'ot*) and the reminder (*zikaron*), but speaks of them in the singular: "And *it* shall serve" instead of the more natural "And *they* shall serve." The odd phrasing is highlighted by Deuteronomy 6:8 and 11:18, the other verses that mention phylacteries, where the head and the hand phylacteries are treated separately.[12] The Mekhilta interprets this weak anacoluthon as indicating the singular nature of the hand phylactery, an indirect testimony that it contains a single scroll of parchment, not four.

The difficulty is that according to the Mekhilta, "TORAH said" to don phylacteries but in fact this command does not appear in the Pentateuch. A number of verses command that God's instructions be bound as a sign on the arm and the forehead (Deut 6:8, 11:18), verses that are later interpreted *by the Rabbis* as referring to phylacteries (tefillin).[13] How, then, can the derashah introduce this commandment as having been spoken by TORAH? Here it is necessary to distinguish the modern, historically informed analysis of the development of tefillin from the understanding of the commandment embodied in this pericope. Though philologically the commandment of tefillin is not stated in Scripture and must be derived midrashically, the author of this derashah considers tefillin a scriptural commandment, as is evident from its status as a decisive proof-text. Like the biblical verses cited in other *'amrah torah* pericopes, the commandment to don tefillin is taken as an unambiguous statement that decides halakhic disputes and does not require proof. The derashah does not try to derive or buttress the commandment to don tefillin; quite the contrary—the tefillin passage provides solid ground from which *other* legal arguments are decided. The language of the derashah makes this point explicitly: "*Since* TORAH says" (הואיל ואמרה תורה). The meaning and authority of TORAH's statement are given, and *since* TORAH said these things, the derashah is free to explore the consequences.[14] TORAH's words are "already spoken" and need only be restated in the context of this derashah, without discussion or interpretation.

A second example of *'amrah torah* introducing a nonbiblical statement is found in the Sifre Numbers §160:

"והוא לא אויב לו ולא מבקש רעתו" (במדבר לה כג): ... אין לי אלא דיאנין [דיינים] שפוסל בהן
סונין [שונאים] וקרובין עדים מנין הרי אתה דן הואיל ואמרה תורה הרוג על פי דיאנין והרוג
על פי עדים מה דיינין שאין הדברים נגמרין על פיהן פוסל בהן סונאין וקרובין עדים שהדברים
נגמרין על פיהן אינו דין שיפסול בהן סונין וקרובין.[15]

"[T]hough he was not an enemy of his" (Num 35:23): . . . I only know regarding judges that enemies and relatives are to be disqualified, whence do I learn this regarding witnesses? You reason thus: Since TORAH said execute on the authority of judges and execute on the authority of witnesses, since judges, whose testimony does not decide the matter, are disqualified in cases of enemies and relatives, witnesses, whose testimony does decide the matter, does it not follow that they should be disqualified in cases involving enemies and relatives? (Sifre Numbers §160, p. 219)

TORAH's words—"execute on the authority of judges and execute on the authority of witnesses"—are not a scriptural citation; rather, they derive from Deuteronomy 17 and its rabbinic interpretation. Deuteronomy 17 expresses a general prohibition against transgressing God's covenant on penalty of death:

If there is found among you . . . a man or woman who has affronted the Lord your God and transgressed His covenant . . . and it has been spoken to you and you have heard it, then you shall make a thorough inquiry. If it is true . . . you shall stone them, man or woman, to death. A person shall be put to death only on the testimony of two or three witnesses. (Deut 17:2–6)

The last verse clearly states that capital punishment can be carried out only if there are two or more witnesses to the transgression. This is the source for the Sifre Numbers' statement that "TORAH said execute on the authority of witnesses." But what of the judges? On what basis does the Sifre Numbers represent TORAH as speaking of the judges' authority?

The answer lies in the rabbinic interpretation of Deuteronomy. The following derashah appears in Midrash Tannaim (a compilation also considered part of the Rabbi Ishmael midrashim) to these very verses:

"וְהֻגַּד לְךָ וְשָׁמָעְתָּ" (דברים יז ד): וכי אפשר לבשר ודם לשמוע אלא מפי הגדה אלא הרי אתה
דן נאמר כאן "וְהֻגַּד" ונאמר להלן "הַגָּדָה" (ויקרא ה א) מה להלן בבית דין אף כאן בבית דין.

"And it has been <u>spoken</u> to you and you have heard" (Deut 17:4): Can a human being hear something save if it was spoken to him [why the apparent redundancy]? Rather you apply an analogy, it says "<u>speak</u>" here and it says "<u>speak</u>" there (Lev 5:1), just as there "speak" refers to a court so here "speak" refers to a court. (Midrash Tannaim, Hoffmann edition, p. 100)

The derashah takes as its focus the apparent redundancy in Deuteronomy 17:4—since the statement has been heard, is it not obvious that it was spoken? The phrase "it has been spoken" is redundant and thus hermeneutically meaningful (more on this below), and the reference to "speaking" links Deuteronomy 17:4 to Leviticus 5:1: "If a person incurs guilt when he has heard a public imprecation and—although able to testify as one who has either seen or learned of the matter—he does not <u>speak</u>, he is subject to punishment." The context of Leviticus 5:1 is unambiguously forensic, and the link to Deuteronomy 17:4 indicates that the latter is also forensic. Whether this is the derashah that underlies Sifre Numbers' assertion that "TORAH said 'execution on the authority of judges'" cannot be known. It is clear, however, that judges are *not* mentioned in Deuteronomy 17:4, yet the Sifre Numbers presents the judges as said "by Torah" and they function as a biblical prooftext. The Sifre Numbers provides no midrashic argument in support of the requirement of judges, employing it alongside the scriptural requirement of witnesses as a certain and decisive fact. Here, too, the Sifre Numbers has incorporated the midrashic argument into Scripture. The consistent hermeneutical employment of the phrases "spoken" by TORAH, even in these exceptional instances, indicates that TORAH speaks legally decisive statements that require no midrashic support. The statements of TORAH are either factually scriptural or are treated as scriptural by the derashah. That TORAH is scriptural may appear an unexceptional conclusion, but it is a point that needs making since (as will be seen below) HA-KATUV is not.

TORAH SPOKE (*dibberah torah*)

Twice in the Rabbi Ishmael midrashim, TORAH's speech is introduced with the formula *dibberah torah*.[16] The first occurs in the Sifre Numbers §23:

"מיין ושכר יזיר" (דברים ו ג): והלא יין הוא שכר ושכר הוא יין. אלא שדיברה תורה
שתי לשונות. כיוצא בו אתה אומר שחיטה היא זביחה וזביחה היא שחיטה קמיצה היא
הרמה הרמה היא קמיצה עמוקה היא שפלה שפלה היא עמוקה אות הוא מופת מופת
הוא אות אלא שדיברה תורה שתי לשונות.

"He shall abstain from *yayin* (wine) and *shekhar* (intoxicant)" (Num 6:3): But
yayin is *shekhar* and *shekhar* is *yayin*, except that the TORAH spoke using two expressions. And similarly *shehitah* (slaughter) is *zebiḥa* (sacrifice) and *zebiḥa* is *shehitah*;
qemitzah (grasping with the hand) is *haramah* (lifting) and *haramah* is *qemitzah*;
'amuqah (a depression) is *shfelah* (a lowland) and *shfelah* is *'amuqah*; *'ot* (a sign) is
mofet (a wonder, sign) and *mofet* is *'ot*, but TORAH spoke using two expressions.
(Sifre Numbers §23, p. 27)

Numbers 6:3 states that the nazirite must abstain from alcoholic beverages. In this passage, Sifre Numbers focuses on the words employed in
the verse—*yayin* and *shekhar*, apparent synonyms for alcoholic beverages.
The Sifre Numbers does not deny the semantic equivalence of *yayin* and
shekhar[17] or imply that synonymity is a form of redundancy and thus
hermeneutically significant. Instead, it embraces the terms' synonymity —"*yayin* is *shekhar* and *shekhar* is *yayin*"—characterizing it as a biblical commonplace and enumerating a list of other synonymous terms.
Synonyms are a matter of style, a biblical *façon de parler*, "TORAH spoke
using two expressions."[18] The second instance of *dibberah torah* is Rabbi
Ishmael's well-known statement in Sifre Numbers §112:

"הכרת תכרת" (במדבר טו לא): "הכרת" בעולם הזה "תכרת" בעולם הבא דברי ר' עקיבה.
אמר לו ישמעאל, לפי שהוא אומר "ונכרתה הנפש ההיא" (במדבר טו ל)[19] שומע אני שלש
כריתות בשלוש עולמות מה תלמוד לומר "הכרת תכרת" דיברה תורה לשון בני אדם.

"[But the person . . . who acts defiantly and reviles the Lord] that person shall
surely be cut off [*hikaret tikaret*] from among his people" (Num 15:31): *Hikaret*
refers to this world, *tikaret* to the world to come, these are the words of Rabbi
Aqiva. Rabbi Ishmael said to him: Since it says, "That person shall be cut off
[*nikhreta*]" (Num 15:30), should I infer, then, that the three instances of [the
root] *karet* correspond to three worlds? What, then, does [Scripture] teach in saying, "*Hikaret tikaret* [surely shall be cut off]?" TORAH spoke the language of man.
(Sifre Numbers §112, p. 121)

The biblical verse in question addresses the punishment of a person who
knowingly transgresses a divine commandment. For an unintentional
transgression (*bi-shegagah*), one must offer a kid as a sin offering (Num
15:27), but in the case of an intentional transgression the offender "shall
surely be cut off." This last phrase is expressed in Hebrew as an infinitive
absolute followed by a finite form of the same root (*k-r-t*), a formulation
that emphasizes the certainty of the punishment.[20] Rabbi Aqiva argues

that the repetition of the root is hermeneutically significant, suggesting that the sinner is to be cut off twice: once in this world and again in the world to come.[21] Rabbi Ishmael counters Rabbi Aqiva's argument by pointing to a third occurrence of the same root in the previous verse, "that person shall be cut off [*nikhreta*]" (Num 15:30). If Rabbi Aqiva understands each of the two forms of *k-r-t* in Numbers 15:31 as corresponding to two worlds, would this logic not dictate that the third form correspond to a third world? Rabbi Ishmael undermines Rabbi Aqiva's interpretation by reductio ad absurdum and concludes, instead, that "TORAH spoke the language of man."

In its two occurrences, *dibberah torah* does not introduce a statement made by TORAH, but rather characterizes TORAH's speech. The formula is not concerned with *what* TORAH says but with *how* it says it. As a result, the hermeneutical function of *dibberah torah* is very different from that of *'amrah torah*. In Sifre Numbers §23, the identity of *yayin* (wine) and *shekhar* (intoxicant) is stated at the outset without the support of a proof-text ("*yayin* is *shekhar* and *shekhar* is *yayin*"). The statement "TORAH spoke in two expressions" is a general support of scriptural synonymity, buttressed by additional examples of this phenomenon. Similarly, in Sifre Numbers §112 the phrase "TORAH spoke the language of man" is not specific to Numbers 15:31. That is, the phrase does not refute Rabbi Aqiva's position; the reductio ad absurdum argument involving the third instance of *k-r-t* does. "TORAH spoke the language of man" explains why Rabbi Ishmael, having rejected Rabbi Aqiva's interpretation, does not present an alternate reading of the infinitive-plus-finite-verb form (*hikaret tikaret*); to wit, it is a permissible mode of speech free of interpretive implications. In both cases, then, *dibberah torah* addresses general hermeneutical issues rather than introducing decisive legal prooftexts, as with *'amrah torah*.

In summary, TORAH's speech is usually introduced by the phrase *'amrah torah* and consists either of verbatim citation of biblical verses or of paraphrases based on what Scripture is understood (by the rabbinic interpreter) to be saying. The content of TORAH's speech is Torah, Scripture, and its words do not need explication or justification; they are hermeneutically self-evident statements applied to *other* verses. There is also a second, rare mode of speech attributed to TORAH—*dibberah torah*—that refers to biblical discourse more generally, suggesting that Scripture possesses a particular style and that not every textual phenomenon justifies interpretation.[22] Aside from the respective functions of the two phrases, the distinction as such is significant, as it suggests that the Rabbi Ishmael midrashim employ interpretive terminology in a deliberate manner.[23]

ACTION OF TORAH

The shift from TORAH's speech to its actions is dramatic. Whereas TORAH speaks in dozens of derashot, it only rarely performs other actions. In fact, the following list is (to the best of my knowledge) exhaustive:[24]

  i. Rabbi Ḥananiah ben Antigonos says: Come and consider the expression that TORAH chose (רבי חנניה בן אנטיגנוס אומר בוא וראה לשון שתפסה תורה). (Mekhilta Baḥodesh 6, p. 224; Lauterbach 2.240–41)
  ii. Since TORAH gave permission for the Temple (הואיל ונתנה תורה רשות לעשות בבית המקדש). (Mekhilta Baḥodesh 10, p. 241; Lauterbach 2.283)[25]
  iii. What did TORAH consider in punishing the thief more severely than the robber? (ומה ראת התורה להחמיר על הגנב יותר מן הגזלן). (Mekhilta Neziqin 15, p. 299; Lauterbach 3.115)
  iv. TORAH gave discernment to the sages so that they expound (נתנה תורה דעת בחכמים לדרוש) (Sifre Numbers §134, p. 179).

The range of activities attributed to TORAH is quite limited. Derashah (i) describes TORAH as speaking, in much the same way as do the 'amrah torah pericopes: the quote is followed by a verse that decides the legal question at hand, and involves no midrashic elaboration. Derashot (ii) and (iii) refer to TORAH permitting or prohibiting (punishing) certain actions, meaning that the actions in question are sanctioned or prohibited by Scripture. As for (iv), it is commonly understood as endowing the reader with a degree of independence from Scripture inasmuch as it provides them with the tools by which to expound Scripture. I will argue below that this interpretation is untenable, but even if one were to grant this reading of (iv), it amounts to a single instance of TORAH not citing or paraphrasing biblical verses.

OBLIQUE ATTRIBUTION

Up to this point, analysis has focused on Torah as the active subject of a verbal clause (TORAH). There are also a significant number of derashot that refer to scriptural speech obliquely, without designating torah as the speaker. Though not directly relevant to the activity of TORAH, these derashot reveal the uneasy relationship of torah to certain kinds of speech. The oblique attribution of speech to torah can be divided into three categories, the first of which involves statements that could be couched as biblical speech but are not:

"תורה אחת יהיה לאזרח ולגר" (שמות יב מט): . . .לפי שהוא אומר "וכי יגור אתך גר

[וְעָשָׂה פֶּסַח]" אין לי אלא פסח שהשווה בו את הגר לאזרח, שאר כל <u>המצות שבתורה</u> מנין,
תלמוד לומר "תורה אחת יהיה לאזרח ולגר.".

"There shall be one law for the citizen and for the stranger who dwells among
you" (Exod 12:49): . . . Since it says: "If a stranger who dwells with you [would
offer the Passover to the Lord]" (Exod 12:48), I might understand that the
stranger is like the born Jew only with respect to the Passover. How about all the
other commandments in the Torah? [Scripture] teaches, saying: "There shall be
one law." (Mekhilta Pisḥa 15, p. 57; Lauterbach 1.128)

The argument of the Mekhilta—that the inclusion of the stranger (*ger*)
in the Passover ceremony is not a unique occurrence but applies to all
the commandments—is not significant for the present analysis. The key
point is that this inclusion is presented as applying to all the commandments "in the Torah" and not to the commandments "that TORAH said."
The commandments are, after all, scriptural statements that could be
attributed to TORAH, as are the other statements that are located by the
Rabbi Ishmael midrashim "within Torah": "all the divine communications [הדברות] in the Torah" (Mekhilta Pisḥa 1, p. 1; Lauterbach 1.1); "all
the prohibitions [איסורים] in the Torah" (Sifre Numbers §23, p. 28); "all
the categories of prohibited work [אבות מלאכות] in the Torah" (Sifre
Numbers §113, p. 122); "all the instances of expiation [סליחות] in the
Torah" (Sifre Numbers §112, p. 119), and more. But while these derashot refer to topics that *could* be presented as spoken by Scripture, the
fact that they are not is not, in and of itself, remarkable.

The second category involves derashot in which the "spoken" nature
of the topic is more pronounced, and are accordingly more marked in
their avoidance of speech. Chief among these are midrashic arguments
that draw a conclusion regarding one instance of a word, and then apply
that conclusion to all the occurrences of the word. For example, the Sifre
Numbers finds evidence in one verse that the word "finger" refers to the
finger of the right hand, then applies that to "all the occurrences of
'finger' in the Torah [בכל אצבעות שבתורה]" (Sifre Numbers §123, p. 154).
This type of argument is also applied to all the occurrences of "take"
(כל הלקיחות שבתורה) (Mekhilta Pisḥa 11, p. 37; Lauterbach 1.83), "all the
occurrences of 'command' in the Torah [לכל הצוואות שבתורה]" (Sifre
Numbers §1, p. 1), "all the occurrences of 'inheritance' in the Torah
[מכל נחלות שבתורה]" (Sifre Numbers §132, p. 174), and more. These
derashot deal directly with the language of Scripture, that is, with the
words "finger," "take," and so on. Nonetheless, these words are not represented as spoken by Torah; they are located within it.

The tendency toward oblique attribution of speech is most evident in
the third category of derashot, which refers explicitly to Torah and

speech in the same clause, but describes the speech as "said *in* the Torah," rather than *by* TORAH, an oblique formulation found time and again in derashot that describe scriptural speech concerning:

    i. "one of the modes of capital punishment <u>stated</u> in the Torah" (באחת מכל מיתות <u>האמורות</u> בתורה). (Mekhilta Neziqin 5, p. 268; Lauterbach 3.49)

    ii. "since several instances of the term 'oath' are <u>stated</u> in the Torah" (הואיל <u>ונאמרו</u> שבועות שבתורה סתם). (Sifre Numbers §14, p. 19)

    iii. "since several instances of the term 'say' are <u>stated</u> in the Torah" (הואיל <u>ונאמרו</u> דברות בתורה). (Sifre Numbers §73, p. 68)

    iv. "since several instances of the term 'enter' are <u>stated</u> in the Torah" (הואיל <u>ונאמרו</u> ביאות בתורה). (Sifre Numbers §107, p. 106)

    v. "since several instances of the term 'fine flour' are <u>stated</u> in the Torah" (הואיל <u>ונאמרו</u> סלתות בתורה). (Sifre Numbers §142, p. 189)

The Hebrew word translated as "stated" is, consistently, the passive form of *'amar*, "say" or "state," the verb whose active form appears in *'amrah torah*, "TORAH said." But despite the willingness to employ *'amrah torah* to introduce cited verses, the Rabbi Ishmael midrashim consistently refuse to attribute other forms of speech to Torah, preferring instead the awkward locution "[the word] spoken in Torah." Why? It appears that the key issue is whether the speech in question can be presented as a biblical quotation. TORAH speaks in quotations or paraphrases a verse, but the Rabbi Ishmael midrashim employ an awkward locution, "spoken in Torah," when dealing with a class of biblical statements. So while individual verses are cited as "TORAH said," the oblique attribution is applied to, for example, *all* the occurrences of the word "commandment" or the several occurrences of "fine flour." And while each individual occurrence of "commandment" could, hypothetically, be introduced as spoken directly by TORAH ("one might think this to be the case but TORAH said: 'commandment'"), the class of all "commandments" lies beyond TORAH's ability as speaker. In distinguishing between statements that can be attributed to Torah as speaker and those that cannot, the Rabbi Ishmael midrashim demarcate the limits of TORAH-as-speaker. TORAH can reproduce biblical verses, but locutions that cannot be presented as quotations cannot be attributed to TORAH.

Ha-Katuv

Like TORAH, HA-KATUV is characterized as speaking by two formulas: [*be-'inyan ploni*] *ha-katuv medabber*, "HA-KATUV speaks [regarding a certain matter]," and *maggid ha-katuv*, "HA-KATUV states."[26]

HA-KATUV SPEAKS [REGARDING A CERTAIN MATTER] ([*be-'inyan ploni*]
ha-katuv medabber)

A survey of the passages in which this phrase appears reveals it as a
technical term with a fixed, definite meaning.[27] The Sifre Numbers
teaches:

"אלה החקים אשר צוה יהוה את משה בין איש לאשתו בין אב לבתו בנעריה בית אביה"
(במדבר ל יז) ור' ישמעאל אומר מאורסה <u>הכתוב מדבר.</u>

"These are the laws that the Lord enjoined upon Moses between a man and his
wife, and as between a father and his daughter while in her father's household
by reason of her youth" (Num 30:17): Rabbi Ishmael says, HA-KATUV speaks of a
betrothed girl. (Sifre Numbers §156, p. 208)

Numbers 30:4–16 describes legal cases involving women who take vows
that are annulled by their fathers or husbands: the first case involves the
vows of a woman who is still in her father's household; the second, a
woman who takes a vow while married; and the third, the vow of a widow
or divorced woman.[28] Numbers 30:17, which concludes the passage, is
glossed with a single sentence: "HA-KATUV speaks of a betrothed girl."[29]
The first issue of note is that, unlike those of TORAH, HA-KATUV's words
are not a scriptural quotation or paraphrase, but a pithy derashah that
introduces information not mentioned in the biblical verse. The brevity
of the derashah obscures the midrashic force of HA-KATUV's argument,
but the hermeneutical activity of HA-KATUV is more visible in longer
derashot:

"כי יכה איש את עבדו" (שמות כא כ): . . . רבי ישמעאל אומר, בכנעני <u>הכתוב מדבר,</u>
את אומר בכנעני הכתוב מדבר או אינו מדבר אלא בעברי, תלמוד לומר "לא יוקם כי כספו
הוא" מה כספו שקנינו קינין עולם וירושתו גמורה לו . . .

"When a man strikes his slave" (Exod 21:20): . . . Rabbi Ishmael says: HA-KATUV
here speaks of a Canaanite slave. You say HA-KATUV speaks of a Canaanite slave,
but perhaps it speaks of a Hebrew slave? [Scripture] teaches, saying: "He is not
to be avenged since he is the other's property" (Exod 21:21). Just as his property
can be acquired by him as a lasting possession, and when acquired by inheritance
is completely his . . . (Mekhilta Neziqin 7, p. 272; Lauterbach 3.57–58)

As with the Sifre Numbers' discussion of Numbers 30:17, the present
derashah establishes the status of a particular legal category—in this
case, the slave. Exodus 21:20 introduces the legal issues that arise "when
a man strikes his slave," but does not specify whether the slave in question is Israelite or Canaanite. Rabbi Ishmael states that, "HA-KATUV here
speaks of a Canaanite slave," but this statement is *not* decisive. HA-KATUV's

assertion is first questioned—perhaps, to the contrary, the verse speaks of a Hebrew slave—then confirmed by midrashic argument. The subsequent verse (Exod 21:21) states that the slave is counted as the owner's property (*kesef*), and property is passed down to future generations as an inheritance. Thus it follows, that the slave must be Canaanite, as Hebrew slaves are released at the Jubilee and not bequeathed to one's children. HA-KATUV's status is very different from that of TORAH. While TORAH's words are accepted without discussion, and function as ultimate authority, the fact that "HA-KATUV speaks of a Canaanite slave" is inconclusive. HA-KATUV's statement is treated as a hypothesis, subject to the same manipulations and questioning as the statements of sages. TORAH is not part of the midrashic process; though cited in the course of a derashah, it is "imported" from Scripture to determine the matter in question. The teachings of HA-KATUV, in contrast, are not an outside authority but part of the midrashic give-and-take.[30]

Here, too, one finds a consistent portrait of HA-KATUV. The phrase "HA-KATUV speaks" provides information omitted by Scripture, concerning the status or the identity of the legal category under discussion, and usually appears at the beginning of the derashah (immediately following the biblical verse). Thus, when Exodus mentions "the Passover offering" (Exod 12:13), the Mekhilta volunteers that "HA-KATUV speaks of the Passover in Egypt and the Passover of subsequent generations" (Mekhilta Pisḥa 15, p. 52; Lauterbach 1.117), and, similarly, "His master shall pierce his ear" (Exod 21:6) is glossed as "HA-KATUV speaks of the right [ear]" (Mekhilta Neziqin 2, p. 253; Lauterbach 3.15).

HA-KATUV STATES (*maggid ha-katuv*)

The second speech-formula associated with HA-KATUV is *maggid ha-katuv*,[31] "HA-KATUV states":

"[ולקח הכהן מים קדושים בכלי חרש] ומן העפר אשר יהיה בקרקע המשכן" (במדבר ה יז)
מגיד הכתוב שאם לא היה שם עפר מביא ממקום אחר ונותנו שם למקום מפני שהמקום
מקדשו.

"The priest shall take sacral water in an earthen vessel and, taking some of the earth that will be on the floor of the Tabernacle, the priest shall put it into the water" (Num 5:17): HA-KATUV states that if there was no earth there he is to bring earth from another site and place it there, for the site [or: God] sanctifies it. (Sifre Numbers, §10, p. 16)

This derashah cites Numbers 5:17 and immediately asserts, "HA-KATUV states that if there was no earth there he is to bring earth from another site and place it there." The Sifre does not make the argument explicit, but the key is the language of the verse, which states that the priest shall

take of the earth "*that will be* on the floor of the Tabernacle" (ומן העפר
אשר יהיה בקרקע המשכן). The phrase "that will be" is superfluous; its omission yields a more natural reading in which the priest shall take "of the
earth on the floor of the Tabernacle" (אשר בקרקע המשכן). HA-KATUV picks
up on this irregularity and argues that even if there is no earth on the
floor of the Tabernacle at first, it "will be" there, that is, it may be brought
to the Tabernacle from elsewhere. The midrashic nature of HA-KATUV's
statement, merely implicit here, is more plainly visible in other derashot:

"וזה לך תרומת מתנם" (במדבר יח יא): <u>מגיד הכתוב</u> שכשם שכלל הכתוב את קדשי קדשים
לנזור דין ולכרות להן ברית כך כלל את קדשים קלים לנזור דין ולכרות להן ברית.

"This, too, shall be yours: the gift offerings of their contributions . . ." (Num
18:11): HA-KATUV states that just as HA-KATUV counted the most holy sacrifices
as a single category with regard to their being intended exclusively [for the
priests] and as a covenant [with the priests] so too it counted the lesser sacrifices as a single category with regard to their being intended exclusively [for the
priests] and as a covenant [with the priests]. (Sifre Numbers §117, p. 136)

The derashah deals with the rights of the priests to various kinds of sacrifices. Earlier in the same chapter, God speaks to Aaron, saying, "I
hereby give you charge of My gifts, all the sacred donations of the
Israelites; . . . [T]his shall be yours from the most holy sacrifices, namely,
every meal offering, sin offering and guilt offering" (Num 18:8–9). In
discussing these verses, the Sifre Numbers (§117, p. 135) concludes that
God sets the most holy sacrifices (*qodshei qodashim*) apart as a covenant
with Aaron and the priesthood, for their exclusive use. When Numbers
18:11 mentions another sacrifice, the gift offering, the Sifre argues that
the conclusions reached earlier concerning the most holy sacrifices (*qodshei qodashim*) apply to these lesser sacrifices as well. In other words, HA-
KATUV draws an analogy from the category of sacrifices introduced in
Numbers 18:8–9 to the category of sacrifices mentioned in Numbers
18:11. It should be noted that HA-KATUV performs two distinct activities:
speaking ("HA-KATUV states . . .") and establishing categories ("HA-
KATUV counted . . . as a single category"). The nonspeech activities of
HA-KATUV will be discussed below, so for the present I will limit the discussion to *maggid ha-katuv*, which functions here much as it does in the
previous derashah (Sifre Numbers §10). *Maggid ha-katuv* follows the biblical verse, introducing the legal conclusion of the derashah—that the
two categories of sacrifice are analogous. Here, however, the midrashic
force of HA-KATUV's statement is explicit, as HA-KATUV arrives at a legal
decision by means of an argument by analogy ("HA-KATUV states that just
as . . . so too . . ."). HA-KATUV's introduction of an overt midrashic argument confirms the interpretation offered above, that HA-KATUV partici-
pates in midrashic discourse.

The contrast between the speech of TORAH and that of HA-KATUV is striking. As discussed above, *dibberah torah* (which occurs only twice) introduces a statement concerning the manner in which Scripture communicates, while the more common formula, *'amrah torah*, introduces either a scriptural citation or what the derashah takes to be the words of Scripture. TORAH reproduces the biblical text, remaining within the purview of what is already provided by Scripture and resorting to the awkward locution "the X that are spoken in the Torah" to avoid attributing to TORAH a speech-act that is not derived from Scripture. HA-KATUV, in contrast, clarifies the legal status of ambiguous biblical categories (*ha-katuv medabber*) and undertakes full-fledged midrashic arguments (*maggid ha-katuv*). HA-KATUV *never* cites a biblical verse. The hermeneutical roles of TORAH and HA-KATUV within the derashah are also quite different. TORAH's words decide the validity of a midrashic interpretation; requiring no justification, they function as a biblical prooftext. HA-KATUV's words *are* the midrashic argument, often elements in a broader midrashic negotiation in need of midrashic justification. TORAH's is a restrained, authoritative voice that restates the words of Scripture, while HA-KATUV actively engages the biblical text, suggesting novel interpretations and readings.

ACTION OF HA-KATUV: INTENTIONALITY AND PEDAGOGY

Another significant difference between TORAH and HA-KATUV is the amount and variety of nonspeech activity in which each engages. HA-KATUV partakes in a wide range of nonspeech activities, the most common of which is teaching—usually introduced by the formula "HA-KATUV comes to teach" (*ba' ha-katuv lelemdekha*) or a close variant.[32] We read in the Mekhilta:

רבי ... :(שמות יב כא)" [ויקרא משה לכל זקני ישראל ויאמר אלהם] משכו וקחו לכם צאן"
ישמעאל אומר, <u>בא הכתוב ללמדך</u> שלעולם נימנין על פסח ומושכין את ידיהם ממנו עד
.שישחט בלבד שיניח את הפסח כל שהוא

"[Moses then summoned all the elders of Israel and said to them], 'Draw out and take lambs'" (Exod 12:21): . . . Rabbi Ishmael says: HA-KATUV comes to teach you that until it is slaughtered people may enroll for partnership in the paschal lamb and withdraw from it; so long as they leave the paschal lamb intact. (Mekhilta Pisḥa 11, p. 36; Lauterbach 1.82–83)

The Mekhilta's derashah is based on the unusual biblical phrase "Draw out and take" from which the Mekhilta learns that one can withdraw (draw out) from a partnership that had been established for the purchase of the paschal lamb. Whatever the merits of this argument, the important point for the present discussion is that it is not made by a rabbinic authority but by HA-KATUV: "HA-KATUV comes to teach you." Rabbi Ishmael is the author of the derashah, but the teaching is not attributed to him but to HA-KATUV.

Bearing in mind Lakoff's findings about the significance of metaphoric and figurative speech,[33] what does this phrase communicate about HA-KATUV? The overall tone is clearly pedagogic—HA-KATUV seeks to impart understanding ("HA-KATUV comes to teach you"). And while the identity of the second-person masculine "you" (presumably the reader) is never fully fleshed out, the direct address endows HA-KATUV's actions with an interpersonal and communicative dimension. The phrase further implies a dynamism on HA-KATUV's part—it "*comes* to teach you" (בא הכתוב ללמדך); HA-KATUV is not always present, but arrives in order to expound the meaning of the ambiguous verse. This may seem a heavy-handed literalization of an innocent idiom, but consider the following. First, the verb "comes" is not needed to convey the notion that HA-KATUV teaches, which could have been expressed in a very natural way with the phrase "HA-KATUV teaches" (מלמד הכתוב). Second, the terminology of arrival is *never* employed with regard to TORAH. And finally, HA-KATUV's "arrival" fits well with the second-person address, creating the impression that HA-KATUV is moved to action by the reader's difficulty with the verse—that HA-KATUV arrives "*in order* to teach you." The precise way in which HA-KATUV teaches will be clarified over the course of this study. For now, it can be stated that a key element in the teaching process is HA-KATUV's tendency to employ interpretive techniques. The following list introduces some of these techniques (it is not exhaustive) while presenting the relationship that holds between HA-KATUV and the biblical verse.

i. Analogy:

"ובשרם יהיה לך כחזה התנופה וכשוק הימין לך יהיה" (במדבר יח יח): בא הכתוב <u>והקיש</u> את הבכור לחזה ושוק שלשלמין [של שלמים].[34]

> "But their meat shall be yours: it shall be yours like the breast of elevation offering and like the right thigh" (Num 18:18): HA-KATUV came and <u>drew an analogy</u> between the firstborn and the chest and thigh of the well-being offerings.[35] (Sifre Numbers §118, pp. 140–41)[36]

ii. Distinguishing between distinct legal cases:

"ואם שור נגח" (שמות כא כט): בא הכתוב <u>לחלוק</u> בין שור תם למועד.

> "If that ox is in the habit of goring" (Exod 21:29): HA-KATUV comes <u>to distinguish</u> between an ox that is not known to have gored and one that is known to have gored in the past. (Mekhilta Neziqin 10, p. 283; Lauterbach 3.82)

iii. Equating analogous legal cases:

"תורה אחת יהיה לאזרח [ולגר]" (שמות יב מט): בא הכתוב <u>והשוה</u> את הגר לאזרח בכל המצות שבתורה.

"There shall be one law for the citizen [and for the stranger]" (Exod 12:49): HA-KATUV comes to <u>declare the proselyte equal</u> to the born Jew with respect to all the commandments in the Torah. (Mekhilta Pisḥa 15, p. 57; Lauterbach 1.128)

iv. Prohibiting:

מה תלמוד לומר "ולא יאכל חמץ" (שמות יג ג): הא לא בא הכתוב אלא <u>לאסרו</u> בהנייה [הנאה].

What does [Scripture] teach in saying: "No leavened bread shall be eaten" (Exod 13:3)? HA-KATUV comes only <u>to prohibit</u> any enjoyment of it. (Mekhilta Pisḥa 16, p. 61; Lauterbach 1.139)

v. Defining the legal status of transgressions:

בא הכתוב <u>לעשות</u> זדון הציבור כשגגה.

HA-KATUV comes <u>to establish</u> that the premeditated transgression of the general public is counted as an inadvertent error. (Sifre Numbers §111, p. 117)

vi. Disqualifying:

תלמוד לומר "איש לפי אכלו תכוסו" (שמות יב ד): <u>שנה</u> עליו הכתוב <u>לפסול</u>.

[Scripture] teaches, saying: "In proportion to the number of persons [you shall contribute for the lamb according to what each household will eat]" (Exod 12:4): HA-KATUV <u>repeats</u> [the paschal command regarding the proportionality of the eaters] <u>to disqualify</u> the sacrifice if the command be transgressed. (Mekhilta Pisḥa 4, p. 12; Lauterbach 1.27)

vii. Establishing a commandment as obligatory:

"בראשון בארבעה עשר יום לחדש בערב תאכלו מצות" (שמות יב יח): <u>קבעו</u> הכתוב חובה.

"In the first month, from the fourteenth day of the month at evening, you shall eat unleavened bread" (Exod 12:18): HA-KATUV <u>establishes</u> it as an obligation [for the first day]. (Mekhilta Pisḥa 8, p. 27; Lauterbach 1.61)

viii. Distinguishing a particular issue from the broader category to which it belongs:

"וכי ישאל איש מעם רעהו" (שמות כב יג): <u>נתק</u> הכתוב השואל מכלל שומר ואמרו עניין בפני עצמו.

"When a man borrows from another" (Exod 22:13): HA-KATUV <u>removes</u> the borrower from the category of the guardian, treating his case as a subject by itself. (Mekhilta Neziqin 16, p. 306; Lauterbach 3.127)

ix. Distinguishing a particular issue from a broader category and in so doing clarifying the severity of the punishment it entails:

"ומכה אביו ואמו מות יומת" (שמות כא טו): ... והרי הכתוב <u>מוציאו מכללו</u> להחמיר עליו שיהא במיתה.

"He who strikes his father and mother shall be put to death" (Exod 21:15): HA-KATUV <u>singles out this case from the general statement</u> ["An eye for an eye" (Exod 21:24)] to declare it a graver, capital, offense. (Mekhilta Neziqin 5, p. 265; Lauterbach 3.41)

With its evident wealth of activities, it should now be clear that HA-KATUV is a very different "actor" from TORAH and that the two constitute distinct personifications of Scripture, not stylistic variation. At the same time, there is no denying that both refer to Scripture. What, then, is the relationship between the two? One way to approach this question is through derashot that refer both to *torah* and *ha-katuv*, providing a context in which the two may be readily compared.

Torah and Ha-Katuv

We begin with the Mekhilta's analysis of Exodus 21:33:

ור' יושיה אומר "איש או אישה" (במדבר ה ו) למה נאמר, אלא לפי שהוא אומר "וכי יפתח איש בור" (שמות כא לג): אין לי אלא איש, אשה מנין, תלמוד לומר "איש או אשה"[37] <u>בא הכתוב והשוה</u> אשה לאיש בכל הנזקין <u>שבתורה</u>.

Rabbi Yoshaiah says "a man or a woman" (Num 5:6), why is this stated? Because it says "When a man opens a pit" (Exod 21:33). From this I know only about a man. But how about a woman? [Scripture] teaches, saying: "a man or a woman," <u>HA-KATUV came and equated</u> women to men in regard to all the laws of damages <u>in the Torah</u>. (Mekhilta Neziqin 6, p. 269; Lauterbach 3.51)[38]

Exodus 21:33 speaks of a man, *'ish*, opening a pit, and details the consequences of that action. Does this mean that this law applies only to men? According to the Mekhilta, the answer is provided by Numbers 5:6, which discusses the case of "a man or a woman" committing a transgression. The Mekhilta presents Numbers 5:6 as HA-KATUV declaring the analogous status of women to men with regard to all the laws of damages that occur <u>in the Torah</u>. Numbers 5:6 is a biblical verse no more and no less than Exodus 21:33 or any other verse communicating biblical tort law. Yet the Mekhilta characterizes the verses differently, as the argument

of the derashah makes clear: Exodus 21:33 contains an ambiguous term
(*'ish*, man) that might lead the reader to a false conclusion (that the laws
of torts apply only to men); Numbers 5:6 clarifies the ambiguity in Exodus 21:33 (the laws apply to both men and women). Exodus 21:33 is characterized as one of the verses that contain the laws of damages "in the
Torah"; Numbers 5:6 is HA-KATUV. From this preliminary sketch, it
appears that one point of contrast between *torah* and *ha-katuv* involves
the passivity of the former and the activity of the latter. Also relevant in
this regard is the Sifre Numbers to Numbers 15:18:

"[וידבר ה' אל משה לאמר דבר אל בני ישראל ואמרת אליהם] בבאכם אל הארץ . . .
"(במדבר טו יח): ר' ישמעאל אומר <u>שינה הכתוב</u> ביאות³⁹ זו מכל <u>ביאות שבתורה</u> . . .
ללמדך שכיון שנכנסו ישראל לארץ מיד נתחייבו בחלה.

"[The Lord spoke to Moses, saying: Speak to the Israelite people and say to
them:] When you enter the land . . ." (Num 15:18): Rabbi Ishmael says, HA-
KATUV altered this instance of the *biy'ah* [arrival formula] in comparison to all
the other *biy'ot* [arrival formulas] in the Torah . . . in order to teach you that
when they entered the land [of Israel] they were immediately obligated to
observe the commandment of *ḥallah* [setting aside the loaf from the first yield].
(Sifre Numbers §110, p. 113)

This derashah will be discussed at length in the following chapter, but it
is important to the present analysis as well for the way that it thematizes
the difference between *torah* and *ha-katuv*. The key element is how the
irregularity of Numbers 15:18 is presented as an intentional act on the part
of HA-KATUV. HA-KATUV alters a biblical formula relative to all the biblical formulas dealing with commandments that take effect, "when you
enter the land." These formulas are "in *torah*" but are not interpreted by
TORAH but rather by HA-KATUV. Finally, consider the interesting argument of Sifre Numbers §107:

"או לאיל תעשה מנחה [סלת שני עשרנים בלולה בשמן שלשית ההין]" (במדבר טו ו):
<u>בא הכתוב לחלק</u> בין נסכי כבש לנסכי איל שהיה בדין בן בקר טעון נסכים ובן צאן טעון נסכים
אם למדתי <u>שלא חלקה תורה</u> בין נסכי עגל לנסכי שור כך לא תחלוק בין נסכי כבש
לנסכי איל תלמוד לומר "או לאיל תעשה מנחה" בא הכתוב לחלוק בין נסכי כבש לנסכי איל.

"In the case of a ram, you shall present as a meal offering [two-tenths of a measure of choice flour with a third of a *hin* of wine as a libation]" (Num 15:6): HA-
KATUV comes to distinguish between the libation of the sheep and the libation of
the ram, since it might be argued that since the cattle require libation and the
sheep require libation, and since TORAH did not distinguish between the libation
of a calf and the libation of an ox, so too it would not distinguish between the
libation of a sheep and the libation of a ram [Scripture] teaches, saying: "In the
case of a ram," HA-KATUV comes to distinguish between the libation of the sheep
and the libation of the ram. (Sifre Numbers §107, p. 109)

This fascinating derashah suggests a division of labor between TORAH and HA-KATUV. The derashah addresses the difference between the libation of the sheep offering, which requires a quarter *hin* of wine (Num 15:5; a *hin* is a measure of volume roughly equivalent to 1.7 gallons or 6.5 liters) and the libation of the ram offering, which requires a third of a *hin* of wine (Num 15:6). This is critical information, since both sacrificial rams and sacrificial sheep require libation, and one might otherwise conclude that the volume of the libation is the same in both cases. This is particularly so in light of the fact that "TORAH did not distinguish between the libation of a calf and the libation of an ox," and the lack of distinction between these animals could be taken as an indication that there is no difference between the sheep and the ram. Thus the need for Numbers 15:6, which, as HA-KATUV, clarifies the matter: the sheep requires only a quarter *hin*, the ram a third of a *hin*. Again, the interpretive activity and passivity of the two personifications is paramount. The non-distinction between the sheep and the bull is the inaction of TORAH, inaction that might suggest no distinction holds between the ram and the sheep. To counter this misunderstanding (and, explicitly, TORAH's inaction), decisive intervention is needed; Scripture must declare that the libation of the ram requires a third of a *hin*, not the quarter *hin* of the sheep, and this is done by HA-KATUV. The seemingly innocent statement that the ram sacrifice requires a third of a *hin* becomes an expression of TORAH's inaction and HA-KATUV's interventionist response.

Before attempting to draw general conclusions, one final difference between TORAH and HA-KATUV should be introduced—namely, their temporal thematization: TORAH acts in the past, and HA-KATUV largely in the present. Regarding the former, TORAH is consistently presented as speaking in the past—the speaking verbs in both the formulas that introduce TORAH's speech (*'amrah torah* and *dibberah torah*) are in the perfect tense. What little TORAH does besides speaking, it also does in the perfect tense: "the expression TORAH chose"; "TORAH gave permission"; "what did the TORAH consider"; "TORAH gave discernment to the sages"; "TORAH designated him a slave."[40]

HA-KATUV, on the other hand, often takes the active participle (which is closely related to the present tense in rabbinic Hebrew),[41] particularly when it speaks. Both HA-KATUV's speech formulas employ the active participle—"HA-KATUV speaks" (*ha-katuv medabber*) and "HA-KATUV states" (*maggid ha-katuv*)—without a single instance of the perfect (*dibber ha-katuv* or *heggid ha-katuv*). HA-KATUV's nonspeech activities are more ambiguous. The phrase "HA-KATUV comes" (*ba' ha-katuv*) is indeterminate with regard to tense, since *ba'* is both the third-person masculine singular active participle (present) and the third-person masculine singular perfect.

Other passages are not decisive, since there are cases of both perfect and imperfect (or participle). Thus one finds:

הרי הכתוב משיאו מכלל היין ובא לו ללמד על התגלחת.

HA-KATUV removes it from the category of the wine and comes to teach regarding the shaving. (Sifre Numbers §25, p. 30)

But also:

בא הכתוב והיקיש את הבכור לחזה ושוק שלשלמין.[42]

HA-KATUV came and drew an analogy between the firstborn and the chest and thigh of the well-being offerings. (Sifre Numbers §118, pp. 140–41)

Even so, there is a consistent (albeit not absolute) division in the temporal characterization of TORAH and HA-KATUV. The actions of TORAH are always past, while HA-KATUV speaks in the present and performs many interpretive activities in the present.

The most basic conclusion from the analysis thus far is that the distinction between *torah* and *ha-katuv* is not merely stylistic, but rather a sustained and consistent rhetorical strategy aimed at establishing two distinct personifications. TORAH is figured almost exclusively as a speaker of scriptural passages, while HA-KATUV never cites Scripture; TORAH is an authoritative voice, deciding halakhic questions, while HA-KATUV is part of the midrashic give-and-take; TORAH's nonspeech actions are very limited, almost nonexistent, while HA-KATUV is presented as an active teacher that employs a wide range of interpretive techniques. In addition, the Rabbi Ishmael midrashim consistently avoid attributing to TORAH speech that cannot be presented as a verse. In these cases, (no longer active) *torah* is presented as the framework in which oaths, commands, and punishments are decreed, while HA-KATUV actively engages these categories in an attempt to determine their underlying halakhic import. Finally, TORAH belongs decisively to the past: its statements already made, its actions (few as they are) already performed, while HA-KATUV is very much part of the present. In light of these distinctions, it would appear that the two personifications of Scripture replicate the relationship between Scripture and its interpretation. TORAH—the past, already spoken, authoritative voice of Scripture—is a metonymy for revelation, and HA-KATUV—the dynamic interpreter and teacher of halakhah—a metonymy for midrash. TORAH is Sinai, and HA-KATUV is the *bet midrash*.

In *Midrash and Theory*, David Stern addresses the issue at the heart of this dual personification of Scripture. According to Stern, the response of the Rabbis to doubts about the authority of their tradition "was to adopt an interpretive posture that is the very opposite of Harold Bloom's idea of the anxiety of influence. The Rabbis consciously—happily, we might say—assume the stance of belatedness. Precisely what they seek to prove is that all the innovations and inventions of their tradition can already be found in the text of the Bible."[43] Stern is certainly right that the Rabbis strive to anchor their views in Scripture, but their belatedness is not only happy—it is anxious as well. The Rabbis can use midrash to anchor their practices and values in Scripture (King David was a Torah scholar, the patriarchs prayed three times a day, and so forth), but these arguments cannot obscure the fact that midrashic argument is *itself* an innovation that stands in need of justification. And it is this need that generates TORAH and HA-KATUV as two distinct voices within Scripture. As the Mishnah observes, tongs are used to forge new tongs, but whence the first tongs? The first set of tongs, the instrument needed for all future metallurgical work, must have been created by God—at dusk prior to the first Sabbath.[44] In the same way, midrash can ground many practices, but not midrash itself. The first midrash, like the first tongs, must be a fixed, ineluctable fact. The inner-scriptural dynamics of TORAH and HA-KATUV accomplish this in a brilliantly simple fashion, collapsing the distance between Scripture and its interpretation. According to the Rabbi Ishmael midrashim, midrashic praxis is neither late nor rabbinic, since Scripture itself—qua HA-KATUV—engages in and thus justifies precisely this type of interpretation. For midrashic interpretation to be ultimately justified, it must become Scripture, and Scripture must become its own interpreter—it must become midrash.[45]

Chapter 2
Inaction and Attention

Bacher, it seems, was only partially right: TORAH and HA-KATUV are two distinct personifications of Scripture, but they are not synonyms. As Chapter 1 demonstrates, they behave differently and play different roles in the explication—or better, the self-explication—of Scripture. Indeed, it is the difference between TORAH and HA-KATUV that first reveals the self-interpretive dynamic attributed to Scripture by the Rabbi Ishmael midrashim and the underlying justification of midrashic interpretation, in which hermeneutical agency is shifted away from the rabbinic reader toward Scripture itself. Scripture, as HA-KATUV, interprets Scripture. What, then, is the role of the reader? To put the same question another way, if HA-KATUV is *bet midrash* to TORAH's Sinai, how is the rabbinic inhabitant of the real, post-70 *bet midrash* to approach Scripture? After all, post-70 midrashic interpretation cannot be wholly effaced—the Rabbi Ishmael midrashim themselves testify to its existence. In what follows, I will argue that these midrashim seek to impose upon the human interpreter a hermeneutic of submission, in which the lead role of Scripture in the interpretive process is constantly acknowledged and fortified. But first I examine how the Rabbi Ishmael midrashim represent biblical interpretation in its ideal state, that is, without the intervention of the human reader. More specifically, I examine a series of pericopes in which the proper response to interpretive difficulties is inaction or attentive openness to Scripture, derashot that counsel passivity or unmediated receptivity to Scripture's words.

Inaction

The clearest expression of the reader's passivity is found in a series of derashot that counsel inaction in the face of interpretive difficulties. The best known of these is the *middah* (commonly translated as "hermeneutical canon")[1] that resolves contradictory verses.

[זו מדה בתורה:]‏[2] שני כתובים זה כנגד זה והרי הן סותרין זה על ידי זה יתקיימו במקומן עד שיבא כתוב אחר ויכריע ביניהם.

This is a *middah* in the Torah: two verses that oppose and contradict each other will remain in their place until another verse comes to decide between them. (Sifre Numbers §58, p. 56)

This *middah* addresses a clear textual difficulty: two verses contradict one another. Since the Rabbis presumably hold that the Torah is not self-contradictory, contradiction ought to justify interpretive action on the part of the reader; for example, the reader might argue with one of the verses against the other, or show that the contradiction is only apparent, or perhaps argue for an altogether different resolution—but some sort of interpretation is required. Yet the *middah* counsels the reader to take the following action: absolutely nothing. The contradictory verses "remain in their place," indefinitely, until a third verse decides the matter. In other words, the reader should not initiate action, but rather wait for Scripture to rectify its own internal difficulties. The procedure is so scriptural that at least one traditional commentator has suggested that it cannot be counted as a *middah* at all. Rabbi Aharon Even Hayyim (d. 1632) writes in *Middot Aharon*, the introduction to *Qorban Aharon*, his commentary on the Sifra: "Rather I hold that the *middah* 'Two Verses Contradict' is not one of the *middot* by which the Torah is explicated, for *middot* are those [techniques] by which we explicate [*dorshim*] and create a matter from the Torah through our reason [*mi-sevaratenu*] and which are not written in the Torah explicitly. Yet when two verses contradict and a third resolves, we do not explicate anything; rather, Scripture [*ha-katuv*(!)] itself explicates and decides the matter."[3]

The interpretive inaction formulated as a general principle in the *middah* is manifested locally in a number of derashot:[4]

"ומקלל אביו ואמו יומת" (שמות כא יז): אין לי אלא אביו אביו ואמו, אביו שלא אמו ואמו שלא אביו מניין⁵... ר' יונתן אומר, משמע שניהם כאחת ומשמע אחד אחד בפני עצמו, עד שיפרוט לך הכתוב באחד.

"He who insults his father and his mother shall be put to death" (Exod 21:17): I thus know only about one who curses both his father and his mother. How about one who curses only his father or only his mother? . . . Rabbi Yonathan says: It can mean both of them together and it can mean either of them until HA-KATUV should expressly decide in favor of one of these. (Mekhilta Neziqin 5, pp. 267–68; Lauterbach 3.47)

The derashah hinges on the ambiguity of the letter *vav* in the phrase "he who insults his father and [*vav*] his mother." The biblical verse may mean that one who insults both his father *and* his mother be put to death, or it may mean that if one insults either his father *or* his mother he shall be put to death. In the former case, the *vav* is conjunctive and both elements need to be present; in the latter, the *vav* is disjunctive and either of the elements suffices. Both meanings of the *vav* exist in biblical Hebrew, so the question cannot be decided on lexical grounds.[6] In addressing this question, the Mekhilta first suggests that both parents must be cursed for the son to be put to death and inquires as to the ruling for a child who curses one parent but not the other. Rabbi Yonathan recognizes that both readings are possible—"It can mean both [parents] together or it can mean either of them [separately]"—but does not attempt to decide the matter. Instead he suggests that the ambiguity remain unresolved "until HA-KATUV should expressly decide in favor of one of these." Again the reader is instructed to avoid interpretation and allow HA-KATUV to act as the interpretive agent.

A similar argument appears in the Sifre Numbers §17:

"[והניף את המנחה] לפני ה'" (במדבר ה כה): במזרח שבכל מקום שנאמר "לפני ה'" הרי הוא
במזרח עד שיפרט לך הכתוב.

"[Then the priest shall . . . elevate the meal offering] before the Lord" (Num 5:25): In the east, for every verse that states "before the Lord" refers to the east unless HA-KATUV specifies otherwise. (Sifre Numbers §17, p. 22)

Numbers 5:25 instructs the priest to elevate the meal offering "before the Lord"—an ambiguous phrase. The Sifre Numbers suggests that the default meaning of "before the Lord" is "in the east," and that meaning holds unless and until HA-KATUV (not the reader) indicates otherwise.[7] Strikingly, then, the Rabbi Ishmael midrashim contain a number of derashot in which the reader, though faced with clear and explicit textual difficulties, is instructed not to interpret but to stand back and allow HA-KATUV to resolve the questions. Though rare, these derashot are important because their explicit and unambiguous demand for interpretive inaction is a distilled expression of the Rabbi Ishmael ideal of scriptural interpretation—a passive reader to complement the active, interpreting HA-KATUV. A more common expression of this ideal is found in a series of formulas that depict the reader listening to Scripture, formulas that contain the Hebrew root *sh-m-'*, "hear."

Hearing Scripture

We Have Heard, We Have Not Heard (*shama'nu, lo' shama'nu*)

The Mekhilta teaches:

"לא תרצח" (שמות כ ין): למה נאמר? לפי שהוא אומר "שופך דם האדם" (בראשית ט ו),
עונש שמענו אזהרה לא שמענו, תלמוד לומר "לא תרצח."

"You shall not murder" (Exod 20:13): Why is this said? Because it says: "Whoever sheds the blood of man [by man shall his blood be shed]" (Gen 9:6). We have heard the penalty for it but we have not heard the warning against it. [Scripture] teaches, saying: "You shall not murder." (Mekhilta Baḥodesh 8, p. 232; Lauterbach 2.260)

Exodus 20:13, the Sixth Commandment, prohibits murder. But the commandment is apparently redundant, since bloodshed has already been prohibited in Gen 9:6 as part of the Noahide laws. According to the Mekhilta, both verses are necessary. Genesis 9:6 states the punishment for murder, but a person cannot be punished without first being warned (an established principle of rabbinic jurisprudence). Exodus 20:13, then, prohibits murder while Gen 9:6 states the punishment for this transgression, but cannot stand on its own since "we have heard the penalty [for murder] but we have not heard the warning against it." Without Exodus 20:13, only the penalty has been heard, not the actual prohibition.

What does it mean, that these statements have been *heard*?[8] One might propose that the hearing imagery depends on their biblical representation as spoken by God.[9] But while the first-person plural *shama'nu*, "we have heard," may describe Israel's auditory experience at Sinai, and the rabbinic author's conviction that he was somehow present at Sinai, this explanation fits Genesis 9:6—addressed to Noah and his family in the postdiluvian world—poorly. As I will argue, the core meaning of "hearing" in the Rabbi Ishmael terminology refers to grasping the meaning of a verse without the need for interpretation. In the derashah at hand, the Mekhilta sets out to explain the relationship between Exodus 20:13 and Genesis 9:6—are they not redundant?—without ever calling into question the meaning of the verses. The meaning of the verses has been "heard" and need not be discussed further. Further analysis reveals that all *shama'nu/lo' shama'nu* (we have heard/we have not heard) derashot consider the meaning of the biblical verse they adduce as obvious, and proceed directly with higher-level analysis. Indeed, a number of derashot implicitly contrast interpreted and uninterpreted understandings of Scripture, characterizing the latter as "heard." Consider the Mekhilta to Exodus 21:13:

"[ואשר לא צדה . . .] ושמתי לך מקום אשר ינוס שמה" (שמות כא יג): אבל לא שמענו להיכן. הרי את דן, נאמר מנוס לשעה ונאמר מנוס לדורות, מה מנוס האמור לדורות, ערי הלוים קולטות, אף מנוס האמור לשעה, מחנות הלוים קולטות.

"[If he did not do it by design . . .] I will assign you a place to which he can flee" (Exod 21:13): But we have not heard where. Thus you reason, refuge was mentioned both in the context of that time and in the context of future generations. And just as in the latter the Levite cities offer refuge, so too in the former do the Levite encampments offer the refuge. (Mekhilta Neziqin 4, p. 262; Lauterbach 3.36)

Exodus 21:12 declares that "he who fatally strikes a man shall be put to death," while Exodus 21:13 qualifies this statement by stating that if the act was unintentional, the perpetrator should not be punished; instead God "will assign" a place to which the inadvertent killer may flee from the vengeance of the victim's family. But no location is assigned, so though Scripture indicates that the location will be assigned, "we have not heard where" and the Mekhilta must decide the matter midrashically. To do so, it cites Numbers 35:6—"The towns that you assign to the Levites shall comprise the six cities of refuge that you are to designate for the manslayer to flee to"—arguing by analogy that just as the cities of refuge were part of the Levite estate, so, too, in the desert period the encampment of Levi served as the place of refuge. In keeping with the proposed meaning of the hearing imagery, note that Exodus 21:13— the verse that is implicitly contrasted with the "unheard" information— is not problematic; it is not made the object of midrashic exposition and, in fact, receives no comment at all. The entire focus of the passage is to provide a midrashic explanation for the omitted information, the information that was "not heard."

As It Is Heard (ki-shmu'o)

Another interpretive term based on the root sh-m-' is ki-shmu'o, literally, "as it is heard."[10] This term is the subject of extensive analysis later in this study,[11] so the present discussion is confined to the question of interpretive activity. The Mekhilta teaches:

"וְעָבַדוּ לְעוֹלָם" (שמות כא ו): . . . מַה תַּלְמוּד לוֹמַר "וְעָבַדוּ לְעוֹלָם"? עַד הַיּוֹבֵל אוֹ "וְעָבַדוּ לְעוֹלָם" כִּשְׁמוּעוֹ[12] תַּלְמוּד לוֹמַר "וְשַׁבְתֶּם אִישׁ אֶל אֲחֻזָּתוֹ" (ויקרא כה י).

"And he shall serve him forever [le-'olam]" (Exod 21:6): . . . what does [Scripture] teach in saying "forever"? "Up to the Jubilee" or "he shall serve him forever" could be taken literally [ki-shmu'o]. But Scripture says: "And you shall return every man to his family" (Lev 25:10). (Mekhilta Neziqin 2, pp. 253–4; Lauterbach 3.17)

This brief derashah raises the possibility of understanding one of the words in Exodus 21:6 ki-shmu'o, but rejects that possibility in light of another verse. The word in question, le-'olam (forever), could be understood ki-shmu'o, but Leviticus 25:10—which states that slaves are freed on the Jubilee year—indicates that le'olam means "up until the Jubilee year." For now, I wish merely to point out that one of the interpretations considered, "up to the Jubilee," is supported with a biblical prooftext, but the other is characterized as ki-shmu'o and nothing more is said. The asymmetry between these readings supports the proposed understanding of

the Rabbi Ishmael *sh-m-'* terminology: the *ki-shmu'o* reading does not require midrashic interpretation because understanding a verse "as it is
heard" means precisely that it does not require midrashic interpretation.
Like the verses that have been "heard" or "not heard," the meaning of a
word "as it is heard" (*ki-shmu'o*) is hermeneutically self-evident and, by
definition, not subject to midrashic explication.

I HEAR (*Shome'a 'Ani*)

Shome'a 'ani, literally, "I hear," is one of the most common formulas in the
Rabbi Ishmael midrashim.[13] Like *ki-shmu'o*, it almost always introduces
an interpretation that is rejected, often because of a conflict with a verse
introduced by *talmud lomar*.[14] *Shome'a 'ani* and *ki-shmu'o* are used in tandem in a number of derashot.[15] Unlike the formulas discussed up to this
point, two derashot appear in which *shome'a 'ani* introduces a midrashic
reading, both of which deal with the silver trumpets described in Numbers 10:1–8:[16]

"עשה לך שתי חצוצרות כסף" (במדבר י ב): למה נאמר פרשה, לפי שהוא אומר "על פי ה'
יחנו ועל פי ה' יסעו" (במדבר ט כג) שומע אני הואיל ונוסעין על פי הדיבר וחונין על פי
הדיבר לא יהו צריכין חצוצרות תלמוד לומר "עשה לך [שתי חצוצרות כסף]", מגיד הכתוב
שאף על פי נוסעין[17] וחונין על פי הדיבר צריכין היו לחצוצרות.

"Have two trumpets made" (Num 10:2): Why was this passage stated? Because it
states, "On a sign from the Lord they made camp and on a sign from the Lord
they broke camp" (Num 9:23). I could understand that since they depart and
encamp according to the divine speech that they do not need trumpets, [Scrip-
ture] teaches, saying: "Have two trumpets made." HA-KATUV states that even
though they decamp and encamp according to the divine speech they still
required the trumpets. (Sifre Numbers §72, p. 67)

And:

שומע אני הואיל ועשאן [את החצוצרות] יהו ירושה לבניו תלמוד לומר "והיו לכם לחקת
[עולם]"(במדבר י ח) לחקה ניתנו ולא לדורות.

I could understand that having made [the trumpets], they would be an inheritance for his sons, [Scripture] teaches, saying: "They shall be for you an
institution for all time throughout the ages" (Num 10:8), they were given as an
institution, not for future generations. (Sifre Numbers §75, p. 70)

In these passages, *shome'a 'ani* clearly introduces statements that require interpretation and so do not fit the proposed meaning of *sh-m-'* terminology.[18] Still, within the context of the two-hundred-plus times that the
phrase occurs in the Rabbi Ishmael midrashim, these two derashot are
clearly the exception. As for the rule, the high incidence of *shome'a 'ani*
makes an exhaustive analysis impractical and, fortunately, unnecessary,

since this phrase exhibits fairly regular interpretive behavior. In what follows, I list—with only the briefest comment—some of the common interpretive roles played by the formula.

    i. *Shomeʿa ʾani* often introduces a reading that is very closely tied to
    the verse it interprets:

"ויאמר ה' אל משה ואל אהרן. . ." (שמות יב א): שומע אני שהיה הדיבר למשה
כשהוא ולאהרן. אומר "ויהי ביום דבר ה' אל משה בארץ מצרים" (שמות ו כו) למשה
היה הדיבר ולא היה הדיבר לאהרן.

"The Lord spoke to Moses and Aaron in the land of Egypt" (Exod 12:1):
From this I might understand that the speech was to Moses and Aaron.
When, however, it says: "For when the Lord spoke to Moses in the land of
Egypt" (Exod 6:28), it shows that the speech was addressed to Moses alone
and not to Aaron. (Mekhilta Pisḥa 1, p. 1; Lauterbach 1.1)

Exodus 12:1 teaches that "the Lord spoke to Moses and Aaron,"
and the *shomeʿa ʾani* interpretation takes this to mean that the
divine speech was to Moses and Aaron. This derashah is not so
much an interpretation as a restatement of the biblical verse.

    ii. *Shomeʿa ʾani* introduces interpretations rejected as too broad or as
    unqualified in light of other biblical statements:

"[כל ימי הזירו לה'] על נפש מת לא יבוא" (במדבר ו ו): שומע אני נפשות בהמה
במשמע תלמוד לומר "לאביו ולאמו לא יטמא" (במדבר ו ז) במה עינין מדבר בנפשות
אדם.

"[Throughout the term of his nazirite oath] he shall not approach a dead
body" (Num 6:6): I might understand this to refer to the corpses of domestic animals, but [Scripture] teaches by saying: "Even if his father or mother
[. . .should die] he must not defile himself for them" (Num 6:7). Of what
matter does it speak? Of human corpses. (Sifre Numbers §26, p. 32)

Since Numbers 6:6 speaks of an indeterminate "dead body," the
Sifre questions how broadly this term is intended. The *shomeʿa ʾani*
reading suggests that the verse could refer to animals, but this view
is rejected as incompatible with the context of the biblical passage,
which deals with human beings.

    iii. Occasionally, *shomeʿa ʾani* introduces an interpretation that is more
    a formulaic gesture than a plausible reading:

"ובבוא משה אל אהל מעד . . . וישמע את הקול" (במדבר ז פט): שומע אני קול נמוך
תלמוד לומר "את הדברים האלה דבר ה' אל כל קהלכם" (דברים ה יט).

"When Moses went into the Tent of Meeting . . . he would hear the voice"
(Num 7:89): I could understand this as meaning [*shomeʿa ʾani*] a quiet

voice, thus [Scripture] teaches, saying: "The Lord spoke these words to your whole congregation" (Deut 5:19). (Sifre Numbers §58, p. 56)

The structure of this derashah is familiar enough: *shome'a 'ani* introduces a reading that is rejected on account of another verse. However, the too-specific understanding of the verse is not clearly anchored in the verse: why would one propose, even as a preliminary hypothesis, that the voice Moses heard in the Tent of Meeting was quiet? Nothing in the verse generates this expectation and consequently, the Sifre's refutation of the low-voice hypothesis appears, prima facie, to be nothing more than a straw man, erected only to be torn down (but see the discussion below).

iv. Similarly, in Sifre Numbers §126:

"[אדם כי ימות באהל כל הבא אל האהל] וכל אשר באהל יטמא שבעת ימים" (במדבר יט יד): שומע אני אף הקש והחרין והעצים והאבנים והאדמה במשמע תלמוד לומר "ולקח אזוב וטבל במים איש טהור" (במדבר יט יח).

"[When a person dies in a tent, whoever enters the tent and] all that is in the tent shall be unclean seven days" (Num 19:14): I could understand this as referring to the straw and the dried branches, and the wood, and the stones, and the earth; thus [Scripture] teaches, saying: "A person who is clean shall take hyssop, dip it in the water" (Num 19:18). (Sifre Numbers §126, p. 162)

Like (ii), the derashah moves from a general or unqualified reading to a scripturally qualified one. The general reading is arguably generated by Scripture, since Numbers 19:14 states that "all that is in the tent" (כל אשר באהל) is unclean. Still, the specific objects cited by the Sifre—"I could understand this as referring to the straw and the dried branches, and the wood, and the stones, and the earth"— appear out of place. Why cite these particular objects, when the verse speaks in undifferentiated generalities? This derashah, too, appears to be at odds with the notion that *shome'a 'ani* introduces an uninterpreted, self-evident understanding of the biblical verse.

Surveying the interpretive functions of *shome'a 'ani*, the first two categories fit my proposal well: in (i), the formula introduces uninterpreted readings of the biblical verse; and (ii), while not a restatement of the biblical verses, introduces a plausible interpretation that requires— and receives—no midrashic support. Derashot (iii) and (iv) are, at first blush, more problematic. The suggestion that "I could understand" the voice in the Tent of Meeting as a quiet voice seems to be a non sequitur. Further consideration, however, suggests that the proposed reading is quite plausible, seeing as the nature of the divine revelation in the Tent of Meeting was the subject of considerable discussion, as evidenced by the extensive analysis in the opening chapters of the Sifra, which also proposes that God spoke in a quiet voice.[19] At stake is the nature of the revelation: if the voice were quiet, only Moses would hear it and the Tent of Meeting would be the site of Moses' private audience with God. The verse introduced by *talmud lomar* rejects this possibility by juxtaposing the revelation at the Tent of Meeting with Deuteronomy 5:9, the most public account of the revelation at Sinai.[20] Removed from the polemic concerning the Tent of Meeting, the reading introduced by *shome'a 'ani* appears arbitrary. But in the context of the time, the Sifre Numbers is responding to an interpretation that was current and thus, for the Sifre, not in need of explanation or justification.

Polemic also appears to be the motivating force behind (iv), since the *shome'a 'ani* interpretation that includes straw and dried branches and earth is the precise halakhic position articulated in the Temple Scroll from Qumran.[21] The polemic context of (iii) and (iv) suggests that though the *shome'a 'ani* readings do not always appear "innocent," sometimes these derashot introduce contemporary interpretations that, as such, do not require midrashic argument or justification. As Moshe Halbertal writes: "While the claim needs to be established more soundly, it should be emphasized that many of the interpretive possibilities rejected in the halakhic midrashim discussed constitute traditions presented by Philo and Josephus."[22] Halbertal's argument is significant inasmuch as it shows that in the few cases that the *shome'a 'ani* readings are not derived from the verse, they are likely responding to existing (and thus, by definition, possible) interpretations. As with the midrashically generated equation of *totafot* and *tefillin*, what counts as a plain or immediate understanding of a verse changes, at times radically, depending on the reader's context. A polemic interpretation advanced by a rival group may be "obvious," inasmuch as its existence is well known, even if it is forced. Overall, then, the Rabbi Ishmael midrashim consistently employ *shome'a 'ani* to introduce readings that, for various reasons, do not require midrashic interpretation.[23]

Finally, the absence of midrashic argument in *shome'a 'ani* interpretations is often highlighted by the contrast with the midrashic explanations that follow it. The midrashic element can consist of nothing more than a verse (*talmud lomar*) and a gloss, as in (ii) above. In other cases, the *shome'a 'ani* interpretation (underlined) is followed by a more explicit midrashic argument, such as analogy (*heqqesh*):

"[כי תקנה עבד עברי] שש שנים יעבוד" (שמות כא ב): שומע אני בין עבדה שיש בה בזיון
בין עבדה שאין בה בזיון תלמוד לומר "כשכיר [כתושב]" (ויקרא כה מ), מה שכיר אין
את רשאי לשנותו מאומנותו, אף עבד עברי אין את רשאי לשנותו מאומנותו.

"He shall serve six years" (Exod 21:2): <u>I might understand this to mean by doing any kind of work whether it is humiliating to him or not.</u> [Scripture] teaches, saying: "as a hired man" (Lev 25:40). Just as the hired man cannot be forced to do anything other than his trade, so, too, a Hebrew slave cannot be forced to do anything other his trade. (Mekhilta Neziqin 1, p. 248; Lauterbach 3.6)

And there are even derashot that omit the refuting biblical prooftext altogether, rejecting the *shome'a 'ani* reading on the basis of logical argument alone. The elaborate halakhic discussion of the following derashah is of no interest for the present discussion; I cite it for the almost comical asymmetry between the uninterpreted *shome'a 'ani* reading (underlined) and its refutation:[24]

"[וכי ישאל איש מעם רעהו ונשבר או מת . . .] אם שכיר הוא בא בשכרו" (שמות כב יג):
<u>שומע אני ישבע ויהיה פטור</u>, הרי את דן הואיל ונושא שכר מהנה והשוכר מהנה אם למדתה
על נושא שכר שנשבע על האונסין ומשלם על הגניבה והאבידה, אף שוכר נשבע על האונסין
וישלם הגניבה והאבדה, והרי שומר חנם יוכיח שהוא מהנה ופטור מלשלם הוא יוכיח על
שוכר שאף על פי שהוא מהנה פטור מלשלם, אמרת הפרש, הואיל ונושא שכר נהנה
ומהנה, והשכיר נהנה ומהנה, אם למדת על נושא שכר שהוא נשבע על
האונסין ומשלם את הגניבה ואת האבדה אף השכיר נשבע על האונסין ומשלם את
הגניבה ואת האבדה, ואל יוכיח שומר חנם שהוא מהנה אבל אינו נהנה והשוכר נהנה
ומהנה, לכך נאמר "אם שכיר הוא בא בשכרו."

"[When a man borrows (an animal) from another and it dies or is injured . . . [and] if it was hired, he is entitled to the hire" (Exod 22:13): <u>I might understand [*shome'a 'ani*] that the hirer should take an oath and be free.</u> Behold, however, you must reason: Since the guardian for hire benefits the owner and the hirer likewise benefits the owner, it follows that inasmuch as you have learned that the guardian for hire takes an oath concerning unavoidable accidents but pays for theft and loss, so also the hirer should take an oath concerning unavoidable accidents and pay for theft and loss. But the case of the gratuitous guardian disproves this. For the latter likewise benefits the owner and yet he is not liable to pay for loss and theft. This should prove concerning the hirer that even though he benefits the owner he should nevertheless be free from liability for theft and loss. You must, however, admit that there is a difference. The guardian for hire benefits himself as well as the owner, and so also the hirer benefits himself as well as the owner. So you cannot cite in argument the case of the gratuitous guardian where the owner derives benefit but does not give any benefit. My argument, then, is simply this: The guardian for hire receives and gives benefit, and the hirer also both receives and gives benefit. Now, inasmuch as you have learned that the guardian for hire takes an oath concerning unavoidable accidents, but pays for theft and loss, so also the hirer should take an oath concerning unavoidable accidents but pay for theft and loss. It is in this sense that it is said: "If it was hired, he is entitled to the hire." (Mekhilta Neziqin 16, p. 307; Lauterbach 3.128–29)

Each of these examples demonstrates the tendency of the Rabbi Ishmael midrashim to present *shome'a 'ani* readings as a foil to explicitly midrashic arguments—a contrast that helps confirm the formula's non-midrashic status. So even though the hermeneutic force of *shome'a 'ani* readings varies—some restate the verse, others respond to issues that lie outside the verse—like the other hearing formulas, it consistently avoids midrashic argument, portraying the interaction with Scripture as passive acceptance of a self-evident verse.

This is not to suggest that the midrashic process as a whole is passive. Each of the hearing formulas can and often does function as the opening salvo in an exchange that concludes with a midrashic argument. "We have heard" merely sets the stage for a midrashic discussion to ascertain that which "we have not heard"; the *ki-shmu'o* reading usually gives way to a reading based on interpretation; *shome'a 'ani* is almost always rejected.

But even though the project writ large is midrashic, it is important, in this case, not to lose sight of the little picture. First, it is obvious that a midrashic collection will only introduce self-evident readings that are to be rejected in favor of midrashic argument. Self-evident readings that do not lead to interpretation have no place in the Sifre Numbers and the Mekhilta. Second, there is no intrinsic reason for a midrash to constantly call attention to the self-evident meaning of the verse, a meaning that is about to be discarded; "hearing" formulas appear hundreds of times in the Rabbi Ishmael midrashim, a constant, almost automatic invoking of the non-interpretive road not taken. Third, in adopting this rhetoric, the Rabbi Ishmael midrashim stand in contrast to other legal midrashim. The Sifra employs a formula in which an interpretation is introduced only to be rejected, "It is possible that . . . but [Scripture] teaches, saying . . ." (. . . תלמוד לומר . . . יכול), and many scholars have treated this as basically equivalent to *shome'a 'ani*. But closer analysis reveals that the Sifra's *yekhol* (it is possible) readings are no more self-evident than the midrashic interpretations that follow them. The resulting contrast is between right and wrong interpretation, not unmediated "hearing" and midrashic interpretation, and so the Sifra does not establish a "plain" or non-midrashic interpretation in the way that the Rabbi Ishmael midrashim do.[25]

The *shome'a 'ani* and *ki-shmu'o* readings are introduced because they manifest the proper hermeneutical hierarchy: the reader first does nothing, accepting without interpretation the "plain" meaning of the verse. Here the importance of the derashot that counsel inactivity becomes apparent, for that is essentially what the "hearing" formulas produce—untampered readings. These readings are rejected in favor of midrashic interpretation, but even though they do not endure, their initial mention indicates that the reader has intervened only after the preferred path of passive receptivity has proven to be untenable. So while both the Rabbi Ishmael midrashim and the Sifra produce midrash, the value, the axiology, of hermeneutical activity in each is profoundly different.

The contrast between listening to Scripture and interpreting it is thematized in a fascinating polemic exchange between Rabbi Ishmael and Rabbi Eliezer, recorded in the Sifra:

"והבגד כי יהיה בו נגע צרעת בבגד צמר או בבגד פשתים [. . . נגע צרעת הוא והראה את
הכהן]" (ויקרא יג מז-נ): אין לי אילא צמר ופשתים המיוחדין מנין לרבות את הכילאיים
תלמוד לומר והבגד; אין לי אילא אחד מן המינים הבא במיקצתו, ומנין לאחד מן המינין הבא
בכולו, כלאים שבא בכולו, כלאים שבא במיקצתו מנין, תלמוד לומר והבגד. אין לי אילא
בגד וארג בו שלוש על שלוש בגד שלוא ארג בו שלוש על שלוש מנין, תלמוד לומר והבגד;
אין לי אלא בגד שיש לו לאיכן שיפשה, בגד שאין לו לאיכן שיפשה מנין, תלמוד לומר
והבגד. דברי ר' אליעזר. אמר לו רבי ישמעאל, ר' הרי את אומר לכתוב שתוק עד שאדרוש.
אמר לו ר' אליעזר, ישמעאל דקל הרים אתה.

"And a garment of wool or linen that contains an eruptive affection [. . . shall be shown to the priest]" (Lev 13:47–49): I know only regarding pure wool and linen, whence do I learn to include mixed fabrics? [Scripture] teaches, saying: "*and* a garment." I know this only regarding the case of a type that is mixed fabric that is only partially mixed; what of fabrics in which the mixture is found throughout it? And as for the case of a mixture that is found throughout the fabric, how do I know that I should include a mixture that is only partially mixed? [Scripture] teaches, saying: "*and* a garment." I only know about a garment in which there are three-by-three fingerbreadths of woven stuff. But what about [the susceptibility of] a garment in which are not three-by-three fingerbreadths of woven stuff? [Scripture] teaches, saying: "*and* a garment." Concerning the garment, I know only about one in which there is room for spreading. How do I know regarding one in which there is not room for spreading? [Scripture] teaches, saying: "*and* a garment." These are the words of Rabbi Eliezer.
    Rabbi Ishmael said to him: "You are saying to HA-KATUV: 'Be silent until I expound [*doresh*].'" Rabbi Eliezer said to him: "Ishmael, you are a mountain-palm."[26] (Sifra Tazri'a, pereq 13.1–2; Weiss 68a)[27]

Leviticus 13:47 reads, "And a garment of wool or linen that contains an eruptive affection [. . . shall be shown to the priest]." Rabbi Eliezer's interpretation hinges on the fact that the verse in question begins with the letter *vav*—"*And* a garment." For Rabbi Eliezer, the *vav* triggers a *ribbui*, a hermeneutical formula in which an unnecessary word or trait indicates that additional conclusions can be drawn from the verse.[28] The *vav* that opens Leviticus 13:47 is unnecessary because it plays no semantic or syntactic role in the sentence. The verse "<u>And</u> a garment of wool or linen that contains an eruptive affection" could just as well have been "A garment of wool or linen that contains an eruptive affection" without affecting the sense of the verse.[29] Rabbi Eliezer employs this *ribbui* quite vigorously, deriving from it a long series of conclusions regarding the type of material used, the weaving style, the attributes of the garment and more, all justified by the superfluous *vav*.
    What is it about Rabbi Eliezer's reading that provokes Rabbi Ishmael to rebuke him, saying, "You are saying to HA-KATUV: 'Be silent until I

expound'"? In light of the interpretive practices of the Rabbi Ishmael midrashim, Rabbi Eliezer could be said to undermine the proper (in Rabbi Ishmael's eyes) relationship between Scripture and interpreter. For Rabbi Ishmael, Scripture speaks and it is incumbent upon the rabbinic interpreter first and foremost to listen: "I hear this to be the meaning," "we have heard . . . but have not heard," this is the meaning "as it is heard." But Rabbi Eliezer silences Scripture while he expounds even though it is the rightful speaker. In speaking out of turn, Rabbi Eliezer places himself above, or prior to, Scripture. Rabbi Ishmael does not oppose midrashic exposition as such, only midrash that is not based on attentive engagement with Scripture's words—an engagement that the Rabbi Ishmael midrashim manifest rhetorically through the hearing formulas. There is a legitimate hermeneutic, but it requires submission to Scripture—a hermeneutic that is guided, and thus legitimated, by Torah itself.

Excursus: Did Rabbi Ishmael Employ *Ribbui?*

In the study of halakhic midrashim, it has generally been accepted that the Rabbi Ishmael midrashim do not employ *ribbui,* the technique employed by Rabbi Eliezer in Sifra to Leviticus 13:47–49 and generally associated with the school of Rabbi Aqiva.[30] Michael Chernick has challenged this position, arguing that Rabbi Ishmael employs *ribbui* and even recognizes words that designate classes as instances of *ribbui*—another trait associated with Rabbi Aqiva.[31] Chernick bases his claim on Sifre Numbers §124, which contains the only instance of the word *ribbui* in the Rabbi Ishmael midrashim:

"[ושרף את הפרה לעיניו את עורה ואת בשרה את דמה על פרשה] ישרף" (במדבר יט ה):
"ושרף" ריבוי אחר ריבוי למעט, דברי ר' ישמעאל.

"The cow shall be burned in his sight—its hide, flesh, and blood shall be burned, its dung included" (Num 19:5): A *ribbui* that follows another *ribbui* indicates a limitation, these are the words of Rabbi Ishmael. (Sifre Numbers §124, p. 155)

The formula "a *ribbui* that follows a *ribbui*" indicates that there are two instances of *ribbui.* One of these is the repetition of the verb "burn"— "The cow shall be *burned* in his sight—its hide, flesh, and blood shall be *burned.*" According to Chernick, the other *ribbui* is the word "cow" itself, proof that classes function as *ribbui* in the Rabbi Ishmael midrashim.[32] That the repetition of "burn" is a *ribbui* is clear enough, but Chernick's second argument is forced and unnecessary. A more plausible reading locates the first *ribbui* in the previous verse (Num 19:4), which reads:

"Eleazar the priest shall take some *of its blood* [the cow's blood] with his finger and sprinkle *of its blood* seven times toward the front of the Tent of Meeting" (ולקח אלעזר הכהן מדמה באצבעו והזה אל נכח פני אהל מועד מדמה שבע פעמים). Here the Hebrew *mi-dammah,* "of its blood," is repeated unnecessarily, as the Sifre itself well recognizes.[33]

Chapter 3

Freedom and Restraint in Midrash Halakhah
Hermeneutic Markedness

On July 31, 1930, the great phonetics scholar Nicolai Trubetzkoy wrote his close friend Roman Jakobson:

Apparently any (or might it not be 'any'?) phonological correlation acquires in the linguistic consciousness the form of a contraposition of the presence of a certain mark to its absence (or of the maximum of a certain mark to its minimum). Thus, one of the terms of the correlation necessarily proves to be 'positive,' 'active,' and the other becomes 'negative,' 'passive . . . In both cases, only one of the terms of the correlation is conceived of as actively modified and positively endowed with a certain mark, while the other is merely conceived of as non-endowed by this mark and thus passively modified.

Jakobson, recognizing the broader cultural implications of Trubetzkoy's insight, replied:

I am coming increasingly to the conviction that your thought about correlation as a constant mutual connection between a marked and unmarked type is one of your most remarkable and fruitful ideas. It seems to me that it has a significance not only for linguistics but also for ethnology and the history of culture, and that such historico-cultural correlations as life~death, liberty~non-liberty, sin~virtue, holidays~working days, etc., are always confined to relations a~non-a, and that it is important to find out for any epoch, group, nation, etc., what the marked element is.[1]

The key insight first articulated in this exchange is that in any opposition, one of the members is perceived as the "natural" or automatic member while the other is distinguished or marked. For example, in the opposition "house-houses" the word "house" is viewed as a regular or self-evident noun and thus the unmarked member, while "houses" is marked as plural. Generally, plural forms are perceived as special cases of the more basic singular form, as though the plural were the singular form with the added characteristic of plurality. Occasionally, though, the single form is marked, as in the case of a graffito or a bacterium. The same holds true for broader cultural patterns. Syntactically, the set {bites, dog, man} can generate two well-formed English sentences whose meaning is determined by word order. In both cases "bites" will be the second word of the sentence with the noun prior to it acting as the subject, the biter, the noun following it as the object, the bitee. Though grammatically very similar, the difference between the two is—according to the journalistic cliché—dramatic. "Dog bites man," is journalistically unmarked, meaning that there is nothing to report. But in the journalistically marked case of "man bites dog"—stop the presses. The thesis of this chapter is that the Rabbi Ishmael midrashim generate an opposition between "hermeneutically marked" and "hermeneutically unmarked" verses and that a textual unit must be "marked" to be legitimately interpretable.

Midrashic Markers

That midrash responds to "gaps and indeterminacies" is well known,[2] and a number of scholars have discussed some of the more typical indeterminacies.[3] A frequently cited example is anomalous spellings:

"ולקחו לטמא מעפר שריפת החטאת" (במדבר יט יז): וכי עפר הוא והלי [והלא]4 אפר הוא מפני מה שינה הכתוב במשמעו מפני שמקישו לדבר אחר.

"Some of the dust from the fire of cleansing shall be taken for the unclean person . . ." (Num 19:17): Is it dust ['*afar*]? It is, after all, ash ['*efer*]. To what end did HA-KATUV change its meaning? Because it employs [the word '*afar*] in an analogy. (Sifre Numbers §128, p. 165)

The biblical word '*afar*, dust, appears where the context indicates that what is being taken from the fire is '*efer*, ash. The Sifre Numbers calls attention to the irregularity ("Is it dust? It is, after all, ash"), arguing that the anomalous spelling intentionally sets the groundwork for a midrashic analogy based on the occurrence of '*afar* here and in the discussion of the suspected adulteress (Num 5:11–31).

Another well-known hermeneutic marker is redundancy. The Sifre Numbers teaches:

"[וזה מעשה המנורה מקשה זהב עד ירכה עד פרחה] מקשה היא" (במדבר ח ד): עוד למה נאמר? והלא כבר נאמר "מקשה זהב" מה תלמוד לומר "מקשה היא"? לפי שמצינו בכלי בית עולמים שאם אין להם מין קשה עושין מין גרוטי שומע אני אף במנורה כן, תלמוד לומר "מקשה היא": שנה עליו הכתוב לפסול.

"[Now this is how the lampstand is made: it is hammered work of gold from base to petal] it is a hammered work" (Num 8:4): Why was this stated additionally, when it has already been stated "hammered work of gold," what then does

[Scripture] teach in saying, "it is a hammered work"? It is because we have found with the Temple utensils that if they do not have hammered material they make them of fragments [*grutei*] so I might hear from this that this is the case with the lampstand as well. Thus it is said, "It is a hammered work," HA-KATUV repeats it to disqualify [the use of anything but hammered work]. (Sifre Numbers §61, p. 59)

The repetition of *miqshah*, "hammered work," in Numbers 8:4 is taken by the Sifre Numbers as a hermeneutic marker, indicating that the verse requires interpretation. "Why was this stated additionally, when it has already been stated?"—asks the derashah, and explains this repetition as an emphatic sign that no analogy can be drawn between the lampstand and other Temple utensils. The repetition authorizes the reader to understand the pericope in a way that would not otherwise be possible.

The standard explanation of this midrashic phenomenon invokes the rabbinic conviction that the Torah is perfect and, as a corollary, that anomalies, contradictions, or any phenomenon that suggests otherwise requires explanation. However, this explanation is wanting with regard to the Rabbi Ishmael midrashim. First, it fails to recognize that the textual markers exist as part of a midrashically constituted dichotomy between hermeneutically marked and hermeneutically unmarked verses. Second, the Rabbi Ishmael midrashim are not so much motivated by the assumption that Scripture is perfect as by the assumption that Scripture is an intentional teacher, a view that ultimately leads back to the attempt to establish Scripture as the lead agent of interpretation.

For the Rabbi Ishmael midrashim, the concept of hermeneutic markedness addresses (even if only partially) the gap between the ideal and the real. In Chapter 1, I argued that the Rabbi Ishmael midrashim constitute HA-KATUV as a teacher and an interpreter, while Chapter 2 examined a series of "hearing" terms based on the root *sh-m-'* that represent the reader as passively accepting the sense of Scripture that requires no interpretation. But, as noted, the "heard" position does not endure; rather, the hearing terms often introduce readings that will be rejected, essentially paving the way for the midrashic readings. Hermeneutic markedness is a mechanism by which interpretations, even when produced by rabbinic readers, can be represented as having been determined by Scripture. Note how the Sifre Numbers characterizes the substitution of *'afar* for *'efer*: "To what end did HA-KATUV change [the verse's] meaning?" According to the Sifre, HA-KATUV intentionally produced the irregular wording of Numbers 19:17 to make possible an analogy between the purification rites and the ordeal of the accused adulteress. Similarly, Sifre Numbers §61, after drawing attention to the repetition of *miqshah* and offering an interpretation of its significance, asserts,

"Thus it is said 'it is a hammered work,' HA-KATUV repeats it to disqualify [the use of anything but hammered work]." The repetition of *miqshah* and the resulting conclusion are framed as HA-KATUV's doing, a pedagogic act intended to teach a halakhic lesson. The question of intentionality is critical. While the connection between textual irregularities and midrashic interpretation is a commonplace, the character of the irregularities (in the Mekhilta and the Sifre Numbers) has not been appreciated. They are not *skandala* to be harmonized away, but pedagogic signs purposely posted by HA-KATUV to signal that a verse is hermeneutically marked, scripturally sanctioning the interpretation of the verse. It is not the perfection of Scripture that justifies the interpretation of textual difficulties, but its pedagogic nature, its desire to guide the reader toward correct interpretations.[5]

A clear example of this tendency is Sifre Numbers §110:[6]

"דבר אל בני ישראל ואמרת אליהם בבאכם אל הארץ אשר אני מביא אתכם"
(במדבר טו יח): ר' ישמעאל אומר שינה הכתוב ביאות זו מכל ביאות שבתורה... ללמדך
שכיון שנכנסו ישראל לארץ מיד נתחייבו בחלה.

"Upon entering the land to which I am taking you" (Num 15:18): Rabbi Ishmael says, HA-KATUV altered this instance of *biy'ah* [entering] in comparison to all the other *biy'ot* [enterings] in the Torah . . . in order to teach you that when they entered the Land [of Israel] they were immediately obligated to observe the commandment of *ḥallah* [setting aside a loaf from the first yield]. (Sifre Numbers §110, p. 113)

The Bible consistently employs the phrase "when you enter into the Land (of Israel)" (*ki tavo'u*) when introducing laws that take effect in Israel. There is a recurrent difference of opinion between Rabbi Aqiva and Rabbi Ishmael with regard to the observance of these laws. According to Rabbi Aqiva these laws went into effect immediately upon entering the Land of Israel, while Rabbi Ishmael holds that the Israelites were not obligated to perform them until the land had been conquered and settled (אחר ירושה וישיבה).[7] Numbers 15:18 introduces the agricultural commandment of *ḥallah* but deviates from the standard formula, using "upon entering" (*bevo'akhem*) instead of "when you enter." Though very minor (nothing that would qualify as a textual difficulty), the Sifre grabs on to this irregularity and casts it as an intentional, pedagogic act: "HA-KATUV altered this instance of *biy'ah* ["entering"] in comparison to all the other *biy'ot* ['enterings'] in the Torah . . . to teach you." Note that the derashah makes a concerted effort to present the biblical verse as marked, as open to interpretation, even *absent* textual difficulties such as redundancy or orthographic irregularities.

WHY WAS THIS STATED (*lammah ne'emar*)? WHAT IS THE
INSTRUCTION (*mah talmud lomar*)? I COULD UNDERSTAND THIS TO
MEAN (*shome'a 'ani*)

Hermeneutical markedness finds expression in a series of formulas that
draw attention to biblical irregularities that are then presented as legit-
imizing interpretive intervention. A prominent example is the formula
lammah ne'emar, one of the most common in the Rabbi Ishmael midrashim.[8] The Sifre Numbers teaches:

"ואת הכבש השני" (במדבר כח ח): למה נאמר לפי שהוא אומר "ושחטו אתו כל קהל
עדת ישראל בין הערבים" (שמות יב ו). איני יודע אי זה יקדום אם תמיד אם פסחים תלמוד
לומר "שני", שני לתמיד ואין שיני לפסח.

"The second lamb [you shall offer at twilight]" (Num 28:8): Why was this stated,
because it says, "and all the assembled congregation of the Israelites shall slaughter it at twilight" (Exod 12:6). I do not know which comes first, the daily burnt
offering or the paschal offering, thus [Scripture] teaches, saying: "second," second to the daily burnt offering, not second to the paschal offering. (Sifre Numbers §143, p. 191)

The question "Why was this stated?" is generated by the repetition of the
phrase "the second lamb" in Numbers 28:

3. As a regular burnt offering every day, two yearling lambs without blemish. 4.
You shall offer one lamb in the morning, and the second lamb (*ha-keves ha-sheni*)
you shall offer at twilight. 5. And as a meal offering, there shall be a tenth of an
ephah of choice flour. 7. The libation with it shall be a quarter of a *hin* for each
lamb. 8. The second lamb (*ha-keves ha-sheni*) you shall offer at twilight, preparing
the same meal offering and libation as in the morning. (Num 28:3–8)

Verse 4 establishes that one lamb is to be offered in the morning and a
second at twilight. Why, then, does the Torah first discuss the meal offering and libation of the first offering, and then repeat the command that
the second lamb be offered at twilight? The Torah could simply have
stated: "These are the procedures for (both) the daily offerings." According to the Sifre, the repetition of "the second lamb" serves to resolve a
potential halakhic conflict. Exodus 12:6 commands the sacrifice of the
paschal lamb at twilight, so the paschal lamb and the daily burnt offering
are to be sacrificed at the same time. What, then, is the order of sacrifice
at the twilight of the fourteenth of Nisan, the eve of the Passover? Is the
paschal lamb sacrificed before the daily offering, or vice versa? Numbers
28:8 responds to this question: the repetition of "the second lamb" indicates that the daily twilight burnt offering remains the second sacrifice of
the day at Passover, that is, it is not pushed down into the third position

by the paschal offering. Why, then, was "the second lamb" stated? Because it resolves an interpretive ambiguity that arises from the juxtaposition of the verse with Exodus 12:6.

The formula *mah talmud lomar* (What is the instruction of this statement?) functions in much the same way, but involves the resolution of misreadings that do not involve other biblical verses.

"[וכי ינצו אנשים ונגפו אשה] הרה ויצאו ילדיה" (שמות כא כב): ומה תלמוד לומר "הרה"?
אלא אם הכה על ראשה או על אחד מאיבריה, שומע אני יהיה חייב, תלמוד לומר הרה,
מגיד שאינו חייב עד שיכנה במקום עוברה.

"[When men fight, and one of them pushes] a pregnant woman [and a miscarriage results] . . ." (Exod 21:22): What does [Scripture] teach in saying "pregnant"? Since I might understand that if he hit her upon the head or upon any other part of her body that he should nevertheless be guilty. Scripture instructs saying "pregnant," thereby stating that he is not guilty unless he hit her upon the part of the body in which the fetus is carried. (Mekhilta Neziqin 8, p. 275; Lauterbach 3.64)

Since Exodus 21:22 deals with a miscarriage, why does Scripture state the obvious fact that the woman in question is pregnant? Because, the Mekhilta argues, the word indicates the kind of blow the woman must suffer for the miscarriage to count as the responsibility of the fighting men—a blow to the stomach. As with *lammah ne'emar, mah talmud lomar* explains the meaning of the biblical word or phrase in terms of its ability to resolve a potential misunderstanding of Scripture. The "instruction" of the verse is its resolution of a hermeneutical problem.

Another formula worth mentioning in this context is *shome'a 'ani*, which was discussed in the previous chapter. It, too, draws attention to a problem in the biblical text and couches the interpretation that follows as a response to this problem. The interpretive work performed by *shome'a 'ani* is, in fact, identical with *lammah ne'emar*, though they approach the issue from the opposite directions. *Shome'a 'ani* begins with the verse that gives rise to the misreading and then introduces (with *talmud lomar*) a clarifying verse: "I could understand the verse to mean *X*, but [Scripture] teaches otherwise, saying *Y*." *Lammah ne'emar*, however, introduces a verse and then uncovers its rationale by locating a potential misreading that arises from another verse, but is resolved by the verse in question. A comprehensive analysis of similar formulas has been performed by Miguel Pérez Fernández,[9] but the list need not be cited here since all the formulas perform the same function: they problematize a biblical verse so that the midrashic reading is presented as a response to the internal needs of Scripture. With these formulas, the Rabbi Ishmael midrashim mark the biblical verse under discussion as needing interpretation, and Scripture itself as responding to that need. For it is not the rabbinic reader making connections between disparate verses, but rather an internal scriptural dynamic: Why did Scripture state *X*? To rectify a possible misreading, to correct an ambiguity within itself.

Finally, it should be noted that the Rabbi Ishmael midrashim's commitment to scripturally sanctioned interpretation stands in sharp contrast to some of the interpretive practices found in the Sifra, as the following pericope demonstrates:[10]

"כי את חזה התנופה ואת שוק תרומה לקחתי מאת בני ישראל" (ויקרא ז לד): "חזה" זה חזה
"תנופה" זו תנופת הסל "שוק" זה שוק "תרומת" זו תרומת תודה.

"For I have taken the breast of elevation and the thigh of contribution from the Israelites" (Lev 7:34): "Breast" this is the breast, "elevation" this is the elevation of the basket, "thigh" this is the thigh, "contribution" this is a contribution of thanksgiving. (Sifra Tzav, pereq 17.5; Weiss 40a)

Leviticus 7:34 speaks of the "breast of elevation" (*ḥazeh ha-tenufah*) and the "thigh of contribution" (*shoq ha-terumah*). Grammatically, both are unambiguous construct chains that signify a single entity—a breast offering that is elevated, a thigh offering that is a gift.[11] Nonetheless, the Sifra treats each phrase as made up of two independent nouns: "elevation" is severed from "breast of elevation" and understood as the elevation of the bread basket, and the "contribution" is detached from "thigh [of contribution]" and understood as the thanksgiving bread offering mentioned in Leviticus 7:11–14.[12] The Sifra is clearly engaged in a meaningful reinterpretation of the verse, but it does not justify or explain its reading, presenting a staccato series of conclusions with only the Hebrew *zeh* (this is) connecting the biblical word and the rabbinic interpretation: "'Breast' this is the breast, 'elevation' this is the elevation of the basket, 'thigh' this is the thigh, 'contribution this is a contribution of thanksgiving." No effort is made to demonstrate the legitimacy of interpretation as such, nor that the issue of legitimate interpretation is an explicit concern. And while the Sifra's breathless jump from word to word might be taken as a sign that *every* scriptural word is marked, this is a meaningless statement, since markedness only exists as one member of a marked-unmarked opposition. If *every* word is hermeneutically marked, *no* word is hermeneutically marked.[13]

Is Every Detail in Torah Significant?

As the discussion of the Sifra indicates, the existence of hermeneutically unmarked verses is a key element in my argument. However, the existence of such verses is far from obvious and, in fact, conflicts with a number of widely held tenets regarding the nature and function of midrash. One is that the Rabbis conceive of the Torah as so suffused with meaning that every aspect of it can and must be interpreted. To cite two recent authors: David Instone Brewer posits as a principle of rabbinic interpretation that "every detail in Scripture is significant,"[14] while Alexander Samely ties a derashah in which the accusative particle *'et* is taken as semantically significant to what he characterizes as the rabbinic expectation that every sign in Scripture means something. "The *nota accusativi* [*'et*] cannot be without relevance—it *can* mean because it *must* mean."[15] These statements, however, move too quickly from a particular derashah or set of derashot to general statements regarding "midrash" or "the Rabbis" as such, without proper appreciation for the diversity of the rabbinic corpus. Samely's example is particularly problematic since the interpretation of the accusative particle is explicitly disputed in rabbinic literature—by none other than Rabbi Aqiva and Rabbi Ishmael.[16] Brewer and Samely are undoubtedly correct that many rabbinic texts support what James Kugel has called the principle of biblical omnisignificance,[17] but many is not the same as all, and, in the Rabbi Ishmael midrashim, interpretation is only one possible (though often realized) course of action.

It is, of course, difficult to demonstrate non-interpretation. Uninterpreted biblical verses are no argument, since they may indicate textual lacunae rather than a conscious statement of the legitimacy of non-interpretation. But as often is the case, the positive is most clearly enunciated when contrasted to the negative. The legitimacy of non-interpretation comes to light most clearly in a series of derashot that discuss textual characteristics that appear to be hermeneutical markers, but in fact are not.[18]

DIVIDE THE ACCOUNT (*lehafsiq ha-'inyan*)

The Sifre Numbers teaches:[19]

"[וְעַתָּה הִרְגוּ כָל זָכָר בַּטָּף וְכָל אִשָּׁה יֹדַעַת אִישׁ] הֲרֹגוּ [וְכֹל הַטַּף בַּנָּשִׁים אֲשֶׁר לֹא יָדְעוּ מִשְׁכַּב זָכָר הַחֲיוּ לָכֶם]" (במדבר לא יז): לָמָּה נֶאֱמַר? לְהַפְסִיק הָעִנְיָין.

"[Now therefore slay every male among the children] and slay [every woman who has known a man carnally and every young woman who has not had carnal relations with a man spare]" (Num 31:17): Why is this said? To divide (or delimit or define) the account, says Rabbi Ishmael. (Sifre Numbers §157, p. 212)

Numbers 31:17 describes the Israelite attack on the Midianites under the leadership of Pinḥas ben Elazar the priest. In the course of the attack, all the Midianite men are slain, but Moses attacks the military leadership for allowing the women to live and commands them: "Now therefore slay every male among the children and slay every woman who has known a man carnally and every young woman who has not had carnal relations with a man spare" (Num 31:17). The verse appears, prima facie, to contain a clear hermeneutic marker—the repetition of the imperative "slay"—and to belong in the same category as, for example, Numbers 8:4, with its redundant assertion that the lampstand be a "hammered work."[20] But the Sifre treats the two pericopes differently. The repetition of "hammered work" in Numbers 8:4 generates a complex derashah, while the repetition of "slay" in Numbers 31:17 generates only the assertion that it serves to "divide the account." Why the different treatment? Consider Numbers 31:17 without the second instance of "slay":

וְעַתָּה הִרְגוּ:
[a] כָּל זָכָר בַּטָּף
[b] וְכָל אִשָּׁה יֹדַעַת אִישׁ
[c] וְכָל הַטַּף בַּנָּשִׁים אֲשֶׁר לֹא יָדְעוּ מִשְׁכַּב זָכָר הַחֲיוּ לָכֶם.

Now therefore slay:
[a] every male among the children
[b] and every woman who has known a man carnally
[c] and every young woman who has not had carnal relations with a man spare.

The sentence opens with the command "slay," which clearly governs [a] so that "every male among the children" is the direct object of "slay." A second command, "spare," concludes the verse, so it is likewise clear that [c], "every young woman," is the direct object of "spare." But [b], "every woman that has known a man carnally", is grammatically indeterminate because of the ambiguity of the *vav* of *ve-khol* (and every). Since both [b] and [c] begin with *vav*, one of them must be a disjunctive *vav* that contrasts the slaying that opens the verse from the sparing that concludes it. Absent additional information, there is no way to determine whether the *vav* of [b] marks continuity with [a] (conjunctive) or with [c] (disjunctive).[21] Without the second "slay," the verse could be translated in two legitimate but incompatible ways:

1. "Now therefore slay every male among the children *and* [conjunctive *vav*] every woman who has known a man carnally *but* [disjunctive *vav*] every young woman who has not had carnal relations with a man spare." On this reading, "slay" governs both male children and sexually adult woman, "spare" governs female children.
2. "Now therefore slay every male among the children *but* [disjunctive *vav*] every woman who has known a man carnally *and* [conjunctive *vav*] every young woman who has not had carnal relations with a

man spare." Here "slay" governs male children, "spare" governs both female adults and children.

The repetition of "slay" clarifies the verse: "Now therefore *slay* every male among the children, and *slay* every woman who has known a man carnally; but every young woman who has not had carnal relations with a man spare." The women who have known a man carnally are to be slain as well. Returning to the comparison with Number 8:4, the surface similarity between the verses is clear—each repeats a key phrase in the sentence: "Now this is how the lampstand is made: it is <u>hammered work</u> of gold, from base to petal it is <u>hammered work</u>"; and Numbers 31:17: "Now therefore <u>slay</u> every male among the children and <u>slay</u> every woman who has known a man carnally, and every woman who has not had carnal relations with a man spare." But while the repetition in Numbers 8:4 serves as a hermeneutic marker—the repetition is explicitly employed by the Sifre to justify its interpretation of the verse—the repetition in Numbers 31:17 does not. The Sifre identifies the repetition, of course, but the resulting gloss does not generate a derashah: it offers no halakhic insights, corrects no potential misreadings. The repetition of "slay" serves a clear purpose within the verse: it punctuates the sentence much as a semicolon distinguishes one phrase from the next. Indeed, this may be the precise meaning of *lehafsiq ha-'inyan*, namely, "to punctuate the discussion," to divide it into recognizable phrases, *pesuqim.* Once this function is recognized, it is clear that the repetition does not entail redundancy, and so there is no legitimate marker to generate a halakhic derashah. Though the verse appears to be hermeneutically marked, it is not and so does not generate a halakhic interpretation.

PRELIMINARY STATEMENTS NOT INTERPRETED (*'ein dorshin teḥilot*)

Another formula that exposes a false hermeneutic marker is *'ein dorshin teḥilot*, which appears in the Mekhilta's commentary to Exodus 25:6–8:[22]

"[כי יתן איש אל רעהו כסף או כלים לשמר וגנב מבית האיש אם ימצא הגנב ישלם שנים.
אם לא ימצא הגנב] ונקרב בעל הבית אל האלהים [אם לא שלח ידו במלאכת רעהו . . . על
כל אבדה אשר יאמר כי הוא זה עד האלהים יבא דבר שניהם אשר ירשיען אלהים ישלים
שנים לרעהו]" (שמות כב ו-ח): הרי אחד, "עד האלהים יבא דבר שניהם" הרי שנים, "אשר
ירשיען אלהים" הרי שלשה, מכאן אמרו דיני ממונות בשלשה, דברי ר' יאשיה. ר' יונתן
אומר, הראשון תחלה נאמר ואין דורשין תחלות."עד האלהים יבא דבר שניהם" הרי אחד,
"אשר ירשיען אלהים" הרי שנים, ואין בית דין שקול, מוסיפין עליהם עוד אחד, הרי שלשה.

"[When a man gives money or goods to another for safekeeping, and they are stolen from the man's house—if the thief is caught, he shall pay double; if the thief is not caught] the owner of the house shall depose before *ha-'elohim* [that he had not laid hands on the other's property . . . or any other loss, whereof one party alleges 'This is it'—the case of both parties shall come before *ha-'elohim*: he whom *'elohim* declares guilty shall pay double to the other]" (Exod 22:6–8): behold this is one. "Both parties shall come before God," this makes two. "He whom God declares guilty," behold this makes three. Hence the sages said: Civil cases [*mammonot*] must be tried by a tribunal of three. These are the words of Rabbi Yoshaiah. Rabbi Yonathan says: As regards the first of these passages—that is the very statement of the subject. And the first statements cannot be employed for any special interpretation. "Both parties shall come before God," this is one. "He whom God declares guilty," this makes two. And since the tribunal must not be evenly balanced, we add one more, thus making three. (Mekhilta Neziqin 15, p. 302; Lauterbach 3.119)[23]

This passage is interesting for what it allows and for what it does not allow. The derashah understands the word *'elohim*—which usually means "God"—as a reference to judges. The strongest proof for this reading occurs later in the same chapter: "You shall not revile *'elohim*, nor put a curse upon a chieftain [*nasi*] among your people" (Exod 22:27), the parallelism suggesting that *'elohim* is semantically similar to *nasi*, a chieftain.[24] Philological fidelity aside, Rabbi Yoshaiah understands *'elohim* as judges, and—building on the notion that repetition is a hermeneutic marker—argues that since "judges" occurs three times, three judges preside in civil cases. Rabbi Yoshaiah reasons that since *'elohim* is stated thrice, the interpreter can legitimately expound upon this repetition, concluding that each instance refers to one of the judges needed in a civil case. Rabbi Yonathan, however, rejects Rabbi Yoshaiah's reasoning, claiming that the first verse cannot be interpreted, since it is "the preliminary statement of the matter." For Rabbi Yonathan (and since he has the last word, this is implicitly the position of the Mekhilta), repetition cannot count as a hermeneutic marker until the word is repeated, that is, until the *second* time it is used. The first occurrence is not hermeneutically marked, since it plays the necessary role of introducing the issue at hand. Only with the second and third occurrences of the word can one speak of redundancy and thus of hermeneutic markedness. Though it yields the correct halakhic conclusion, Rabbi Yoshaiah's approach is rejected: the two *redundant* occurrences of *'elohim* yield only two judges, but since an odd number of judges is required to avoid a hung bench, a third is added.

It must be emphasized that in this debate, Rabbi Yonathan accepts redundancy as a hermeneutic marker. Indeed he applies it in his derashah, using the second and third mention of the *'elohim* (judges) as proof of the need for two judges. He takes Rabbi Yoshaiah to task for *conflating repetition and redundancy*. It is incumbent upon the interpreter to demonstrate the redundancy of each occurrence of the word, and since there can be no redundancy until the second occurrence, the first is, by definition, ineligible. Clearly, then, Samely's statement that "the mere fact of repetition . . . brings about the reading"[25] does not hold for Rabbi Yonathan, whose refutation of Rabbi Yoshaiah stands unchallenged. It is not the mechanics of repetition that serve as a hermeneutic marker, but the semantics of redundancy.

FREED FOR THE SAKE OF ANALOGY (*mufneh lehaqish*)

The Mekhilta teaches:

"כי תקנה עבד עברי [שש שנים יעבד ובשבעת יצא לחפשי חנם]" (שמות כא ב): בבן ישראל
הכתוב מדבר או אינו מדבר אלא בעבדו של עברי, ומה אני מקיים "והתנחלתם אותם
לבניכם אחריכם" (ויקרא כה מו) בנלקח מן הגוי, אבל בנלקח מן ישראל שומע אני יהיה
עובד שש ויצא בשביעית, תלמוד לומר "כי ימכר לך אחיך [העברי או העבריה ועבדך שש
שנים ובשנה השביעת תשלחנו חפשי מעמך]" (דברים טו יב), שאין תלמוד לומר העברי
שכבר נאמר אחיך, ומה תלמוד לומר העברי, אלא מפני [מופנה] להקיש לדון גזירה
שוה. נאמר כאן עברי ונאמר להלן עברי, מה עברי שנאמר להלן בבן ישראל הכתוב מדבר,
אף עבד עברי האמור כאן בבן ישראל הכתוב מדבר.

"When you acquire an *'eved* [slave] *'ivri* [Hebrew] [he shall serve six years; in the seventh year he shall go free, without payment]" (Exod 21:2): Scripture deals with a slave who is an Israelite. Perhaps, however, it deals only with the [non-Israelite] slave of an Israelite? And to what am I to apply the passage: "You may keep them [the slaves] as a possession for children after you" (Lev 25:46)? To a slave purchased from among the Gentiles, but regarding a slave purchased from among Israel[26] I might understand this to mean that he should serve only six years and come out free in the seventh year. [Scripture] teaches, saying: "If your brother, a fellow Hebrew, a man or a woman, be sold to you [he shall serve you six years and in the seventh you shall set him free" (Deut 15:12). Now, having said "your brother" there seems to be no purpose in saying "a fellow Hebrew." Why, then, does Scripture say "a fellow Hebrew"? Merely to furnish an expression free to be used in formulating the following *gezerah shavah*: Here the expression "Hebrew" is used, and there the expression "Hebrew" is used. Just as there when using the expression "Hebrew" HA-KATUV deals with an Israelite, so also here when using the expression "Hebrew" HA-KATUV deals with an Israelite. (Mekhilta Neziqin 1, p. 247; Lauterbach 3.3–4)

The derashah opens by suggesting that the phrase *'eved 'ivri* refers to an Israelite slave. Grammatically, this means that *'eved* (slave) is understood to be a noun and *'ivri* (Hebrew) an adjective modifying it. But a second possibility is raised, according to which both *'eved* and *'ivri* are nouns (*'ivri* can mean "a Hebrew"), and their conjunction, *'eved 'ivri*, is a construct chain meaning "the slave of a Hebrew," which could include gentile slaves. On this reading, Exodus 21:2 commands that any slave— Hebrew *and Gentile*—owned by a Hebrew be set free on the seventh year. The derashah resolves the ambiguity by citing Leviticus 25:46, according to which gentile slaves[27] may be passed down as inheritance to future generations, ergo they are not released on the seventh year and Exodus 21:2 refers only to Hebrew slaves. For reasons that are not fully clear to me,[28] the Mekhilta then proposes a second solution based on an analogy between Exodus 21:2 ("When you acquire an *'eved 'ivri* he shall serve six years; in the seventh year he shall go free, without payment") and Deuteronomy 15:12 ("If your brother, a fellow Hebrew [*'ivri*], a man or a woman, be sold to you he shall serve you six years and in the seventh you shall set him free"). Both speak of an *'ivri*, a Hebrew slave being set free on the seventh year, but in Deuteronomy the grammatical force of *'ivri* is unambiguous—it can only be an adjective. The Mekhilta draws an analogy from the adjectival use of *'ivri* in Deuteronomy 15:12 to Exodus 21:2, concluding that *'ivri* in the latter is also an adjective. Only Hebrew slaves are set free on the Jubilee year.

The halakhic question is resolved, but the hermeneutical question remains open. The word *'ivri* occurs, after all, more than a dozen times in the Pentateuch; could an interpreter not find a nominal *'ivri*, use it as a basis for analogy, and arrive at the opposite conclusion? Is the choice of analogue arbitrary? No, replies the Mekhilta, because Scripture hermeneutically marks Deuteronomy 15:12, "freeing up" *'ivri* and purposely making it a legitimate analogue for Exodus 21:2. Deuteronomy 15:12 is a conditional clause, whose prodosis is "If your brother, a fellow Hebrew [*'ivri*] . . . ." According to the Mekhilta, "brother" refers to a Hebrew, and so *'ivri* is pleonastic and thus free from the immediate context of Deuteronomy 15:12. This freedom allows it to serve as the basis of the analogy (*gezerah shavah*) with Exodus 21:2. According to Saul Lieberman, in characterizing a word as *mufneh lehaqish*, the derashah asserts: "The word [in the Torah] is vacant [for the purpose] of juxtaposing it and deducing a *gezerah shavah* from it."[29] The word *'ivri* has been *mufneh* (literally, emptied, made *panuyi*), that is, freed so that it can be employed for the analogy.[30]

The hermeneutical ideology underlying *mufneh lehaqish* is identical to that of *'ein dorshin tehilot* (preliminary statements of the matter cannot be used for interpretation) and *lehafsiq ha-'inyan* (to divide the account). In the latter, apparent redundancies are shown to be relevant to the verse, thus hermeneutically unmarked—and the verse does not produce any halakhic analysis on the basis of the repeated words. With *mufneh lehaqish*, the derashah must show that a term is redundant and thus extraneous to the understanding of its home verse—otherwise it cannot be employed in an analogy. These formulas insist that Scripture is not inherently interpretable; it must be shown that a textual unit is open to interpretation—that it is not otherwise engaged—before interpretation can proceed. Not every detail in Scripture is hermeneutically meaningful.

The word that appears in different verses cannot be used for analogy at will, and even repeated words within a verse—an outstanding hermeneutic marker in most situations—are inadmissible if they are critical for understanding the basic sense of their "home" verse. These formulas regulate the economy of biblical meaning by ascertaining that the word in question is not "bound," that is, its services are not otherwise required for understanding its home verse. For the Rabbi Ishmael midrashim, Scripture is not saturated with meaning, the legitimate object of varied and potentially infinite interpretation. Instead, a division of labor is evident: interpretation ventures only into areas that Scripture has vacated of meaning, but recedes in the face of meaning.

This view conflicts with two other widely held views regarding midrash. The first is that the Rabbis interpret Scripture without regard for context. Early in the twentieth century, G. F. Moore wrote that midrash is "atomistic exegesis" that "interprets sentences, clauses, phrases and even single words independently of the context . . . [and] combines them with other similarly detached utterances and makes use of analogy of expression, often by purely verbal association."[31] Some seventy years later, these words are still cited without qualification, and the thesis roundly endorsed.[32] The second view attributes to the Rabbis the view that the Torah is polysemic. As David Stern has written: "The idea of Scriptural polysemy . . . represents a virtual ideological cornerstone of midrashic exegesis. The concept does not appear to have changed or developed perceptibly through the classical Rabbinic period."[33] These views are incompatible with—or at least stand in tension to—the notion of hermeneutic markedness. Markedness requires distinctions and delimitations, whereas thoroughgoing polysemy and a disregard for context suggest that there are no limitations on, respectively, the number or type of interpretations offered.

CONTEXT AND *Ki-shmu'o*

Above, I argued that the Rabbi Ishmael midrashim establish hermeneutic markedness by problematizing a verse and presenting another verse as a resolution of the problem. They repeatedly interrogate an isolated verse, laying bare its apparent shortcomings, only to show that these may be overcome by reading the verse in connection with another verse—indeed, that the second verse exists for this very purpose. Thus, interpretation is presented as a response to the needs of Scripture. The conceptual possibility of this procedure rests on the observation that the Rabbi Ishmael midrashim understand the biblical verse as contextually determined, obtaining its full meaning only within the broader context of Scripture. This view is explicit in the function of *ki-shmu'o*, a formula whose meaning requires further investigation. Returning to a derashah discussed briefly above, the Mekhilta teaches:[34]

"ועבדו לעולם" (שמות כא ו):... מה תלמוד לומר "ועבדו לעולם"? עד היובל או "ועבדו
לעולם" כשמועו תלמוד לומר "ושבתם איש אל אחוזתו" (ויקרא כה י).

"And he shall serve him forever [*le-'olam*]" (Exod 21:6): ... What does [Scripture] teach in saying "forever"? Up to the Jubilee, or "he shall serve him forever" could be taken literally [*ki-shmu'o*]. But Scripture says: "And you shall return every man to his family" (Lev 25:10). (Mekhilta Neziqin 2, pp. 253–54; Lauterbach 3.17)

Halakhically, the issue here is the duration of time that a slave is to remain enslaved to his master. Exodus 21:6 states that the slave is to serve the master *le-'olam*, that is, "forever."[35] The Mekhilta questions whether this phrase means "up to the Jubilee" or, on a literal reading, "forever." The matter is resolved by Leviticus 25:10, which states that every man is to return to his family at the Jubilee. According to this interpretation of the derashah, the hermeneutical issue at stake is whether to adopt the literal reading of *le-'olam*. This, in any case, is how Lauterbach understands the derashah, translating *ki-shmu'o* as "literally". But this translation is erroneous, as in all but a small number of cases, *ki-shmu'o* contrasts context-sensitive to context-blind interpretations, and demonstrates a consistent preference for the former.

The *Oxford English Dictionary* defines "literal" as "the distinctive epithet of that sense of interpretation (of a text) which is obtained by taking the words in their natural or customary meaning . . . opposed to *mystical*, *allegorical* etc."[36] The *OED*, then, defines "literal" partially by way of its opposite. And rightly so, since the notion of a literal sense or a literal interpretation is only meaningful when its opposite (the figurative or the symbolic or the mystical) is a viable alternative. In other words, a literal reading is only possible for texts that include figurative reading as a cultural possibility. Like the marked-unmarked opposition, both the figurative and the literal need to exist for either to be meaningful. For example, a baker who meticulously follows the instructions for baking a cake, understanding "sugar" as the sweet substance $C_{12}H_{22}O_{11}$ (and not as a term of affection: "hey, sugar") and "egg" as an oval reproductive body consisting of an embryo and a protective covering (and not as British slang for a person: "he's a good egg")—would not be considered a literalist. Recipes, along with tax forms, road signs, assembly instructions for children's toys and more, are not as a rule interpreted figuratively, and so literal adherence to the text is not seen as a cultural choice but as the natural or commonsense reading. A second-century Jew who reads the biblical dietary laws as binding, rejecting current allegorical readings (Paul, Philo), is a literalist; a twenty-first-century Jew who reads tax laws as binding is not, because no allegorical interpretation of the tax code is rejected in the process. The upshot is that, to identify a literal interpretation of a verse, one must establish that it is rejecting a figurative reading. To clarify this question, I will briefly examine a patently allegorical reading by Clement of Alexandria (ca. 150–215 C.E.):

Such are the injunctions of Moses: "These common things, the sow, the hawk, the eagle and the raven, are not to be eaten."[37] For the sow is the emblem of voluptuous and unclean lust of food, and lecherous and filthy licentiousness in venery, always prurient, and material, and lying in the mire, and fattening for slaughter and destruction. . . .

And when he says "Thou shalt not eat the eagle, the hawk, the kite and the crow," he says, Thou shalt not adhere to or become like those men who know not how to procure for themselves subsistence by toil and sweat, but live by plunder and lawlessly. For the eagle indicates robbery, the hawk injustice, and the raven greed.[38]

Using Clement's interpretation as an example, I would like to distinguish three key assumptions of the figurative (or symbolic, in Clement's terminology) mode of interpretation:

   i. Biblical language bears a second stratum of meaning. In this passage, the correct understanding of the commandment not to eat eagle is arrived at by recognizing that "eagle," "hawk," and "raven" refer not only to particular birds but also to allegorical characteristics: "the eagle indicates robbery, the hawk injustice," and so on. The text is "turned" to discover the meaning beneath the "plain meaning." As Gerald Bruns has written: "On the face of [the text], or in that portion that faces you, there is nothing to be found— nothing, anyhow, of much importance—but if you turn it slightly you will be able to glimpse what is hidden on its nether side."[39]

   ii. The figurative has axiological priority over the literal. Once the second, figurative, meaning is uncovered, it becomes *the* reading, while the literal meaning is secondary or discarded altogether. For Clement, the literal, legal sense of the biblical passage is annulled once the figurative reading is adduced, and the verses cease to count as laws. The assertion that the eagle signifies robbery, the hawk injustice, and the raven greed is not an additional stratum of meaning that enriches the prohibition against eating them—it annuls the prohibition.

  iii. Clement's reading requires a hermeneutical key or code not provided by the biblical text, without which the Bible cannot be properly understood. In arguing that "eagle" signifies greed or rapaciousness, Clement does not cite, for example, Habakkuk 1:9:

"Like eagles rushing toward food, they all come, bent on rapine."
Rather than anchor his reading in the biblical text, Clement assumes
external knowledge that is applied to the interpretation of Scripture, what Clement calls the (lowercase g)[40] gnostic exposition of
Scripture.[41]

Though this discussion of allegory is brief and rudimentary, it does set
out the main characteristics of the figurative-literal division in Clement
and provides a measure by which to judge whether allegory is the opera-
tive category in Rabbi Ishmael's *ki-shmu'o*/non-*ki-shmu'o* readings. I
believe that this question is, on the whole, to be answered in the negative, but there are a few derashot that come close to the literal-interpretive
opposition, and I begin with them. The most famous of these discusses
the biblical law governing the case of a man who claims that his new
bride was not a virgin on their wedding night, saying: "I married this
woman; but when I approached her, I found that she was not a virgin"
(Deut 22:14). The bride's father defends his daughter's virginity by producing the bloodied night garment before the town elders, saying:
"[H]ere is the evidence of my daughter's virginity" (Deut 22:17) and they
"spread out the cloth before the elders of the town" (Deut 22:17). In the
Sifre Deuteronomy, the biblical procedure is transformed to conform
to rabbinic legal standards: the husband's accusation is interpreted to
mean that he has witnesses who will testify that his new bride had sexual
relations while still in her father's care, and similarly the night garment
is interpreted as opposing witnesses that refute the testimony of the husband's witnesses. At this point, the Sifre Deuteronomy states:[42]

"והוציאו את בתולי הנערה" כמשמעו . . . "ופרשו השמלה" יחוורו דברים כשמלה זה אחד
מן הדברים[43] שהיה רבי ישמעאל דורש מן התורה במשל כיוצא בו "אם זרחה השמש עליו
דמים לו" (שמות כב ב) וכי עליו השמש זורחת. . . [אלא] מה השמש שלום לעולם אף זה
אם היה יודע שהוא שלום ממנו והרגו הרי זה חייב, כיוצא בו "אם יקום והתהלך בחוץ על
משענתו" (שמות כא יט) על בוריו.

"[The girl's father and mother] shall display the girl's virginity [before the elders
of the town at the gate]" (Deut 22:15): Literally [*ki-shmu'o*] . . "And they shall
spread out the garment before the elders of the town" (Deut 22:17): The witnesses must make their accounts as clear as if the garment itself were exhibited.
This is one of the instances in which R. Ishmael interpreted the Torah symbolically. Another instance is: "If the sun has risen on him, there is bloodguilt in that
case" (Exod 22:2). Does the sun rise only upon him? . . . [Rather] just as the sun
has peaceful intentions toward the entire world, so, too, if the householder knew
that the thief had peaceful intentions toward him, yet slew him nevertheless,
he is liable. Another instance is: "If he gets up and walks outdoors upon his staff
[his assailant shall go unpunished]" (Exod 21:19), meaning, if he is restored to
health. (Sifre Deuteronomy §235, p. 268; Hammer, p. 245, followed by §237, p. 269)

The Sifre Deuteronomy present two views. One, *ki-shmu'o*, and the other Rabbi Ishmael's views that the biblical reference to the dress is symbolic of the clarity of the matter. Rabbi Ishmael's readings, characterized as instances of *mashal*, exhibit the three characteristics enumerated above. First, they bring into play a second level of meaning: the biblical night garment is understood as a description of the legal argument, the sun is understood as peaceful intentions, and the staff is understood as health. Second, the literal sense of the verse—the bloodied garment, the sun, and the staff—is not preserved; the *mashal* interpretation replaces it altogether. Third, the interpretations are gnostic. Each presupposes knowledge of a symbolic code that is not derived from the biblical text: the dress refers to a witness, the staff is really well-being, the sun designates peaceful intentions. In these respects, Rabbi Ishmael's *mashal* interpretations are analogous to Clement's assertion that the pig signifies sloth and the eagle robbery.

The analogy, however, is not perfect. Allegory interprets a nonfigurative element and attributes to it figurative or allegorical meaning. For Rabbi Ishmael, the situation is reversed—the biblical verse contains a figurative element that is endowed with a technical, legal sense. The whiteness of the garment is not made figurative by the witnesses, nor the beneficence of the sun by the thief's intentions, nor is the support of the staff made more figurative by health. To the contrary, in each of these instances the biblical image provides a figurative description for the nonfigurative matters that Rabbi Ishmael's *mashal* introduces. The biblical text provides an image that, as it were, expands and elaborates upon the dry, legal rabbinic interpretation, and in this respect it is Scripture that offers the figurative reading, not the interpreter.[44] Nonetheless, the *mashal* interpretations do exhibit key traits of figurative or allegorical interpretation.

Turning to *ki-shmu'o*, Reuven Hammer translates it as "literally," and in his notes opposes this reading to the figurative reading of other sages: "This is the opinion of R. Eliezer ben Jacob (b. Ketubot 46a). The Rabbis, however, interpret these words symbolically: bring witnesses and make the matter as clear as if the stained garment itself had been shown."[45] As Hammer rightly notes, the dichotomy between literal and figurative is applicable in this case. The *ki-shmu'o* reading stands in contrast to the figurative reading proposed by Rabbi Ishmael and thus may to be considered literal. But the question remains as to whether "literal" is the only, or even the primary, meaning of *ki-shmu'o*. Does this pericope justify the translation of *ki-shmu'o* as "literally" elsewhere? The derashah itself suggests that this is not the case, since the dress interpretation is one of only three pericopes that Rabbi Ishmael interpreted as a *mashal*. On its own, this statement indicates that for (at least) one rabbinic interpreter, the scope of the *mashal* interpretation was strictly limited.

With this in mind, we return to the Mekhilta's (non-*mashal*) interpretation to Exodus 23:4:

"וְעָבְדוֹ לְעֹלָם" (שמות כא ו). . . מה תלמוד לומר "וְעָבְדוֹ לְעֹלָם"? עד היובל או "וְעָבְדוֹ לְעֹלָם"
כשמועו תלמוד לומר "וְשַׁבְתֶּם אִישׁ אֶל אֲחֻזָּתוֹ" (ויקרא כה י).

"And he shall serve him forever [*le-'olam*]" (Exod 21:6): . . . What does [Scripture] teach in saying "forever"? Up to the Jubilee or "he shall serve him forever" could be taken literally [*ki-shmu'o*]. But Scripture says: "And you shall return every man to his family" (Lev 25:10). (Mekhilta Neziqin 2, pp. 253–54; Lauterbach 3.17)

In this derashah, the opposition between the *ki-shmu'o* and the non-*ki-shmu'o* reading is not that of literal versus figurative readings. The *ki-shmu'o* reading, "forever," is not rejected because the Hebrew *le'olam* has a deeper, symbolic sense, but because the reading is contradicted by Leviticus 25:10, and there is nothing figurative about releasing a slave on the Jubilee year; it is a concrete, physical action. The correct interpretation, moreover, does not involve any extra-textual knowledge—it is based on a straightforward reading of Leviticus. Two characteristics of figurative reading (the assumption that language has a second, figurative level of meaning and the use of an extra-scriptural key to decode the text) are not applicable. The rejection of the *ki-shmu'o* interpretation in favor of the non-*ki-shmu'o* is similar to Clement's rejection of the literal in favor of the allegorical, but the rejection is not an essential component of *ki-shmu'o*, as the following two derashot—taken together—attest:

"כִּי תִפְגַּע [שׁוֹר אֹיִבְךָ אוֹ חֲמֹרוֹ תֹעֶה הָשֵׁב תְּשִׁיבֶנּוּ לוֹ]" (שמות כג ד): שומע אני כשמועו,
תלמוד לומר "כִּי תִרְאֶה [שׁוֹר שֹׂנַאֲךָ]" (שמות כג ה).

"When you encounter [your enemy's ox or ass wandering you must take it back to him]" (Exod 23:4): I might understand this *ki-shmu'o*, but [Scripture] teaches, saying: "When you see [the ass of your enemy lying under its burden]" (Exod 23:5). (Mekhilta Kaspa 20, p. 323; Lauterbach 3.163)

Exodus 23:4 commands that one return an enemy's ox or ass *ki-tifga'*, "when you encounter" the beast. *Tifga'* also means "strike," so the sense seems to be of a very close physical encounter. The derashah proposes a *ki-shmu'o* understanding—perhaps the verse refers only to cases in which I bump in to the animal—but rejects it in light of Exodus 23:5, the next verse. This verse also deals with obligations toward the beast of one's enemy, but "activates" the command *ki-tir'eh*, upon seeing the beast. The second verse provides, then, a broader context in which to understand the first, and in so doing indicates that *ki tifga'* is not restricted to physical contact. The Mekhilta then offers the following interpretation of Exodus 23:5:

"כי תראה [חמור שנאך רבץ תחת משאו . . . עזב תעזב עמו]" (שמות כג ה): שומע אני אפילו
רחוק הימנו מלא מיל, תלמוד לומר "כי תפגע [שור אויבך או חמורו]" (שמות כג ד).

"When you see [the ass of your enemy lying under its burden . . . you must raise
it with him]" (Exod 23:5): I might understand this to mean even at a distance of
a mile. But [Scripture] teaches, saying: "When you encounter [your enemy's ox
or ass wandering]" (Exod 23:4). (Mekhilta Kaspa 20, p. 323; Lauterbach 3.165)

This derashah is, in a sense, the mirror image of its predecessor. The
Mekhilta investigates the distance at which a sighted beast obligates one
to aid in raising it. Exodus states the obligation begins *ki-tir'eh*, upon seeing the beast; is one, then, obligated to assist an ox viewed from a mile
away? No, says the Mekhilta, since Exodus 23:4 states that a similar obligation occurs *ki tifga'*, that is, "when you encounter" your enemy's ox. Now
the roles are reversed: Exodus 23:4 provides the context for understanding Exodus 23:5, instructing the reader that *ki tir'eh* does not refer to just
any sighting, but rather requires a degree of physical proximity.

Together, these sequential derashot demonstrate that no fixed trait
(syntactic, semantic, morphological) identifies a verse as inherently a *ki-
shmu'o* reading or as a non-*ki-shmu'o* counterexample. The *ki-shmu'o* reading of the first derashah functions as the conditioning or contextualizing
verse of the second, while the contextualizing verse of the first derashah
becomes the *ki-shmu'o* reading of the second, now determined by the
verse that it had "earlier" contextualized.[46] Such a reversal is unthinkable
in literal-figurative interpretations. First, because the literal meaning is
always the more generally accepted lexical sense of the word, and the
figurative rarer. In Clement's discussion of "bird" and "robbery" as two
senses of "eagle," "bird" *must* be the literal meaning and "robbery" the
figurative. Second, the hermeneutical vector of literal-figurative interpretation always runs from the common meaning to the uncommon,
from the material to the spiritual. The figurative sense cannot "change
places" with the literal and provide insight into its meaning. A dietary
injunction against eating eagle may be, figuratively understood, a prohibition against stealing, but it is impossible to read the commandment
against theft as actually (or, literally) a prohibition not to eat eagle. In
this respect, too, the *ki-shmu'o*/non-*ki-shmu'o* distinction is unlike the lit-
eral/figurative opposition. For the vast majority of its occurrences, the
ki-shmu'o reading does not assume that Scripture bears a second layer
of meaning, does not require extra-scriptural (gnostic) knowledge, and
does not obviate the reading it replaces. In short, in all but a handful of
cases, the distinction between *ki-shmu'o* and non-*ki-shmu'o* does not mirror the distinction between literal and figurative, and *ki-shmu'o* should
not be understood (or translated) as "literally."

The *ki-shmu'o* readings, then, are not rejected for being literal. Why are they rejected? The answer is provided by the *ki-shmu'o* formula: "Verse P could be understood *ki-shmu'o*, but Scripture states: verse Q." On its own, verse P could be understood in its basic, uninterpreted sense. However, verse P does not exist on its own; rather, it is part of an interdetermining web of verses that make up the Torah and must be understood within that context. Building on the earlier analysis of the root *sh-m-'*, the rejection of *ki-shmu'o* can be framed as follows: the first interpretive course of action is to listen to Scripture, to understand the verse as it is heard, that is, *ki-shmu'o*. This understanding must, however, be qualified by other verses, since scriptural truth is not found in discrete verses but in Scripture's discourse as a whole. The Hebrew *le-'olam* means "forever," and thus "he shall serve him forever" is a lexically correct rendering of Exodus 21:6. This interpretation is unobjectionable on its own, but the verse does not exist "on its own"; it is always situated within the broader biblical context. Rather than literal-figurative, *ki-shmu'o/non-ki-shmu'o* distinguishes lexical readings from contextual or syntactical readings,[47] and in so doing undercuts the notion that "the Rabbis" interpret Scripture without concern for context. To be sure, context no longer denotes the single verse but Torah (the Pentateuch) in general; but this is context nonetheless, and for the Rabbi Ishmael midrashim, context is the chief guide in understanding the meaning of Scripture.[48]

THE INTERPRETATION IS UNWARRANTED (*'eino tzarikh*)

The interpretive practices outlined above (*'ein dorshin teḥilot, lehafsiq ha-'inyan, mufneh lehaqish*) also suggest that the Mekhilta and Sifre Numbers do not subscribe to the idea that scriptural verses can bear multiple, even contradictory interpretations, a premise that enjoys wide currency in scholarly literature. A formula that addresses the issue of polysemy more directly is *'eino tzarikh*:[49]

"ולא תעלה במעלות על מזבחי" (שמות כ כג):... אין לי אלא עלייה, ירידה מנין, תלמוד
לומר "אשר לא תגלה ערותך עליו" הא לא עלייה ולא ירידה גרמה אלא כסוי גורם. רבי
ישמעאל אומר אינו צריך הרי הוא אומר "ועשה להם מכנסי בד לכסות בשר ערוה"
(שמות כח מב) ומה תלמוד לומר "אשר לא תגלה ערותך עליו" שלא יפסע בו פסיעה יתירה
אלא גודל בצד עקב ועקב בצד גודל.

"Do not ascend my altar by steps [that your nakedness may not be exposed upon it]" (Exod 20:23):[50] . . . From this passage I would know only about ascending. How about descending? [Scripture] teaches, saying: "that your nakedness may not be exposed upon it" (Exod 20:23), hence it matters not whether it is at going up or at coming down. What does matter is being covered. Rabbi Ishmael says: This is unnecessary, for it has already been said: "You shall also make for [the priests] linen breeches to cover their nakedness" (Exod 28:42). What, then, does Scripture teach by saying: "that your nakedness may not be exposed upon it"?

That one is not to take big steps on it but walk heel to toe and toe to heel. (Mekhilta Baḥodesh 11, pp. 244–45; Lauterbach 2.291)

Exodus 20:23 prohibits ascending the altar by steps. The Mekhilta notes that Scripture only prohibits ascent and inquires as to the source of the prohibition against descending the altar by steps.[51] The derashah proposes that this prohibition is to be found in the second half of the verse ("that your nakedness may not be exposed upon it"), which indicates that it is not ascent as such but revealing nakedness that is at stake; ergo descent is prohibited as well. But Rabbi Ishmael rejects this reasoning on the grounds that it is unwarranted, 'eino tzarikh, since Exodus 28:42 commands that the priests wear breeches to cover their nakedness. As a result, the midrashic attempt to use Exodus 20:23b ("that your nakedness may not be exposed upon it") to explain the language of Exodus 20:23a ("do not <u>ascend</u> my altar by steps") fails. Outright nakedness is prohibited elsewhere. What, then, does Exodus 20:23b mean, given that the priests are already garbed in breeches? Rabbi Ishmael explains the verse as an additional stricture instructing that the priests walk in a modest fashion, heel to toe, as opposed to striding boldly and perhaps immodestly.

Rabbi Ishmael's argument reflects the conviction that the same legal ruling cannot be derived from two verses. Note that Rabbi Ishmael fully accepts the halakhic validity of the conclusion, namely, that priests must cover their nakedness, but rejects its application to the verse in question. The rejection is generated by a hermeneutical principle: once the prohibition against nakedness is located in Exodus 28:42, it is no longer possible to interpret Exodus 20:23b as making the same point. The derashah may be well reasoned and well argued, but, 'eino tzarikh, it is not warranted and must be rejected. As with lehafsiq ha-'inyan and 'ein dorshin teḥilot, Rabbi Ishmael will only accept midrash where it is otherwise free and unneeded. Unlike lehafsiq ha-'inyan and 'ein dorshin teḥilot, here the object is not the biblical word or verse, but the halakhic conclusion itself. If mufneh lehaqish, lehafsiq ha-'inyan and 'ein dorshin teḥilot verify that a verse or phrase is only to be interpreted if it is not already in use elsewhere, 'eino tzarikh prohibits two derashot from generating the same legal conclusion: each biblical verse produces a single interpretation, and each interpretation derives from a single verse.

Rabbi Ishmael and the Hammer on the Rock

The present study deals with the legal midrashim associated with Rabbi Ishmael; it does not cover statements associated with Rabbi Ishmael throughout rabbinic literature. And, as the formulas discussed in this chapter indicate, the Rabbi Ishmael midrashim do not interpret

Scripture as a polysemic text. But the narrow focus on the Mekhilta and the Sifre Numbers is difficult to maintain, as the Babylonian Talmud attributes a polysemic manifesto to the school of Rabbi Ishmael.[52] B. Sanhedrin 34a teaches:

אמר אביי דאמר קרא "אחת דבר אלהים שתים זו שמעתי כי עז לאלהים" (תהלים
סב יב) מקרא אחד יוצא לכמה טעמים ואין טעם אחד יוצא מכמה מקראות. דבי ר'
ישמעאל תנא "וכפטיש יפוצץ סלע" (ירמיה כג כט) מה פטיש זה מתחלק לכמה
ניצוצות אף מקרא אחד יוצא לכמה טעמים.

Abbaye said: The verse says, "One thing God has spoken, two things have I heard: that might belongs to God [and faithfulness is Yours, O Lord]" (Ps 62:12). A single verse [*miqra'*] results in several meanings [*te'amim*] but a single meaning does not result from several verses.

It was taught in the school of Rabbi Ishmael: "Behold, My word is like fire, declares the Lord, and like a hammer that shatters rock" (Jer 23:29). Just as this hammer produces [literally, divides into] many sparks, so a single verse has several meanings.

This passage lies outside the scope of the present study: it is recorded in the Talmud, and is chronologically (at least as far as its final redaction) later than the Rabbi Ishmael midrashim; it is not attributed to Rabbi Ishmael but to his school, an amorphous entity whose relationship to the historical tanna is unclear; and the context is not clearly halakhic. These are legitimate arguments for ignoring the testimony of the Babylonian Talmud altogether, but to do so would be tantamount to discarding the principle that the Rabbi Ishmael midrashim be, as a heuristic procedure, read alongside statements attributed to Rabbi Ishmael. This approach is particularly important in this case since the difference between the Babylonian Talmud's statement and image of Rabbi Ishmael throughout tannaitic literature is so deep. Both the explicit hermeneutical statements of Rabbi Ishmael and the practices of the Rabbi Ishmael midrashim portray a very sober and restrained interpreter. How, then, did the polysemic statement par excellence come to be associated with this figure?

There is a tension between Jeremiah's simile—"like a hammer that shatters rock"—and the rabbinic image of the hammer on the rock.[53] The problem, already noted in the Tosafot to Sanhedrin 34a, has a long history in later commentaries.[54] The basic problem is that the rabbinic gloss introduces sparks, not found in Jeremiah, and the dispersed element is no longer the rock but the sparks that fly when the rock is struck by the hammer. David Stern has argued that the introduction of the sparks serves to resolve the problematic presence of two similes in a single biblical verse: Jeremiah states that God's word is both like fire and like a hammer shattering the rock.[55] According to Stern, the sparks unify the two images so that God's word is the fiery product of a hammer striking rock. For my part, I am not convinced that the presence of two similes in Jeremiah constitutes a problem for the Babylonian Talmud, especially since there are established rabbinic formulas for dealing with pleonastic or redundant biblical expressions and these formulas are not adduced. The difficulty that leads the Talmud to introduce the sparks is rooted, I suggest, in the shift from the biblical verse to the rabbinic gloss.

Jeremiah speaks of the power of God's word, describing the prophetic experience in violent and destructive images that distinguish the true prophet from self-styled prophets who report mere dreams. "How can straw be compared to grain?—says the Lord. Behold, My word is like fire, declares the Lord, and like a hammer that shatters rock" (Jer 23:28–29). The force of God's word is here likened to the mighty hammer, the shattered rock bearing witness to its power and distinguishing it from the fleeting, illusory dreams of the false prophets. The rabbinic gloss of this verse attributes a polysemic abundance to the word of God, a plurality of meanings generated from a single verse. As a result, the word of God no longer shatters something external to it, but is itself fragmented into different interpretations. Using only the inventory of images provided by Jeremiah 23:29 to communicate the idea of scriptural polysemy, the word of God—the polysemic element—is represented as fragmenting, corresponding to the shattered rock. But this image is problematic: Can one suggest that the word of God is shattered? At this point, the Babylonian Talmud pulls back, refusing to present God's word as shattered like a rock struck by a hammer, and instead introduces the sparks produced by the blow—perhaps, as Stern suggests, an association that stems from the fire in the first part of the verse. The sparks provide the plurality and dispersion required of scriptural polysemy, without compromising the integrity of God's word. The derashah exhibits an anxiety rooted in the conflicting desires to present God's word as open to different interpretations, on the one hand, and to maintain its integrity, on the other. It insists on introducing the notion that a single biblical verse can be read in incompatible ways, despite the unwanted consequences this entails, consequences that the spark imagery seeks to blur. Can this insistence on biblical polysemy—attributed to the school of Rabbi Ishmael—be reconciled with the hermeneutical practices of the Rabbi Ishmael midrashim?

One way to approach this question is to contextualize the polysemic credo of Sanhedrin 34b within other statements attributed to Rabbi Ishmael and thus show that it is not as aberrant as might appear. This is the approach adopted by Hananel Mack in an article that traces the roots of the saying "Torah has seventy aspects."[56] Mack, it should be emphasized, is not directly concerned with the question under discussion here. Rather, he argues that "Torah has seventy aspects" is a late (post-amoraic) saying that evolved from two earlier sayings: "Torah is expounded in forty-nine aspects of purity and forty-nine aspects of impurity" and the talmudic expositions of Jeremiah 23:29. In discussing this verse, Mack outlines the history of the polysemic interpretation of Sanhedrin 34b, arguing that it "originates in the tannaitic literature from the school of Rabbi Ishmael," more specifically the Mekhilta's interpretations of Exodus 15:11 and 20:8,[57] each of which is here examined in turn.

MEKHILTA TO EXODUS 15:1

"מי כמכה באלים ה'" (שמות טו יא): מי[58] כמוכה באילו שאחרים קורין אותם אלוהות ואין
בהן ממש ועליהם נאמר "פה להם ולא ידברו ונער לא יהגו בגרונם" (תהלים קטו ה) אילו
פה להם ולא ידברו אבל מי שאמר והיה העולם אינו כן אלא אמר הקב"ה שני דברים בדיבור
אחד מה שאין איפשר לבשר ודם לומר כן שנאמר "אחת דבר אלהים שתים זו שמעתי"
(תהלים סה יב), "הלא כה דברי כאש נאם ה'" (ירמיהו כג כט) וכתיב עד [עוד] "והגה מפיו
יוצא" (איוב לז ב).

"Who is like you, O Lord, among the gods" (Exod 15:11): Who is like you among those whom others call gods, in whom there is no substance and of whom it is said: "They have mouths but cannot speak" (Ps 115:5). These have mouths and cannot speak but He who spoke and created the world is not thus, rather the Holy One Blessed be He speaks two statements [*devarim*] in a single saying [*dibbur*], which is impossible for human beings, as it is written "One thing God has spoken, two things have I heard" (Ps 62:12), "Behold, My word is like fire" (Jer 23:29), and it is further written "[Listen to the noise of his rumbling] and a sound comes out of His mouth" (Job 37:2). (Mekhilta Shirata 8, p. 143; Lauterbach 2.60)

The connection between this passage and the polysemic midrash in tractate Sanhedrin is clear enough—both cite Jeremiah 23:29 alongside Psalm 65:12. In its current form, however, the connection between the Mekhilta's gloss and the biblical verse is obscure. On what basis does the verse "Who is like you, O Lord, among the gods" lead to the comparison between the speechless state of the other gods and the superabundant speech of God? The missing element is provided a few lines earlier when the same biblical verse is glossed: "?'Who is like you among the Gods, O Lord'—Who is like you among the mute ones" (מי כמוך באלים ה'-מי כמוך באלמים). The phonetic similarity of 'elim (gods) and 'ilmim (mute ones) generates the comparison between the muteness of the idols and God's speech. The Mekhilta contrasts the silent "gods" (or idols) that stand below humanity in speech capacity, and the superabundant speech of God, who "speaks two statements [*devarim*] in a single saying [*dibbur*], which is impossible for human beings."

The play on 'elim/ 'ilmim clarifies the connection between Exodus 15:11 and the power of God's speech, but why is God characterized as speaking twofold speech? What are the two statements that God speaks in a single saying? Nothing in Exodus 15:11 or the surrounding verses concerns God's speech or hints at a twofold enunciation. As for the prooftexts, the first (Psalm 62:12) fits this description of God's speech very well, but the other two less so. Jeremiah 23:29,which here appears with no gloss, likens God's words to fire, and Job 37:2 is apparently cited because it contains an imperative followed by an internal accusative (שִׁמְעוּ שָׁמוֹעַ), perhaps connoting a twofold hearing of God's word. The resulting derashah states that God speaks two statements and provides prooftexts in support of this statement, but this view of divine speech is not connected to the biblical verse under discussion. Indeed, the obscurity of God's twofold speech is evidenced from the Mekhilta's own attempt to explain it in the subsequent derashah:

לא כמדת בשר ודם מדת הקדוש ברוך הוא. מדת בשר ודם אינו יכול לומר שני דברים כאחד⁵⁹ אבל מי שאמר והיה העולם אמר עשרת הדברות בדיבור אחד שנאמר "וידבר אלהים את כל הדברים האלה לאמר" (שמות כ א).

God's character is unlike the character of human beings. A human being cannot speak two statements in a single saying, but the Holy One blessed be He spoke the Ten Commandments at once, as it is said: "God spoke all these statements, saying" (Exod 20:1). (Mekhilta Shirata 8, p. 142; Lauterbach 2.62)⁶⁰

In keeping with the discussion that precedes it, the derashah contrasts human beings and God with regard to their speech, as the former are unable to speak two statements in a single saying. The Mekhilta then provides the apparent context for this contrast, suggesting that Exodus 20:1—"God spoke all these statements"—indicates that the Ten Commandments were spoken in a single statement. This argument, however, is an interpretive non sequitur. The derashah glosses the assertion that God can speak two statements at once by proving that God spoke ten statements in a single utterance. Surely, if this were the context of the previous derashah, the number of statements would have been ten, not two, and the prooftext Exodus 20:1, not Exodus 62:12, Jeremiah 23:29, and Job 37:2. This derashah does not explain God's twofold speech so much as demonstrate the need for an explanation.

MEKHILTA TO EXODUS 20:8

The second derashah cited by Mack is the Mekhilta's interpretation of Exodus 20:8, "Remember the Sabbath day and keep it holy":⁶¹

"זכור" (שמות כ ה) ו"שמור" (דברים ה יב): שניהם בדיבור אחד נאמרו, "מחלליה מות יומת" (שמות לא יד) "וביום השבת [שני כבשים]" (במדבר כח ט) שניהם נאמרו בדיבור אחד. "ערות אשת אחיך" (ויקרא יח טז) ו"יבמה יבא עליה" (דברים כה ה) שניהם נאמרו בדיבור

אחד. "לא תלבש שעטנו" (דברים כב יא) ו"גדילים תעשה לך" (דברים כב יב) שניהם בדיבור
אחד. מה שאי איפשר לבשר ודם לומר כן, שנאמר "אחת דבר אלהים שתים זו שמענו"
(תהלים סב יב) ואומר "הלא כה דברי כאש נאם ה'" (ירמיה כג כט).

"Remember" (Exod 20:8) and "observe" (Deut 5:12): Both were said in a single
saying [*dibbur*]. "He who profanes [the Sabbath] shall be put to death" (Exod
31:14) and "[On the Sabbath day] two yearling lambs" (Num 28:9) were both
said in a single saying. "[Do not uncover] the nakedness of your brother's wife"
(Lev 18:16) and "Her husband's brother shall unite with [the levirate wife]"
(Deut 25:5) were both said in a single saying. "You shall not wear cloth combin-
ing wool and linen" (Deut 22:11) and "You shall make tassels on the four corners
of your garment" (Deut 22:12) were both said in a single saying. Which is impossible for human beings to do so, as it is written: "One thing God has spoken, two
things have we [MT: 'I'] heard" (Ps 62:12), and it states "Behold, My word is like
fire" (Jer 23:29). (Mekhilta Baḥodesh 7, p. 229; Lauterbach 2.252)

This derashah enumerates four pairs of contradictory statements and
asserts each pair was said "in a single saying," implying that this characterization refers to God's ability to pronounce contradictory statements
while maintaining the veracity of each statement. The contradictory
statements are followed by Psalm 62:12 and Jeremiah 23:29, two of the
three prooftexts cited in the Mekhilta's discussion of Exodus 15:11. The
derashah is problematic. For one thing, there is a significant difference
between the first pair of verses and the three that follow.[62] The first
pair—the pair that generates the derashah—juxtaposes the two versions
of the Fourth Commandment: the Exodus Decalogue commands the
Israelites to "remember" (*zakhor*) the Sabbath while Deuteronomy commands them to "observe" (*shamor*) it. The next three pairs, however,
establish a completely different pattern. The first verse is, in each case, a
sweeping prohibition: not to profane the Sabbath, not to uncover the
nakedness of one's brother's wife, and not to wear fabrics that contain
wool and linen (*sha'atnez*). The second verse is an exception to the prohibition: priests are to offer sacrifices during the Sabbath, it is obligatory
to marry one's brother's wife if she has become levirate, and tassels
may be made of conjoined wool and linen.[63] The difference between the
first pair and the subsequent three is not addressed by the derashah,
which instead presents the entire set as having been said "in a single saying." But it is not clear why the last three pairs are characterized in this
way. Two of the three contain verses that appear in different contexts in
the Bible. If they form a single saying qua part of the biblical (or Penta-
teuchal) corpus, and the point of the derashah is that God can speak
contradictions, then surely there are more glaring contradictions in the
Bible. If, on the other hand, there is something unique about these
verses that distinguishes them as "said in a single saying," this uniqueness
is not identified in the derashah. Furthermore, there is no explanation

as to why it is "impossible for human beings" to speak in the manner of the last three pairs. Human legislation allows for exceptions, particularly when there has been a clear shift in the relevant circumstances. There is nothing particularly divine about prohibiting fire on the Sabbath except for the purpose of making offerings, or that a prohibition against sexual relations with a brother's wife be rescinded upon the brother's death, or that ceremonial objects be exempt from certain restrictions. Taken together, these difficulties indicate that the last three verses fit the derashah poorly, and may not be original to it.

The first pair of verses, however, cites the commands to observe and remember the Sabbath, commands that are not contradictory as the Hebrew roots sh-m-r and z-k-r overlap semantically.[64] The issue is rather their dual enunciation—the biblical narrative represents them as spoken simultaneously by God—two versions of the Fourth Commandment, both spoken at Sinai (Horeb). And simultaneous communication of distinct words *is* impossible for human beings. The derashah juxtaposes the two Sabbath commandments, thematizing the problematic, only to affirm that, wondrously, both were said in a single speech-act. As it is written: "One thing God has spoken, two things have we [MT: 'I'] heard" (Ps 62:12).[65] The uniqueness of twofold speech—it only occurs at Sinai— suggests that the three subsequent pairs of verses are extraneous additions to the derashah. Without them, the derashah makes good sense: it presents a genuine textual difficulty (*shamor* and *zakhor* spoken at the same time), explains it as a reflection of the unbridgeable gap between human and divine speech, and provides a prooftext that suits the situation perfectly (Psalm 62:12). But for the present discussion, the perfect fit of Psalm 62:12 to the Mekhilta's argument is problematic, for Jeremiah 23:29 does *not* address the dual nature of God's speech at Sinai, and it is unclear why the verse is cited alongside Psalm 62:12. To summarize:

i. The Mekhilta's interpretation of Exodus 20:8 is the likely source of the formula "both were said in a single saying," since it is here that we find the relevant biblical context—the two versions of the Sabbath Commandments (*shamor ve-zakhor*) spoken by God at Sinai. The Mekhilta to Exodus 15:11 employs "both were said in a single saying" as an already established motif by which to elevate God's speech and better contrast it to the silence of the idols.

ii. Both derashot bear the marks of a heavy editorial hand. In the Mekhilta to Exodus 15:11, the editing is evident in the break between the *'elim* (gods) / *'ilmim* (mute ones) gloss and the derashah that develops this motif by comparison with the silent idols. In the Mekhilta to Exodus 20:8, it is the insertion of the three additional pairs of verses forming a distinct pattern of prohibition and exception that is unrelated to the notion that "both were said in a single saying."

iii. Jeremiah 23:29 is out of place in both derashot. The Mekhilta's discussion of Exodus 20:8, the singular speech of God that yields a twofold understanding, is perfectly complemented by Psalm 62:12, but Jeremiah 23:29 adds little as a prooftext.

These findings suggest that rather than the Mekhilta shedding light on the Babylonian Talmud's juxtaposition of Psalm 62:12 and Jeremiah 23:29, it is more likely that the awkward reference to Jeremiah 23:29 in the Mekhilta is a late addition, the *result* of the talmudic juxtaposition. This possibility is strengthened by a number of textual considerations. First, Jeremiah 23:29 is absent from some of the textual witnesses to the Mekhilta to Exodus 20:8.[66] Second, the Sifre Deuteronomy preserves a parallel derashah that cites Psalm 62:12 but not Jeremiah 23:29.[67] Finally, if these derashot were the source of the pericope in the Babylonian Talmud, why would the interpretation of Jeremiah 23:29 be attributed to the school of Rabbi Ishmael but Psalm 62:12 cited in the name of Abbaye?

Even if the various textual and literary difficulties were somehow resolved and Jeremiah 23:29 shown to be an integral part of the derashot, the interpretation of the verse is completely different in the Mekhilta and the Talmud. The Mekhilta uses this verse (if it does) to explain a unique crux in the Bible—the distinct speech-acts at Sinai. It is not, by any means, a statement about the polysemic nature of the biblical text as such. Indeed, it suggests an underlying non-polysemic understanding of the Torah, since in a polysemic context the dual speech of the Sabbath Commandment spoken at Sinai might be held up as a particular instance of the general principle,[68] but this is not done. Even the biblical verses best suited for a polysemic derashah, which appear as prooftexts for such arguments in amoraic literature, are not cast in this role by the Mekhilta. It appears then, that the path Mack traces from the Mekhilta to the polysemic credo in the Talmud is not viable. Rather than point to the early roots of polysemy in the Rabbi Ishmael midrashim, the derashot under discussion demonstrate how differently Jeremiah 23:29 functions in the Mekhilta and in the polysemic context in Sanhedrin 34a, all of which serves to underline the perplexing attribution of a polysemic hermeneutic to the school of Rabbi Ishmael.

SEVENTY LANGUAGES OF TORAH

The answer to the apparent contradiction between the restrained interpretive practices found in the Rabbi Ishmael midrashim and the attribution of a polysemic hermeneutic to the school of Rabbi Ishmael, may

be arrived at by comparing b. Sanhedrin 34a with two other texts. The
first is the so-called parallel in b. Shabbat 88b:

תני דבי ר' ישמעאל "וכפטיש יפוצץ סלע" (ירמיה כג כט) מה פטיש זה נחלק לכמה ניצוצות
אף כל דיבור ודיבור שיצא מפי הקב"ה נחלק לשבעים לשונות.

It was taught in the school of Rabbi Ishmael: "[Behold, My word is like fire,
declares the Lord, and] like a hammer that shatters rock" (Jer 23:29). Just as this
hammer produces many sparks [when it strikes the rock], so each and every
statement[69] that came from the mouth of the Holy One blessed be He divides into
seventy languages.

Though clearly similar, the two versions exhibit significant differences.
In tractate Sanhedrin, a verse (*miqra'*) has several meanings (*te'amim*),
while in tractate Shabbat each divine statement (*dibbur*) divides into seventy languages (*leshonot*). The term *lashon* can mean "proposition" as
well as language,[70] but "seventy *leshonot*" is a formula that means all the
languages in the world, which suggests that the derashah speaks of languages, not propositions.[71] These differences become more significant
when a third source is introduced, a Genizah fragment published by
Solomon Schechter from the Mekhilta Deuteronomy, the no-longer-
extant midrash to Deuteronomy associated with the school of Rabbi Ishmael.[72] In it we find:

בו ביום עברו ישראל את הירדן ונטלו את האבנים והעבירום והעמידום וכתבו על [האבנים]
את כל דברי התורה [הזאת באר היטב] (דברים כז ח). ר' ישמעאל אומר בשבעים
לשון כתבו . . . ר' שמעון בן יוחאי אומר לא כתבו עליה [א][ל][א את משנה] תורת משה שנאמר
"ויכתב שם על האבנים את משנה תורת משה" (יהושע ח לב).

On that day the Children of Israel crossed the Jordan and took the stones and
carried them across and erected them and wrote on [the rocks] "all the words of
[this] Teaching [*torah*] [most distinctly]" (Deut 27:8). Rabbi Ishmael says: they
wrote in seventy languages. Rabbi Shimon ben Yohai says, they wrote [only the
copy of the] teaching of Moses, as it is written "And there, on the stones, he
inscribed a copy of the teaching that Moses had written for the Israelites." (Josh
8:32)[73]

The context of this saying is Deuteronomy 27:2–8, the command to
construct an altar upon crossing the Jordan, and Joshua 8:30–35, where
Joshua carries out this command. Deuteronomy specifies that the stones
of the altar are to be covered with plaster and that "you shall inscribe
every word of this teaching [*divrei ha-torah*] most distinctly [*ba'er heitev*]"
(Deut 27:8). Rabbi Ishmael interprets the phrase "most distinctly" as
indicating that *divrei ha-torah* were written in seventy languages, that is,
in all languages. This view is also attested in m. Sotah 7.5: "[after the
blessings and curses at Gerizim and Ebal] they wrote thereupon all the

words of the Law in seventy languages, as it is written, 'most distinctly' [*ba'er heitev*] (Deut 27:8)."[74]

The contexts of the Genizah fragment and b. Shabbat 88b are, of course, very different. Nonetheless, the linguistic similarity of the two sources is apparent. In the Genizah fragment, *kol divrei* (all the words) are written in seventy languages, while in the Talmud, *kol dibbur* (every saying) appears in seventy languages. And the statements are attributed to Rabbi Ishmael or to his school, respectively. There are also two key differences: first, the verse with which each saying is associated is different—the Mekhilta Deuteronomy discusses Deuteronomy, while Shabbat 88b cites Jeremiah 23:29. The second and more important difference is that the Genizah fragment contains no mention of scriptural polysemy. In other words—and this point is absolutely key—we have here a derashah that is attributed to Rabbi Ishmael and contains the notion of the Torah appearing in seventy languages in the very concrete context of Joshua's altar. Rabbi Ishmael's statement in the Mekhilta Deuteronomy fragment deals with scriptural polyglossia, not polysemy.

Sanhedrin 34a shares with Shabbat 88b the association with Jeremiah 23:29, but subtly and significantly alters the seventy languages into *kamah te'amim*, several justifications or meanings.[75] The outcome is that Sanhedrin 34a breaks with the polyglossic language of the Mekhilta Deuteronomy and Shabbat 88b and replaces it with a statement that can be understood as advocating a thoroughly polysemic view of Torah. With this shift, Sanhedrin 34a is no longer tied to the Genizah fragment: terminology, prooftexts, polyglossia versus polysemy—the two have nothing in common. Nothing, that is, except the attribution to Rabbi Ishmael or his school.

The relationship between the three pericopes may be reconstructed as follows: the tannaim debated the writing on the altar erected after crossing the Jordan—one view held that the Torah was written in seventy languages. This position is attributed to Rabbi Ishmael in the Genizah fragment from the Mekhilta Deuteronomy and appears anonymously in m. Sotah 7.5. As we know from James Kugel's work on midrash aggadah, rabbinic discussions can detach from their textual-exegetic moorings and drift into other contexts, while Jeffrey Rubinstein's work demonstrates that the Babylonian Talmud draws on traditions from various sources in constructing an argument, often without attending to the original context.[76] This is, I believe, what happened here. The notion of the Torah appearing in seventy languages broke free from Joshua's altar and became an independent motif, which appears in b. Shabbat 88b. This passage preserves the basic terminology of the Rabbi Ishmael derashah from the Genizah, the polyglossic notion that each *davar/ dibber* appears in seventy languages, but does not describe Torah as such, and is associated with Jeremiah's hammer on the rock.[77] The final step occurs in b. Sanhedrin 34b, where polyglossia is recast as polysemy, producing the well-known polysemic manifesto. What started out as a very clearly defined statement by Rabbi Ishmael regarding the writing on the altar after crossing the Jordan was ultimately transformed into a polysemic manifesto.[78] The conclusion is that, while polysemy *is* rabbinic, it is not rabbinic ab initio (and thus not *essentially* rabbinic), at least not in the school of Rabbi Ishmael.

Chapter 4
The Role of the Reader I

As this study proceeds, one dominant theme is emerging—the Rabbi Ishmael midrashim struggle to bridge the gap between the ideal of scriptural self-interpretation and the persistent need for an interpreter. The ideal situation is discussed in the first two chapters: HA-KATUV interprets Torah, while the reader abstains from interpreting, engaging Scripture as a passive hearer. The establishment of the hermeneutical markedness of a textual unit prior to its interpretation indicates that the ideal situation is only rarely attained. The interpreter does intervene, and so the pressing need is to establish a hermeneutic of submission in which the reader's actions are guided or even determined by Scripture. Scripturally sanctioned hermeneutic markedness is a necessary first step but not sufficient, since taken alone it merely sanctions the interpretation of a verse without exerting any control over the interpretive process that follows. In this chapter and the following, I discuss the different formulas employed by the Mekhilta and the Sifre Numbers to limit the hermeneutical freedom of the interpreter and to distinguish Scripture as the lead agent in its self-exposition. I begin with a discussion of the two kinds of analogy found in the Rabbi Ishmael midrashim, their distinct hermeneutical functions, and the concomitantly different responses they elicit.

Analogy by *Heqqesh*

The first, *heqqesh*, involves the derivation of legal conclusions from the proximity of the terms within a single biblical verse or passage:

"שבעת ימים שאור לא ימצא" (שמות יב יט): אין לי אלא דברים שהן משום בל ימצא, בל
יראה מנין תלמוד לומר "לא יראה לך שאור [בכל גבולך]" (דברים טז ד). אין לא אלא שאור
בל יראה ובל ימצא חמץ מנין תלמוד לומר "לא יראה לך חמץ [ולא יראה לך שאור]"
(שמות יג ז). הקיש על שאור לחמץ וחמץ לשאור מה זה בל יראה אף זה בל יראה ומה
זה בל ימצא אף זה בל ימצא.

"No leaven shall be found in your houses" (Exod 12:19): From this I know only that it is under the prohibition of being found. How do we know that it is also under the prohibition of being seen? [Scripture] teaches, saying: "No leaven shall be seen in all your territory" (Deut 16:4). So far I know only that leaven is under the prohibition of being seen and of being found. How about leavened bread? [Scripture] teaches, saying: "No leavened bread shall be seen with you and no leaven shall be seen" (Exod 13:7). [Scripture] draws an analogy from leavened bread to leaven and from leaven to leavened bread. Just as the one, leaven, is under the prohibition of being seen and of being found, so also is the other, leavened bread. (Mekhilta Pisḥa 10, pp. 33; Lauterbach 1.76)

The derashah seeks to reconcile two Passover commands: Exodus 12:19 states that "no leaven [*śe'or*] shall be *found* in your houses" while Exodus 13:7 orders that "no leavened bread [*ḥametz*] . . . and no leaven [*śe'or*] shall be *seen*." Both verses prohibit leaven and occur in relative proximity, but the Mekhilta distinguishes between them—the one prohibits the possession of leaven, and the other prohibits the presence (visibility) of leaven. The second part of the derashah inquires as to the status of leavened bread (*ḥametz*), which is not mentioned in Exodus 12:19, leaving open the possibility that only its sight is prohibited, not its possession. Not so, the Mekhilta argues, since by citing leavened bread (*ḥametz*) and leaven (*śe'or*) in the same verse, Exodus 13:7 "draws an analogy from leavened bread to leaven and from leaven to leavened bread," indicating that legal rulings that are established with regard to the one apply to the other as well. The Mekhilta characteristically suggests that the juxtaposition of the terms is an intentional pedagogic device that leads the reader to recognize their analogous legal status. The analogizing agent is not named here, but it is fairly certain that this is an elliptic reference to HA-KATUV: first, because HA-KATUV performs interpretive work throughout the Mekhilta and the Sifre Numbers; and second, because the specific phrase "*heqqish* HA-KATUV" appears elsewhere in the Mekhilta.[1] Once Scripture's (or HA-KATUV's) juxtaposition of the terms has been recognized as hermeneutically meaningful, the difficulty is resolved and the possession of leavened bread is also prohibited. The Mekhilta states the conclusion, no dissenting readings are proposed—the *heqqesh* argument is conclusive. The proximity of "leaven" and "leavened bread" in Exodus 13:7 is, then, an argument in and of itself.

The compelling force of the argument—for the Rabbi Ishmael midrashim, of course—is brought to light in the following derashah:

"אלה החוקים [אשר צוה ה' את משה בין איש לאשתו בין אב לבתו]" (במדבר ל, יז):
על כורחך אתה מקיש את האב לבעל ואת הבעל לאב בכל מה שאמרנו.

"These are the laws [that God commanded Moses concerning a husband and wife and a father and daughter]" (Num 30:17): You are compelled to draw an analogy from the father to the husband and the husband to the father in all that has been stated. (Sifre Numbers §156, p. 208)

Numbers 30:4–16 deals with the laws governing a woman who has taken a vow, particularly the right of her father or husband to annul her vow. After presenting the laws, the section concludes with the anaphoric statement, "These are the laws that God commanded Moses concerning a husband and wife and a father and daughter" (Num 30:17). Since the verse mentions the father and the husband together, the Sifre characterizes it as a *heqqesh*, and the rules governing the father are applied to the husband and vice versa. Notable is the lack of interpretive freedom allotted the reader who encounters the *heqqesh*—the move from the verse to the midrashic conclusion is wholly determined: "*You are compelled* to draw an analogy . . . in all that has been stated." The presence of both husband and father in Numbers 30:17 *forces* the reader to equate the two. Even though the putative agent of this derashah is the reader ("you draw an analogy") and not HA-KATUV, the deep structure is identical in both derashot since the reader merely makes manifest the argument latent in the biblical text. The "compulsion" to draw the analogy shifts the interpretive agency to the biblical text, so that, ultimately, *heqqesh* is generated by the biblical text, not the reader. This shift is only possible because of the nature of the *heqqesh*, which is based on the proximity of two terms within a verse—a scriptural phenomenon that does not require human intervention.[2] The thoroughly textual determination of the analogous elements and the concomitant marginalization of the reader's contribution reduce the need for strictures or guidelines for *heqqesh* arguments. Not so with the second type of analogy, *gezerah shavah*.

Analogy by *Gezerah Shavah*

Like *heqqesh*, *gezerah shavah* is a midrashic analogy, but rather than establish a connection between two elements that appear in a single verse, it connects two disparate verses on the basis of a shared word or phrase.[3] Unfettered, *gezerah shavah* could be applied to any two biblical verses that have a word in common, and posit a halakhically significant analogy between them. The result would be a much freer and more open interpretive tool than *heqqesh*, one that allows the reader a great deal of discretion.[4] Rabbi Ishmael recognizes this difficulty and limits the application of *gezerah shavah* by means of *mufneh lehaqish*. This constraint, discussed above, posits that at least one of the elements used in an analogy must be shown to be "empty" of meaning, and so freed for interpretation, before it can be used in *gezerah shavah*.[5] In the example discussed in Chapter 3, the Mekhilta argued that Deuteronomy 15:12—"If your brother, a fellow Hebrew, a man or a woman, be sold to you he shall serve you six years and in the seventh you shall set him free"—contains a superfluous term, "Hebrew," which is already understood from "your

brother." "Why then does Scripture say "a fellow Hebrew"? Merely to furnish an expression free to be used in formulating the . . . *gezerah shavah*"
(Mekhilta Neziqin 1, p. 247; Lauterbach 3.3–4).

Requiring one of the terms in the verbal analogy to be *mufneh lehaqish*
drastically reduces the number of verses that are candidates for this argument and, accordingly, reduces its currency.[6] More importantly, *mufneh
lehaqish* shifts the agency of the analogy from the reader to Scripture. In
the example above, the decision to employ Deuteronomy 15:12 is legitimate because the grounds for such an analogy have been laid by Scripture itself: "Why then does Scripture say 'a fellow Hebrew'? . . . [Because]
just as when using the expression 'Hebrew' HA-KATUV deals with an
Israelite, so also here when using the expression 'Hebrew' HA-KATUV
deals with an Israelite." Once this pattern is recognized, the halakhic conclusion is foregone and the Mekhilta attributes the entire argument to
HA-KATUV. The reader cannot roam the biblical text in search of paired
terms to interpret, but must carefully attend to the language of Scripture,
seeking out redundancies that free up words for *gezerah shavah*. No independent interpreter, the reader carries out the exegetic instructions
already inscribed in the text.

No Punishment from Logical Argument
(*'ein 'onshin min ha-din*)

The contrast between *heqqesh* and *gezerah shavah* is telling. The inherently
scriptural nature of *heqqesh*—the proximity of two words in a verse—
allows the Rabbi Ishmael midrashim to accept this type of analogy as it
stands. But *gezerah shavah*, with its potential for unfettered interpretation, requires a delimiting condition. This pattern, wherein a potentially
open-ended interpretive technique is reined in, repeats throughout these
midrashim, including with *qol va-ḥomer*,[7] the argument from the lesser to
the greater (*de minore ad maius*). According to *qol va-ḥomer*, once a legal
rule is established for a category that is less severe, it can be applied to a
category that is more severe (and vice versa in the case of leniencies).[8]
The following is a typical example:

"ואם מזבח אבנים תעשה לי" (שמות כ כב): רבי ישמעאל אומר, כל אם ואם שבתורה רשות
. . . והרי דברים קל וחומר ומה אם מזבח החמור אם רצה לשנות ישנה קל וחומר לשאר
כל הכלים.

"And if you make for Me an altar of stones" (Exod 20:22): Rabbi Ishmael says:
Every "if" in the Torah refers to a voluntary act . . . . Now, by using the method
of *qol va-ḥomer*, one can reason: If in the case of the altar, which is a weighty matter (*ḥomer*),[9] a change in the material is permitted, how much more should this
be permitted in the case of other Temple utensils. (Mekhilta Baḥodesh 11, pp.
243–44; Lauterbach 2.288)

This derashah contains two separate arguments. According to Rabbi Ishmael, the term "if" ("And *if* you make for Me an altar of stone") marks the injunctions surrounding the altar as nonbinding: one may build the altar of stone, but it can also be made of other material. The derashah goes on to argue, by *qol va-ḥomer*, that the material makeup of other Temple utensils is also nonbinding: if the most important instrument of the Temple service may be made of other material, how much more so for less central utensils.

Qol va-ḥomer is widely considered an outstanding example of rabbinic logic, and modern interpreters often treat it as a formal argument like the syllogism.[10] Its authority, however, does not derive from human reasoning but from its explicit use in the Torah. Numbers 12 recounts Miriam and Aaron's attack against Moses following his marriage to a Kushite woman. Though Moses says nothing, God is furious and strikes Miriam with a skin affliction. Moses then calls upon God to heal his sister, which God apparently does (though this is not stated), and then speaks to Moses, saying: " 'If her father spat in her face, would she not bear her shame for seven days? Let her be shut out of camp for seven days, and then let her be readmitted.' So Miriam was shut out of camp seven days; and the people did not march on until Miriam was readmitted" (Num 12:14–15). God's rhetorical question is understood by rabbinic readers as a *qol va-ḥomer* argument: since Miriam would retreat in shame seven days if her father had spat in her face, how much more so if God strikes her with a skin affliction. In short, the Book of Numbers records a *qol va-ḥomer* argument made by no less an authority than God, and this argument is cited as precedent for the rabbinic *qol va-ḥomer*. Indeed, Numbers 12 is cited in the *Baraita of Rabbi Ishmael*, which appears at the beginning of the Sifra to Leviticus, the only example of the Bible *employing* an interpretive technique. But despite its divine origin, *qol va-ḥomer* presents the Rabbis with a number of difficulties, including its applicability:

"והביא האיש את אשתו אל הכהן" (במדבר ה טו): מן התורה האיש מביא את אשתו אל הכהן אלא אמרו מוסרין לו שני תלמידי חכמים בדרך שלא יבא עליה ורבי אומר בעלה נאמן עליה מקל וחומר, ומה נידה שחייבין על ביאתה כרת בעלה נאמן עליה, סוטה שאין חייבין על ביאתה כרת אינו דין שיהא בעלה נאמן עליה. אמרו לו, לא אם אמרת בנידה שיש לה התר אחר איסורה תאמר בסוטה שאין לה התר אחר איסורה, כל שכן הואיל ואין חייבים על ביאתה כרת לא יהא בעלה נאמן עליה.

"He shall bring his wife to the priest" (Num 5:15): The biblical ordinance is that the husband brings his wife to the priest, but [the sages] said: Two disciples of the sages are to accompany him on the way lest he have intercourse with her. Rabbi [Yehudah] says, her husband is deemed reliable as may be learned by *qol va-ḥomer*. Since in the case of a menstruant the husband is deemed reliable, and that is a transgression whose punishment is *karet* [cutting off], in the case of the suspected adulteress, [intercourse with whom] is not punishable by *karet*, does it not stand to reason that her husband be deemed reliable with regard to her? They said to him, No, for if that is the case for a menstruant who is permissible after the prohibition, then surely it is thus with the suspected adulteress who is not permissible after her prohibition, and, moreover, since intercourse with the wife is not punishable by *karet*, the husband is not deemed reliable with regard to her. (Sifre Numbers §8, p. 13)

Numbers 5:15 refers to the suspected adulteress, whose husband is bringing her to the priest to undergo the ordeal of the bitter waters. In reworking the biblical instructions, the Rabbis stipulate that two scholars accompany the couple to ensure that they do not have sexual relations en route to Jerusalem. Rabbi Yehudah questions the need for the chaperones, arguing that husbands are routinely trusted with sexual restraint without oversight when their wives are menstruating, an offense punishable by *karet*, while sexual relations with a wife suspected of adultery has no stated punishment. If, Rabbi Yehudah argues, the husband is trusted in the weighty matter of refraining from intercourse with his menstruant wife, should he not be trusted in the lesser matter of a suspected adulteress? But Rabbi Yehudah's respondents argue that it is *precisely* the severity of intercourse with a menstruating wife that makes the husband reliable on that matter. Absent the fear of *karet*, the husband ceases to be reliable. The anonymous respondents reverse the force of Rabbi Yehudah's *qol va-ḥomer* argument, such that the severity of the *ḥomer* (the *karet* punishment for intercourse with a menstruant) makes the legal conclusion inapplicable to the *qol*. The derashah does not pursue the hermeneutic question further, but the issue is critical to the viability of *qol va-ḥomer*, an argument predicated on the possibility of drawing legal conclusions from varying degrees of severity. Though not elaborated in the derashah, the response to Rabbi Yehudah's argument calls into question the general applicability of *qol va-ḥomer*, for if the disparity between the "weighty" and "light" can be argued in both directions, is *qol va-ḥomer* not, ultimately, an arbitrary argument? The Rabbi Ishmael midrashim respond to this interpretive freedom as they are wont—by formulating a stricture:

"וכי יפתח איש בור [או כי יכרה איש בור ולא יכסנו . . . בעל הבור ישלם]" (שמות כא לג): אין
לי אלא פותח, כורה מנין, תלמוד לומר "או כי יכרה איש" עד שלא יאמר יש לי בדין,
אם הפותח חייב הכורה לא יהיה חייב, הא אם אמרתה כן ענשת מן הדין, לכך נאמר "או כי
יכרה" ללמדך שאין עונשין מן הדין.

"When a man opens a pit [or digs a pit and does not cover it . . . the one responsible for the pit shall make restitution]" (Exod 21:33): I thus know only about one who opens a pit. How about one who digs a pit? [Scripture] teaches, saying: "Or digs a pit." But even before it said this, I could have reasoned: If the one who opens a pit is responsible, shall the one who digs a pit not be responsible? But if you say so, you would be decreeing punishment merely on the basis of logical argument. Therefore it is said: "Or digs a pit," thus teaching you that punishment cannot be decreed on the basis of logical argument. (Mekhilta Neziqin 11, p. 288; Lauterbach 3.91)

The derashah concerns Exodus 21:33, which reads in full: "When a man opens a pit, or digs a pit and does not cover it, and an ox or an ass falls into it, the one responsible for the pit must make restitution." The Mekhilta understands Exodus to be making two distinct legal statements: first, the uncoverer of a ditch is liable for damages incurred as a result of his actions; and second, the digger of a ditch is similarly liable. But the second statement can be derived—by *qol va-ḥomer*—from the first: if the person who uncovers an *existing* ditch is liable, how much more so is the person who dug it liable. In other words, Scripture need only have stated the liability of the uncoverer, since that of the digger could be inferred from it. Why, then, does Scripture state that the digger is liable? Because, the Mekhilta argues, the attribution of liability in tort law entails punishment, and whenever punishment is involved *qol va-ḥomer* arguments are not admissible: *'ein 'onshin min ha-din*, "punishment cannot be decreed on the basis of logical argument." The Mekhilta does not question the general legitimacy of *qol va-ḥomer*, or the specific argument of the derashah; the derashah assumes the liability of the digger *can* be correctly inferred from that of the uncoverer. But as with *gezerah shavah*, *qol va-ḥomer* places too much freedom in the hands of the reader and thus must be checked, even when it can produce halakhically correct conclusions. It can be employed to elucidate verses only so long as the resulting conclusions do not decide a punishable transgression.

A General Statement Followed by a Particular Instance (*kelal u-feraṭ*)

The Babylonian Talmud preserves the following in the name of Rabbi Yoḥanan: "Rabbi Ishmael studied under Rabbi Nehunia ben Haqanah who expounded the entire Torah by *kelal u-feraṭ* [a general statement followed by a particular instance] and he, too, expounds by *kelal u-feraṭ*" (b. Shevu'ot 26a).[11] The biographical value of this statement is questionable, but it is true that the Rabbi Ishmael midrashim make frequent use of *kelal u-feraṭ* arguments. The two most common are *kelal u-feraṭ* (a general statement followed by a particular instance), in which the general statement is limited to those particulars that are stated explicitly (אין בכלל אלא מה שבפרט); and *kelal u-feraṭ u-khelal* (a general statement followed by a particular instance and another general statement), in which the general statements can only include particulars that share an (unstated) trait with the particulars cited (אין אתה דן אלא כעין הפרט).[12] Like the *heqqesh*, the hermeneutical force of these techniques lies in their close connection with the biblical text. When Scripture states that "in all charges of misappropriation—pertaining to an ox, an ass, a sheep, a garment—or in any other loss . . . the case of both parties shall come before God [*'elohim*]" (Exod 22:8), the reader plainly sees a general statement ("in all charges") followed by a set of particular instances ("an ox, an ass . . .") and a second general statement ("any other loss"). If we accept that the structure of general-particular-general (*kelal u-ferat u-khelal*) indicates that the category in question contains elements that are essentially similar to the instances enumerated, then Scripture has gone a long way in interpreting itself. It is for the reader to determine the essential trait, and this can be a matter of controversy, but the process is far more structured then it would otherwise be. Still less is required of the reader when the pattern is general-particular (*kelal u-ferat*), since the instances cited in the verse *constitute* the class of objects included in the general statement.

The difference between the two patterns, along with the leading role of Scripture in the interpretive process, is addressed in the following derashah:

"[איש או אשה כי יפלא לנדר נדר נזיר נדר להזיר לה'. . . מיין ושכר יזיר חמץ יין וחמץ שכר לא ישתה . . . מכל אשר יעשה מגפן היין] מחרצנים ועד זג" (במדבר ו ג-ד): למה נאמר לפי שהוא אומר "מכל אשר יעשה מגפן היין" כלל "מיין ושכר יזיר חומץ יין חומץ שכר" פרט, כלל ופרט אין בכלל אלא מה שבפרט, מה הפרט מפורש פרי ופסולת פרי אף אין לי אלא פרי ופסולת פרי להביא את החרצנין ואת הזוגין שהם פרי ופסולת פרי . . . אם זכיתי מן הדין מה תלמוד לומר "מחרצנים ועד זג לא יאכל" אלא ללמדך, כל שמוסף על הפרט ואי אתה יכול לדון כעין הפרט להוציאו מן הכלל עד שיפרוט לך הכתוב כדרך שפרט לך בנזיר.

"[If anyone, man or woman, explicitly utters a nazirite's vow, to set himself apart for the Lord . . . he shall abstain from wine and any other intoxicant; he shall not drink vinegar of wine or any other intoxicant . . . and he may not eat anything that is obtained from the grapevine,] from the seed to the skin" (Num 6:3–4): Why was this stated? Because it states, "anything that is obtained from the grapevine"—this is a general statement, "he shall abstain from wine and any other intoxicant; he shall not drink vinegar of wine or any other intoxicant"—this is a particular instance, in the case of a general statement followed by a particular instance, there is nothing in the general statement except for [the elements enumerated in] the particular instance. Just as the particular instance consists of the fruit and the waste of the fruit so all the other elements will be fruit and the waste of the fruit, thus including the seed and the skin, which are fruit and the waste of the fruit . . . but if I have arrived at this conclusion by logical argument, what does [Scripture] teach by saying, "from the seed to the skin"? Rather, this teaches you that with regard to a general statement that appears in conjunction with a particular instance, you cannot infer [regarding the other elements in it] from the trait of the particular instance, thus removing it from the general statement, until HA-KATUV makes this explicit, as it made it explicit for you in the matter of the nazirite. (Sifre Numbers §24, pp. 29–30)

The Sifre begins its discussion of the phrase "from the seed to the skin" by pointing to the general-particular pattern (*kelal u-ferat*) in Numbers 6:3 (the preceding verse), in which the general statement refers to the produce of the grapevine, and the particular instances to wine, other intoxicants, and wine vinegar. The standard formula is then adduced—"there is nothing in the general statement except for [the elements enumerated in] the particular instance." But instead of limiting the elements to the elements cited, the derashah proceeds *as though* dealing with a general-particular-general pattern (*kelal u-ferat u-khelal*), identifying the salient characteristics of the particular element. The (provisional) conclusion is that the *ferat* includes both the fruit of the grapevine (wine) and its waste (vinegar), criteria that would include the skin and seeds of the grape, but this conclusion is short-lived. If the prohibited status of the skin and the seeds can be inferred from the general categories of fruit of the grapevine and its waste, why does Scripture explicitly state that they are prohibited? The original argument leads to an apparent redundancy and so produces the grounds for its own undoing, though this undoing is itself significant. Scripture has led the reader into error in order to demonstrate a general hermeneutical truth—one does not apply the *kelal u-ferat u-khelal* procedure to instances of *kelal u-ferat*: "with regard to a general statement that appears in conjunction with a particular instance, you cannot infer [regarding the other elements in it] from the trait of the particular instance." Such a procedure is only permitted if the interpretive agent is ultimately authoritative, that is, when "HA-KATUV makes this explicit, as it made it explicit for you in the matter of the nazirite." If HA-KATUV cites a second particular, the reader may deduce the common characteristic that unites the two particulars and extrapolate to other, unstated, particulars.

The derashah is hermeneutically limiting in two ways. First, it presents standards of interpretation for scriptural patterns of general statements and particular instances, an approach that minimizes the reader's input and allows Scripture to serve as the main interpretive agent. Second, the interpretive primacy of HA-KATUV is affirmed, since deviation from this pattern is permitted only when HA-KATUV provides explicit permission to do so.[13]

No Hermeneutically Derived Conclusion as Basis for Argument (*lamed min ha-lamed*)

Another restrictive formula that is unique to the Rabbi Ishmael midrashim is *lamed min ha-lamed*, a prohibition against using a hermeneutically derived conclusion as the basis for another argument.[14] It appears in the following lengthy passage, whose English translation I divide into four sections:[15]

[ונשאל דבר זה לפני ר' טרפון בכרם ודרש כך][16] אמרו לו תלמידיו, רבינו למדינו, אמר להן, בכור קדשין קלין ושלמין קדשין קלין מה שלמים נאכלין לב' ימים ולילה אחד אף הבכור יהא נאכל לשני ימים ולילה אחד. היה ר' יוסי הגלילי שם כשבא תחילה לשמש את חכמים. אמר לו, רבי, חטאת מתנה לכהן ובכור מתנה לכהן, מה חטאת נאכלת ליום ולילה אף הבכור יהא נאכל ליום ולילו. אמר לו, בני, אלמוד דבר מדבר ואדון דבר מדבר. אלמוד דבר שהוא קדשין קלין מדבר שהוא קדשין קלין ואל אלמוד דבר שהוא קדשין קלין מדבר שיהא קדשי קדשים. אמר לו, רבי, אלמוד דבר מדבר ואדון דבר מדבר. אלמוד דבר שמתנה לכהן מדבר שמתנה לכהן ואל אלמוד דבר שמתנה לכהן מדבר שמתנה שלכל [של כל] אדם. נסתלק ר' טרפון וקפץ ר' עקיבה ואמר לו, בני, כך אני דורש. "ובשרם יהיה לך [כחזה התנופה]" (במדבר יח יח), בא הכתוב והיקיש את הבכור לחזה ושוק שלשלמין. מה חזה ושוק שלשלמין נאכל לשני ימים ולילה אחד אף הבכור יהא נאכל לשני ימים ולילה אחד. אמר לו, רבי, אתה מקישו לחזה ושוק שלשלמין ואני אקישנו לחזה ושוק שלתודה. מה חזה ושוק שלתודה נאכל ליום ולילו אף הבכור יהא נאכל ליום ולילו. אמר לו, בני, כך אני דורש, "ובשרם יהיה [לך כחזה התנופה]" אין תלמוד לומר לך יהיה אלא ריבה הכתוב הוויה אחרת שיהא נאכל לשני ימים ולילה אחד. אמר לו ר' ישמעאל [שנית],[17] וכי תודה מאין למידה? לא משלמים? ודבר הלמד ממקום אחר אתה בא ללמוד ממנו. למד מן הלמד. האין [הא אין] עליך לומר כלשון אחרון אלא כלשון הראשון . . . מה חזה ושוק שלשלמין נאכלין לשני ימים ולילה אחד, אף הבכור יהא נאכל לשני ימים ולילה אחד.

[A] [The question (for how long can a sacrifice of the firstborn be eaten) was put to Rabbi Tarfon in the vineyard (of Yavne), and he explained the matter (*darash*) thus (namely, that they can be eaten over a period of two days and a night).] His students said to him, teach us, our master. He said to them, the first-born are minor sacrifices [*qodashim qalim*] and the well-being offerings are like-wise minor sacrifices. Just as sacrifices of well-being are eaten for two days and a night, so too the firstborn is to be eaten for two days and a night. Rabbi Yose the Galilean was there, as he was starting to serve under the sages. He said to him, my master, the sin offering is a gift to the priest and the firstborn is a gift to the priest. Just as the sin offering is eaten for a day and a night, so too the firstborn is eaten for a day and a night. He said to him, my son, I will learn a matter from [a similar] matter and infer from one matter to [a similar] matter. I will learn regarding a minor sacrifice from a matter that is itself a minor sacrifice and will not learn regarding a minor sacrifice from a matter that is a major sacrifice [*qodshei qodashim*]. He said to him, Rabbi, I will learn a matter from [a similar] matter and infer from one matter to [a similar] matter. I will learn regarding a gift to the priest from another matter that is a gift to the priest and will not learn regarding a gift to the priest from a matter that is a gift for any person. Rabbi Tarfon departed.

[B] Rabbi Aqiva jumped up and said, My son, this is how I explicate [*doresh*]: "But their meat shall be yours: yours shall it be like the breast of elevation offer-ing and like the right thigh" (Num 18:18). HA-KATUV came and drew an analogy between the firstborn and the breast and thigh of the sacrifices of well-being, just as the breast and thigh of the well-being offering are eaten over two days and a night, so too the firstborn is to be eaten over two days and a night. He said to him, My master, you draw an analogy to the breast and thigh of the well-being offering, and I draw an analogy to the breast and thigh of the thanksgiving offer-ing. Just as the breast and thigh of the thanksgiving offering are eaten during a day and a night, so too the firstborn is to be eaten over a day and a night.

[C] He said to him, My son, this is how I explicate [*doresh*]: "But their meat shall be yours: yours shall it be." [Scripture] teaches nothing by saying, "yours shall it be." Rather, HA-KATUV is expanding [*ribbah ha-katuv*] a single issue so that it can be eaten over two days.

[D] Rabbi Ishmael said to him, You are wrong. For whence do we learn regarding the thanksgiving offering? Is it not from sacrifices of well-being? You are taking a matter that has been learned from another passage and using it as a source for learning. Learning from that which has been learned. Thus you should accept the first [interpretation] and not the last, namely, "But their meat shall be yours." HA-KATUV draws an analogy from the firstborn to the breast and thigh of the sacrifices of well-being. Just as the breast and thigh of the sacrifices of well-being are eaten over two days and a night, so too the firstborn is to be eaten over two days and a night. (Sifre Numbers §118, p. 141)

A question is posed before the Rabbis: How long does one have to eat a sacrifice made following the birth of a firstborn? The derashah enumerates four responses, corresponding to sections A–D in the above translation, along with challenges by Rabbi Yose the Galilean, who is characterized as a recent arrival on the rabbinic scene. As I will demonstrate below, section C is an interpolation.

In section A, Rabbi Tarfon responds to the question by drawing an analogy between sacrifices of the firstborn (*bekhor*) and sacrifices of well-being (*shelamim*), based on the fact that both are minor offerings (*qodashim qalim*). On this analogy, the sacrifices of the firstborn may be eaten over a period of two days and a night. Rabbi Yose challenges this analogy and suggests another in its place—between the firstborn and the sin offering (*hata't*). Rabbi Tarfon counters that the first analogy (to the sacrifices of well-being) is justified by an inherent similarity between the two sacrifices ("I will learn a matter from a [similar] matter"), implying that Rabbi Yose's is not. But the matter is not so simple, since Rabbi Yose's analogy is based on the fact that firstborn offerings and sin offerings are sacrifices that are given exclusively to priests, whereas Rabbi Tarfon's analogy yokes together sacrifices eaten by priests with those given to lay people. Which trait is more pertinent: the degree of sanctity or the identity of the eater? Unable to provide a conclusive argument for why his analogy is to be preferred, Rabbi Tarfon departs. Section A ends in aporia.

Section B contains a similar exchange between Rabbi Yose and Rabbi Aqiva. Rabbi Aqiva answers Rabbi Yose's challenge by citing Numbers 18:18: "But [the meat of the firstborn offering] . . . shall be like the breast of elevation offering and like the right thigh." According to Rabbi Aqiva, the "breast of elevation" and the "right thigh" belong to the sacrifices of well-being (*shelamim*), and since these are known to be eaten over a period of two days and a night, the same holds for the firstborn offerings. In other words, Rabbi Aqiva uses a *heqqesh* argument to justify Rabbi Tarfon's analogy. Again Rabbi Yose challenges the analogy, arguing that the unspecified thigh and breast sacrifice in Numbers 18:18 refers to the thanksgiving offering, not the well-being offering, in which case the permitted consumption time is one day and one night only.

In its current form the derashah records a second response by Rabbi Aqiva, section C, where the helping verb *yehieh* (shall it be) in Numbers 18:18 functions as a *ribbui*, indicating that the eating can occur over the span of two days.[18] A number of factors suggest that this is an interpolation.

i. The section does not fit the narrative structure of the derashah: Rabbi Aqiva attempted an explanation in B, was refuted, but appears again in C with the same emphatic "this is how I explicate," as though he had not just essayed to explicate the same verse in the preceding section.

ii. Section C is stylistically discontinuous as well, breaking with the dialogue format of A and B, in which the established sage refers to Rabbi Yose as "my son" and he responds, "my master." The first address is present, but Rabbi Yose never responds. The lack of response from Rabbi Yose would suggest that Rabbi Aqiva's argument is conclusive, yet section D continues the argument as though no conclusion has been reached.

iii. The most telling evidence comes from section D. In its current configuration, Rabbi Ishmael's statement—"You are wrong. For whence do we learn regarding the thanksgiving offering?"—must be a response to Rabbi Aqiva's last statement in C. This is, for example, the understanding of the text of the Sifre Numbers reflected in Rabbenu Hillel's (Hillel ben Elyaqim; twelfth-century Greece) commentary *ad loc.*,[19] which has Rabbi Ishmael say: "Go forth and say to Rabbi Aqiva, you are wrong." But Rabbi Ishmael's statement does not refer to Aqiva's *ribbui* argument in C, but rather to Rabbi Yose's argument in B, that the thanksgiving offering could be substituted for the well-being offering as the analogue to Numbers 18:18 (more on D below). In other words, Rabbi Ishmael defends the legitimacy of Rabbi Aqiva's analogy, as the conclusion of the derashah makes clear: "Thus you should speak after the matter of the first and not the last. . . . HA-KATUV draws an analogy from the firstborn to the . . . sacrifices of well being"—a repetition of Rabbi Aqiva's conclusion in B. In other words, D does not "know of" C; it responds directly to B, indicating that C is an interpolation.[20]

Turning to the content of the final argument, it becomes apparent that the pericope grapples with the use of analogy in legal argument. Both Rabbi Aqiva and Rabbi Tarfon respond to Rabbi Yose's question by drawing an analogy between sacrifices of the firstborn and sacrifices of well-being, but are reduced to aporia because they cannot justify this move. Rabbi Yose accepts the legitimacy of analogy—he employs it himself—but challenges the procedure by exposing the danger of insufficiently grounded application. Why, then, is this the salient characteristic rather than another? As noted, his demand for justified midrash is met only by Rabbi Ishmael.

In order to understand Rabbi Ishmael's response, a detailed examination of his argument is in order. Numbers 18:18 states that the offering of the firstborn is analogous to the raised offering, but without specifying the identity of the latter. Rabbi Aqiva suggests that the verse refers to the well-being offering which is raised or elevated by the priest: "The offering to the Lord from a sacrifice of well-being must be presented by him who offers his sacrifice of well-being to the Lord. . . . The breast [is] to be elevated as an elevation offering" (Lev 7:29–30). Rabbi Yose's counterargument, that the raised offering of Numbers 18:18 is not the well-being offering but the thanksgiving offering, assumes that the latter is similarly counted among the raised offerings, a point that Rabbi Aqiva tacitly concedes but Rabbi Ishmael rejects. For unlike the offering of well-being, Scripture does not state that the thanksgiving offering is raised, a fact learned by analogy from the sacrifices of well-being, as the Sifra testifies:

"[כי את חזה התנופה ואת שוק] התרומה [לקחתי מאת בני ישראל מזבחי שלמיהם . . .]"
(ויקרא ז לד): זו תרומת תודה.

"[For I have taken the breast of elevation offering and the thigh of] contribution offering [from the Israelites, from their sacrifices of well-being . . .]" (Lev 7:34): . . . This refers to the contribution offering of thanksgiving. (Sifra Tzav, pereq 17.5; Weiss 40a)

Though this may not be the derashah that Rabbi Ishmael has in mind, so to speak, the Sifra's argument indicates that the elevation of the thanksgiving offerings is not scripturally given but learned by midrashic analogy. But if this is the case, Rabbi Yose's analogy between the firstborn offering and the thanksgiving offering cannot stand, since it takes a legal conclusion learned midrashically (the thanksgiving offering is raised) and uses it as the basis for a different argument (the thanksgiving and firstborn offerings are analogous since both are raised). This procedure transgresses Rabbi Ishmael's hermeneutical rule against using a midrashic conclusion as the basis for a new analogy (*lamed min ha-lamed*). Rabbi Yose's challenge to Rabbi Aqiva's argument collapses, and Rabbi Aqiva's original position (in section B) is accepted: the analogy to the well-being offerings indicates that firstborn offerings are to be eaten over two days and a night. Thus Rabbi Ishmael resolves the halakhic question *and* the hermeneutical question regarding the status of analogy by introducing the stricture: a midrashic conclusion cannot serve as the basis for further interpretive speculation.

The refusal to accept a midrashic conclusion as the basis for analogy is motivated by the ineluctable contingency of human interpretation, a matter raised time and again by the midrashim themselves. An attentive reading of Scripture, one that recognizes points of hermeneutic markedness and that follows HA-KATUV's own arguments, will yield well-founded interpretations. But even though Scripture's guidance minimizes the role of the reader and the accompanying potential for arbitrary arguments, it does not eliminate them altogether, as Rabbi Aqiva's and Rabbi Tarfon's inability to ground their own (halakhically correct!) arguments clearly demonstrates. Even a correct interpretation remains an interpretation—it does not become Scripture, and so cannot serve as the basis for a new midrashic analogy. To confuse the human and the divine voice is to err theologically and, as a result, hermeneutically. Torah speaks the language of man, but man does not speak the language of Torah.

Numbers §134

The central contention of the present chapter, namely, that the Rabbi Ishmael midrashim regulate interpretive activity and curtail the freedom of the reader, seems to be contradicted by Sifre Numbers §134,[21] an apparent celebration of interpretive freedom:

"[ואם אין אחים לאביו ונתתם את נחלתו לשארו הקרוב אליו ממשפחתו וירש אותה] והיתה
לבני ישראל לחקת משפט" (במדבר כז יא):. . . נתנה תורה דעת בחכמים לדרוש ולומר כל
הקרוב בשאר קודם בנחלה.

"[If his father has no brothers, you shall assign his property to his nearest relative in his own clan, and he shall inherit it.] This shall be the law of procedure for the Israelites . . ." (Num 27:11): . . . TORAH gave reason [da'at] to the sages to expound the meaning of Scripture and state that whoever is nearer as relative is prior with regard to the property. (Sifre Numbers §134, p. 179)

Abraham Heschel characterizes this derashah as follows: "This saying, that was observed in the school of Rabbi Ishmael, claims priority for logic in understanding Torah, and opens a path [for understanding] Rabbi Ishmael's hermeneutic system [shitah]."[22] According to Heschel, the phrase "TORAH gave reason to the sages to expound the meaning of Scripture" means that Rabbi Ishmael sanctions the use of logic in midrash as such, giving the sages the keys to the interpretive kingdom. But this understanding of Sifre Numbers §134 is problematic for a number of reasons. First, Heschel fails to address the curious characterization of *torah* as endowing the sages with "reason" (*da'at*). What exactly does this mean? If Heschel is right and this term refers to the logical faculties, shouldn't it be God who gives this ability to man? Second, the interpretive context in which the saying appears does not support Heschel's reading: the saying glosses Numbers 27:11, a verse that does not refer to logical argument or to interpretation, so it is curious that the Sifre would read it as Heschel suggests. Finally, Heschel only cites the first half of the rabbinic saying, omitting the second. The full statement is: "TORAH gave reason to the sages to expound the meaning of Scripture *and state that whoever is nearer as relative is prior with regard to the property.*" The content of the sages' exposition is known—the degree of proximity determines the relative's place in the inheritance. The Sifre's statement does not invite human reason to engage Scripture so much as describe the conclusion drawn from Numbers 27:11—a conclusion that closely echoes the language of the verse. Numbers 27:11 reads: "If his father has no brothers, you shall assign his property to his nearest relative in his own clan, and he shall inherit it," and the sages conclude that "whoever is nearer as relative is prior with regard to the property." To the extent that the Sifre's gloss—almost a restatement of the verse—counts as interpretation, it is very restrained.

Indeed, hermeneutical restraint—not freedom—is the point of the derashah. Numbers 27:11 states that "if his father has no brothers, you shall assign his property to his nearest relative in his own clan, and he shall inherit it," and then characterizes this statement as "the law of procedure [*mishpaṭ*]." The rabbinic gloss generalizes the biblical statement—where Scripture specifies the case of a father who has no brothers, the sages state that the nearer relative receives priority in inheritance. Even this generalization, however, needs to be anchored in Scripture, and this, argues the Sifre, is the meaning of the second half of the verse, which characterizes "if his father has no brothers" as a "law of procedure." The rabbinic gloss is justified because Scripture itself characterizes the verse as the basis for a general legal position (*mishpaṭ*). Scripture does not endow the sages with reason to apply logical argument to the biblical text—quite the contrary. Scripture *permits* them to interpret the specific verse in question by characterizing the phrase "if his father has no brothers" as a "law of procedure," thus indicating that it may be generalized. The interpretive freedom of the reader is minimized: even legitimate techniques are regulated, their scope limited, deferring as much as possible to Scripture itself.

(Legal) Midrash and Theory

Since Susan Handelman's *Slayers of Moses*[23] and Hartman and Budick's *Midrash and Literature* appeared in the early and mid-eighties, there has been a sustained dialogue between midrash and literary theory. One of the foci of this dialogue emphasizes the independence and freedom of rabbinic interpretation, often drawing parallels with contemporary theories of interpretation that make similar claims.[24] It should be clear by now that I do not believe that such claims are relevant for the halakhic interpretation of the Mekhilta and the Sifre Numbers. But this position should not be taken as a rejection of the relevance of literary theory as such—it is only that the theorists who are usually invoked shed little light on this particular corner of rabbinic literature. But there are other theorists.

In his introduction to *The Role of the Reader*,[25] Umberto Eco positions himself between two extremes in literary interpretation. He begins by describing the suspicion that "The Poetics of the Open Work," one of his earlier works, aroused in Claude Lévi-Strauss. True to his structuralist sensibilities, Lévi-Strauss viewed "the idea of taking into account the role of the addressee [as] a disturbing intrusion, disquietingly jeopardizing the notion of a semiotic texture to be analyzed in itself and for the sake of itself."[26] Eco deftly counters these objections and shows that Lévi-Strauss himself assumes the presence of a reader in his and Roman Jakobson's well-known interpretation of Baudelaire's "Les Chats," apparently championing the involvement of the reader in the interpretive process. As the introduction proceeds, however, it becomes clear that while Eco invokes the role of the reader, he is not concerned with empirical readers, but with what he calls the Model Reader. Eco writes: "To organize a text, its author has to rely upon a series of codes that assign given contents to the expressions he uses. To make his text communicative, the author has to assume that the ensemble of codes he relies upon is the same as that shared by his possible reader. The author has thus to foresee a model of the possible reader (hereafter Model Reader) supposedly able to deal interpretatively with the expressions in the same way as the author deals generatively with them."[27]

The Model Reader is an idealized entity envisioned by the author as someone who can properly decode the "ensemble of codes" that the author employs in writing. Eco proposes this terminology to distinguish two possible relationships between the author and the Model Reader, and the texts each generates. There are writers who aim at "pulling the reader along a predetermined path, carefully displaying their effects so as to arouse pity or fear, excitement or depression at the due place and at the right moment."[28] These writers produce "closed texts" that assume the reader's responses can be controlled by the text and are oblivious to the possibility that their codes can be subverted. An open text, on the other hand, is encoded in a way that recognizes and even embraces a reader "able to master different codes and eager to deal with the text as with a maze of many issues."[29] The open text contains consciously and productively ambiguous statements that invite different interpretations, creating a Model Reader who is not limited to a single proper response.

Eco rejects the structuralist notion that a literary work is approached "as an object which, once created, [has] the stiffness—so to speak—of a crystal."[30] But he rejects the idea that texts are inherently open to any interpretation. Even open texts manipulate the reader: "An open text, however 'open' it be, cannot afford whatever interpretation. An open text outlines a 'closed' project of its Model Reader as a component of its structural strategy."[31] Far from embracing an inherent openness of texts as such, Eco denies the legitimacy of indeterminate reading and criticizes readers who fail to recognize their "proper" place. As he writes in a later essay on Joyce: "It is impossible to say what is the best interpretation of the text, but it is possible to say which ones are wrong. . . . Before a text is produced, every kind of text could be invented. After a text has been produced, it is possible to make a text say many things—in certain cases a potentially infinite number of things—but it is impossible—or at least critically illegitimate—to make it say what it does not say. Texts frequently say more than their authors do but less than what many incontinent readers would like them to say."[32]

Here Eco identifies his polemic opponents, the "incontinent readers" who think they can make a text say anything they please. Eco recognizes potentially infinite legitimate readings, but that does not mean that all readings are legitimate.[33] Legitimacy is a function of sovereignty; all interpretations are legitimate so long as they recognize the sovereignty of the text: "[I]n a world dominated by Übermensch readers, let us first rank with the Slave. It is the only way to become, if not the Masters, at least the respectfully free Servants of Semiosis."[34]

This brief excursus is not meant as an exhaustive survey of theoretical analogues to the "Ishmaelian" hermeneutics, or even a full discussion of Eco's position, but rather a brief affirmation that there are contemporary theorists whose work can shed light on legal midrash (and perhaps vice versa). For it is clear that Eco's polemic is easily transposed into the Ishmaelian register. Eco's "Übermensch readers" are those who say to the text, "Be silent until I expound," rather than adopt attentive submission to the text. Why second-century rabbinic Palestine produced reading practices so similar to those of twentieth-century Europe and America—that is an investigation unto itself. What can be stated is that rabbinic literature records a variety of interpretive ideologies, and there are surely analogies to be made to contemporary proponents of interpretive freedom, but that—then as now—one can also hear the voices of those who oppose these practices.

Chapter 5

The Role of the Reader II
Middot

Appended to the Sifra, the halakhic midrash to Leviticus, is a short baraita known as the *Baraita of Thirteen Middot* or the *Baraita of Rabbi Ishmael* (a baraita is a passage that is attributed to tannaitic figures but not part of the Mishnah). The opening line of the *Baraita*—"Rabbi Ishmael says: By thirteen *middot* is the Torah explicated"—has rightly been characterized as "probably the most famous saying of Ishmael in the whole of rabbinic literature."[1] The *Baraita* opens with a list of *middot*—hermeneutical rules or canons—that constitute a rabbinic interpretive logic, followed by examples of each *middah*. The list of the *middot* is as follows:[2]

1. קול וחומר

Inference from minor to major premises

2. גזירה שוה

Analogy based on similar words or phrases

3. בנין אב מכתוב אחד

A comprehensive principle derived from a specific passage

4. בנין אב משני כתובים

A comprehensive principle derived from two passages

5. כלל ופרט

A general statement followed by a particular instance

6. פרט וכלל

A particular instance followed by a general statement

7. כלל ופרט וכלל אי אתה דן אלא כעין הפרט

A general statement followed by a particular instance and then by a general statement, you must interpret according to the character of the particular instance

8. כלל שהוא צריך לפרט

A general statement that requires a particular instance [to be interpreted]

9. פרט שהוא צריך לכלל

A particular instance that requires a general statement [to be interpreted]

10. כל דבר שהיה בכלל ויצא מן הכלל ללמד לא ללמד על עצמו יצא אלא ללמד על הכלל כלו יצא

If a matter is included in a general statement and then made an exception to it, this is not to teach regarding this matter alone but regarding the general statement as a whole.

11. כל דבר שהיה בכלל ויצא לטעון טען אחר שהוא כעינו יצא להקל ולא להחמיר

If a matter is included in a general statement and then made an exception to it in order to teach regarding a similar matter, this is done for the sake of leniency, not strictness.

12. כל דבר שהיה בכלל ויצא לטעון טען אחר שלא כעניינו יצא להקל ולהחמיר

If a matter is included in a general statement and then made an exception to it in order to teach regarding a dissimilar matter, this is done for the sake of both leniency and strictness.

13. כל דבר שהיה בכלל יצא לדון בדבר חדש אי אתה יכול להחזירו לכללו עד שיחזירנו הכתוב לכללו

If a matter is included in a general statement and then made an exception to it in order to deal with a new matter, you cannot return it to the general statement until HA-KATUV does so.

14. דבר הלמד מענינו

A matter that is learned from its context

15. דבר הלמד מסופו

A matter that is learned from its conclusion

16. שני כתובים המכחישים זה את זה יעמדו במקומם עד שיבוא כתוב שלישי ויכריע ביניהם

Two verses that contradict each other will remain in their position until a third verse comes and decides between them.

This list has been the subject of much scholarly analysis, most of it concerned with the identity and provenance of the *middot*. The identity of the *middot* is evidently problematic because the *Baraita*'s statement that there are thirteen *middot* is followed by sixteen rules.[3] Discussion of the *middot*'s provenance focuses on the logical nature of the *middot* and the possibility that they are either historically or conceptually related to Greek logic—more on which below. For now, it should be noted that the *Baraita* presents a challenge to the view that Rabbi Ishmael identifies Scripture as the primary agent of interpretation and delimits the role of the reader. The *Baraita of Thirteen Middot* assumes that the reader approaches Scripture with a ready set of interpretive rules and proceeds to apply them to the text; Scripture is the object of interpretation, playing no role in the process. Moreover, the *Baraita* knows nothing of the interpretive practices of the Mekhilta and the Sifre Numbers: there is but minimal mention of HA-KATUV, no listening to Scripture, no hermeneutic markedness. In short, the *middot* are grounded in human reason, not Scripture.

Before examining whether the *Baraita of Thirteen Middot* and the Rabbi Ishmael midrashim can be reconciled, it needs first be asked whether they need be reconciled, that is, whether the *Baraita* belongs to the Rabbi Ishmael corpus. The *Baraita* is an independent unit that is not part of the Mekhilta and the Sifre Numbers and so, on a strict reading, is outside the purview of this study. But as in previous cases of potentially relevant material associated with Rabbi Ishmael, the possibility that there is a significant connection between the *Baraita* and the Rabbi Ishmael midrashim must be examined—especially when the text in question deals directly with legal hermeneutics. In examining the relationship between the *Baraita* and the midrashim, one must be aware of two dangers: circular reasoning and insensitivity to distinctions of genre. If certain criteria define the "Rabbi Ishmael corpus" and these criteria are absent from the *Baraita of Thirteen Middot*, it does not follow that the *Baraita* is not part of the corpus—perhaps the criteria are wanting. As for generic distinctions, terms may appear in full-fledged midrashic analysis (the Mekhilta and Sifre Numbers) but be absent from synopses (like the *Baraita*), even though the two originate in the same circles.[4] That said, it is clear that the phrase "Rabbi Ishmael says" does not in and of itself guarantee that the statement that follows belongs to the same tradition as the legal midrashim associated by modern scholars with Rabbi Ishmael. A set of criteria is needed by which to weigh comparable elements within the *Baraita* and the midrashim and determine whether they belong to the same tradition. In the following discussion, I employ three criteria: the interpretive techniques that count as *middot* in the midrashim and the *Baraita*; the tradition that the *middot* number thirteen; and the terminology used to characterize them.

The *Baraita of Rabbi Ishmael* and the Midrashim

THE IDENTITY OF THE *Middot*

Gary Porton's study of the traditions of Rabbi Ishmael in the Mishnah, the Babylonian Talmud, and the Palestinian Talmud counsels caution when it comes to the *middot*, as he has found that Rabbi Ishmael employs only six of the *middot* listed in the *Baraita of Thirteen Middot*.[5] Indeed, there are clear discrepancies in what counts as a *middah* in the Rabbi Ishmael midrashim versus the *Baraita of Thirteen Middot*. The following is a list of the pericopes in which the term *middah* or *middot* is used in a hermeneutical sense in the Mekhilta and the Sifre Numbers:[6]

1)

[זו מדה בתורה]:[7] שני כתובים זה כנגד זה והרי הן סותרין זה על ידי זה יתקיימו במקומן עד שיבא כתוב אחר ויכריע ביניהם.

This is a *middah* in the Torah: Two verses that oppose and contradict each other will remain in their place until another verse comes to decide between them. (Sifre Numbers §58, p. 56)[8]

2)

זו אחת מן המדות שהתורה נדרשת בהן, מכלל שהוא צריך לפרטו ופרט שהוא צריך לכללו.

This is one of the thirteen *middot* for interpreting the Torah. There are instances in which not only does the general term need its specific term, but the specific term also needs its general term. (Mekhilta Pisḥa 16, p. 57; Lauterbach 1.28)

3)

זו מדה בתורה פרשה שנאמרה במקום אחד וחסר בה דבר אחד וחזר ושנאה במקום אחד לא שנאה אלא על שחיסר בה דבר אחד.

This is a *middah* in the Torah, any discussion stated in one place, that omits a specific matter, and is then repeated in another place—this repetition is only for the sake of the omitted matter. (Sifre Numbers §2, p. 4)

4)

אמרת, זו מדה בתורה, כל מיתה בתורה סתם, אין את רשאי למושכה להחמיר עליה אלא להקל . . . [או] כל מיתה[9] שנאמרה סתם הרי זו בחנק.

You must say—this is a *middah* in the Torah: Whenever a death penalty is mentioned in the Torah with the mode of execution undefined, you are not allowed to extend its meaning to include a severer mode . . . [or] every undefined death is strangulation." (Mekhilta Neziqin 5, pp. 265–66; Lauterbach 3.45–46)

There is little overlap between these *middot* and the *middot* listed in the *Baraita of Thirteen Middot*. The vast majority of the *middot* listed in the *Baraita of Thirteen Middot* are absent from the Mekhilta and Sifre Numbers. Only two—"a general statement followed by a particular instance" and "two verses that contradict each other"—are identified as *middot* in the Rabbi Ishmael midrashim, a surprising paucity considering that the Mekhilta and Sifre Numbers are the natural setting for applying hermeneutical rules.

The corollary incongruity is equally significant; the Rabbi Ishmael midrashim characterize as *middot* two procedures that do not appear in the *Baraita*. One of them, "a repeated discussion that omits a specific matter," is a general interpretive rule that conforms to the tone of the *Baraita*. Less so the second—number 4 on the list above—which addresses unspecified references to capital punishment. Not only is this rule not counted among the *middot* of the *Baraita*; it is not clear that it could be since it concerns verses with specific content, rather than a general, formal, hermeneutical procedure.

Finally, the Mekhilta and the Sifre Numbers frequently employ formulas listed among the *middot* of the *Baraita* (for example, *kelal u-ferat*, *gezerah shavah*, and *qol va-ḥomer*), without ever referring to them as *middot*. And while the admittedly *e silentio* absence cannot be a decisive argument, it is nonetheless curious that the Rabbi Ishmael midrashim specify certain techniques as *middot*—so the term is known and current—but not the techniques identified as *middot* by the *Baraita*. In light of these incongruities, the criterion of the identity of the *middot* does not indicate that the *Baraita of Thirteen Middot* and the Rabbi Ishmael midrashim belong to the same tradition.

The Number and Characterization of the *Middot*

A key element in the *Baraita* is the number thirteen. That the "thirteen" *middot* seem to number sixteen—a discrepancy that has generated innumerable solutions (proof positive that no one has been wholly satisfactory)—does not undermine the centrality of this tradition. Quite the contrary; the discrepancy suggests that the number thirteen is not an empirical characterization arrived at by counting the *middot*, but rather an ideological statement imposed upon the list. Yet the Rabbi Ishmael midrashim are unaware that the *middot* number thirteen. The Sifre Numbers makes no reference to this tradition; the Mekhilta uses the phrase "thirteen *middot*" twice, but both are late interpolations. One occurrence is in the Mekhilta's interpretation of Exodus 20:13:

"לא תגנוב" (שמות כ ינ): . . . הרי זה אזהרה לגונב נפש. אתה אומר הרי זה אזהרה לגונב נפש או אינו אלא אזהרה לגונב ממון, כשהוא אומר "לא תגנובו" (ויקרא יט יא) הרי זה אזהרה לגונב ממון והלה אזהרה לגונב נפש. אמרת, צא ולמד משלש עשרה מדות שהתורה נדרשת בהן; ועוד אמרת, שלש מצות נאמרו בעניין, שתים מפורשות ואחת סתומה. נלמד סתומה ממפורשות, מה מפורשות מצוות שחייבין עליהן מיתות בית דין, אף סתומה מצוה שחייבין עליה מיתות בית דין. הא אין עליך לומר כלשון אחרון אלא כלשון ראשון, הרי זה אזהרה לגונב נפש והלה אזהרה לגונב ממון.

"You shall not steal" (Exod 20:13): . . . This is a warning against stealing persons. You interpret this to be a warning against stealing persons, but perhaps it is a warning against stealing money [*mammon*]? When it says "All of you shall not steal" (Lev 19:11), behold there you have the warning against stealing property. You must reason: <u>Go and learn it by one of the thirteen *middot* according to which the Torah is interpreted</u>. And further it says, there are three laws mentioned here, two of them explicit and one non-explicit. Let us learn regarding the non-explicit from the explicit ones. Just as the explicit ones incur the death penalty, so also the non-explicit incurs the death penalty. Thus you must say that this verse is a prohibition against stealing a person, and that one against stealing money. (Mekhilta Baḥodesh 8, pp. 232–33; Lauterbach 2.260–61)

The derashah asks whether "You shall not steal" (the Eighth Commandment) refers to stealing people or property. The Mekhilta suggests that Exodus 20:13 warns against stealing people and Leviticus 19:11 ("You shall not steal") warns against stealing property, but immediately questions why the roles cannot be reversed. The answer lies in the broader context of the verse. While the prohibition against stealing is ambiguous, it is one of three prohibitions in Exodus 20:13 and the other two—the prohibitions against murder and adultery—are both capital offenses. Thus, "Let us learn regarding the non-explicit from the explicit," that is, one can infer that the prohibition against theft is a capital crime as well. Since property theft is not a capital offense but stealing people is, Exodus 20:13 prohibits theft of people.

The argument is elegant and to the point, and therein lies the problem. As the preceding summary demonstrates, the phrase "go and learn it by one of the thirteen *middot*"—located, jarringly, between the presentation of the problem and its solution—does not play a role in the argument and is clearly out of context. The Mekhilta exhorts the reader to learn the matter by one of the thirteen *middot*, but never specifies which, or how the *middah* resolves the question. Moreover, the reference to thirteen *middot* is followed by the non sequitur "And further it says," so the thirteen *middot* are hermeneutically meaningless and out of context. These difficulties strongly suggest that the reference to the thirteen *middot* is not an integral part of this text, but has been imported from b. Sanhedrin 86a:[10]

תנו רבנן "לא תגנוב" בגונב נפשות הכתוב מדבר. אתה אומר בגונב נפשות או אינו אלא
בגונב ממון. אמרת צא ולמד משלש עשרה מדות שהתורה נדרשת בהן דבר הלמד מעניינו.
במה הכתוב מדבר, בנפשות, אף כאן בנפשות.

Our masters teach: "You shall not steal" (Exod 20:13), Scripture speaks of stealing persons. You interpret this as stealing persons, but perhaps it refers to stealing money. You say: Go and learn it by one of the thirteen *middot* according to which the Torah is interpreted—a matter is learned by its context. What is Scripture discussing? Capital offenses. Thus here, too, it discusses a capital offense.

In this passage, the Babylonian Talmud presents the same argument as the Mekhilta, but employs different terminology. The appeal to context is introduced by the formula "A matter is learned by its context," which is one of the *middot* enumerated in the *Baraita of Thirteen Middot*. Here the phrase "go and learn it by one of the thirteen *middot*" makes perfect sense: the *derashah* cites one of the *middot*, and then uses it to resolve the problem. Borrowing a page from Rabbi Ishmael, we can use the clear passage to shed light on the obscure and conclude that a scribe familiar with the argument of the Talmud interpolated the thirteen *middot* into the Mekhilta. As such, the reference to the number thirteen cannot be counted as proof that the Mekhilta knows of the thirteen *middot* tradition.

The second *derashah* that links the *middot* to the number thirteen occurs in the Mekhilta's discussion of Exodus 13:

"וידבר ה' אל משה וגו' קדש לי כל בכור" (שמות יג א-ב): זו אחת משלש עשרה מדות
שהתורה נדרשת בהן כלל שהוא צריך לפרטו ופרט שהוא צריך לכללו.

"The Lord spoke further to Moses saying, Consecrate to Me every firstborn" (Exod 13:1–2): This is one of the thirteen-*middot* for interpreting the Torah. There are instances in which not only does the general term need its specific term, but the specific term also needs its general term." (Mekhilta Pisha 16, p. 57; Lauterbach 1.128)

In this *derashah*, the *middah* does play an integral role, but the number thirteen is absent from MS Oxford, the best manuscript of the Mekhilta.[11] Instead of "this is one of the thirteen *middot*," MS Oxford (and the medieval midrashic compilation *Yalqut Shim'oni*) read: זו אחת מן המדות שהתורה נדרשת בהם, "this is one of the *middot* by which the Torah is interpreted." Since MS Oxford dates from the late thirteenth century, when the *Baraita of the Thirteen Middot* was well known, a scribe would have no reason to omit the number thirteen attested in the other witnesses, so it is unlikely that MS Oxford altered an earlier tradition of thirteen *middot*. To the contrary, the absence of the number thirteen makes MS Oxford the *lectio dificilior*—suggesting that the other manuscripts incorporated the number thirteen to conform to the *Baraita of Thirteen Middot*. If so, "this is a *middah* in the Torah" is the earlier formula and "this is one of thirteen *middot* by which Scripture is interpreted" the later. This argument finds additional support in the Munich Mekhilta, MS Munich 117.1 (see figure 1), which reads:[12]

 וידבר יי' קדש לי בכור זו אחת מן י"ג מדות ש'
שבתורה נדרשת הן בכלל שהוא צריך לפרטו

The following hyper-literal translation is meant to suggest the ungrammatical nature of the passage, though the ensuing discussion resists translation altogether and is presented in Hebrew:

The Lord spoke: "Consecrate to Me firstborn": This is one of thirteen *middot* that are in the Torah is explicated them, by a general term that needs a specific

In the MS, the words זו אחת מן י"ג מדות (this is one of thirteen *middot*) are visibly smeared, and the letter ה faintly visible under the י" and immediately preceding מדות. This ה strongly suggests that the phrase י"ג מדות is overlaid on an earlier המדות and that the original phrase in the Munich Mekhilta was זו אחת מן המדות שבתורה. The shift from שבתורה מן המדות זו אחת

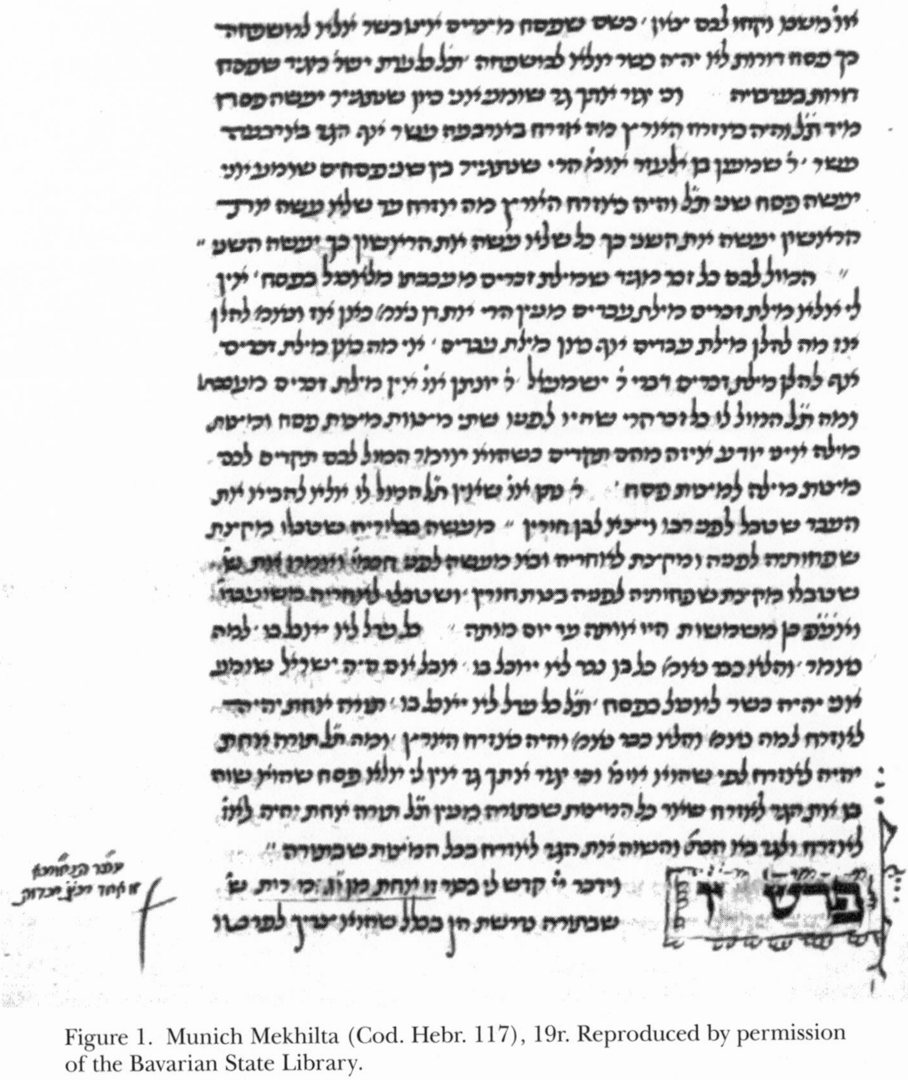

Figure 1. Munich Mekhilta (Cod. Hebr. 117), 19r. Reproduced by permission of the Bavarian State Library.

(one of the *middot* in the Torah) to the current זו אחת מן י"ג מדות (one of the thirteen *middot*) also explains the odd: שבתורה נדרשת הן instead of שהתורה נדרשת בהן. The first word, שבתורה, is a relic from the phrase זו אחת מן המדות שבתורה (one of the *middot* in the Torah). As for הן in lieu of בהן, this could be due to objective space problems that arise from the need to insert the phrase נדרשת בהן, though it is also possible that once the phrase appeared as שבתורה נדרשת בהן the scribe unconsciously compensated for this additional ב by omitting the ב that should precede הן.

Finally, there is a marginal notation in a different hand that reads זו אחד מי"ג מדות עמ"ד תנחומ"א. As Goldin notes in his introduction, עמ"ד stands for עיין מדרש and the notation—a limited critical apparatus—refers the reader to Midrash Tanḥuma' where the reading is אחד מי"ג מדות (one of thirteen *middot*).[13] An early reader of the manuscript found the language of the Munich Mekhilta remarkable and refers the reader to a text that reads אחד מי"ג מדות (one of thirteen *middot*) except that this *is* what the Munich Mekhilta now reads. Since the annotator would not have referred to an identical and otherwise unremarkable version, it is clear that the note was made when the Munich Mekhilta's version (still discernable under the changes) was *not* "one of thirteen *middot*," but rather, as argued above, זו אחת מן המדות שבתורה (this is one of the *middot* in the Torah), without reference to the number thirteen. The textual witnesses consulted—MS Oxford, MS Munich, and the marginal reference to Midrash Tanḥuma'—indicate that the number thirteen is not original to the Mekhilta at Exodus 13:1–2. Rather, they suggest a general shift toward the number thirteen, and a concomitant move from "this is a *middah* in the Torah" to "this is one of the thirteen *middot* by which Scripture is interpreted," with the latter superimposed upon the former. The significance of this shift will be discussed below. For now, these are the main points of difference between the Rabbi Ishmael midrashim and the *Baraita of Thirteen Middot*:

i. The Rabbi Ishmael midrashim employ only two of the sixteen (or thirteen) *middot* listed in the *Baraita*.

ii. The midrashim refer to various interpretive procedures not listed in the *Baraita* as *middot*.

iii. Interpretive procedures characterized as *middot* in the *Baraita* appear in the midrashim without this designation.

iv. The midrashim are unaware of the tradition that the *middot* number thirteen.

v. The *Baraita* and the midrashim use different introductory phrases. The former speaks of the thirteen *middot* "by which the Torah is interpreted," while the Rabbi Ishmael midrashim characterize them as *middot* "in the Torah."

Taken together, these findings strongly suggest that, *pace* the *Baraita*'s attribution to Rabbi Ishmael, it belongs to a different tradition from the Mekhilta and the Sifre Numbers. For the current discussion, it does not matter whether the differences are the result of chronology, geography, ideology, or some combination of these, only that the analysis of the *middot* in the Rabbi Ishmael midrashim need not include the *Baraita of Thirteen Middot*. Of greater significance is the conceptual analysis that is now needed. The regnant understanding of the *middot* as logical formulas is derived from the *Baraita of Thirteen Middot*. With the disassociation of the *Baraita* from the midrashim, the meaning of the *middot* in the latter becomes a topic of investigation in its own right.

Are the *Middot* Logic?

In 1953, Louis Jacobs published "The Aristotelian Syllogism and the Qal wa-Homer,"[14] in which he argues that the *qol va-ḥomer* is unlike the syllogism in a number of respects: *qol va-ḥomer* contains an element of "how much more so" that is absent from the syllogism; it deals with precepts rather than the relationship between genus and species; and more. That same year, Jacobs presented a similar argument in his "The Talmudic Hermeneutical Rule of 'Binyan 'Abh' and J. S. Mill's 'Method of Agreement.'?"[15] The argument: *binyan 'av* (*middah* number three and four in the list that opens this chapter) is not a form of analogy, and "a more fruitful way of explaining the principle is to compare it with John Stuart Mill's method of agreement, to which it bears a striking resemblance."[16] Setting aside the fact that neither formula is referred to as a *middah* in the Rabbi Ishmael midrashim, Jacobs's articles are of interest for the way they frame the investigation of the *middot*. Is *qol va-ḥomer* like a syllogism, and if not, which argument is? Should *binyan 'av* be studied as a form of analogy or does Mill's logic provide a better approach? For Jacobs, the scholarly desideratum is ascertaining the precise type of logic with which the *middot* should be identified, while their identification with logic as such is self-evident and passed over without comment.

Jacobs's position reflects both the continuity and the change in *middot* scholarship over the past century and more. On the one hand, he has broken with the view of earlier scholars[17] that the logical structure of the *middot* means that they can be traced to Aristotle's logic, a view refuted by scholars such as David Daube and Saul Lieberman, who argue that no scholar "has been able to discover definite Greek influence on [the *middot*]."[18] But even in breaking with the Greeks, the *middot* (again, largely under the influence of the *Baraita of Thirteen Middot*) were still viewed as providing general, formal rules of interpretation anchored in human reason; a logic of interpretation. Though not Greek, they remain logical in the broader sense of the word. Thus Lieberman, in the very same study that argues that the *middot* are not of Greek provenance, writes, "We can safely assert that the Jews possessed their *rules of logic* for the interpretation of the Bible in the second half of the first century B.C.E."[19] One scholar, Rabbi David Cohen (*ha-Rav ha-Nazir*), developed a theory of a uniquely Jewish logic, a logic based largely on the *middot* that is philosophically and spiritually opposed to Greek thought.[20] The starting point for these studies is invariably the *Baraita of Thirteen Middot*, and, while the interpretive rules of this text may be logical, it is not clear that this is true of the Rabbi Ishmael midrashim.

For one thing, the *middot* in the Rabbi Ishmael midrashim do not make the broad claims of logic, since they apply only to Scripture. Some *middot* in the *Baraita of Thirteen Middot* could be used as general rules of inference (*qol va-ḥomer*) or analogy (*gezerah shavah*) and, in fact, appear in non-scriptural contexts in rabbinic literature. To cite just one example from m. Keritot 3.7:

אמר רבי עקיבה שאלתי את רבן גמליאל ואת ר' יהושע . . . הבא על אחותו ועל אחות אביו
ועל אחות אמו בעלם אחד מה הוא חייב אחת על כולן או אחת על כל אחת ואחת
אמרו לו לא שמענו, אבל שמענו בבא על חמש נשיו נידות בעלם אחד שהוא חייב על כל
אחת ואחת ורואים אנו שהדברים קל וחומר.

Rabbi Aqiva said: I asked Rabban Gamliel and Rabbi Yehoshua . . . if a man had intercourse with his sister and his father's sister and his mother's sister during one bout of forgetfulness, what happens?—is he liable to one offering for them all or to one offering for each of them? They said to me, We have not heard, but have heard [a tradition] that if a man had intercourse during one spell of forgetfulness with his five wives who were menstruants, he is liable for each one of them; and we consider that this applies still more [*qol va-ḥomer*] in the other case. (m. Keritot 3.7; Danby, p. 567)

The case that Rabbi Aqiva raises before his teachers has no precedent in extra-scriptural tradition—Rabban Gamliel and Rabbi Yehoshua acknowledge this. But there is an analogous case, which is cited as the basis for a *qol va-ḥomer* argument that decides Rabbi Aqiva's question. The Mishnah here is concerned with non-scriptural tradition (no verse is cited), which is evidently a legitimate area for *qol va-ḥomer* arguments.

Strikingly, the formulas that could be (and are) used in non-scriptural contexts are not called *middot* in the Rabbi Ishmael midrashim. The Mekhilta and Sifre Numbers designate as *middot* only arguments anchored in the biblical text.[21] These *middot* present a variety of interpretive strategies, some responding to content-specific issues in the biblical text (unspecified modes of execution), and others to more abstract relations between general and specific terms and the like. Indeed, it appears the basic function of the *middah* is hermeneutical, or more accurately, meta-hermeneutical: it controls the interpretive process by eliminating potentially problematic hermeneutical possibilities. Setting aside the *middah* "two verses contradict, a third resolves," consider each *middah* in turn:

Middah (2)[22] (the need for general and specific terms) refers to the two procedures that can be undertaken when faced with a general term and a specific term, *kelal u-ferat* and *kelal u-ferat u-khelal*. As discussed above,[23] the specific statement (the *perat*) restricts the general statement to differing degrees based upon the *middah* employed. *Kelal u-ferat* requires the general statement to correspond to the specific instances provided, while *kelal u-ferat u-khelal* requires that it be essentially similar but not co-extensive. In both cases, the *middah* limits the interpretive possibilities of a potentially very open statement. *Middah* (3) (a section is repeated for the sake of the new element in it) also delimits the interpretive freedom of the reader, limiting the scope of the hermeneutic markedness of the repeated passage. *Middah* (4) (unspecified forms of capital punishment are strangulation) is the clearest example of this pattern, since it denies that unspecified modes of execution are subject to interpretation.

In each case, the *middot* fix upon the most open element in the biblical text and transform it into a marker of closure. This is most explicit in *middah* (4), in which the biblical verse contains an *unspecified* form of capital punishment, which would otherwise open the verse to any number of interpretations. The *middah* solves this problem by making the lack of specificity an "anti-hermeneutic marker." That is, rather than the unspecified capital punishment indicating the verse is open to interpretation, the lack of specificity is identified as the marker that elicits a fixed reading. The indeterminacy of the verse is explicitly identified as the element that sets in motion the *middah* that introduces a closed, determined meaning.

In considering *kelal u-ferat*, it is important to recall Michael Chernick's observation that in tannaitic literature the "biblical passage that makes up the general statement (*kelal*) contains the word *kol* (all or every) or a noun whose meaning is general and inclusive."[24] In other words, the *middah* is applied to verses that contain an inclusive element and are inherently open to interpretation as to what constitutes all instances of a given category. The *middah* transforms such verses into closed, or at least much less open, readings. Rather than indicate—as the semantics of biblical Hebrew would suggest—that a verse applies to all instances, the word *kol* invokes a rule by which the general statement is delimited by the specific. This transformation negates the indeterminate character of the universal qualifier by subsuming its meaning to that of the specific instances. Like the unspecified capital punishment, the word *kol* is turned against itself—its inherent openness transformed into a marker of closure.

This reversal also characterizes *middah* (3). As discussed in Chapter 2, the Rabbi Ishmael midrashim consider redundancy (though not repetition as such) a hermeneutic marker. When, however, entire passages are repeated and the interpreter is free to interpret every word, the *middah* reverses the valence of the repetition. Rather than legitimate interpretation, the repetition of the passage indicates that the entire passage is intended for the sake of the one novel element, marking the only *nonredundant* element as the legitimate object of interpretation. Each of these formulas then deals with the perceived threat of excessive interpretation where moderation is required, or with the perceived threat of moderate interpretation where none is required. And in each case, the *middah* isolates the open element in the verse and reverses its hermeneutical significance so that it yields a fixed, closed interpretation.[25]

TWO VERSES CONTRADICT AND A THIRD RESOLVES (*shnei ketuvim*)

The remaining *middah* appears in the Rabbi Ishmael midrashim in the following form: [26]

שני כתובים מכחישין זה את זה עד שיבוא הכתוב השלישי ויכריע ביניהם.[27]

Two verses contradict [literally, deny] each other until a third verse comes and decides between them.

As mentioned above, this is one of the *middot* that appear in the *Baraita of Thirteen Middot* and is considered an outstanding example of rabbinic logic. After all, the *middah* deals with contradiction, a logical issue par excellence, functioning as an algorithm that instructs the reader as to the proper procedure when faced with contradictory verses. Curiously, however, most of the derashot in the Mekhilta and the Sifre Numbers that resolve biblical contradictions do *not* follow the hermeneutical procedure outlined in the *middah*. They appear, rather, in the following form:

כתוב אחד אומר "את עולותיך ואת שלמיך" (שמות כ כד) וכתוב אחד אומר "ועשית עולותיך הבשר והדם" (דברים יב כז) הא כיצד יתקיימו שני כתובין. אמר רבי יוסי ברבי יהודה, מחצי המזבח ולצפון בצפון, ומחצי המזבח ולדרום בדרום.

One verse states, "[Sacrifice] your burnt offerings and your sacrifices of well-being" (Exod 20:24 [in some Bibles, 20:21]), while another verse states, "You shall offer your burnt offerings, both the flesh and the blood" (Deut 12:27). How can both verses be maintained? Rabbi Yose the son of Rabbi Yehudah said, from the middle of the altar northward counts as north, from the middle of the altar southward as south. (Mekhilta Baḥodesh 11, p. 242; Lauterbach 2.286)[28]

Or, in an aggadic context:

כתוב אחד אומר "ישא ה' פניו אליך" (במדבר ו כו) וכתוב אחד אומר "אשר לא ישא פנים"

(דברים י יז). כיצד יתקיימו שני כתובים הללו כשישראל[29] עושין רצון מקום "ישא ה' פניו
אליך" וכשאין ישראל עושים רצונו של מקום "אשר לא ישא פנים."

One verse states, "May the Lord show His favor to you" (Num 6:26) and another
verse states, "[God] shows no favor" (Deut 10:17). How can both these verses be
maintained? When Israel does the will of God, "May the Lord show His favor to
you" and when they do not do the will of God, "[God] shows no favor." (Sifre
Numbers §42, p. 45)[30]

These derashot explicitly address the issue of contradiction and use
the same terminology as "two verses contradict and a third resolves"
("one verse states . . . the other verse states . . . how can both be maintained?").[31] But despite the thematic and terminological similarity, the
derashot do not follow the *middah*'s "recommended" procedure, that is,
they do not appeal to a third verse. Instead, they resolve the contradiction with ad hoc arguments, appropriate only to the particular issues
at hand, making no claims to general validity. Such ad hoc arguments
are relatively numerous, appearing dozens of times in the Mekhilta and
the Sifre Numbers.[32] As for the "proper" procedure, "two verses contradict and a third resolves," it occurs twice in the Mekhilta of Rabbi Ishmael, and once in the Sifre Numbers.[33] Of these, one occurrence is
attributed to Rabbi Aqiva but immediately rejected by Rabbi Ishmael.
Since Rabbi Ishmael is the dominant rabbinic figure of the Mekhilta, the
attribution to Rabbi Aqiva and explicit rejection by Rabbi Ishmael indicate that the teaching does not belong to the "Ishmaelian" corpus, but is
cited as a foil.[34]

The paucity of "two verses contradict and a third resolves," relative to
the total number of derashot dealing with biblical contradictions, is puz-
zling. If "two verses contradict and a third resolves" is a canon of interpretation, why isn't it employed more consistently? Why is the *middah*
used only twice while the ad hoc explanations appear much more frequently? What distinguishes these derashot?

Sifre Numbers

According to the Horovitz edition, Sifre Numbers §58 begins as
follows:

"ובבוא משה אל אהל מועד לדבר אתו" (במדבר ז פט): למה נאמר? לפי שהוא אומר "וידבר
ה' אליו מאהל מועד לאמר" (ויקרא א א). שומע אני מאהל מועד ממש, תלמוד לומר
"ונועדתי לך שם ודברתי אתך מעל הכפורת" (שמות כה כב), אי אפשר לומר מאהל מועד.

"When Moses went into the Tent of Meeting to speak with Him" (Num 7:89):
Why is this said? Because it says: "The Lord called to Moses and spoke to him
from the Tent of Meeting" (Lev 1:1). I could understand this as referring to the

Tent of Meeting in an unqualified sense, but [Scripture] teaches, saying: "There I will meet with you from above the cover of the Ark" (Exod 25:22). It is impossible to hold that [God spoke from] the Tent of Meeting.

This passage, which is followed by the "two verses contradict and a third resolves" argument, is a mixture of two different derashot. It begins with the phrase *lammah ne'emar*, "Why was this stated?," a formula that introduces a hermeneutical procedure whose structure is as follows: the biblical verse in question is cited, followed by the question "Why was this stated?" and then a second biblical verse is adduced. The derashah then argues that the second verse is susceptible to misinterpretation and that the first verse—the object of inquiry—clarifies the ambiguity, thus steering the reader clear of a potential error. The derashah concludes with a second citation of the verse in question, its hermeneutical function now apparent and the initial question, *lammah ne'emar*, answered. Miguel Pérez Fernández, who has studied derashot of this type, distinguishes several subcategories according to the terminology that introduces the second, potentially misunderstood verse, and all conclude with the biblical verse that opens it.[35] Sifre Numbers §58 follows this pattern to a point, opening with Numbers 7:89 ("When Moses went into the Tent of Meeting"), and presenting the question *lammah ne'emar*, "Why is this said?". It then cites Leviticus 1:1 ("The Lord called to Moses and spoke to him from the Tent of Meeting"), and suggests that this verse may be misinterpreted as referring to the Tent of Meeting in an unqualified sense (*mamash*). At this point, however, the structure of the derashah collapses. Instead of explaining how Numbers 7:89 helps avoid this misunderstanding and concluding with a second citation of the verse, a third verse, Exodus 25:22, is introduced and the discussion breaks off in a new direction.

Besides breaking with the established structure of *lammah ne'emar*, this sequence renders the derashah nonsensical: it sets out to investigate the hermeneutical role of Numbers 7:89, hints that the answer lies in its relationship to Exodus 25:22, but ultimately leaves the initial question—Why was Numbers 7:89 stated?—with no response. What we have here is a mixture of two midrashic arguments. The derashah can be made to fit the structure of *lammah ne'emar* either by having the *talmud lomar* formula introduce Numbers 7:89 instead of Exodus 25:22, or by having the derashah open with Exodus 25:22 instead of Numbers 7:89. Which of these is to be preferred is not germane to the present discussion. What is important is to recognize the *lammah ne'emar* argument and isolate "two verses contradict and a third resolves" from it. Since the contradictory verses are cited in the body of the argument, the reconstruction of "two verses contradict and a third resolves" requires only that these verses be cited at the introduction, as follows:

כתוב אחד אומר "ונועדתי לך שם ודברתי אתך מעל הכפורת" (שמות כה כב) וכתוב אחד
אומר "וידבר ה' אליו מאהל מועד" (ויקרא א א). אי אפשר לומר מאהל מועד שכבר נאמר
מעל הכפורת, ואי אפשר לומר מעל הכפורת שכבר נאמר מאהל מועד, כיצד נתקיימו
שני כתובים זה כנגד זה והרי הן סותרין זה על ידי זה. יתקיימו במקומן עד שיבא כתוב אחר
ויכריע ביניהם. מה תלמוד לומר "ובבוא משה אל אהל מועד [לדבר אתו]" (במדבר ז פט)
מגיד הכתוב שהיה[36] משה נכנס ועומד באהל וקול יורד משמי שמים לבין שני הכרובים
והוא שומע את הקול מדבר אליו מבפנים.

One verse says: "There I will meet with you from above the cover of the Ark"
(Exod 25:22), and another verse says, "The Lord called to Moses and spoke to
him from the Tent of Meeting" (Lev 1:1). It is impossible to hold that [God spoke
from] the Tent of Meeting since it has been said "above the cover of the Ark,"
and it is impossible to hold that [God spoke from] above the cover of the Ark
since it has been said "from the Tent of Meeting." How can these two verses be
maintained as they contradict one another? They remain in their place until
another verse comes to decide between them. What does [Scripture] teach by
saying, "When Moses went into the Tent of Meeting to speak with Him" (Num
7:89)? HA-KATUV states that Moses would enter into the Tent of Meeting and
stand there, and the voice descended from the highest heavens to between the
two cherubs [situated above the cover of the Ark] and he heard the voice speaking to him from within. (Sifre Numbers §58, pp. 55–56)

The two contradictory verses are "The Lord called to Moses and spoke
to him from the Tent of Meeting" (Lev 1:1) and "There I will meet with
you from above the cover of the Ark" (Exod 25:22). The question is how
the third verse, "When Moses went into the Tent of Meeting to speak with
Him" (Num 7:89), resolves the contradiction.

Since the publication of Meir Friedmann's posthumous and incomplete edition of the Sifra in 1915,[37] scholarship on "two verses contradict
and a third resolves" has been shaped by Friedmann's claim that the
schools of Rabbi Ishmael and Rabbi Aqiva employ the third verse differently. According to Friedmann, Rabbi Aqiva cites a third verse that supports one of the contradictory positions, tilting the scales in its favor and
excluding the opposing view. Rabbi Ishmael, on the other hand, cites a
third verse that contains elements from each of the two positions, harmonizing the contradictory verses. For Rabbi Aqiva, the third verse
resolves by exclusion, and for Rabbi Ishmael by harmonization. Regarding the derashah at hand, Friedmann argues that it constitutes an exclusive resolution in which Numbers 7:89 ("When Moses went into the Tent
of Meeting") sides with Leviticus 1:1 ("The Lord called to Moses and
spoke to him from the Tent of Meeting") against Exodus 25:22 ("There
I will meet with you from above the cover of the Ark")[38]—the two "tent"
verses outweighing the one "ark" verse. More recently, David Henshke
has argued against this reading, suggesting that it fails to consider the
third verse in its entirety.[39] Henshke shows Friedmann's claim that Numbers 7:89 excludes Exodus 25:22 is based on the partial citation adduced

by the Sifre Numbers, "When Moses went into the Tent of Meeting," while the full verse reads: "When Moses went into the Tent of Meeting to speak with Him, he would hear the voice addressing him from above the cover of the Ark." Once the verse is considered in its entirety, Henshke argues, the harmonizing nature of the decision becomes evident: Numbers 7:89a agrees with Leviticus 1:1 (Tent of Meeting) while Numbers 7:89b agrees with Exodus 25:22 (above the cover of the Ark).[40]

Before proceeding to my own analysis of the third verse, it is worth noting that these readings—Henshke's no less than Friedmann's—fail to provide a satisfactory account of the Sifre's assertion that Exodus 25:22 and Leviticus 1:1 are contradictory. For Friedmann and Henshke, the question involves the location of God when speaking to Moses, and the contradiction lies in the different accounts given in Exodus (God spoke to Moses from above the cover of the Ark) and Leviticus (God spoke to Moses from the Tent of Meeting). But these are not contradictory statements, as the Ark is located *within* the Tent of Meeting, so any event that takes place above the Ark occurs, ipso facto, within the Tent of Meeting. By way of analogy: if one were to ask two people about Jane's whereabouts and be told by one that she is at home and by the other that she is in her room, these statements would not be considered contradictory. They are fully compatible descriptions, differing as to the specificity of the information they provide. Other tannaitic sources saw this clearly:

"מאהל מועד" (ויקרא א א): יכול מכל הבית, תלמוד לומר "מעל הכפורת" (שמות כה כב) או מעל הכפורת יכול מעל הכפורת כולה, תלמוד לומר "מבין שני הכרובים" (שם) דברי ר' עקיבה.

"From the Tent of Meeting" (Lev 1:1): Does this refer to the entire Tabernacle? [Scripture] teaches: "Above the cover of the Ark" (Exod 25:22). If, then, it is above the cover of the Ark, does this mean above the whole cover of the Ark? [Scripture] teaches by saying: "From between the two cherubs" (Exod 25:22), the words of Rabbi Aqiva. (Sifra Nedava, pereq 2.12; Weiss 4a)

For the Sifra, the relationship between Leviticus 1:1 and Exodus 25:22 is one of generality versus specificity. Leviticus 1:1 describes the general location of God's speech, the Tent of Meeting, while Exodus 25:22 provides progressively more precise descriptions—first from above the cover of the Ark and then from between the two cherubs. None of these descriptions contradicts any of the others.[41] Why, then, should a verse locating God above the cover of the Ark be said to contradict a verse locating God in the Tent of Meeting?

In an earlier version of this argument, I concluded that there was no real contradiction generating this derashah.[42] Since then, one of the University of Pennsylvania Press readers suggested, in commenting on this manuscript, that a contradiction may exist after all. Leviticus 1:1 is to be understood against the backdrop of the statement at the very end of Exodus that Moses could not enter the Tent of Meeting because it was filled by God's presence: "Moses could not enter the Tent of Meeting because the cloud had settled upon it and the Presence of the Lord filled the Tabernacle" (Exod 40:35). In light of this statement, "The Lord called to Moses and spoke to him <u>from</u> the Tent of Meeting" (Lev 1:1) indicates that Moses stood *outside* the Tent while the Lord spoke to him from within. Exodus 25:22 has God saying to Moses, "There <u>I will meet with you</u> from above the cover of the Ark," suggesting that Moses is *inside* the Tent.[43] The Sifre resolves this contradiction by citing Numbers 7:89, which locates Moses squarely within the Tent of Meeting, emphasized by the concluding observation of the derashah, that Moses "heard the voice speaking to him from within."

This is an interesting and original interpretation, though I am not fully convinced that the Sifre says this. Simply put, if the derashah revolves around Moses' inability to enter the Tent, in one case, and his presence within the Tent, in another, why cite Leviticus 1:1 as an example of the former? "The Lord called to Moses and spoke to him from the Tent of Meeting" *could* mean that Moses was outside, but why not adduce the explicit statement in Exodus 40:35, "Moses could not enter the Tent of Meeting"? Moreover, when the Sifre states, "It is impossible to hold 'the Tent of Meeting' since it has been said '<u>above the cover of the Ark</u>,'" the contrast seems to involve God's location, not Moses'. Why, in sum, present the contradiction so obscurely as to escape even the discerning eyes of Abraham Ibn Ezra, the great Bible commentator, who wrote in his commentary to Exodus 25:22: "I do not understand how this verse (Exod 25:22) contradicts '[The Lord called to Moses] and spoke to him from the Tent of Meeting' (Lev 1:1), for the Tent of Meeting is a term that includes the Ark and everything else in it, so there is no need for a resolution."[44]

Despite these qualifications, the reader's interpretation identifies a contradiction between Exodus 25:22 and Leviticus 1:1 and thus makes sense of the derashah's own claims. This is a major advantage to any interpretation, but even if it is accepted it must come with an important qualification: the derashah is not exclusively (or even primarily) concerned with resolving a scriptural contradiction—and the proof is in the third, resolving verse.

According to the reading just presented, the function of the third verse is to establish that Moses meets with God within the Tent of Meeting. Numerous verses could be used to make this argument. Some verses affirm that the Tent of Meeting is the site in which God and Moses are to meet: "Place [the altar] in front of the curtain that is over the Ark of the Pact . . . where I will meet with you" (Exod 30:6). Other verses describe God speaking to Moses from within the Tent: "On the first day of the second month . . . the Lord spoke to Moses in the wilderness of Sinai, in the Tent of Meeting" (Num 1:1). Yet the Sifre chooses a verse that is textually fragmented and out of place and, curiously for a verse intended to locate God and Moses in the Tent of Meeting, does not explicitly mention God's presence in the Tent: "When Moses went into the Tent of Meeting to speak with Him, he heard the voice addressing him from above the cover that was on top of the Ark of the Pact between the two cherubim." At first sight, this comment may appear trivial, since God, while not mentioned explicitly, is obviously introduced through the voice that speaks to Moses. Martin Noth, in his commentary on Numbers, speaks of "'the voice' (sc. of God)," without offering any argument for this addition, no doubt because the precedent for this reading goes back to the Septuagint.[45] God is, moreover, referred to in the pronominal phrase לדבר אתו, "to speak with Him," or as Philip J. Budd glosses the verse: "And when Moses entered the Tent of Meeting to speak with him (Yahweh) . . ."[46]

Indeed, virtually all translators and interpreters have "introduced" God into the verse in one of these two ways. The near universal acceptance of this practice does not, however, count as a conclusive argument in its favor, for Numbers 7:89 does not support either claim. First, because the failure to mention God is marked: that God speaks to Moses, that Moses hears God, and that God has a voice are all uncontroversial assertions attested throughout the Pentateuch. Yet Numbers 7:89 states that Moses heard "*the* voice" rather than "God" or "God's voice." As for "to speak with him" referring to God, this claim fails to take into account the isolated and discontinuous status of Numbers 7:89 within its broader context. The entirety of Numbers 7 is devoted to the offerings brought by the tribes in honor of the completion and dedication of the Tent of Meeting, concluding with the herd animals brought for the burnt offerings and the sacrifices of well-being (*shelamim*): "Total of herd animals for sacrifices of well-being, twenty-four bulls; of rams, sixty; of he-goats, sixty; of yearling lambs, sixty. That was the dedication offering for the altar after its anointing" (Num 7:88). This statement is followed by Numbers 7:89: "When Moses went into the Tent of Meeting to speak with Him, he heard the voice addressing him from above the cover that was on top of the Ark of the Pact between the two cherubim; thus He spoke to him." In the following verse, Numbers 8:1, the narrative sets off in a new direction: "The Lord spoke to Moses saying, Speak to Aaron and say to him, When you mount the lamps, let the seven lamps give light at the front of the lampstand." A. H. McNeile's description of the contextual difficulties that Numbers 7:89 presents is apt: "An isolated and mutilated fragment describing the intercourse of God with Moses in the sanctuary. . . . The verbs 'went,' 'heard' and 'spake' are not frequentative, describing what usually happened. It is a single incident, introducing some words of Jehovah which have been lost. They cannot be the commands in the following chapter, for in that case v. 1 [of chapter 8 of Numbers] would be meaningless repetition."[47]

The isolation of Numbers 7:89 from any context makes it impossible to link "with him" to God in a direct, grammatical sense, since God was last mentioned in Numbers 7:11, almost eighty verses earlier and is not the preceding noun. Since, grammatically speaking, neither the voice nor the pronominal "with him" necessarily refers to God, the assertion that the speaker in Numbers 7:89 is God is ultimately theological, not grammatical. The assertion is also common sense; after all, who but God would be speaking to Moses in the Tent of Meeting? But common sense is not always the best guide in these situations, so it is worth noting that from a strictly grammatical perspective, it is possible to read Numbers 7:89 as claiming that Moses entered the Tent of Meeting to speak with the same entity that spoke to him, namely "*the* voice," understood as a divine intermediary.

Whether or not this is a plausible interpretation of Numbers 7:89 is not relevant to the present discussion. The argument is that (plausible or not)[48] this is the interpretation found in the Sifre Numbers. Note how the biblical "voice" is picked up by the Sifre's gloss:

Numbers 7:89:"When Moses went into the Tent of Meeting to speak with Him, he heard the voice . . ."
Sifre Numbers:"HA-KATUV states that Moses would enter into the Tent of Meeting and stand there, and the voice descended from highest heavens to between the cherubs, and he heard the voice speaking to him from within."

The Sifre Numbers is alive to God's absence from Numbers 7:89 and reproduces this absence in the gloss—Moses hears "the voice" speaking in the Tent. More importantly, the Sifre provides additional information on the voice, information unrelated to the contradictory verses: upon Moses' entry into the Tent of Meeting, the voice "descended from the highest heavens"—where it presumably resides at other times. If the intention of the derashah were merely to argue that Moses encounters God inside the Tent of Meeting, why use a prooftext that does not mention God but only a voice, and then—compounding what should be an unfortunate omission—make no reference to God in the derashah but rather pick up on the voice leitmotiv? Because that is precisely the point of the derashah: a voice, a divine voice that regularly resides in the highest heavens, descends to speak with Moses in the Tent of Meeting, serving as an intermediary and thus allowing God to remain divorced from human affairs. The theological dimension of the derashah will be discussed more fully below. For now, note that the derashah does not so much resolve a scriptural contradiction as use the contradiction as a pad from which to launch a third, theologically driven, view.

MEKHILTA OF RABBI ISHMAEL

The second "two verses contradict and a third resolves" derashah occurs in the Mekhilta to Exodus 20:22:

"כי מן השמים דברתי עמכם" (שמות כ כב): כתוב אחד אומר "כי מן השמים" וכתוב
אחד אומר "וירד ה' על הר סיני אל ראש ההר" (שם יט כ). כיצד יתקיימו שני כתובין?
הכריע "מן השמים השמיעך את קולו ליסרך" (דברים ד לו), דברי ר' ישמעאל.

"[You yourselves saw that] I spoke to you from the very heavens" (Exod 20:22):[49] One verse says: "From the very heavens" and one verse says: "The Lord came down upon Mount Sinai" (Exod 19:20). How can both these passages be maintained? The matter is decided by the verse: "From the heavens He let you hear His voice to discipline you" (Deut 4:36). These are the words of Rabbi Ishmael. (Mekhilta Baḥodesh 9, p. 238; Lauterbach 2.275)[50]

The Mekhilta does not gloss the third verse, so the manner in which the derashah resolves the contradiction must be determined by analysis of the verse and its relationship to the contradictory verses. Essentially, the task at hand is to determine whether this passage presents the same hermeneutical argument (and perhaps the same theological agenda) as Sifre Numbers §58.

The derashah identifies "I spoke to you from the very heavens" (Exod 20:22) and "The Lord came down upon Mount Sinai" (Exod 19:20) as the contradictory verses while "From the heaven He let you hear His voice to discipline you" (Deut 4:36) is the third, deciding verse. Did God speak from the heavens, as Exodus 20:22 suggests, or was God on Mount Sinai, in keeping with Exodus 19:20? Previous treatment of the derashah reveals a very similar dynamic to that found in the discussion of the Sifre Numbers §58, with the issue again being framed as whether the third verse resolves the contradiction by exclusion or by harmonization. A number of scholars read this as an exclusive decision in which Deuteronomy 4:36 (from the heavens) sides with Exodus 20:22 (the very heavens) against Exodus 19:20 (upon Mount Sinai), the two "heavens" verses tilting the scales against the one "Sinai" verse.[51] David Henshke again rejects this view as based on an incomplete reading of the third verse. Once the verse is considered in full, Henshke argues, it becomes clear that the third verse seeks to harmonize the contradiction: "From the heaven He let you hear His voice to discipline you and on earth He showed you His great fire." On Henshke's reading, Deuteronomy 4:36a ("From the heavens He let you hear His voice") corresponds to Exodus 20:22 ("I spoke to you from the very heavens"), while 4:36b ("on earth He showed you His great fire") echoes Exodus 19:20 ("The Lord came down upon Mount Sinai"). The derashah cites a third verse that contains elements of the two contradicting verses and thus is a harmonizing resolution.

But while Henshke's criticism of earlier scholarship is (again) valid, his own reading fails—on two counts. First, Henshke overlooks the revisionist dynamic at work in Deuteronomy 4:36. He recognizes that Deuteronomy alludes to the Sinai narrative of Exodus 19, but mistakes allusion for agreement. Deuteronomy 4:36a—"From the heavens He let you hear His voice"—does indeed correspond to "I spoke to you from the very heavens" (Exod 20:22), but "on earth He showed you His great fire" is *opposed* to "The Lord came down upon Mount Sinai" (Exod 19:20). As so often in Deuteronomy's reworking of earlier themes, the adoption of the fire motif from Exodus 19 serves Deuteronomy's own revisionist reading.[52] This becomes evident once we consider the theological role of the fire in the Exodus narrative: "Now Mount Sinai was all in smoke, for the Lord had come down upon it in fire" (Exod 19:18). The difference between this account and that of Deuteronomy is critical: in Exodus, God descended upon the mountain in a fire; in Deuteronomy, God sends the fire to earth while remaining in the heavens above. As Moshe Weinfeld has written: "[The author] combines the speaking from heaven with the fire on the mountain in order to advance his abstract notion of the revelation: neither did God descend upon the mountain nor did the Israelites see any image during the revelation, they only heard God's words from the fire."[53] Deuteronomy 4:36 does not openly challenge Exodus 19's account of revelation. Instead, it incorporates the notion of a fiery presence on the mountain in a way that relieves God of the need to be present on earth. In other words, Deuteronomy suggests that Exodus 19 is right about the fire on the mountain but errs in taking the fire as a sign of God's presence. The thrust of Deuteronomy 4:36b is to reverse Exodus 19:20's assertion that God came down upon Mount Sinai: God was in heaven (as Deuteronomy 4:36a explicitly states), and on earth the Israelites saw *only* God's fire. In terms of the argument of the Mekhilta, then, both parts of Deuteronomy 4:36 correspond to the theological position of Exodus 20:22—God was in the heavens and did not descend upon Mount Sinai.[54] It is, of course, possible that the Mekhilta missed this dynamic altogether and, in a gross misreading, yoked together theologically opposing verses. But one should only impute such a mistake to a commentary if no viable alternatives exist, and that is not the case here.

The second difficulty with Henshke's interpretation involves the same criticism he levels at his predecessors—the failure to consider the third verse in its entirety. Henshke's harmonizing interpretation demands symmetry between the positions of the contradictory verses, on the one hand, and the distinct elements of the third verse, on the other. He finds this symmetry by matching "I spoke to you from the very heavens" (Exod 20:22) with "From the heavens He let you hear His voice" (Deut 4:36a), and "The Lord came down upon Mount Sinai" (Exod 19:20) with "On earth He showed you His great fire" (Exod 4:36b). In doing so, however, he commits the same offense as his predecessors, for these are only the first two of the *three* elements that make up Deuteronomy 4:36. The whole verse reads: "From the heavens He let you hear His voice to discipline you, on earth He showed you His great fire <u>and from amidst that fire you heard His words</u>."

The third stich profoundly alters the verse. Structurally, it disrupts the bipartite symmetry that Henshke's position requires; the three discrete units of Deuteronomy 4:36 can no longer be said to correspond to the two contradictory verses of the derashah. More importantly, Deuteronomy 4:36c subtly but significantly alters the theological position of the verse.[55] The words in question are the Ten Commandments, which, the verse indicates, were not heard directly from God. God was in the heavens, and His words, the Decalogue, were heard "from the fire." Deuteronomy 4:36 posits a twofold distantiation of God from the Sinai/Horeb theophany: the visible fire on the mountain does not indicate God's presence, since God is still in the heavens, and the Decalogue is not heard directly from God but from the great fire that God has made visible. The first denies that the Israelites saw God on the mountain, the second that they heard God speak. The words were God's, but they were conveyed through the mediation of God's great fire.[56]

Though not all scholars accept the understanding of Deuteronomy 4:36 outlined here,[57] there is a broad consensus that Deuteronomy 4 seeks to distance God from the site of revelation. See, in addition to Weinfeld, R. E. Clements's statement that Deuteronomy's account contains "no suggestion . . . of a descent of Yahweh in any fashion, but only of the appearance of fire and of a voice out of the fire."[58] Though Jeffrey Tigay does not state outright that Deuteronomy 4:36 involves intermediation, his assertion that the verse "states that there was indeed something on the earth when God spoke but it was not God," comes very close.[59]

Returning to the "Two Verses Contradict a Third Resolves" argument, if one accepts that the Mekhilta understood the claims of Deuteronomy 4:36 no less clearly than do contemporary scholars, the derashah is similar to Sifre Numbers §58 in several ways. Thematically, both deal with the role of God in revelation; theologically, both adopt a position of divine transcendence and revelation by intermediaries (the more widely accepted intermediary position of the Mekhilta perhaps strengthening the intermediary-voice reading of the Sifre Numbers); and hermeneutically, they argue for this position in similar ways. Both derashot cite two verses expressing different views concerning God's role in revelation (at Mount Sinai or in the Tent of Meeting) and characterize them (with varying degrees of clarity) as contradictory. The juxtaposition of the contradictory verses introduces revelation as a problem while indicating the need to look beyond the cited verses for a third, more definitive, statement on the matter. This dynamic complicates the traditional question of whether the derashot resolve the contradiction through harmonization or exclusion; it seems, rather, that both the contradictory positions are rejected and a third, novel view is introduced instead.[60] Finally, the theological force of "two verses contradict and a third resolves" may also explain its infrequent use. Though the *middah* resolves scriptural contradictions, logic is not its primary concern, and it certainly is not an algorithm for resolving contradictions. As a result, many contradictory verses are resolved using ad hoc arguments, while the *middah* is only employed in the theologically charged context of divine revelation.[61]

A *Middah* in the Torah

The analysis thus far suggests that the *middot* used in the Rabbi Ishmael midrashim are not logic. Three of the four limit the interpreter's freedom, intervening in situations of potential hermeneutical indeterminacy to provide fixed, closed readings. The fourth is not concerned with logic as such, but rather is motivated by theological concerns. The break with the notion that the *middot* are logic raises the question of their authority. The *middot*, after all, represent a claim to authority, but on what grounds?[62] More generally, what *are* the *middot*? The first step toward an answer is to recognize that the term *middah* does *not* mean "hermeneutical rule or canon" anywhere in tannaitic literature outside the *Baraita of Thirteen Middot* and the Tosefta's account of the seven *middot* that Hillel argued before Bnei Batira.[63] Instead, the word *middah* covers three semantic areas:

i) The core meaning of *middah* in tannaitic Hebrew preserves the biblical meaning of מ־ד־ד "measure, extent."[64] This is the most common sense and is not relevant for the present analysis.
ii) *Middah* can also refer to the "measure" that one receives for good or bad actions, that is, reward or punishment.[65] This meaning, too, is irrelevant.
iii) Finally, *middah* signifies the character or nature of a person or thing:

ארבע מידות באדם: האומר שלי שלי ושלך שלך—מדה בינונית . . . שלי שלך ושלך
שלי—עם הארץ וכו'.

Four characters [*middot*][66] among people: He who says, what is mine is
mine and what is yours is yours—this is the common type . . . What is mine
is yours and what is yours is mine—this is *'am ha-'aretz*, etc. (m. Avot 5.10;
Danby, p. 457)

Or:

ארבע מדות בלמידים: ממהר לשמוע וממהר לאבד—יצא שכרו בהפסדו; קשה לשמוע
וקשה לאבד—יצא הפסדו בשכרו וכו'.

Four characters [*middot*] among the disciples: Quick to learn and quick to
forget—his gain is canceled by his loss; slow to learn and slow to forget—
his loss is canceled by his gain, etc. (m. Avot 5.12; Danby, p. 457)

The similarity of these phrases (and others like them)[67] to the *middot*
formula in the Rabbi Ishmael midrashim is readily apparent, as in both
cases the *middah* is followed by the preposition ב, whose root meaning is
"in" or "with respect to." This is significant since the phrase "This is a
middah in the Torah" (זו מידה בתורה) cannot mean that the *middot* are
listed in the Torah, since they are not. The Avot passages use *middah* + ב
to refer to typical modes of behavior of people, students etc., and this, I
propose, is precisely the meaning of זו מידה בתורה: "This is the typical
mode of behavior of Scripture." Applying this meaning to the *middot* of
the Rabbi Ishmael midrashim yields, for example: "This is the typical
mode of behavior of Scripture: any discussion stated in one place, which
omits a specific matter and is then repeated—the repetition is only for
the sake of the omitted matter." Or: "It is typical for Torah to have a general term need a specific term, and so on." On this reading, the *middot*
are not imposed upon the biblical text; they emerge from recognizing a
mode of expression as typical of Scripture.[68] Here, too, then, the lead
agent of interpretation is Scripture, and it is from Scripture that the
interpreter takes his cues.

Chapter 6
Presponsive Torah

The contours of Rabbi Ishmael's hermeneutics are now visible. Scripture has priority—hermeneutical, chronological, ontological—over the reader. When Scripture speaks clearly, the reader listens without interpreting. At times, the reader must avoid interpreting manifest textual difficulties; at other times, the reader can interpret but only when Scripture sanctions this course of action. When interpreting, the reader must comply with established rules, authorized by—and often patterned in—Scripture. Possible support for this interpretation comes from the work of Jacob Neusner, who has examined the relationship between the interpreter and the biblical text in the introduction to his translation of the Sifre Numbers.[1] His conclusion is that the Sifre Numbers proves logic's inability to interpret Scripture or, at least, to do so unaided: "Scripture stands paramount, logic, reason, analytical processes of classification and differentiation, secondary. Reason not built on scriptural foundations yields uncertain results."[2] For Neusner, this approach is true of legal midrash as such, and he makes much the same argument in his analysis of the Sifra, a problematic position that does not take into account significant differences between the Rabbi Ishmael midrashim and the Sifra.[3] Be that as it may, in discussing the Sifre Numbers, Neusner presents a series of derashot that thematize the relationship between reader and text, often representing human reason with the term *din* (reasoned argument) or its verbal cognates *dan, ladun,* and the like.[4] As Neusner demonstrates, the derashot often come down in favor of Scripture, demonstrating the interpretive shortcomings of the reader—and this is true of the Mekhilta as well. The Rabbi Ishmael midrashim make two distinct critiques of reasoned argument. The first involves a *din* argument leading to an erroneous conclusion:

"מחרצנים ועד זג לא יאכל" (במדבר ו ד): מגיד שלא פטר בו אכילת צער. שהיה בדין יום
הכפורים שהוא חמור פטור בו אכילת צער נזיר הקל אינו דין שיפטור בו אכילת צער?
תלמוד לומר "מחרצנים ועד זג לא יאכל" מגיד שלא פטר בו אכילת צער.

"[The nazirite] may not eat anything . . . even seeds or skin" (Num 6:4): It states that it does not exempt cases of eating to avoid physical suffering. Since one could argue that if on *yom ha-kippurim*, which is the weighty case, one is exempt from fasting that causes physical suffering, then with respect to the nazirite, which is the light case, is it not *din* that he be exempt from fasting that leads to physical suffering? [Scripture] teaches, saying: "[The nazirite] may not eat anything . . . even seeds or skin," it states that it does not exempt cases of eating to avoid physical suffering. (Sifre Numbers §24, p. 29)

Numbers 6:4 is a very detailed prohibition: "Throughout his term as nazirite, he may not eat anything that is obtained from the grapevine, even seeds or skin." Why, the Sifre asks, does Scripture state "even the seeds or skin" when the grape has already been prohibited? The answer: Scripture employs this phrase to drive home the severity and scope of the prohibition, denying the otherwise plausible *din* argument (*qol va-ḥomer*)[5] that the nazirite be exempt from fasting that results in pain. The *din* argument is introduced, but rejected as halakhically incorrect.

The second critique involves the inability of reasoned argument to ground itself:

"סקול יסקל השור ולא יאכל את בשרו" (שמות כא כח): . . . אין לי אלא שהוא אסור באכילה, מנין שהוא אסור בהנאה, אמרת קל וחומר הוא, ומה אם עגלה ערופה שהיא מכפרת על שפיכות דמים הרי היא אסורה בהנייה ושור הניסקל שהוא שופך דמים דין הוא שיהא אסור בהנייה. או חילוף, אם שור הניסקל שהוא שופך דמים מותר בהנאה ועגלה ערופה שהיא מכפרת על שפיכות דמים, אינו דין שתהא מותרת בהנייה, תלמוד לומר "וערפו שם את העגלה [בנחל]" (דברים כא ד). דנתי חילפתי בטל החילוף וזכיתי לדון כתחילה, מה אם עגלה ערופה שהיא מכפרת על שפיכות דמים, הרי היא אסורה בהנייה ושור הנסקל שהוא שופך דמים דין הוא שיהא אסור בהנייה.

"[When an ox gores a man or a woman to death,] the ox shall be stoned and its flesh shall not be eaten" (Exod 21:28): . . . I thus know that it is forbidden to be eaten. How do I know that it is also forbidden to have any benefit from it? You reason by using the method of *qol va-ḥomer*. If the heifer whose neck is broken, which atones for the shedding of blood, is forbidden to be made use of, it can be derived by *din* [*qol va-ḥomer*] that the ox that is stoned, being a shedder of blood, should surely be forbidden to be made use of. Or perhaps the reverse holds true. If the stoned ox, though being a shedder of blood, is permitted to be made use of, is it not *din* that the heifer whose neck is broken, which atones for the shedding of blood, should surely be permitted to be made use of? For this [Scripture] teaches, saying: "There, in the wadi, they shall break the heifer's neck" (Deut 21:4). I have set forth an argument, and considered the opposite position, and the opposite position has been refuted and I have proven right the first argument. If the heifer whose neck is broken, which atones for the shedding of blood, is forbidden to be made use of, it can be derived by reasoned discourse [*din*] that the ox that is stoned, being a shedder of blood, should surely be forbidden to be made use of. (Mekhilta Neziqin 10, p. 282; Lauterbach 3.79)

An ox that has gored and been put to death—what is the status of its corpse? Exodus 21:28 prohibits eating the corpse, but can it be used in other ways (for example, tanning)? The derashah offers a preliminary hypothesis, that the status of the ox is analogous to that of the heifer that is slain when a corpse is found outside the city limits (Deuteronomy 21). The heifer is purer than the ox—she atones for spilled blood while the ox is a spiller of blood—so if her corpse cannot be used, it stands to reason that the ox must not be used either. But this argument is found wanting since the prohibition against using the heifer is not grounded in Scripture, so it is possible that the ox *can* be used for utility, in which case the *qol va-ḥomer* would be reversed: "How much more so would the [less severely restricted] heifer be utilized." The result is aporia. Both arguments are valid, and there is no logical way to determine which is correct. The aporia must be decided by the biblical text. Deuteronomy 21:4 states that the heifer is to be killed in the wadi, which the Mekhilta apparently takes to mean that it is to be buried there and not carried back to the city to be used.[6] Thus Scripture indicates that the heifer may not be used, justifying the initial argument and proving that the goring ox is analogously not to be used. Scripture confirms the original hypothesis.

This derashah possesses a logical structure evident in its terminology—"I have set forth an argument and considered the opposite position, and the opposite position has been refuted, and I have proven right the first argument." Yet, ultimately it argues against the use of *din* independently of Scripture; for all the logical rigor of the derashah, the reader comes to aporia that cannot be resolved without recourse to Scripture. Left to its own devices, reason could not decide whether the ox or the heifer should serve as the basis for the analogy. The reversal of the argument points to an inherent weakness of *din*—an arbitrariness inherent in the application of interpretive principles to Scripture. Ultimately, *din* is unable to arrive at definitive conclusions, or even establish the structure of its own argument, without the aid of Scripture; *din* is not self-grounding.

In summary, *din* can fail by leading to false halakhic conclusions or it can lead to aporia, underlining its inherently ungrounded nature. In each case, Scripture sets matters aright, providing the correct conclusion, the correct interpretive process, or the necessary grounding, supporting the claim that the Rabbi Ishmael midrashim downplay the role of the human reader in the interpretive process. Indeed, Neusner's thesis that "reason not built on scriptural foundations yields uncertain results" is particularly appealing, since it implies that even apparent contributions by the interpreter are ultimately aimed at proving Scripture's priority.

The Legitimacy of *Din*

Unfortunately, Neusner's sweeping conclusion is based on a very partial sample of derashot and cannot be accepted as currently formulated, for there are derashot that teach the contrary. The most obvious examples are derashot that employ reasoned argument successfully, as with the formula "you must reason thus" (*harei 'atah dan*). This formula is quite common, appearing some two dozen times in the Sifre Numbers—the book upon which Neusner bases his argument—and more than thirty times in the Mekhilta:[7]

"[ורצע אדניו את] אזנו [במרצע ועבדו לעולם]" (שמות כא ו): בשל ימין הכתוב מדבר אתה אומר בשל ימין הכתוב מדבר או אינו אלא בשל שמאל הרי את דן, נאמר כאן אזנו ונאמר להלן אזנו מה להלן בימין אף כאן בימין.

"[His master shall pierce his] ear [with an awl; and he shall remain his slave for life]" (Exod 21:6): HA-KATUV speaks of the right ear. You say HA-KATUV speaks of the right ear, but perhaps it speaks only of the left ear? You must reason thus: Here it is said "ear" and there (Lev 14:17) it says "ear."[8] Just as there the act is performed on the right ear, so also here the act is performed on the right ear. (Mekhilta Neziqin 2, p. 253; Lauterbach 3.15–16)

The derashah presents a reasoned argument (by analogy) that yields the correct halakhic conclusion, employs the correct interpretive procedure, and is not inherently ungrounded or in any way problematic. This derashah, typical of "you must reason thus" arguments, undermines Neusner's assertion that human reason is portrayed as inadequate for explicating Scripture. Moreover, a number of derashot present reasoned argument not only as legitimate, but as a necessary foil to the *shortcomings of Scripture*:

"ושמתי לך מקום" (שמות כא ינ): אבל לא שמענו להיכן. הרי את דן, נאמר מנוס לשעה ונאמר מנוס לדורות, מה מנוס האמור לדורות ערי הלוים קולטות אף מנוס האמור לשעה מחנות הלוים קולטות.

"I will assign you a place [to which he can flee]" (Exod 21:13): But we have not heard where.[9] You must reason thus: A refuge for the use of that period was ordered and a refuge to be used from future generations was ordered. Just as in the case of the refuge for the future generations it was the cities of the Levites that offered it, so also in the case of the refuge for that period it was the camps of the Levites. (Mekhilta Neziqin 4, p. 262; Lauterbach 3.36)[10]

In this derashah,[11] it is the reader who does the most important work, since listening to Scripture—non-interpretive engagement of Scripture—fails to provide critical information. Scripture states that God will "assign you a place," but none is assigned. The lacuna can only be filled by ceasing to listen to Scripture and pressing an argument—in this case, an analogy to Numbers 35:6. The second-person singular imperative "you must reason thus" thematizes Scripture's failure to provide the requisite information and the need for the reader to intervene and determine the exact place of refuge. The roles that Neusner assigns reason and Scripture are reversed: Scripture leads to aporia while the reader resolves the difficulty.

These derashot, which demonstrate the legitimacy—even necessity—of reasoned argument, present a challenge to two theses: Neusner's and my own. The Rabbi Ishmael midrashim appear to speak in two voices, often providing intricate arguments that demonstrate the frailty of reason as a source of interpretive authority, while elsewhere presenting reason as a vital and necessary tool for dealing with scriptural lacunae. One could explain these differences as inconsistency,[12] but this explanation is unsatisfying in light of the Rabbi Ishmael midrashim's broad and consistent attempts to limit the interpretive freedom of the reader. If reasoned argument is an unproblematic complement to Scripture, why require that analogy (*gezerah shavah*) be *mufneh lehaqish* when other tannaim impose no such strictures? Why stipulate that a conclusion reached through argument cannot serve as the basis for another (*lamed min ha-lamed*) or as the basis for punishment (*'ein 'onshin min ha-din*)?

Ha-Katuv's Interpretive Instruction

To resolve this difficulty, a deeper understanding of the relationship between Scripture and the reader is needed, and in particular of Scripture's role as teacher. It has already been observed that Scripture, figured as HA-KATUV, is a teacher of halakhah. Time and again, the Rabbi Ishmael midrashim employ the phrase *ba' ha-katuv lelamdekhah*, "HA-KATUV comes to teach you," to introduce a legal conclusion. But, not all of HA-KATUV's lessons are halakhic:

"וכי יתן איש אל רעהו חמור או שור או שה [וכל בהמה לשמר]" (שמות כב ט): אין לי אלא
חמור ושור ושה ושאר כל בהמה מנין תלמוד לומר "וכל בהמה לשמר." אני אקרא
"וכל בהמה" ומה תלמוד לומר "חמור או שור או שה" שאם אני קורא כל בהמה שומע
אני לא יהיה חייב עד שיפקד אצלו כל בהמה, תלמוד לומר "חמור או שור או שה" לחייב
כל אחד ואחד בפני עצמו ועל זה בפני עצמו, ומה תלמוד לומר "וכל בהמה" אלא <u>בא הכתוב</u>
<u>ללמדך שכל הכלל שהוא מוסיף על הפרט הכל בכלל.</u>

"When a man gives to another an ass, an ox, a sheep [or all animals to guard] . . ." (Exod 22:9): I thus know only about an ass, an ox, and a sheep. How about any other beast? [Scripture] teaches, saying: "Or all animals to guard." I read, then, "All animals to guard." What does it teach by saying, "an ass, an ox, a sheep"? Because if it had read only "all animals" I might have understood that the keeper is liable only if all beasts have been put in his care. Therefore it says, "an ass, an ox, a sheep," to declare him liable for each one by itself. And what does [Scripture] teach by saying, "all animals"? <u>HA-KATUV comes to teach you that a general statement that is added to a specific statement includes everything.</u> (Mekhilta Neziqin 16, pp. 302–3; Lauterbach 3.121)

Exodus 22:9 begins by listing the domestic animals that a person might lend his fellow—an ass, an ox, a sheep—and then states "or all animals," and the Mekhilta seeks to explain this apparent redundancy: Why does Scripture enumerate specific animals only to state that the case holds for all animals? Because, the Mekhilta argues, the absence of either could lead to confusion: the general statement is necessary lest one think that the case pertains only to the three animals cited, and the enumeration is necessary lest one think that the case pertains only to a person who guards "*all* animals." With both a general statement and a list of particulars, Scripture communicates that the case holds for any and all animals, thus resolving the halakhic questions. Interestingly, the derashah does not end at this point, but introduces an additional conclusion, this one hermeneutical: "HA-KATUV comes to teach you that a general statement that is added to a specific statement includes everything." Here the familiar trope of HA-KATUV acting as instructor appears in a slightly different light, as HA-KATUV moves beyond the legal content of the verse, instructing the reader as to the hermeneutical rule that emerges from the derashah.

Another instance of HA-KATUV teaching interpretive lessons is found in the Mekhilta's reading of Exodus 21:22:

"וכי יריבון אנשים" (שמות כא יח): למה נאמר, לפי שהוא אומר "עין תחת עין"
(שמות כא כד) אבל שבת וריפוי לא שמענו, תלמוד לומר "וכי יריבון אנשים . . . אם יקום
[והתהלך בחוץ . . . ורפא ירפא . . .]" (שמות כא יט) <u>בא הכתוב ללמד בו דברים מחוסרין בו.</u>

"When men quarrel" (Exod 21:18): Why is this section stated? Because it says "An eye for an eye" (Exod 21:24), but we have not heard about indemnity for the loss of time and for the expenses of healing. Therefore [Scripture] teaches, saying: "When men quarrel . . . if he then gets up [and walks outdoors . . . he must pay for his idleness and his cure]" (Exod 21:19). <u>HA-KATUV comes to teach regarding matters that had been omitted.</u> (Mekhilta Neziqin 6, p. 269; Lauterbach 3.51)

The Mekhilta questions the function of Exodus 21:18 ("When men quarrel"), since it is followed by a very similar clause that begins "When men fight" (Exod 21:21). Aren't these verses addressing the same circumstances? The Mekhilta suggests that Exodus 21:24 ("an eye for an eye"; part of the second clause) provides the basis for the tannaitic interpretation that one is liable for the pain and the damage inflicted on another, but does not mandate liability for compensation of lost wages and medical expenses. These matters are learned from Exodus 21:19, and so the repetition is justified as both clauses contribute toward a full and correct halakhic conclusion. The Mekhilta then characterizes HA-KATUV's teaching in the derashah, and it is not halakhic but hermeneutical: "HA-KATUV comes to teach you regarding matters that had been omitted."

In these derashot, HA-KATUV moves beyond the role of halakhic teacher. In resolving halakhic matters, HA-KATUV employs interpretive practices, and these practices—or, more precisely, the principles that underlie them—become the ultimate content of its teaching. Strikingly, in each case the lesson that HA-KATUV teaches echoes a principle formulated elsewhere as a *middah*: the lesson of Mekhilta Neziqin 16 ("HA-KATUV comes to teach you that a general statement that is added to a specific statement includes everything") corresponds to the *middah* "There are instances in which not only does the general term need its specific term, but the specific term also needs its general term,"[13] while Mekhilta Neziqin 6 ("HA-KATUV comes to teach regarding matters that had been omitted") echoes the *middah* "Any discussion stated in one place, that omits a specific matter, and is then repeated in another place—this repetition is only for the sake of the omitted matter."[14] In light of the understanding of *middah* proposed in Chapter 5, the correlation between HA-KATUV's interpretive practices and explicit *middot* is not surprising. As argued in Chapter 5,[15] the term *middah* refers to typical or characteristic behavior of Scripture, and as we see here the *middot* find expression in HA-KATUV's interpretations, presented as the content of its instruction to the reader. These derashot reveal a new pedagogic dimension of HA-KATUV, as it instructs through the example of its own interpretive activities.

Just as HA-KATUV Specifies

HA-KATUV's status as interpretive model is most evident in the derashot that employ the phrase "Just as HA-KATUV specifies . . . so too I specify." Consider the Mekhilta to Exodus 22:10:[16]

"שבועת יי תהיה בין שניהם" (שמות כב י): מיכן את דן כל השבועות שבתורה סתם ,ופרט [לך הכתוב][17] באחת מהן שאינה אלא ביו"ד ה"י פורט אני בכל השבועות שבתורה שאינן אלא ביו"ד ה"י.

"[A]n oath of YHWH shall be between the two of them" (Exod 22:10): An oath by the Tetragrammaton. From this you can conclude with regard to all the oaths in the Torah. Since all the oaths in the Torah were stated without specification and HA-KATUV specifies for you with regard to one that it must be by the Tetragrammaton, so too I specify with regard to all the oaths in the Torah that they must be by the Tetragrammaton. (Mekhilta Neziqin 16, p. 303; Lauterbach 3.122–23)

Exodus 22:10 deals with a man who entrusts his possessions to another and they go inexplicably missing. Though the guardian claims that they were stolen, no thief is found, and so both must take an "oath of YHWH." The explicit mention of the name of God used in the oath generates a derashah that contains two distinct interpretive moments. The first revolves around this being the only verse that specifies the name of God employed in oaths.[18] As the Mekhilta states, Scripture records many oaths *stam* but one that is explicit. What is the force of this *stam?* The term has essentially the same meaning as its cognate *satum*—closed, sealed, and, by extension, hermeneutically opaque[19]—so the resulting structure is curious: *all* oaths are unspecified except for the *single* example at hand. The creation of two separate sets—the set of all-but-one biblical oaths (*stam*) and the one-member set (explicit)—functions as a hermeneutic marker, a marker not anchored in a word or a phrase but in the relationship that holds between larger textual units. Once the marked nature of the structure is recognized, the reader extends the conclusion of the derashah—that the oath in Exodus 22:10 invokes the Tetragrammaton—to the other (*stam*) oaths, but only by citing HA-KATUV's precedent as justification: "HA-KATUV specifies . . . so too I specify." Though the reader appears to play an active role in determining the meaning of Scripture, in fact HA-KATUV sets the interpretation in process and through its own actions makes the reader's interpretation possible. HA-KATUV provides one explicit statement regarding the nature of biblical oaths, thus creating the hermeneutically marked opposition (all-but-a-single-case *stam* vs. one explicit) that legitimizes the reader's extension. Then its own interpretation is cited as precedent.

The Rabbis, like all people, tend to go about their business without stopping at every turn to explain to themselves or others the conceptual schemata that inform their practices. It is, as a rule, only in disputes or moments of cultural anxiety that these schemata come to light. The advantage of the passages cited above is their explicit characterization of Scripture as teacher of midrash, as an interpreter whose practices set precedent and are to be emulated.[20] But a broader view suggests that the same dynamic exists in other derashot as well. So even though HA-KATUV's teachings are usually halakhic, these, too, instruct the reader in the proper engagement of Scripture. For when the Rabbi Ishmael midrashim state, "HA-KATUV comes to draw an analogy between the first-born and the breast and thigh of the sacrifices of well-being" (בא הכתוב והקיש את הבכור לחזה ושוק של שלמים), or "HA-KATUV singles out this case from the general statement to declare it a graver, capital, offense" (הרי הכתוב מוציאו מכללו להחמיר עליו שיהא במיתה),[21] the instruction is twofold. HA-KATUV communicates the halakhic conclusion and, with it, the proper way to arrive at said conclusion. HA-KATUV becomes the source of legal decision, but also of legal midrash.

Presponsive Scripture

So while the primacy of Scripture is affirmed, the affirmation is more nuanced than Neusner's argument allows. The division between Scripture and human reason is not an antagonistic, zero-sum game; there can be a fruitful cooperation between the two. Indeed, human reason plays a vital role in the interpretive process, but only if the reader recognizes the primacy of Scripture and sets out to identify and then adopt HA-KATUV's own interpretive methods. The interpretive collaboration between HA-KATUV and the reader is particularly evident in the following derashah from the Sifre Numbers:

"והשורף אותה יכבס בגדיו" (במדבר יט ח): בא הכתוב ולימד על שורף הפרה שמטמא בגדים. הא עד שלא יאמר יש לי בדין אם המשליך את האזוב מטמא בגדים השורף את הפרה לא יטמא בגדים? אם זכיתי מן הדין מה תלמוד לומר "והשורף אותה יכבס בגדיו"? בא הכתוב ולימד על העסיקין[22] בפרה מתחילה ועד סוף שיהיו טעונין תכבוסת בגדים ורחיצת הגוף והערב שמש.

"He who performed the burnings shall wash his garments" (Num 19:8): HA-KATUV came and taught regarding the one who burns the cow that his clothes are impure. [But] even before it states this I can derive it by reasoned argument, for if the person who hurls the hyssop defiles his clothing, will the one who burns not defile his clothing? If I have arrived at this conclusion by reasoned argument, what does [Scripture] teach in saying, "He who performed the burning shall wash his garments"? HA-KATUV came and taught that those who have contact with the cow from the outset to the end are required to wash their clothing and bathe their bodies and will remain impure until evening. (Sifre Numbers §124, pp. 156–57)

Numbers 19:8 is part of the instructions for the slaughtering and burning of the red heifer whose ashes are to be mixed with water and used for purification:

> 5. The cow shall be burned in [the priest's] sight—its hide, flesh, and blood shall be burned, its dung included—6. and the priest shall take cedar wood, hyssop, and crimson stuff, and throw them into the fire consuming the cow. 7. The priest shall wash his garments and bathe his body in water; after that the priest may reenter the camp, but he shall be unclean until evening. 8. He who performed the burning shall also wash his garments in water, bathe his body in water, and be unclean until evening. (Num 19:5–8)

The derashah opens by suggesting that Numbers 19:8 teaches that the priest's clothes have become impure—"HA-KATUV came and taught regarding the one who burns the cow that his clothes are impure." This suggestion is met with the following objection: the preceding verse, 19:7, states that the priest who throws the hyssop (and the cedar and the crimson stuff) into the fire must wash his clothes. Would not reasoned argument (*qol va-ḥomer*) indicate that the priest who performs the actual burning of the heifer be likewise required to wash his garments? And if so, why does Scripture state the matter explicitly? The Sifre responds that Numbers 19:8 indeed does not teach that the clothing of the second priest is impure, since this fact *is* obviously derivable from the preceding verse. Rather, "HA-KATUV came and taught that those who have contact with the cow from the outset to the end" are impure and required to wash.

The derashah raises two issues. One is the repetition of the phrase "HA-KATUV came and taught." The phrase appears at the opening of the derashah, where HA-KATUV teaches that the clothes of the priest who burns the cow are impure. This is a straightforward attribution to HA-KATUV—Numbers 19:8 states that the priest should wash his garments, and so HA-KATUV teaches that the garments are impure. After HA-KATUV's first teaching is challenged on the grounds that the same conclusion could be reached through *qol va-ḥomer*, a new interpretation is proposed in its stead, but this interpretation, too, is introduced with the formula "HA-KATUV came and taught." The attribution of the second interpretation to HA-KATUV is curious, considering that HA-KATUV's original interpretation was rejected by a *din* argument and this rejection led to the correct interpretation. The *qol va-ḥomer* argument that rejected HA-KATUV's initial reading—and the conclusion it yields—should, by all rights, be in opposition to HA-KATUV. Nonetheless, the derashah indicates that "HA-KATUV came and taught" with regard to the final conclusion as well.

The second issue is the status of the *din* argument. The derashah hinges on the notion that if a conclusion can be learned via reasoned argument from one verse (*'im zakhiti min ha-din*), it is unnecessary for Scripture to state the conclusion.[23] Thus, the Sifre rejects HA-KATUV's straightforward reading of Numbers 19:8 ("HA-KATUV came and taught regarding the one who burns the cow that his clothes are impure") on the grounds that the same conclusion could be reached by a *qol va-ḥomer* from Number 19:7. This line of reasoning is similar to *'eino tzarikh* (it is not necessary), a formula discussed in Chapter 3, in which a midrashic interpretation is rejected on the grounds that its conclusion has already been stated in Scripture, as when Rabbi Ishmael rejected the notion that the priests' nakedness prohibits them from descending the step of the altar, since Exodus 28:42 addresses priestly modesty explicitly.[24] There is, however, a significant difference between *'im zakhiti min ha-din* and *'eino tzarikh*. The latter rejects an interpretation of one biblical verse because the same conclusion is stated more directly by a different biblical verse, implicitly valorizing Scripture over interpretation. The former, however, rejects HA-KATUV's teaching because a midrashic argument *could have been* applied to a different verse and yielded the same conclusion. On what grounds does a *din* argument—one that "could have been" made at that—obviate HA-KATUV's scriptural teachings? Do *din* and HA-KATUV enjoy equal status?[25]

The answer to these difficulties—the status of the *din* argument and its attribution to HA-KATUV—lies in recognizing that the Rabbi Ishmael midrashim do not view *din* and Scripture as opposing elements but as a complex interpretive agent ultimately grounded in Scripture. The *din* argument can obviate HA-KATUV's teaching because both are ultimately Scripture. Sifre Numbers §124 attributes the *din* argument to HA-KATUV because on a certain level it is made by HA-KATUV. By this, I mean that the reader's responses are so patterned after and determined by HA-KATUV's actions that the border between Scripture and interpreter is blurred: the interpreter becomes, in effect, an extension of HA-KATUV.

The last statement is not intended figuratively. There is a strict technical sense in which Scripture incorporates the reader's interpretation into its own (self-)explication. This behavior can be expressed as a maxim: *Scripture is aware of the hermeneutical responses it will elicit in the reader who is properly trained in Rabbi Ishmael's hermeneutics, and Scripture intentionally incorporates these future responses into its own arguments.* Consider, once again, the argument of Sifre Numbers §124:

  i. According to HA-KATUV, Numbers 19:8 teaches that the clothing of the priest who burns the heifer is impure.
  ii. An objection is raised on the grounds that the same conclusion may be learned by applying *qol va-ḥomer* to Numbers 19:6–7.
  iii. Step (ii) assumes that Scripture knows that Numbers 19:6–7 leads to this conclusion and that the reader will recognize this apparent redundancy, but that Scripture nonetheless provides the same information in Numbers 19:8. As a result, HA-KATUV's interpretation of Numbers 19:8 is redundant and HA-KATUV's teaching in (i) is rejected.
  iv. A new reading of Numbers 19:8 is put forward—that all who come into contact with the heifer are impure.
  v. Since the entire argument—including the *din*—has been determined by Scripture, the conclusion is attributed to HA-KATUV ("HA-KATUV came and taught . . .").

The Sifre's logic requires that the biblical statement "He who performed the burnings shall wash his garments" (Num 19:8) is intended, *from the very outset*, as redundant in light of the (potential) *qol va-ḥomer* of the preceding verse. The *qol va-ḥomer* argument is not "sprung upon" Scripture by the reader. It is a necessary step in an argument laid out in advance by Scripture; it "frees" Numbers 19:8, thus allowing it to communicate the correct halakhic teaching (all who come into contact with the heifer are impure). Within these parameters, *din* functions as a hermeneutical sub-contractor of Scripture, as it were, and this relationship resolves the two issues raised earlier: the status of the *qol va-ḥomer* argument and the attribution of the *din* argument to HA-KATUV. The *qol va-ḥomer* argument can—indeed, must—reject HA-KATUV's interpretation because the entire procedure—the *qol va-ḥomer*, the redundancy and the new conclusion—is "built in" to the biblical passage and as such sanctioned by Scripture. Similarly, the attribution of the second conclusion to HA-KATUV is appropriate, since the entire argument unfolds under the guidance of Scripture. The reader may have rejected HA-KATUV's preliminary reading, but this rejection is itself part of a prescripted argument, a step in a dance choreographed by Scripture. The reader's responses are assumed and accounted for in the biblical text, while Scripture does not so much respond to the interpreter as *prespond*; for the Mekhilta and the Sifre Numbers, the Torah is a *presponsive* text.

A more detailed demonstration of Scripture's presponsive nature is found in the Mekhilta to Exodus 21:33:[26]

"וכי יפתח איש בור [או כי יכרה איש בור ולא יכסנו . . . בעל הבור ישלם . . .]" (שמות כא לג):
אין לי אלא פותח, כורה מנין, תלמוד לומר "או כי יכרה איש" "עד שלא יאמר יש לי בדין, אם
הפותח חייב הכורה לא יהיה חייב, הא אם אמרתה כן ענשת מן הדין, לכך נאמר "או
כי יכרה" ללמדך שאין עונשין מן הדין.

"When a man opens a pit [or digs a pit and does not cover it . . . the one responsible for the pit must make restitution]" (Exod 21:33): I thus know only about one who opens a pit. How about one who digs a pit? [Scripture] teaches, saying: "Or digs a pit." But even before it said this, I could have reasoned: If the one who opens a pit is responsible, shall the one who digs a pit not be responsible? But if you say so, you would be decreeing punishment merely on the basis of *din*. Therefore it is said: "Or digs a pit," to teach you that punishment cannot be decreed on the basis of *din*. (Mekhilta Neziqin 11, p. 288; Lauterbach 3.91)

Like Sifre Numbers §124, the Mekhilta deals with a verse whose halakhic teaching could have been arrived at by applying reasoned argument to another verse.[27] Exodus 21:33 reads: "When a man opens a pit, or digs a pit and does not cover it, and an ox or an ass falls into it, the one responsible for the pit must make restitution." The derashah understands the first verse to be making two distinct legal statements: that the uncoverer of a ditch is liable for damages incurred as a result of his action, and that the digger of a ditch is liable for damages incurred as a result of his action. The problem is that the second statement—the liability of the digger—can be derived (by *qol va-ḥomer*) from the first. If the uncoverer is liable then surely the one who dug the ditch is liable. As with Sifre Numbers §124, the initial interpretation ("I thus know only about one who opens a pit") is rejected because of a *qol va-ḥomer* argument, and the final conclusion of the derashah is characterized as a lesson from Scripture ("therefore it is said . . . to teach you"), despite the role of reasoned argument. The derashah can be cast as an exchange between two interpreters whose intentions and reactions are transparent to each other.

    i. Scripture fashions Exodus 21:33 such that the second part of the verse (the guilt of the digger) can be derived from the first part (the guilt of the uncoverer) by *qol va-ḥomer*. Scripture does this, knowing that the reader will recognize that the first half of the verse supplies the basis for a *qol va-ḥomer* argument that makes the second half redundant.

    ii. The reader recognizes the relationship between the two halves of the verse and knows that it is the result of an intentional act on Scripture's part and that Scripture knows that the reader will apply a *qol va-ḥomer* argument to the first half.

    iii. The reader applies the *qol va-ḥomer*, making the second half of the verse redundant. As this redundancy is achieved under Scripture's guidance, it functions as a hermeneutic marker and Exodus 21:13 stands in need of interpretation.

    iv. Since Exodus 21:33 states the punishment for uncovering a pit, the Mekhilta concludes that the explicit statement of the digger's guilt is necessary to avoid a situation in which a *din* argument determines punishment, which would be the case if the guilt of the digger were established by *qol va-ḥomer*.

    v. The final conclusion is presented as a lesson of Scripture: "Therefore it is said: 'or digs a pit,' to teach you that punishment cannot be decreed on the basis of *din*."

It must be emphasized that the hermeneutical negotiations are not a dialogue between two independent voices; the reader is not a partner in interpretation but a trained assistant carrying out the instructions prescripted by Scripture. The training process, which, as now becomes visible, has been the subject of this study up to this point, consists of two stages. First, Scripture trains the reader in the arts of interpretation both through explicit pronouncements regarding proper practices and, more importantly, by example. HA-KATUV's interpretive practices—the employment of hermeneutical rules and techniques—provide the reader with an apprenticeship of sorts. The readers identify the patterns, the characteristic modes of behavior of HA-KATUV, and employ them in their own interpretation ("this is a *middah* in the Torah"; "since HA-KATUV specifies . . . so too I specify"). Second, Scripture instructs the reader as to the proper application of these techniques by using irregularities (misspellings, redundancies, inconsistencies and the like) to hermeneutically mark the appropriate verses. As a result of this double engagement, Scripture knows which verses the (properly trained and attentive) readers will interpret as well as which interpretive techniques they will use, thus controlling the two key moments of the interpretive process and creating a hermeneutic of submission; the reader is active but not independent.

Within this framework, the role of the interpreter is vital but strictly delimited, analogous to that of a cryptographer, working to crack the code, i.e., to discover the appropriate practices and the verses to which they apply. The cryptographer is important but only inasmuch as the message is decoded correctly. That is, Scripture is not presponsive to interpretation "as such," but rather engages the reader who knows the code, that is, who is *properly trained in Rabbi Ishmael's hermeneutics*. In the Mekhilta's discussion of Exodus 21:33, the interpreter recognizes that the second half of the verse can be derived through *qol va-ḥomer* and further recognizes that Scripture knows that the *qol va-ḥomer* argument will be applied and will produce a redundancy. The interpreter must know, then, that applying a particular technique (here, *qol va-ḥomer*) to a particular verse (Exod 21:33) is the proper response, indeed the *only* proper response. An incorrect response would collapse the argument: without *qol va-ḥomer*, there is no redundancy, no hermeneutic markedness, and ultimately no scriptural guidance to the proper conclusion, namely, that it is prohibited to decree punishment based on logical argument.[28]

Implicit Presponsiveness

Once identified, Scripture's presponsive nature can be discerned in many derashot. Some of the derashot that follow have been discussed, and I return to examine the manifestation of presponsive Torah in each. Consider the Mekhilta's interpretation of Exodus 22:15:

"וכי יפתה איש בתולה" (שמות כב טו): בא הכתוב ללמד על מפותה שישלם עליה קנם. והדין נותן, הואיל ותפושה ברשות אביה ומפותה ברשות אביה, אם למדת על תפוסה שהוא משלם עליה קנם, אף מפותה ישלם עליה קנם. לא, אם אמרתה בתפוסה שעבר על דעתה ועל דעת אביה, לפיכך הוא משלם עליה קנם, תאמר במפותה שלא עבר אלא על דעת אביה, לפיכך לא ישלם עליה קנם, <u>הא לפי שלא זכיתי מן הדין צרך הכתוב להביאו</u>.

"If a man seduces a virgin [. . . he must make her his wife by payment of a bride price]" (Exod 22:15): Ha-katuv comes to teach concerning the seduced girl, that in her case also he must pay the fine. But mere logical reasoning would prove this: Since the law of rape applied only to a girl under the jurisdiction of her father and the law of seduction applies only to a girl under the jurisdiction of her father, it follows that inasmuch as you have learned that in the case of rape he has to pay a fine, he would likewise pay a fine in the case of seduction. No! If you cited the case of rape—that is different, for there he sinned against her own wish and against her father's wish. Therefore he should pay the fine for raping her. But will you argue the same in the case of seduction? There he has only sinned against her father's wish and therefore in her case he should not pay that fine. Thus, since I could not succeed in proving it by logical inference [*din*], HA-KATUV has to cite it. (Mekhilta Neziqin 17, pp. 307–8; Lauterbach 3.129–30)

Briefly, the derashah opens by questioning whether the instruction of Exodus 22:15 (that a seducer must pay a bride price) is necessary, since this conclusion could be drawn from Deuteronomy 22:28–29, which deals with the punishment of the rapist. But further consideration indicates that this analogy is faulty. In one case (rape), the act is performed against the wills of father and daughter alike, while in the other (seduction) against the will of the father alone. Since the analogy to rape is rejected, the payment of the bride price is stated explicitly;[29] *din* is unable to interpret and requires Scripture. The key element is the concluding statement: "Thus, since I could not succeed in proving it by logical argument [*din*], HA-KATUV has to cite it." Note the causal force of this sentence: *since* the analogy failed, HA-KATUV must step in to provide the necessary information. Logicians rightly argue that *post hoc* does not imply *propter hoc*, but *propter hoc* surely entails *post hoc*—if event P occurs as a result of Q, then it is subsequent to Q. Since HA-KATUV's intervention is precipitated by *din*'s failure, it must, in some sense, be subsequent to *din*. The Mekhilta is obviously not suggesting that the composition of Exodus 22:15 is subsequent to the rabbinic discussion of the verse. Rather, in presenting the biblical verse as a response to the failed argument, the Mekhilta figures Scripture as presponsive to the reader, responding in advance to his interpretations.

The reversed causality between the interpreter and Scripture that characterizes presponsiveness appears in various formulas throughout the Rabbi Ishmael midrashim, including one of the most common, *lammah ne'emar* (why was this stated?), which explains the hermeneutical significance of a verse as a response to a potential misinterpretation of another verse:

"ואת הכבש השני [תעשה בין הערבים]" (במדבר כח ח): למה נאמר לפי שהוא אומר "ושחטו אותו כל קהל עדת [ישראל בין הערבים]" (שמות יב ו). איני יודע אי זה יקדום אם תמיד אם פסחים תלמוד לומר שני, שני לתמיד ואין שיני לפסח.

"The second lamb [you shall offer at twilight]" (Num 28:8): Why was this stated, because it says, "and all the assembled congregation of the Israelites shall slaughter it at twilight" (Exod 12:6). I do not know which comes first, the daily burnt offering or the paschal offering. [Scripture] teaches, saying: "Second," second to the daily burnt offering, not second to the paschal offering. (Sifre Numbers §143, p. 191)

As discussed above,[30] the Sifre explains the repetition of "second lamb" as a response to a potential ambiguity concerning the twilight sacrifice of the paschal lamb. If both the paschal lamb and the daily burnt offering are offered at this time, what is the proper order of sacrifice at the twilight of the fourteenth of Nisan, the eve of the Passover? To clarify this point, Scripture separates the first and second sacrifice and states each separately, emphasizing the phrase "the second lamb" to teach that the daily offering remains second even at Passover. Like the derashot discussed above, *lammah ne'emar* explains the biblical verse as responding to the interpreter. The verse was stated because "I do not know which comes first"— that is, the interpreter's failure elicits Scripture's response. Scripture knows that the reader will arrive at aporia and presponds appropriately.

Scripture's responsiveness to the interpretive needs of the reader is also visible in the most common formula of the Mekhilta and the Sifre Numbers:

"[בהעלתך את הנרות אל מול פני המנורה] יאירו שבעת הנרות" (במדבר ח ב): שומע אני שיהו דליקין"[31] לעולם <u>תלמוד לומר</u> "מערב עד בקר" (ויקרא כד ג).

"When you mount the lamps, let the seven lamps give light" (Num 8:2): <u>I could understand</u> this to mean that they burn perpetually, <u>but [Scripture] teaches, saying</u>: "[The lamps shall burn] from evening to morning" (Lev 24:3). (Sifre Numbers §59, p. 57)

In this derashah, as in most *shome'a 'ani . . . talmud lomar* passages,[32] an erroneous teaching is introduced by *shome'a 'ani*—here that the lamps of the lampstand are to burn perpetually. However, Scripture responds to the potential error on the reader's part and provides another verse that clarifies the matter—in this case, Leviticus 24:3, which states that the lamps are to burn only from evening to morning. Though the causal link between the reader's error and Scripture's response is less explicit, the formula fits the general pattern established in the Rabbi Ishmael midrashim (a pattern absent from other midrashim, even if they employ phrases similar to *shome'a 'ani*), in which biblical verses are presented as a response to potential errors on the part of the interpreter.[33]

On Belatedness

The practices and assumptions I have labeled "presponsive Scripture" arise from a tension inherent in the enterprise of biblical commentary, a tension born of the commentators' need to be at once identical with the biblical text and other than it. On the one hand, the commentators must be identical with Scripture, since the authority and legitimacy of the commentary depends on its fidelity to the biblical text, in having faithfully realized its sacred message without introducing any extraneous elements. On the other hand, the interpreters must acknowledge their otherness from the Bible, since this otherness undergirds interpretation as such. The Rabbis, like all interpreters, are—borrowing David Stern's phrase—belated. The Bible already exists as a source of religious authority when the commentator arrives on the scene. Full and complete identity with any sacred text is reproduction—like Borges's Pierre Menard composing *Don Quixote*—and so renders the interpreter superfluous.[34] Scripture is already available to the reader, and to justify the composition of an ineluctably belated commentary—why read the commentary when you can "simply" read the Bible?—the commentary must be non-scriptural; it must be productive and novel rather than wholly reproductive.

The need to be both the same as and other than Scripture may be conceived in terms of the tension between authority and relevance. The authority of the commentary lies in its fidelity to Scripture, but the claim to relevance implicit in its very composition means that the commentary cannot be "only" Scripture. Even the rallying cry *sola Scriptura* is not itself Scripture. This tension animates the Rabbi Ishmael midrashim, and is the key to the complex relations between HA-KATUV and the interpreter. The Mekhilta and the Sifre Numbers (like all rabbinic midrash) openly acknowledge their otherness from Scripture by portraying the interpreter as an active participant in the midrashic process.[35] But at the same time, the Rabbi Ishmael midrashim (and this is not true of all rabbinic midrash) inscribe the interpreter within a dense web of scripturally determined practices. Through the mechanisms described above, these midrashim present Scripture as the authority that determines what verses are to be interpreted as well as the legitimate interpretive techniques to be applied, producing a hermeneutic of submission by which the midrashic reader—and legal midrash itself—is ultimately incorporated into Scripture.

Imitatio Scripturae: Hermeneutics and Theology

Before turning to the historical context of Rabbi Ishmael's hermeneutical practices, a few brief comments are in order on the theological dimension of these practices. The central argument of Heschel's *Theology of Ancient Judaism* is that Rabbi Ishmael and Rabbi Aqiva represent opposing theological views. Rabbi Aqiva emphasizes God's proximity and similarity to mankind and Israel, while Rabbi Ishmael represents God as transcendent. These differences are reflected in a wide range of issues, among them sacrifice, prophecy, and the possibility of speaking about God,[36] and while Heschel's work has been criticized for various shortcomings, there is no question that rabbinic literature represents these two rabbinic figures as engaged in theological debate. Here, too, the heuristic association of the tanna Rabbi Ishmael with the Mekhilta and the Sifre Numbers is illuminating, and the hermeneutics of the Rabbi Ishmael midrashim can be seen as elements of a broadly understood transcendent theology.

Throughout this study, the role of HA-KATUV has been contrasted to that of the human reader. But personified Scripture also serves to distance God from the interpretive process—there is no need to approach the author of a self-explicating text—and thus HA-KATUV fulfills many of the explanatory functions that an author would usually be called upon to perform. The self-sufficiency of Scripture weakens, on some level, the connection between author and text, God and Torah. This is not to suggest that the Rabbi Ishmael midrashim question the divine authorship of the Torah, but rather that God's role is akin to that of the poet in a New Criticism interpretation. New Criticism accepts that a poem was composed by a particular poet, living at a particular time, but it denies that this information is relevant or legitimate in interpreting a poem. Once composed, the author is no longer accessible to the reader and, for both New Criticism and the Rabbi Ishmael midrashim, the object of study is solely the text; it is not legitimate to look elsewhere.

But surely, one could protest, Scripture *is* the word of God and so analysis of Scripture does provide access to God. This dissent holds much commonsense appeal, but the matter is not so clear when it comes to the Rabbi Ishmael midrashim. For one thing, the tendency to distance God from revelation is attested elsewhere in the Rabbi Ishmael midrashim, most clearly in the two derashot that employ the *middah* "Two Verses Contradict a Third Resolves." As discussed in Chapter 5, Sifre to Numbers 7:89 suggests that a voice descended into the Tent of Meeting to speak with Moses, not God, and the Mekhilta to Exodus 20:18 argues that the Israelites did not hear the Decalogue from God's mouth, but from God's great fire manifest on the earth.[37] It is worth noting that the midrashic argument and its conclusion—the medium and the message— are mutually enforcing. The derashot teach God's transcendence, the same transcendence that makes direct communication impossible and requires that HA-KATUV provide the reader with instruction.

Or consider Sifre Numbers §112, which deals explicitly with the divine status of Torah:

"כי דבר ה' בזה [ואת מצותו הפר]" (במדבר טו לא): . . . ר' ישמעאל אומר בעבודה זרה הכתוב מדבר שנאמר "כי דבר ה' בזה" שביזה על דיבור הראשון שנאמר למשה מפי הקב"ה שנאמר" אנכי ה' אלהיך לא יהיה לך [אלהים אחרים על פני]" (שמות כ ב-ג).

"Because he has spurned the word [*davar*] of the Lord [and violated His ordinance]" (Num 15:31): . . . Rabbi Ishmael says, HA-KATUV speaks of idol worship, for it is said "Because he has spurned the word [*davar*] or the Lord," he has spurned the first commandment [*dibbur*] that was spoken to Moses from the mouth of the Holy on Blessed be He, as it is written: "I am the Lord your God . . . . You shall have no other gods besides Me" (Exod 20:2–3). (Sifre Numbers §112, p. 121)

Numbers 15:31 is part of the biblical discussion of witting and unwitting transgressions and refers to witting transgressions, characterizing them as more severe since they entail a rejection of God's word and a violation of His commandment. The biblical context of this verse suggests that the verse refers to the divine laws and instructions that the sinner so blatantly disregards. But Rabbi Ishmael offers a different interpretation based on the single form of "the word of the Lord" (*dvar 'adonai*) and "His ordinance" (*mitzvato*), rather than the plural "words" and "commandments." Rabbi Ishmael suggests that the (single) statement and (single) commandment refer to the First Commandment of the Decalogue—"I am the Lord your God. . . . You shall have no other gods besides Me." The phrase *dvar 'adonai* (word of the Lord) lends itself to this interpretation, since each of the Ten Commandments is called a *dibber* (similar to *davar*) and the first introduces God as Lord (*'adonai*). But Rabbi Ishmael's gloss includes an additional element, the description of the First Commandment as spoken to Moses from the mouth of God. Grammatically, this statement is ambiguous. It can mean that the commandment in question is the first of the Ten Commandments, all of which were spoken to Moses from God ("the first commandment that [just like the nine that follow] was spoken to Moses from the Mouth of the Holy on Blessed be He"). But on this reading, Rabbi Ishmael has added an appositive statement that does not distinguish the First Commandment in any way; it is one of ten statements made by God at Sinai. Moreover, if the derashah is generated by the linguistic similarities between Numbers 15:31 and Exodus 20:2 (*davar-dibber* and the recurrence of *'adonai*), it stands to reason that they would be emphasized, but they are not. A more natural reading results if the phrase "that was spoken to Moses from the mouth of of the Holy on Blessed be He" emphasizes the unique status of the First Commandment as God's communication, strengthening its identification as "the word of the Lord" and "His [single] ordinance." On this reading, which I think is the plain sense of the derashah, "word of the Lord" is linked to the First Commandment because the First Commandment is *the* word of God inasmuch as it was spoken to Moses by God while the other commandments were not.

   The idea that most of the commandments were not spoken directly by God is not a rabbinic *skandalon*. It appears in b. Makkot 24a, where Rav Hamnuna identifies "I am the Lord your God" and "You shall have no other Gods before Me" as the statements heard from God's mouth.[38]

But there is an important difference between the Sifre's position and Rav Hamnuna's, as the latter says, "We heard them from the mouth of God" (מפי הגבורה שמענום), allowing for the interpretation that the remaining commandments were not addressed directly to the people but that God spoke them to Moses.[39] The Sifre, in contrast, suggests that the First Commandment was the only one spoken *to Moses* directly from the mouth of God, and this is a more radical distancing of God from Sinai.[40]

Finally, consider midrash as a religious ideal. According to the Rabbi Ishmael midrashim, the role of the interpreter is to listen attentively to the teachings of Scripture, learn its (interpretive) ways, and adopt them: "Just as HA-KATUV specifies [and draws analogy, employs *kelal u-ferat*, and so forth], so too I . . . ." If midrash is, in fact, a religious ideal, then the model presented by the Mekhilta and the Sifre Numbers denies the ideal of *imitatio Dei*—not possible with a transcendent God—and replaces it with *imitatio Scripturae*. The religious ideal is not to cleave to the *middot* (the attributes) of God, but to learn and then apply the *middot* of Scripture.[41] As Rabbi Ishmael says: *dibberah Torah leshon benei 'adam*, "Torah spoke the language of man." It is *only* Torah that speaks the language of man; the language of God is radically, categorically, unattainable.

Chapter 7

Rabbi Ishmael and the Rabbis

Having set forth the interpretive practices of the Rabbi Ishmael mid-rashim, I now turn to a preliminary discussion of some of the relevant historical and cultural contexts of these practices. My aim in the next two chapters is to map these practices onto the religious landscape of late Second Temple and post-70 Palestine and environs, focusing first on the Rabbis and then on nonrabbinic groups.[1] Such analysis does not entail a shift toward a naïve, historicist reading of the texts. The phrase "Rabbi Ishmael" still functions first and foremost as a shorthand desig-nation for the distinctive practices and terminology of the Mekhilta and Sifre Numbers, and only in a qualified, heuristic fashion to the histori-cal tanna. But doubts as to the authorship of a text are not doubts as to the historical situatedness of that text; whatever their ultimate prove-nance, the ideas and practices of these texts were situated within a broader cultural and intellectual context.

Rabbi Ishmael and the Question of Extra-Biblical *Halakhah*

For Rabbi Ishmael, Scripture is doubly authoritative. The teachings of the Torah are divine, and HA-KATUV is the authoritative interpreter of Scripture. The result is a hermeneutic that presents itself as depending almost exclusively on Scripture, which is both authoritative text and authoritative interpreter. This description may not seem problematic at first blush, so accustomed are we to totalizing theories of rabbinic textu-ality—but it does, in fact, raise a key question: If Scripture functions as both text and interpreter, what role does extra-scriptural tradition—which will later come to be known as "Oral Torah"—play?[2] This question is raised explicitly by the Mekhilta:

"ורצע אדניו את אזנו במרצע" (שמות כא ו): בכל דבר, התורה אמרה "ורצע אדוניו את אזנו במרצע" והלכה אמרה בכל דבר.

"His master shall pierce his ear with an awl" (Exod 21:6): With any instrument. TORAH says: "His master shall pierce his ear with an awl," but *halakhah* says: It may be with any instrument. (Mekhilta Neziqin 2, p. 253; Lauterbach 3.16)

Exodus discusses the instrument used to bore the ear of the slave who chooses to stay in his master's custody. Exodus 21:6 states that an awl must be used, while *halakhah* allows the action to be performed by any instrument, presenting the master with a wider range of options than Exodus would allow.[3] Here *halakhah* refers to (and is probably an ellipsis of) *halakhah le-moshe mi-sinai*, an extra-scriptural tradition originating at Sinai. The contrast between *halakhah* and Scripture ("Scripture says . . . but *halakhah* says . . .") is typical.[4] The question of the boring implement also appears as part of a fuller discussion of *halakhah* and Scripture in a derashah attributed to Rabbi Ishmael and preserved in the Sifre Deuteronomy §122:

"ולקחת את המרצע" (דברים טו יז): מיכן היה רבי ישמעאל אומר בשלושה מקומות הלכה עקפת על המקרא. התורה אמרה "ושפך את דמו וכסהו בעפר" (ויקרא יז יג) והלכה אמרה בכל דבר שמגדיל צמחין, התורה אמרה "וכתב לה ספר כריתות" והלכה אמרה בכל דבר שהוא בתלוש, התורה אמרה "במרצע" והלכה אמרה בכל דבר.

"You shall take an awl" (Deut 15:17): This was the source of Rabbi Ishmael's saying: In three places *halakhah* circumvents Scripture: the Torah says, "He shall pour out its blood and cover it with earth" (Lev 17:13) while *halakhah* says, with anything that grows plants; the Torah says, "He writes her a document of divorce" (Deut 24:1) while *halakhah* says, [he may write] on anything that was separated from the ground; the Torah says "with an awl" (Exod 21:6), while the *halakhah* says, with anything. (Sifre Deuteronomy §122, Finkelstein, p. 180; Hammer, p. 167)[5]

This passage teaches that the conflict between the scriptural injunction and the ultimate ruling of the *halakhah* was, for Rabbi Ishmael, one of three instances in which *halakhah* bypasses Scripture. To appreciate the meaning of this statement, one must recognize that the structure "rule with three exceptions" is a pattern in the Mekhilta and the Sifre Numbers:

   i. "This is one of the three instances in which Rabbi Ishmael interpreted the accusative particle *'et*." (Sifre Numbers §32, p. 38)

   ii. "Rabbi Ishmael says: Every *'im* ['if'] in the Torah refers to a voluntary act with the exception of three [which refer to obligatory acts]." (Mekhilta Baḥodesh 11, p. 243; Lauterbach 2.287–288)

   iii. "This is one of three expressions in the Torah that Rabbi Ishmael used to interpret as a *mashal* [allegory]." (Mekhilta Neziqin 6, p. 270; Lauterbach 3.53)

   iv. "Thus you must say that Aaron was not directly addressed in any of the divine communications in the Torah, with the exception of three." (Mekhilta Pisḥa 1, p. 1; Lauterbach 1.1)

   v. "Rabbi says: Even when Scripture does not use the expression 'saying' or 'and you shall say unto them,' the commandment is for

all generations, with the exception of three instances." (Mekhilta
Beshalaḥ 1, p. 83; Lauterbach 1.187)[6]

In each of these derashot, the three exceptional cases are exhaustive,
that is, the rule holds except for three cases and three cases alone. The
statement that *halakhah* bypasses Scripture in three places fits this pattern, so the three instances cited appear to be the only exceptions to the
(implicit) rule that *halakhah does not bypass Scripture*. In an article dealing with this passage, David Henshke recognizes this pattern[7] and its
challenge to the traditional view that extra-scriptural tradition was a
foundational principle of rabbinic ideology. In response, he argues first
that each of the three cases in which "*halakhah* bypasses Scripture"
responds to the contradictory halakhic positions of other rabbis and so
must be seen as polemic in nature. Second, he argues that Rabbi Ishmael
"does not characterize the general rule between *halakhah* and Scripture,
but rather deals with the exceptions to the rule."[8] But these arguments
explain little. That the legal positions enunciated in Rabbi Ishmael's
three *halakhah* rulings are a matter of dispute is hardly significant—
many of the legal decisions enunciated in midrashic literature are a matter of dispute. Moreover, the midrashim have many tools at their disposal
by which to make explicit the disputed nature of a decision—citing the
contrary position, questioning the validity of the hypothesis, linking
different views together with the phrase *davar aḥer* (another account)—
none of which is employed. So while there may be halakhic disputes concerning these statements, the derashah does not present them *as* controversial or disputed. As for Henshke's statement that the cases in question
are exceptions, this is true, but trivially so—the derashah identifies the
cases as exceptions. The significant issue is that they are exceptions to a
rule, and in this case the rule is that *halakhah*—extra-scriptural tradition—does not bypass Scripture.

This conclusion is of critical importance because *halakhah* functions
as an independent source of authority only inasmuch as it *does* bypass
Scripture, for only then does *halakhah* provide information that cannot
be arrived at by interpreting the biblical text. If *halakhah* represents a
non-scriptural authority, Rabbi Ishmael's dictum ultimately means that
there are only three cases in which there is *halakhah*; for all other cases,
Scripture provides the requisite information, obviating the need for an
"external" *halakhah*.

In keeping with this explicit statement, the Rabbi Ishmael midrashim
do not bear witness to the existence of an extra-scriptural tradition, as
traditions are not cited without scriptural justification. The only exceptions are Mishnaic citations that are appended to the midrashic argument and appear to be late additions.[9] The absence of such traditions in

the Mekhilta and the Sifre Numbers may appear obvious, since they
are midrashim that deal with scriptural interpretation rather than extra-
scriptural tradition. But, in fact, the Sifra does cite statements of rabbis
divorced from scriptural argument. Often these are extended quotations
from the Mishnah that do not even gesture toward Scripture, as in the
discussion of the order of benedictions in Sifra 'Emor parshata 11.3–5
(Weiss 101b), which is a verbatim citation of the Mishnah (Rosh ha-
Shanah 4.5). A more telling inclusion of non-interpretive statements
occurs in disputes that involve scriptural and non-scriptural statements:

"[ואיש כי יאכל] קדש [בשגגה]" (ויקרא כב, יד): מה קודש אמור להלן בקודשי הגבול הכתוב
מדבר, אף קודש אמור כן [כאן] בקודשי הגבול הכתוב מדבר. "בשגגה" פרט למזייד. אמר
ר' יוסה, שמעתי באוכל מבשר קדשי קדשים לאחר זריקת דמים שהוא משלם את הקרן
לכהנים והכהנים לוקחין בדמיו שלמים.

"[If a man eats of] the sacred donation [unwittingly]" (Lev 22:14): Just as elsewhere the "sacred donation" (Deut 26:13) refers to the donations consumed outside the Temple, so too here [Scripture] speaks of donations consumed outside
the Temple. "Unwittingly" this excludes the premeditated transgression. Rabbi
Yose said, I heard regarding one who eats the meat of the holiest offerings after
the dashing of the blood that he pays the principle to the priests and the priests
use the money to purchase well-being offerings. (Sifra 'Emor, pereq 6.4; Weiss 97b)

The first argument in this passage is a *gezerah shavah*, arguing by the analogy of the term "sacred donation" in Leviticus and Deuteronomy that
both cases involve a particular class of offerings. This is followed by a
gloss that is not a full-fledged midrashic argument but at least involves
Scripture. Then comes Rabbi Yose's statement that he "heard," that is,
received an extra-scriptural tradition, involving the case of one who eats
an offering meant for the priests, an explicitly non-midrashic statement.
    Here too, the evidence of the Rabbi Ishmael midrashim accords
with the rabbinic representation of the tanna Rabbi Ishmael. The non-
midrashic tannaitic corpus, the Mishnah and the Tosefta, do not contain
a single statement attributed to Rabbi Ishmael "in the name of" (משום or
משם) another sage.[10] Indeed, there is no tannaitic record of Rabbi Ishmael learning a *halakhah* (an extra-scriptural tradition) from an earlier
sage. As Marcus Petuchowski writes: "Just as the Talmud teaches us little
about Rabbi Ishmael's origins, so too there is a paucity of information
regarding his youth and education."[11] According to the Babylonian Talmud, Rabbi Ishmael did have a teacher, Rabbi Nehunia ben ha-Qana.
"R. Yohanan said: Rabbi Ishmael who was the disciple of Rabbi Nehunia
ben ha-Qana, who explicated the entire Torah in *kelal u-ferat*, he too
[Rabbi Ishmael] explicates by *kelal u-ferat*."[12] But note that Rabbi Ishmael's discipleship involves the reception of exegetic principles, not extra-
scriptural legal teachings. There are no teachings cited in the name of

Nehunia ben ha-Qana in the Rabbi Ishmael midrashim, and certainly none preserved by Rabbi Ishmael. It must be emphasized that the issue has nothing to do with naïve biographical reconstruction and everything to do with cultural representation: in a religious system that recognizes extra-scriptural tradition as authoritative, and in a literary corpus that deals explicitly with this authority (most famously in m. Avot 1.1), scholarly genealogy is a critical component of the authority of the individual rabbi. The absence of such information regarding Rabbi Ishmael and the absence of *halakhah*-based practices attributed to him suggest that the tanna, too (as represented in rabbinic literature), does not establish his authority from extra-scriptural sources.

It could also be argued that the evidence of the Mishnah and Tosefta is not conclusive, since these collections are traditionally attributed to the school of Rabbi Aqiva,[13] and so the traditions of Rabbi Ishmael are to be sought in Mishnah-like collections of that school. However, no such collection is extant and it appears that none was written. As David Weiss Halivni has written:

R. Yehudah Hanassi, the editor-anthologizer of the Mishnah, knew the teachings of R. Ishmael's students, and he is quoted in their Midrashim almost as often as he is quoted in the Midrashim that stem from the school of R. Akiba. Even more important, in his Mishnah he quotes statements from the Mekhilta of R. Ishmael verbatim. Why, then, are the students of R. Ishmael not mentioned in the Mishnah? Is it merely an accident that we are not in possession of Mishnah from the school of R. Ishmael (although we do have Midreshei Halakhah from both schools), or was there no Mishnah in the school or R. Ishmael? The evidence seems to favor the latter solution.[14]

In light of the Scripture-centered interpretive practices of the Mekhilta and the Sifre Numbers, it is possible that no such text exists because the group that produced the Rabbi Ishmael midrashim does not (except for rare exceptions) recognize legal argument divorced from the authority of Scripture.

To summarize the argument thus far, there are a number of strong indications that "Oral Law" (as it would come to be called) is marginal, at best, both for the Rabbi Ishmael midrashim and for the figure of Rabbi Ishmael:

i. The Rabbi Ishmael midrashim exhibit a consistent Scripture-centered ideology, seeking to anchor legal decisions in the Written Torah.

ii. The Mekhilta contains an explicit statement about *halakhah* circumventing Scripture, an idea expanded in Rabbi Ishmael's derashah in the Sifre Deuteronomy that limits the instances of extra-scriptural tradition to three.

iii. No traditions are quoted in the name of earlier tradents in the Mekhilta and the Sifre Numbers (unlike the Sifra).

iv. No reports of traditions in the name of earlier tradents are attributed to Rabbi Ishmael in other tannaitic sources. Indeed, he seems to have no teachers of *halakhah*.

v. The school of Rabbi Ishmael did not produce a non-scriptural codex such as the Mishnah and the Tosefta.

It is notoriously difficult to prove absence, and perhaps inevitably, some of the arguments adduced above (iii–v) are *e silentio*. There is, however, strong evidence that extra-scriptural traditions are absent from the Rabbi Ishmael midrashim because there is no conceptual "room" for them. At issue are numerous terms and phrases that appear in both the Rabbi Ishmael midrashim and the Mishnah, but whose surface identity obscures a profound difference: the Mishnah employs these terms in the context of extra-scriptural traditions, but the Mekhilta and the Sifre Numbers employ them in scriptural interpretation.

The Terminology of *Halakhah* and of Exegesis

We Have Heard/Not Heard (*shama'nu/lo' shama'nu*)

The centrality of the hearing motif for the Rabbi Ishmael midrashim has been discussed at length in the present study, including the formula "we have heard/not heard." This formula presents Scripture as the speaker and the interpreter as listening to Scripture. When Scripture fails to provide requisite information, the interpreter has no recourse but to acquire it by other—namely, midrashic—means.[15] In the Mishnah, the same phrase serves a different function:[16]

אמר רבי עקיבה שאלתי את רבן גמליאל ואת ר' יהושע . . . הבא על אחותו ועל אחות אביו ועל אחות אמו בעלם אחד מה הוא חייב אחת חייב על כולן או אחת על כל אחת ואחת אמרו לו לא שמענו, אבל שמענו בבא על חמש נשיו נידות בעלם אחד שהוא חייב על כל אחת ואחת רואים אנו שהדברים קל וחומר.

Rabi Aqiva said: I asked Rabban Gamliel and Rabbi Yehoshua . . . if a man had intercourse with his sister and his father's sister and his mother's sister during one bout of forgetfulness, what happens?—is he liable to one offering for them all or to one offering for each of them? They said to me, We have heard not heard, but have heard [a tradition] that if a man had intercourse during one spell of forgetfulness with his five wives who were menstruants, he is liable for each one of them; and we consider that this applies still more (*qol va-ḥomer*) in the other case. (m. Keritot 3.7; Danby, p. 567)[17]

The Mishnah recounts an exchange in which Rabbi Aqiva presents to his teachers the case of a man who has committed repeated sexual offenses during a single bout of forgetfulness: Does this count as a single offense or as three separate offenses? Rabban Gamliel and Rabbi Yehoshua respond, *lo' shama'nu*, "we have not heard" about this particular case, but they do know of an analogous case that can be used as a model for Rabbi Aqiva's question. The Mishnah uses the same phrase as the Mekhilta to express the absence of pertinent halakhic information, and in both cases the absence of information sanctions the use of a hermeneutical argument (*gezerah shavah* in the Mekhilta, *qol va-ḥomer* in the Mishnah). The key difference lies in the identity of the (unheard) speaker: for the Rabbi Ishmael midrashim, "we have not heard" refers to Scripture's silence on a particular point; for the Mishnah, it means that the sages have not received an extra-scriptural tradition regarding the case in question.[18]

THE CASE UNDER DISCUSSION (*hoveh*)

Another example of a phrase that appears in the context of extra-scriptural traditions in the Mishnah but appears in scriptural contexts in the Rabbi Ishmael midrashim is "the case under discussion." Consider the following debate between the Houses of Hillel and Shammai in Yevamot:

האשה שהלכה היא ובעלה במדינת הים, שלום בינו לבינה ושלום בעולם, באת ואמרה מת בעלי תינשא, מת בעלי תתיבם . . . בית הילל אומרים, לא שמענו [אלא][19] בבאה מן הקציר בלבד. אמרו להם בית שמי, אחד הבאה מן הקציר ואחד הבאה מן הזיתים ואחד הבאה ממדינת הים. לא דיברו [חכמים][20] <u>בקציר אלא בהוה.</u>

If a woman and her husband went beyond the sea and there was peace between him and her and peace in the world, and she came back and said "My husband is dead," she may marry again. [If she said] "My husband died [childless]," she may contract levirate marriage. . . . The House of Hillel say: We have heard no such tradition save of a woman who returned from the harvest. The House of Shammai answered: It is all one whether she returned from the harvest or from the olive picking or from beyod the sea; [the sages] spoke of the harvest only <u>because that was the case under discussion</u>. (m. Yevamot 15.1–2; Danby, p. 241)

The Mishnah records a disagreement between the Houses of Hillel and Shammai in the case of a woman who returns from overseas and states that her husband has died. The House of Shammai holds that her testimony is valid and she is allowed to remarry or to contract a levirate marriage, depending on the circumstances. The House of Hillel objects, since they have "not heard"[21] regarding this particular case, but only the case of a woman who returns from the harvest. The House of Shammai rejects this objection and argues that the cases are analogous—the precise details surrounding the woman's absence are immaterial, and since her testimony is accepted in the one case it is to be accepted in the others as well. The House of Shammai (or the anonymous voice of the

Mishnah) then adds a brief statement as to why the earlier sages spoke of the harvest: "The sages spoke of the harvest only because that was the case under discussion" (לא דברו חכמים אלא בהווה). The earlier tradition does not restrict the scope of the legal decision to harvesting wives; rather, that happened to be the case before the court. Strikingly, the Mekhilta employs the same formula to explain why Scripture gives particular examples:[22]

"ובשר בשדה טרפה [לא תאכלו]" (שמות כב ל): אין לי אלא בשדה בבית מנין, תלמוד לומר
"נבלה וטרפה" (ויקרא יז טו), הקיש טריפה לנבלה מה נבלה לא חלק בה בין בבית ובין
בשדה אף טריפה לא נחלק בה בין בבית בין בשדה, הא מה תלמוד לומר "ובשר בשדה
טרפה" דיבר הכתוב בהווה.

"You must not eat flesh torn by beasts in the field" (Exod 22:30): I thus know only about the field. How about the house? [Scripture] teaches, saying: "[Any person . . .] who eats what has died or been torn by beasts shall [. . . remain unclean until evening]" (Lev 17:15). [HA-KATUV][23] draws an analogy between an animal torn of beasts and an animal dying of itself. Just as in the case of an animal dying of itself it makes no difference whether it dies in the house or in the field, so also in the case of an animal torn of beasts, there is no difference whether it is torn in the house or in the field. Why then does [Scripture] teach, in saying: "You must not eat flesh torn by beasts in the field"? HA-KATUV spoke of the case under discussion. (Mekhilta Neziqin 20, pp. 320–21; Lauterbach 3.157)

The Mekhilta questions why Exodus 22:30 specifies that one is not to eat flesh torn by beasts in the field, when the prohibition holds in other locations as well. The legal issue is clarified by Leviticus 17:15, which classifies as unclean both the (non-slaughtered) carcass (nevelah) and the animal killed by a beast (ṭrefah). The appearance of both the nevelah and the ṭrefah in the same verse indicates that the latter is generally prohibited, that is, that its prohibition is not limited to the field but holds in the household as well. The legal question resolved, the Mekhilta asks why, then, Exodus 22:30 speaks of the animal whose flesh is torn by beasts in the field. The answer is that "HA-KATUV spoke of the case under discussion" (דיבר הכתוב בהווה), explaining Scripture's behavior in the same way as the Mishnah explains that of the sages.

WITHOUT EXPLANATION (stam) [FOLLOWED BY INTERPRETATION]

Another term that appears in the Mishnah and the Rabbi Ishmael midrashim is stam, which refers to a statement made without explication. In the Mishnah, it refers to an extra-scriptural tradition:

רבי אליעזר אומר, עגלה בת שנתה, ופרה בת שתים . . . אמר ר' יהושע לא שמעתי אלא
שלשית אמרו לו מה הלשון שלשית אמר להם כך שמעתי סתם. אמר בן עזיי, אני אפריש

R. Eliezer says: The red heifer [whose neck is to be broken] must be [not more than] one year old; and the [red] heifer [not more than] two years old. . . . R. Yehoshua said: I have never heard that any [was valid] save a "three-year-old" (*sheloshit*). They said to him, Why do you use the term *sheloshit?* He said to them, thus have I heard it but <u>without explanation</u> (*stam*). Ben Azzai said, I will explain it (*'afaresh*). (m. Parah 1.1; Danby, p. 697)

The broader context of this mishnah—the laws concerning the red heifer—is not pertinent to the present discussion. The key issue is that Rabbi Yehoshua uses an unusual term, *sheloshit* (a three-year-old heifer), to characterize the heifer, and when asked why he uses this term, he replies, "Thus I have heard it but without explanation [*stam*]" That is, he is transmitting a genuine tradition, though one that he received without explanation, and so he can only reproduce the tradition verbatim. Another sage, ben Azzai, then proposes an explanation whose specifics do not concern us here. In contrast, we find in the Mekhilta and Sifre Numbers that it is Scripture that speaks *stam* and requires interpretation, as in the phrase: "Since all the oaths in the Torah were stated without specification [*stam*] and HA-KATUV specifies for you with regard to one that it must be by the Tetragrammaton."[24] This passage from the Mekhilta has been discussed at length and the argument need not be repeated here, except to point out that the term *stam* (without specifications) parallels the Mishnah's "without interpretation," with the former referring to Scripture and the latter to *halakhah*.[25]

More could be said about each of the preceding derashot, but the pattern is, I hope, clear.[26] The same terms that designate extra-scriptural traditions in the Mishnah appear in an interpretive and scriptural context in the Mekhilta and the Sifre Numbers. At this point, I am not interested in the question of influence, that is, whether one paradigm preceded and influenced the other, or whether both developed from a shared source. Rather, I wish to show that the extra-scriptural traditions recorded in the Mishnah not only *do* not appear in the Rabbi Ishmael midrashim, they *cannot.* The terminological and conceptual framework in which these traditions are couched does not exist for the Rabbi Ishmael midrashim and could not, in principle (as opposed to historical accident) be integrated into these midrashim because there is no conceptual "space" for them. Many key terms are represented: "we have not heard," *stam* as opposed to explicit, "the case under discussion," but in each case, the subject is Scripture, not extra-scriptural tradition.

Interpretation and Extra-Scriptural Tradition in the Sifra

It must be emphasized that the contrast being drawn here is not between midrash "as such" and the apodictic formulations of the Mishnah. As

I've argued throughout this study, many of the tools used to delimit the interpretive role of the reader and establish Scripture (HA-KATUV) as the prime agent in interpretation are not found in the Sifra. The Sifra does not contain phrases such as *lehafsiq ha-'inyan* (divide the account), *mufneh lehaqish* (freed for the sake of interpretation), or *'ein dorshin tehilot*. It does not present interpretation as an option adopted following the failure of an unmediated "listening" to Scripture, as the Mekhilta and the Sifre Numbers do with the *sh-m-'* formulas (*shome'a 'ani, ki-shmu'o, shama 'nu/lo' shama'nu*). Nor, finally, does the Sifra establish the opposition between hermeneutically marked and unmarked verses: for the Sifra, every verse is open to interpretation (often to numerous interpretations), so there is no need to justify each reading by presenting it as a response to a scriptural need. The same holds true for the terminological contrast I've suggested between the language of *halakhah* in the Mishnah and that of midrash in the Mekhilta and the Sifre Numbers: the phrase "Scripture speaks of the case under discussion" (*dibber ha-katuv ba-hoveh*), the distinction *shama'nu/lo' shama'nu*, and the use of *stam* to pave the way for interpretation—all these are characteristic of the Rabbi Ishmael midrashim but not of the Sifra.

But the most important distinction is found in the Sifra's own discussions of interpretation and its relationship to extra-scriptural tradition. As noted, I plan to devote a separate study to this question, so for now I will limit my discussion to two examples in which the Sifra lauds Rabbi Aqiva's interpretive skills. The first involves the Sifra's discussion of Leviticus 1:5 ("The bull shall be slaughtered before the Lord; and Aaron's sons, the priests, shall offer the blood, dashing the blood against all sides of the altar that is at the entrance of the Tent of Meeting"). Rabbi Aqiva argues that phrase "Aaron's sons, the priests" forms an analogy with Numbers 3:3 ("These are the names of Aaron's sons, the priests, the anointed ones") and so teaches that the collecting of the blood must be done by a ritually fit priest (*kasher*) using a consecrated vessel. Rabbi Tarfon, however, rejects Rabbi Aqiva's use of Exodus 1:5 as the basis for study regarding the collecting of the blood (*qabbalat ha-dam*) since the verse refers only to the dashing of the blood against the altar, and, Rabbi Tarfon argues, collecting and dashing are substantively different (and thus unfit for analogy):

אמר לו ר' טרפון עקיבה עד מתי אתה מגביב ומיביא עלינו. איקפח את בניי אם לא שמעתי הפריש בין קבלה לוריקה ואין לי לפרש.

Rabbi Tarfon said to him: Aqiva, how much longer will you gather up words against us. May I lose my sons if I did not hear a clear distinction expressed between the collection of the blood and its tossing, but I cannot explain it. (Sifra Nedava, parshata 4.5; Weiss 6a)

Rabbi Aqiva responds by enunciating the difference between the reception and the dashing of the blood. First, intentional collection of blood does not count as a sacrifice, so if an animal was slaughtered in the wrong time and its blood collected, it does not yet count as an improper sacrifice (*piggul*), but if the blood has been dashed with the intention of offering a sacrifice at the wrong time, the animal counts as an improper sacrifice. Second, the slaughter and collection of blood outside the Temple is not a transgression against the laws of cult centralization, whereas dashing the blood makes it a transgression. Rabbi Tarfon accepts this explanation and lauds Rabbi Aqiva's interpretive abilities:

אמר לו ר' טרפון אקפח את בניי שלא היטיתה ימין ושמאול אני הוא ששמעתי ולא היה לי
לפרש אתה דורש ומסכים לשמועה, הא כל הפורש ממך כפורש מחייו.

Rabbi Tarfon said to him: May I lose my sons! You have not swerved to the right or the left. It was I who received the tradition but was unable to explain while you explicate [*doresh*] and agree with the tradition. Indeed, to depart from you is to depart from life itself. (Sifra Nedava, parshata 4.5; Weiss 6a)

Focusing on the interpretive dynamic between Rabbi Aqiva and Rabbi Tarfon, the derashah contrasts the latter's authority as an eyewitness to the Temple service to the former's interpretive acumen. Rabbi Tarfon initially rejects Rabbi Aqiva's interpretation, stating bluntly: "May I lose my sons if I did not hear a clear distinction," which apparently contradicts Rabbi Aqiva's position. Once Rabbi Aqiva explains that, in fact, the distinction in question does not contradict his position, Rabbi Tarfon responds: "It was I who received the tradition but was unable to explain while you explicate [*doresh*] and agree with the tradition." For our purposes, the key element in this exchange is that Rabbi Aqiva's brilliance lies in correlating Scripture to an existing, and clearly authoritative, extra-scriptural codex. As Rabbi Tarfon states explicitly, "You explicate [*doresh*] and agree with the tradition." Though midrashically derived, Rabbi Aqiva's findings are traditional in the most literal sense of the word—they affirm the existing tradition.[27]

The second example is Rabbi Aqiva's well-known midrashic interpretation of *kikar ha-shelishi*, the impurity of the third loaf:

"כל אשר בתוכו יטמא" (ויקרא יא, לג): ר' עקיבה אומר אינו אומר טמא אילא יטמא לטמא
את אחירים וללמד על הככר השני שיטמא את השלישי . . . אמר רבי יהושע מי יגלה עפר
מעיניך רבן יוחנן בן זכאי שהיית אומר עתיד דור אחר לטהר את ככר השלישי שלא מן
התורה (!)[28] והרי עקיבה תלמידך הביא לו מקרא מן התורה שהוא טמא "כל אשר
בתוכו יטמא."

"[And if any of (the unclean dead creatures) falls into an earthen vessel] everything inside it shall be unclean [יטמא]" (Lev 11:33): Rabbi Aqiva says: It does not say "is unclean" [יִטְמָא] but "shall be unclean" [יְטַמֵּא] meaning that it transmits uncleanness to other objects, indicating that the loaf of bread that has second-level uncleanness imparts third-level uncleanness to other objects. Rabbi Yehoshua said: Who will remove the earth from your eyes, Rabbi Yohanan ben Zakkai, for you used to say that a future generation will declare the third-level loaf clean since it is not scriptural—but your disciple Rabbi Aqiva adduced a scriptural prooftext for its impurity, as it is written "everything inside it shall be unclean [יִטְמָא]." (Sifra Shemini, parshata 7.12; Weiss 54a)[29]

The legal issue is as follows: if a dead impure animal falls into a vessel, the vessel becomes "directly" impure—this is the first level of impurity. In addition, any object that was in the vessel, such as a loaf of bread, also becomes unclean—the second-level of impurity. Rabbi Aqiva interprets Leviticus 11:33 as indicating that the second level impure loaf then transmits (third-level) impurity if it comes into contact with another object (loaf). This interpretation hinges on the ambiguous vocalization of the verb יטמא, translated above as "shall be unclean," a translation that assumes the Hebrew is vocalized as a *qal* (יִטְמָא), following the MT. The same consonants can, however, be vocalized as a *pi'el* (יְטַמֵּא), in which case the verb would have a causal force, implying that the loaf within the vessel would transmit impurity, and this is the reading proposed by Rabbi Aqiva.[30] For the present discussion, the legal conclusion is less important than the role of midrash in the passage, a role made explicit by the response it evokes in Rabbi Yehoshua, one of Rabbi Aqiva's teachers. Rhetorically addressing Rabbi Yohanan ben Zakkai, Rabbi Yehoshua allays his dead teacher's fears lest the *halakhah* concerning the transmission of third-level impurity be forgotten, since it has no scriptural basis. Now, Rabbi Yehoshua continues, a scriptural mnemonic has been discovered, and so the ruling is secure. Rabbi Yehoshua's words make it abundantly clear that Rabbi Aqiva's midrash did not establish that the second-level impure loaf imparts third-level impurity—that ruling was known to earlier generations who had no knowledge of the biblical prooftexts. Indeed, the absence of biblical support is explicitly lamented by Rabbi Yohanan ben Zakkai, but not because, as Halivni would have it, "[n]o law is really binding on the Jew unless it can be shown to have its origin in the Bible,"[31] but rather because without scriptural anchoring the *halakhah* might be forgotten. Rabbi Aqiva's midrash is explicitly presented as a mnemonic accomplishment; the non-scriptural tradition has priority (both chronological and axiological) over legal midrash, which is understood (at least in this passage) as a memory aid to existing *halakhot*.

The contrast between the Sifra (and its midrashist hero, Rabbi Aqiva), on the one hand, and the Mekhilta and Sifre Numbers (with Rabbi Ishmael as model), on the other, is stark. Rabbi Ishmael (as the source of the saying "in three places [only three places] *halakhah* bypasses Scripture")

and the Rabbi Ishmael midrashim (in their interpretive practices) mini-
mize the role of extra-scriptural *halakhah* and establish midrash as the
legitimate source of legal decisions. The Sifra, on the other hand, extols
Rabbi Aqiva's interpretive prowess precisely because he is able to anchor
existing extra-scriptural *halakhot* in Scripture, thereby making Scripture
the handmaiden and support of extra-scriptural traditions.

Chapter 8

The Non-Rabbinic Landscape

Rabbi Ishmael and Qumran

In an important article, Steven Fraade has studied the social institutions of interpretation at Qumran, demonstrating how authoritative—indeed, constitutive—biblical exegesis was to the community:[1]

   i. The founding figure of Qumran, the Teacher of Righteousness, is portrayed as a divinely inspired interpreter to whom the secrets of Scripture are known.[2]

   ii. The community presents itself as a group devoted to biblical interpretation.

   iii. The community demands of new members an oath of fidelity to the study of Torah.

   iv. The community establishes ritualized study as a central activity of the members.

These traits clearly bespeak the centrality of Torah and Torah interpretation to the Qumran community—a possible point of affinity between the Rabbi Ishmael midrashim and Qumran.[3] The similarity would be strengthened if one could flesh out more specific parallels between Rabbi Ishmael's legal midrash and the legal interpretations of Qumran. An exhaustive comparison is beyond the scope of the present study, but I shall argue that a number of shared traditions are evident in *Miqṣat Ma'aśe Ha-Torah* (4QMMT), the legal letter discovered in Qumran cave 4 and published ten years ago.[4]

SHARED LEGAL AND INTERPRETIVE TRADITIONS

a) B 25–28

‫[כי לבני] הכו[הנ]ים ראואין[להש[מ]ר בכול הד[ברים [האלה בשל שלוא יהיו] משיאים את‬
‫העם עוון [וע]ל שא כתוב [איש כי ישחט במחנה או ישחט] מחוץ למחנה שור וכשב ועז.‬

[For the sons] of the priests should [take care] concerning all [these] practices, [so as not to] cause the people to bear punishment. [And concerning] that it is written: [if a person slaughters inside the camp, or slaughters] outside the camp cattle or sheep or goat.

Leviticus prohibits the non-ritual slaughter (*ḥullin*) and consumption of animals:

איש איש מבית ישראל אשר ישחט שור או כשב או עז במחנה או שאר ישחט מחוץ למחנה
ואל פתח אהל מועד לא הביאו להקריב קרבן לה' לפני משכן ה' דם יחשב לאיש ההוא דם
שפך ונכרת האיש ההוא מקרב עמו. (ויקרא יז ג-ד)

If anyone of the house of Israel slaughters an ox or sheep or goat in the camp, or does so outside the camp, and does not bring it to the entrance of the Tent of Meeting to present it as an offering to the Lord, before the Lord's Tabernacle, bloodguilt shall be imputed to that man: he has shed blood; that man shall be cut off from among his people. (Lev 17:3–4)

This is the reading that underlies 4QMMT, which goes on (B 29–31) to identify the camp in question as the city of Jerusalem, suggesting that the *ḥullin* prohibition is still in force, despite the apparently contradictory statement in Deuteronomy 12: "When the Lord enlarges your territory, as He has promised you, and you say, 'I shall eat some meat,' for you have the urge to eat meat, you may eat meat whenever you wish" (כי ירחיב ה' אלהיך את גבולך כאשר דבר לך ואמרת אכלה בשר כי תאוה נפשך לאכל בשר בכל אות נפשך תאכל) (Deut 12:20). In rabbinic literature, the question of *ḥullin* is a matter of controversy, with opposing views attributed to Rabbi Ishmael and Rabbi Aqiva in the discussion of Deuteronomy 12:20:

רבי ישמעאל אומר, מגיד שבשר תאוה נאסר להן לישראל במדבר ומשבאו לארץ
התירו הכתוב[5] להם. רבי עקיבה אומר, לא בא הכתוב אלא ללמדך מצות האמורות בו.

Rabbi Ishmael says: From this we learn that meat for profane consumption was forbidden to Israel in the wilderness, but when they came to the (Holy) Land, HA-KATUV permitted it. Rabbi Aqiva, however, says: The purpose of HA-KATUV is to do nothing but teach you the commandments set forth in it. (Sifre Deuteronomy §75, pp. 139–40; Hammer p. 128)[6]

The justification for Rabbi Aqiva's position—that there never was a prohibition against slaughtering *ḥullin*—is not relevant for the present discussion.[7] What is important is that Rabbi Ishmael reads Leviticus 17 as prohibiting *ḥullin*, like 4QMMT. So while 4QMMT and Rabbi Ishmael differ as to the "contemporary" legal question of whether it is proper to eat *ḥullin*, they share (against Rabbi Aqiva) the interpretation of Leviticus 17:3 as a prohibition against *ḥullin*.

b) B 36–38

[ועל העברות אנחנו חושבים שאין לזבוח א[ת האם ואת הולד ביום אחד .]. . . ועל
האוכל אנח]נו חושבים שׁאיאכל את הולד [שבמעי אמו לאחר שחיטתו ואתם
יודעים שהו]א כן.

[And concerning pregnant (animals) we are of the opin[ion] that] the mother
and its fetus [may not be sacrificed] on the same day . . . . [And concerning] eating (a fetus): we are of the opinion that the fetus [found in its (dead) mother's
womb may be eaten (only) after it has been ritually slaughtered. And you know
that it is] so.

In 1857, Abraham Geiger published *Urschrift und Übersetzungen*, in which
he argued that rabbinic halakhah, beginning with Hillel and culminat-
ing with Rabbi Aqiva, represents a break with an earlier legal tradition—
the ancient halakhah—reflected in the Septuagint, Samaritan legal traditions, and elsewhere outside rabbinic literature.[8] But while the new
halakhah became the dominant voice in rabbinic literature, traces of the
old are still visible, according to Geiger, most clearly in the Rabbi Ishmael
midrashim.[9] Geiger identifies a number of legal disputes that reflect the
break between the old halakhah and the new, one of them being the
legal status of the fetus. Generally, rabbinic halakhah holds that the fetus
is part of the mother and not an independent entity, a matter that finds
legal expression with regard to both human and animal fetuses. In the
case of humans, the issue arises in the case of a person who has struck a
pregnant woman and caused her to miscarry. The general rule is that
there is liability toward the mother but not toward the fetus. The Mekhilta, however, contains a trace of the old halakhah according to which
the fetus is a legal agent:

"וכי ינצו אנשים [ונגפו אשה הרה ויצאו ילדיה ולא יהיה אסון ענוש יענש כאשר
ישית עליו בעל האשה ונתן בפלילים. ואם אסון יהיה ונתתה נפש תחת נפש]"
(שמות כא כב-כג): . . . ומה תלמוד לומר "וכי ינצו אנשים" לפי שהוא אומר "ואיש
כי יכה כל נפש אדם" (ויקרא כד יז) שומע אני אף בן שמונה במשמע, תלמוד לומר
"וכי ינצו אנשים" מגיד <u>שאינו חייב עד שיהרג בר קיימא</u>.

"When men fight [and one of them pushes a pregnant woman and a miscarriage
results, but no other damage ensues, he shall be fined according as the woman's
husband may exact from him, the payment to be based on reckoning. But if other
damage ensues, the penalty shall be life for life] (Exod 21:22–23): What does
[Scripture] teach, in saying: "When men fight"? Because it says, "If anyone kills
any human being" (Lev 24:17), which I might understand to mean even if he kills
a child born after only eight months of pregnancy. Thus [Scripture] teaches, saying: "When men fight," [Scripture] states that he is not guilty unless he kills a
viable fetus. (Mekhilta Neziqin 8, p. 275; Lauterbach 3.63)

The assumption that underlies this derashah is that (contrary to general rabbinic halakhah) the fetus is an independent entity, and a person who causes the death of a fetus is legally liable. The possibility that is introduced by *shome'a 'ani* is that there is liability in the death of a fetus even when it is not at full term, that is, liability can be pushed back to earlier stages of the pregnancy, but the Mekhilta argues that there is only liability if the fetus was viable. The stricter view is that there is blanket liability for the fetus, the more lenient that the fetus must be liable; the possibility that there is no liability is unknown to the derashah. After discussing the rabbinic dispute regarding the status of the human fetus, Geiger writes: "And if we investigate more deeply we will find that there is another ancient dispute that revolves around this distinction, for all that we have said regarding man, the very same matter holds for the animals, namely the controversy whether the fetus is an integral part [literally: thigh] of its mother and the slaughter of its mother purifies it, or whether it is an independent entity that requires separate slaughter."[10]

From the passage cited above, it is clear that 4QMMT prohibits the slaughter of pregnant animals and further stipulates that a fetus must be slaughtered before it is eaten. For Geiger the issue concerns the status of the fetus as such, and this view is endorsed by Qimron and Strugnell, who write: "These laws should be viewed in the framework of the general juridical problem of whether the embryo is a living creature or merely a part of the mother."[11] If so, the Mekhilta agrees with 4QMMT that the fetus is an independent entity,[12] a particularly notable agreement, as it comes against the broader backdrop of opposing rabbinic halakhah.[13]

c) B 62–63:

ואף על מ[טעת עצ]ין המאכל <u>הנטע בארץ ישראל</u> כראשית הוא לכוהנים.

And concerning the (fruits of) trees with edible fruit <u>planted in the Land of Israel</u>: they are to be dealt with like first fruits belonging to the priests.

In a recent article, Aharon Shemesh examined the meaning of the rabbinic phrase *mitzvoth ha-teluyot ba-'aretz*, "commandments in force in (literally: dependent upon) the Land (of Israel)."[14] Shemesh argues that the phrase originally referred to commandments whose biblical enunciation is preceded by the phrase "when you enter" (or a cognate phrase). But this meaning did not endure, and the midrashim associated with Rabbi Aqiva regularly interpret "when you enter" as a reference to the commandments by whose observance Israel merits entrance into Israel. Aside from the commandments that deal with agricultural obligations (whose exclusively Palestinian observance the Sifra recognizes), the Rabbi Aqiva midrashim disassociate the biblical "when you enter" from the notion of exclusive observance in the Land of Israel.[15] This tendency is not shared by the Rabbi Ishmael midrashim, which consistently gloss the biblical "when you enter" as "HA-KATUV refers to [the time] after the conquest and settlement." In this way, the Rabbi Ishmael midrashim strengthen the connection between the verse and the observation of the commandment in question and preserve, Shemesh argues, the earlier interpretative tradition.

One of Shemesh's proofs for the relative antiquity of this tradition is 4QMMT B: 62–63, cited above. 4QMMT's statement is based on Leviticus 19:23: "when you enter the land and plant any tree for food, you shall regard its fruit as forbidden for you, not to be eaten." The key issue is that "when you enter the land" is glossed by 4QMMT glosses as "[And concerning the (fruits of) trees with edible fruit] planted in the Land of Israel." This gloss indicates that the Qumran community equates the biblical "when you enter" with observance of the commandment in Israel, the view preserved in the Rabbi Ishmael midrashim but rejected in those associated with Rabbi Aqiva.[16]

d) B 13–16[17]

וְאַף עַל טׇהֳרַת פָּרַת הַחַטָּאת הַשּׁוֹחֵט אוֹתָהּ וְהַשּׂוֹרֵף אוֹתָהּ וְהָאוֹסֵף אֶת אֶפְרָהּ וְהַמַּזֶּה אֶת [מֵי] הַחַטָּאת לְכֹל אֵלֶּה לְהַעֲרִי[בוֹ]ת הַשֶּׁמֶשׁ לִהְיוֹת טְהוֹרִים בְּשֶׁל שֶׁא יְהִיֶה הַטָּהֵר מִזֶּה אֶל הַטְמֵא.

And concerning the purity regulations of the cow of the purification offering (i.e., the red cow): he who slaughters it and he who burns it and he who gathers its ashes and he who sprinkles the [water of] purification—it is at sun[se]t that all these become pure so that the pure man may sprinkle upon the impure one.

At issue is the status of the priest who burns the red heifer whose ashes are used for purification (Numbers 19), which rabbinic literature presents as a subject of debate between the Pharisees and the Sadducees. According to the former, the priest had to be in the status of *tevul yom*, that is, he had to be ritually immersed in water and then purified by the setting of the sun, while the latter held that the setting of the sun alone was necessary (without the immersion). According to the Mishnah, the polemic was so sharp that during the heifer ritual, "The elders of Israel . . . rendered unclean the priest who should burn the heifer, because of the Sadducees: that they should not be able to say, 'It must be performed only by them on whom the sun has set.'"[18] 4QMMT B 13–16 indicates that for the Qumran community the purity of the purifying priest is determined by sunset, corresponding to the position attributed by the Mishnah to the Sadducees. As Menahem Kister has shown, the same legal position is found in two other Qumran fragments:

i. 4Q277, which contains the phrase: איש טהור מכל טמאת ערב

ii. 4QD^d+4QD^f, which contains the phrase: איש טהור מכל טמאתו אשר
יעריב א[ת השמש]

Moving from Qumran to the Rabbi Ishmael midrashim, the Sifre Numbers records a derashah attributed to Rabbi Ishmael that deals with this topic:

"טהור": שר' ישמעאל אומר טהור למה נאמר, הא עד שלא יאמר יש לי בדין,
אם המזה טהור, האוסף לא יהא טהור הא מה תלמוד לומר "טהור" מכל טומאה,
ואי זה זה, זה טבול יום.

"Pure" (Num 19:9): As Rabbi Ishmael says "pure," why was this stated? For until it says thus I could reason that if the sprinkler is pure, should the gatherer not be pure? Thus what does [Scripture] teach, saying "pure"? Pure of all impurity, and which is that? That is the *tevul yom.* (Sifre Numbers §124, p. 157)

The derashah is difficult. Rabbinic law does not consider the *tevul yom* the highest level of purity—the *tevul yom* is not even allowed to eat the *terumah* offerings (the contribution dedicated to the priests)—so it is curious that the Sifre would identify *tevul yom* as "pure of all impurity." The motivation for this counterintuitive reading, Kister persuasively argues, is polemic: the Sifre is struggling with an earlier interpretive tradition, a tradition reflected in 4QMMT and fragments (i) and (ii). The Sifre reinterprets the language of this tradition to produce a "rabbinic" conclusion, namely, that sunset alone is not enough to purify the priest. As with B 25–28 (the question of *hullin* slaughter), the legal conclusion of Rabbi Ishmael is *not* the same as 4QMMT's, but the discussion nonetheless reflects a familiarity with the interpretive traditions preserved in the Qumran writings (though their ultimate provenance may lie elsewhere).

The Role of *Katuv/Ha-Katuv*

In the critical edition of 4QMMT, Elisha Qimron calls attention to what he takes to be the anomalous use of *katuv* (כתוב) in 4QMMT: "The word is known in [Mishnaic Hebrew] as a technical term introducing scriptural citations. In 4QMMT, it never introduces biblical verses."[19] The second of these statements—the categorical assertion that 4QMMT does not introduce biblical verses—has been challenged by other Qumran scholars. Moshe Bernstein cautiously notes: "That כתוב need not introduce a quotation in 4QMMT is clear; whether it can is another issue."[20] George Brooke offers a more vigorous challenge, arguing that *katuv* introduces verbatim biblical citations (at B 70, C 6) or scriptural citations with only minor changes (at B 66–67, C 12–16 and more).[21] Even Brooke admits, however, that some statements introduced by *katuv* are patently non-biblical, particularly B 38, הדבר כתוב עברה, "the matter is written concerning a pregnant [animal]," which concludes the discussion of the status of the fetus, discussed above. As the editors note, the biblical prohibition underlying this passage is Leviticus 22:28, ושור או שה אתו ואת בנו לא תשחטו ביום אחד ([N]o animal from the herd or from the flock shall be slaughtered on the same day with its young). The Bible prohibits slaughtering אתו ואת בנו, literally, "him and his son," on the same day. 4QMMT, however, interprets this verse such that the biblical אתו (him) refers to pregnant animals and בנו (his son) refers to the fetus. The legal unclarity regarding the animals referred to in Leviticus 22:28 is resolved by 4QMMT, which specifies pregnant animals as the subject of the verse by asserting that "the matter is written [*katuv*] concerning a pregnant [animal]." So while Qimron's initial statement may be overly broad, *katuv* does introduce statements that are not quotations, and so the basic problem of *katuv* employed in non-scriptural context stands.

But the problem of *katuv* introducing non-biblical statements is more apparent than real, at least as far as the Rabbi Ishmael midrashim are concerned, since they *never* introduce biblical citations by *ha-katuv* (or, HA-KATUV).[22] Indeed, one of the formulas used by Rabbi Ishmael—"HA-KATUV speaks" (הכתוב מדבר)—functions similarly to *katuv* in B 38. In statements such as "HA-KATUV speaks of a betrothed girl," "HA-KATUV speaks of the Passover in Egypt and the Passover of subsequent generations," or "HA-KATUV speaks of the right [ear],"[23] HA-KATUV clarifies the status or identity of an ambiguous biblical subject. This is precisely the function of "the matter is written [*katuv*] concerning a pregnant [animal]."

There are, to be sure, differences between this phrase and Rabbi Ishmael's terminology. In 4QMMT *katuv* is the past participle, and in the Rabbi Ishmael midrashim it is the nominal subject; the Rabbi Ishmael midrashim employ the definite form, and 4QMMT the indefinite; and perhaps most significantly, in the Rabbi Ishmael midrashim HA-KATUV functions as part of the opposition TORAH-HA-KATUV, whereas the word *torah* does not appear in the legal section of 4QMMT.[24] Nonetheless, for both 4QMMT and the Rabbi Ishmael texts (*ha-*)*katuv* is employed to clarify the nature or status of the otherwise ambiguous subject of a biblical verse.

In conclusion, 4QMMT and the Rabbi Ishmael midrashim exhibit a significant number of common elements. Some of the shared elements involve both the presentation of the question and the halakhic conclusion, as in the question of whether the *re'shit* belongs to the priest. But even when the conclusions are different, as with the slaughter of *ḥullin* and the purity of *tevul yom*, Rabbi Ishmael is struggling with the same legal and

interpretive traditions as the author of 4QMMT. Add to this the terminological similarity in the non-scriptural employment of *katuv/ ha-katuv*,
and there begins to appear a much closer connection between Rabbi
Ishmael and Qumran than is usually attributed to Qumran and "the
Rabbis." Strikingly, the Rabbi Ishmael midrashim often side "with" Qumran against other rabbinic interpretations, a dynamic that holds even
regarding the priority of scriptural authority over transmitted tradition.

Torah and Wisdom: Ben Sira

In his recent book, *Torah for the Entire World*, Marc Hirshman argues
for the existence of a universalistic current within tannaitic literature.[25]
Hirshman examines a series of issues such as the dissemination of Torah
among the Gentiles, the legitimacy of gentile Torah observance,[26] and
the status of converts, and identifies a position that emphasizes the universal scope of Torah. Hirshman then shows that this universal tendency
is associated with the figure of Rabbi Ishmael and found in the Rabbi Ishmael midrashim. In searching for the roots of this approach, Hirshman
draws a number of parallels between the universalism of the Rabbi Ishmael school and the Wisdom tradition whose exemplar is Ben Sira, parallels involving the role of Torah in the school of Rabbi Ishmael and that
of Wisdom for the Book of Ben Sira (composed circa 175 B.C.E.).[27]
Specifically, both believe that Wisdom/Torah is universal and the patri-
mony of all mankind, but that the gentile nations have refused to accept
what is theirs. For this rejection, the nations qua collectives merit God's
wrath, but non-Jewish individuals who draw near Wisdom/Torah are to
be welcomed.[28]

Other points of contact suggest that Rabbi Ishmael and the Rabbi Ishmael midrashim are heirs, in some sense, to the Wisdom tradition. A
possible terminological marker is found in Rabbi Ishmael's statement in
the Mishnah that "he who wishes to gain wisdom should study property
laws; there is no greater field in the Torah, as they are like a gushing
fountain" (הרוצה שיחכים ילמד דיני ממונות שאין לך מקצוע בתורה גדול מהן שהן כמעין
הנובע),[29] where the study of Jewish law is presented as the medium by
which to attain wisdom—the only such statement in tannaitic literature.
Moreover, the dictum identifies the fluvial nature of property laws as the
characteristic that makes them suited for the acquisition of wisdom ("as
they are like a gushing fountain"). The gushing fountain imagery, which
is different from likening Torah to life-giving water, is not common in
tannaitic literature and may have its roots in the association of Wisdom
with rivers, as when Ben Sira compares wisdom to the four rivers that
depart from Eden in Genesis 2 (Pishon, Giḥon, Tigris and Euphrates) as
well as to the Nile and Jordan (Ben Sira 24:25–27). Commenting on this

verse, John Collins writes that the "comparison with foreign rivers may be significant. Wisdom was always an international phenomenon, and its character is not changed in that respect by the identification with Jewish law."[30]

There is also a shared theological motif with the Sifre Numbers, namely Ben Sira's description of Wisdom residing "in the highest heavens" (24:4) but descending and spreading "like the odor of incense in the Tent [of Meeting]" (24:15). Di Lella observes that the latter verse "adds a new dimension to Wisdom. . . . [I]t is an intermediary between God and human beings."[31] This description is strikingly similar to the Sifre Numbers' interpretation of Num 7:89, in which an intermediary voice descends from "the highest heavens" into the Tent of Meeting to communicate to Moses, an intermediary between God and humanity.[32]

More significant than any shared motif or image is the overall characterization of Scripture. As discussed above, the Rabbi Ishmael midrashim figure Scripture, HA-KATUV, as an active, intentional teacher that comes to clarify potentially misunderstood biblical passages, as well as instruct regarding proper modes of interpretation. This portrait of Scripture is unique to the Rabbi Ishmael midrashim and suggests an affinity between Torah and the personified teacher par excellence, Wisdom. The issues surrounding the figure of personified Wisdom are complex and the scholarly literature they have produced immense,[33] but the points relevant to the present discussion are basic and uncontroversial: Wisdom is a divine being that functions as an intermediary that comes to instruct humanity. The biblical *locus classicus* of this tradition is Proverbs 8:

> [25] YHWH created me at the beginning of His course
> As the first of His works of old.
> [26] In the distant past I was fashioned,
> At the beginning, at the origin of earth . . .
> [27] I was there when He set the heavens in place;
> When He fixed the horizon upon the deep;
> [28] When He made the heavens above firm,
> And the fountains of the deep gushed forth;
> [29] When He assigned the sea its limits,
> So that its waters never transgress His command;
> When he fixed the foundations of the earth,
> [30] I was with Him as a confidant,
> A source of delight every day,
> Rejoicing before Him at all times,
> [31] Rejoicing in His inhabited world,
> Finding delight with mankind.
> [32] Now, sons, listen to me;
> Happy are they who keep my ways.

³³ Heed discipline and become wise;
Do not spurn it.
³⁴ Happy is the man who listens to me,
Coming early to my gates each day,
Waiting outside my doors.
³⁵ For he who finds me finds life
And obtains favor from YHWH.
³⁶ But he who misses me destroys himself;
All who hate me love death.

Verses 25–31 describe Wisdom's role as the primordial consort of Yahweh and witness to Creation. At verse 32, the poem shifts to a hortative address to humanity, urging the readers to "keep the ways" of Wisdom and extolling the benefits of a life devoted to Wisdom. At this point, the critical issue is that Wisdom is both the speaker that calls humanity to learning and the content of the learning; Wisdom exhorts the readers to study Wisdom.

Ben Sira adopts many of the Wisdom motifs found in Proverbs, most clearly in chapter 24, but also introduces key innovations. Wisdom's residence on earth is successful, and it occurs within a particular national context:

⁶ Over waves of the sea, over all the land,
over every people and nation I held sway.
⁷ Among them all I sought a resting place:
in whose inheritance should I abide?
⁸ Then the Fashioner of all gave me His command,
and He who made me chose ᵗhe spot for my tent,
Saying "In Jacob make your dwelling,
In Israel your inheritance."
⁹ Before the ages, from the first, He created me,
and through the ages I shall not cease to be.
¹⁰ In the holy Tent I ministered before Him,
and then in Zion I took up my post.
¹¹ In the city He loves as He does me, He gave me rest;
In Jerusalem is my domain.
¹² I have struck a root among the glorious people;
in the portion of the Lord is my inheritance.

Wisdom's success in finding a terrestrial home contrasts with the more usual account of its inability to find a place on earth, an account found most explicitly in 1 Enoch 42:1–2 ("Then Wisdom went out to dwell with the children of the people; but she found no dwelling place"),[34] but with echoes throughout Second Temple literature.[35] The second innovation comes in the precise form that Wisdom takes in its terrestrial existence:[36]

> [23] All this is true of the book of the Most High's covenant,
> the Law which Moses enjoined on us
> as the heritage for the community of Jacob.

Wisdom descends upon the earth as Torah, or, to put it differently, the Torah *is* Wisdom. Ben Sira's identification of Torah and Wisdom (repeated in the later apocryphal Book of Baruch)[37] may be derived from Deuteronomy 4:5–6, where laws are characterized as the wisdom of Israel. It is unclear, however, whether Ben Sira adopts Deuteronomy's identification or polemicizes against it.[38] Whatever the motivation, Ben Sira's identification of Torah and Wisdom appears throughout the book:

i. The commandments of the Torah are the path to Wisdom ("If you desire wisdom, keep the commandments, and the Lord will lavish her upon you," 1:26).
ii. Wisdom entails the Law ("The whole of wisdom is fear of the Lord, and in all wisdom there is the fulfillment of the law," 19:20).
iii. Fear of God is paralleled by adherence to the Law ("Whoever fears the Lord will do this, and whoever holds to the law will obtain wisdom," 15:1).[39]

The critical point for the present study is that Ben Sira identifies Torah, and specifically Torah as legal corpus, with Wisdom—the outstanding personified instructor of Second Temple Judaism. Ben Sira, like Rabbi Ishmael, holds that Scripture is a personified instructor.[40] Indeed, for both Ben Sira and the Rabbi Ishmael midrashim, Wisdom and Scripture, respectively, are both the instructor and the content of instruction. Wisdom appears on earth in order to teach humanity wisdom, while Scripture (HA-KATUV) comes to teach the meaning of Scripture (*torah*). Conceptually, then, the Mekhilta and Sifre's active, instructing Scripture can be seen as an elaboration on Ben Sira's identification of Torah with Wisdom.

Rabbi Ishmael and the Priesthood

As with the section on Ben Sira, discussion begins with Marc Hirshman's book *Torah for the Entire World*, which argues that the universalism of Rabbi Ishmael and the Rabbi Ishmael midrashim is, in some sense, priestly. Hirshman is well aware of the difficulties inherent in historical analysis of tannaitic literature and is careful to avoid historicist assumptions, while insisting on the shared motifs with priestly sources.[41] Having come to the same conclusion independently of Hirshman's book, I believe the findings of the present investigation support this hypothesis.

The similarities between personified, instructing Scripture (HA-KATUV) of the Mekhilta and the Sifre Numbers, and the personified, instructing Torah (Wisdom) in Ben Sira are relevant here. After all, Ben Sira was (as Hirshman notes) closely connected to the priesthood: he discusses sacrifices (31:21–32:20)—a topic absent from other Wisdom literature—urges the reader to give the priests that which is due them according to biblical law (7:29–31), and privileges the Aaronide priesthood over the Davidic kingship (45:23–26). Helge Stadelmann interprets these passages as evidence that Ben Sira was a priest, and subsequent scholars, among them Saul Olyan and Benjamin Wright, share this view.[42] Even John Collins, who rejects Stadelmann's conclusion, admits Ben Sira's sympathy for the priesthood, which, Collins suggests, "can be explained by supposing that he depended on the patronage of the High Priest."[43] In either case, it is clear that Ben Sira was intimately familiar with the priesthood and its traditions, either as a priest or as a sympathetic member of the priestly milieu.

The same holds true for the similarities between Rabbi Ishmael and the author of 4QMMT.[44] The Qumran community was, after all, priestly in its self-understanding and, most likely, in its historical origins. The Qumran documents "teem with references to priestly figures, practices, and concerns."[45] The shared elements between 4QMMT and the Rabbi Ishmael midrashim may point to a common legal and hermeneutical heritage that is, broadly understood, priestly.

A third link, which has not been discussed up to now, is Targum Pseudo-Jonathan. Ephraim Itzchaky has compared the halakhic pluses in Pseudo-Jonathan with the rabbinic legal midrashim, and has demonstrated that the language and legal positions of Pseudo-Jonathan bear a striking resemblance to the Rabbi Ishmael midrashim, but not to the midrashim associated with Rabbi Aqiva (the Sifra and the Sifre Deuteronomy).[46] These findings are of particular interest in light of Beverly Mortensen's examination of the priestly elements in Pseudo-Jonathan and her conclusion that the Targum "addresses itself to a readership of priests."[47] Though the matter requires additional investigation, the identification of Pseudo-Jonathan as both Ishmaelian and priestly is notable.

It is also worth noting, even with all the well-known caveats regarding rabbinic biography, that rabbinic literature presents Rabbi Ishmael as a scion to a priestly family. In the Tosefta, Rabbi Ishmael swears by the priestly garb worn by his father, suggesting that his father served in the Temple,[48] and a later amoraic source preserves a mnemonic phrase— ישמעאל כהנא מסייע כהני—that presupposes his priestly status.[49] Among modern scholars, there is some controversy as to whether Rabbi Ishmael was the son or the grandson of a high priest, but for the present purposes it need only be established that Rabbi Ishmael is represented as being of (broadly understood) priestly origin.[50] Indeed, scholars are increasingly recognizing the durability of priestly traditions, identity, and institutions after the destruction of the Second Temple, suggesting that the question at hand is less how the Rabbis saw their *predecessors*, and more how they interacted with their contemporaries.[51] The vitality of priestly religious and literary traditions has recently been argued by Rachel Elior, whose ambitious analysis covers biblical, Qumran and Hekhalot literature.[52]

More important than any of the thematic connections to priestly sources is the single most dominant trait of the Rabbi Ishmael midrashim, their insistence on the centrality of Scripture and concomitant marginalization of extra-scriptural traditions. The relationship between these two modes of authorization has been central to the modern study of rabbinics since its inception.[53] During the first half of the twentieth century, the question was debated by two of the greatest rabbinics scholars in Israel. J. N. Epstein argued that midrashic argument was secondary to extra-scriptural tradition: Scripture was consulted to buttress or provide mnemonic support for existing *halakhot*, but midrash did not generate legal norms.[54] Chanoch Albeck argued, to the contrary, that Scripture was—at least in certain cases—an integral part of the legal process and that there were legal decisions that were made on the basis of scriptural interpretation alone.[55] Nearly half a century ago, Ephraim Urbach argued that each of these scholars had identified significant phenomena that reflected part of the reality of the rabbinic period, but both erred in trying to generalize from these partial data.[56] According the Urbach, Pharisaic circles were originally committed to the preservation of extra-scriptural tradition, as is clear from a number of ancient sources, chiefly Josephus's description of the Pharisees and their priestly opponents: "What I would now explain is this, that the Pharisees have delivered to the people a great many observances by succession from their fathers, which are not written in the law of Moses; and for that reason it is that the Sadducees reject them and say that we are not to esteem those observances to be obligatory which are in the written word, but are not to observe what are derived from the tradition of our forefathers."[57]

Alongside Josephus, the Pharisaic commitment to extra-scriptural tradition is also evident in the New Testament and finds expression in rabbinic literature in the "chain of tradition" in m. Avot 1.1.[58] At the same time, there were other, non-Pharisaic, circles committed to scriptural study: "All the extant evidence proves that there was a class of scribes who copied the biblical books and preserved the scriptural tradition, the teachers and expositors of Scripture. There are indications that these early scribes were associated with the Temple and it appears they were priests."[59] Over time, the priestly practice of scriptural exposition penetrated into the Pharisaic—and then rabbinic—circles, and Urbach shows that the change was met with resistance on the part of those committed to the Pharisaic model. I find Urbach's thesis, on the whole, correct, though it requires some adjustment for the Rabbi Ishmael midrashim. For the community that produced these texts was not struggling to accept the legitimacy of biblical exegesis; it was committed to exegesis as the primary, almost exclusive form of legitimate argument. Nor do the Rabbi Ishmael midrashim show traces of the previous dominance of *halakhah*; to the contrary, they suggest that there is only very limited room for non-scriptural argument. In this respect, the Mekhilta and the Sifre Numbers do not fit Urbach's historical reconstruction, though this can be interpreted in two ways: either Urbach's thesis is incorrect—the Rabbis, as heirs to the Pharisees, did not struggle to recognize the legitimacy of midrash (as opposed to extra-scriptural tradition). This interpretation is very problematic since there is ample evidence that throughout tannaitic times, the Sages prefer extra-scriptural traditions to biblical exegesis as a source for halakhic ruling, including the passages from the Sifra discussed above, which reflect the superiority of extra-scriptural *halakhah* over midrash.[60] The second possibility is that Urbach is correct overall, but the struggle of which he speaks has left no trace in the Rabbi Ishmael midrashim because these texts were produced in a circle that was not heir to Pharisaic ideology but rather to the Scripture-centered views of priestly circles; the biblical and Second Temple priest was, after all, the authorized interpreter of Torah.[61] This direction is ineluctably speculative: there is very little solid historical information on the Pharisees or the priesthood, or even what "priestly" means post-70. Nonetheless, the dominance of scriptural interpretation and marginalization of *halakhah* in the Rabbi Ishmael midrashim (along with the other arguments) may indicate that while the majority of the tannaim emerged from Pharisaic groups, there was also a group that was heir, in some sense, to priestly practices.

Torah and Logos: Clement of Alexandria

The historical divide separating the Rabbi Ishmael midrashim from Ben Sira makes any comparison necessarily speculative—some 250 turbulent and poorly documented years separate Ben Sira from the historical Rabbi Ishmael, more from the final redaction of the Mekhilta and Sifre. There are, however, more contemporary intellectual traditions that employ the idea of personified, instructing Scripture—namely, the patristic tradition of Christ as teacher, the *Christos Didaskalos* tradition, surveyed by

Friedrich Normann.[62] According to Normann, the *Christos Didaskalos* tradition has its roots in a number of key New Testament passages such as the characterization of Jesus as the teacher with authority (ἐξουσία) in Mark 1:27, Jesus' statement to the crowds and to his disciples that they "have one teacher" (Matt 23:8), and Jesus' assertion that his teachings are "not mine, but His who sent me" (John 7:16). Out of these verses there developed scattered references to Christ as teacher, and Normann adduces a wealth of passages from the epistolary literature of Paul, Clement of Rome, Ignatius, and Polycarp. These thinkers, however, do not incorporate Jesus' role as teacher into broader theological structures, and so cannot count as representatives of a mature *Christos Didaskalos* tradition. The closest one gets is Clement of Rome's statement that Christ "Himself by the Holy Ghost thus addresses us: 'Come, ye children, hearken unto Me; I will teach you the fear of the Lord'" (1 Clement 22).[63] This statement portrays Christ as a preexistent teacher, but, as Normann notes, this concept is not developed further in Clement of Rome's writings.[64] It is only with the second century writings of Justin Martyr that the *Christos Didaskalos* tradition comes into its own, and it peaks shortly thereafter, with Clement of Alexandria, who is the subject of the following analysis.

Clement of Alexandria (c. 150–c. 215) was head of the catechetical church in Alexandria. His main literary works are the *Protreptikos* (Exhortation to the Pagans), the *Paedagogue* (Instructor) and the *Stromata* (Tapestries, or Miscellanies). The first two works are apparently parts of a trilogy whose third volume was to be the *Didaskalos* (Teacher), the planned culmination of an educational process: first an exhortation to the pagans to accept Christ, followed by the lessons of the pedagogue, the propaedeutic instructor, and finally, the more complex teachings of the *Didaskalos*. The last book was never composed, and many of its teachings made their way into the *Stromata*. But the original outline plan of Clement's writings reflects two of his fundamental convictions: that religious perfection is a matter of education and that the ideal Christian is also the true gnostic, the true knower. According to Clement, the path to religious perfection involves the acquisition of divine knowledge—and so the Christian is called upon to master the gnosis (knowledge) imparted to mankind by God or, more accurately, by the Logos.[65] This educational process culminates in the knowledge imparted by Christ in the gospel. But the revelation of the gospel is not an unannounced leap but itself part of an educational process that recognizes two significant, though ultimately unsuccessful, precedents: Greek philosophy and the Old Testament. The role of philosophy is less important for the current study and will not be discussed in any detail;[66] rather, the focus is on Clement's understanding of the Hebrew Bible and its relation to the New Testament.

Clement emphasizes the continuity of the Old and New Testaments. For Clement, the Hebrew Bible is an educational tool authored by the Logos as part of its mission to instruct humanity.[67] For the instructor is none other than the Logos, as Clement clearly states in the opening of *The Instructor*: "Let us then designate this Logos appropriately by the one name instructor."[68] As such, Clement regularly refers to the Logos's authorship of the Hebrew Bible in introducing biblical citations: "And the instructor, as I think, very beautifully says through Moses: 'And if any man die very suddenly by him . . .' (Num 6:9)."[69] The Logos's role as author of Scripture is addressed explicitly later in the same book: "Now the Law [*nomos*, Torah] is ancient grace given through Moses by the Logos. Wherefore also Scripture says 'The Law was given *through* Moses not by Moses' (John 1:17) but *by* the Logos and through Moses His Servant."[70]

By emphasizing the Logos's authorship of the Torah, Clement binds together the Old and New Testaments as two works of the same author and twin elements in a single educational process.[71] Clement returns to the commonality of the two testaments time and again. Their overt theological message is the same—"one God and omnipotent Lord [is] truly preached in the Law [Torah] and the prophets [and] the blessed Gospel"[72] —and they contain the same inner meaning since "Law, prophets and Gospel converge into one knowledge [*gnosis*]."[73]

Yet the common origin and pedagogic unity of the two testaments cannot obscure the important differences in status that each enjoys within Clement's broader theological system. The Hebrew Bible is merely propaedeutic. Its role is to inculcate right and lawful behavior among the children of Israel, paving the way for the appearance of Christ, the Logos incarnate: "But since God deemed it advantageous, that from the law and the prophets, men should receive a preparatory discipline by the Lord, the fear of the Lord was called the beginning of wisdom, being given by the Lord, through Moses, to the disobedient and the hard of heart. . . . [T]he instructing Logos, foreseeing from the first, and purifying by each of these methods, adapted the instrument suitable for piety."[74]

The Torah plays a critical role in the education of Israel, but Torah alone is not sufficient to lead Israel to redemption. Right behavior is necessary, but not the ultimate end of God's instruction, as the following passage makes clear: "Who then is perfect? He who professes abstinence from what is bad. Well, this is the way to the Gospel and to well-doing. But gnostic perfection in the case of the legal man is the acceptance of the Gospel. . . . Now in the Gospel the gnostic attains proficiency not only by making use of the law as a step, but by understanding and comprehending it."[75] In this passage, Clement distinguishes between two levels of perfection. The Hebrew Bible teaches proper living, and as a result the legal man—the man of *nomos*, of Torah—attains a certain degree of perfection, one that follows from "abstinence from what is bad." But there exists a higher perfection, one that requires *understanding* Scripture, and the Hebrew Bible is unable to lead the reader to this perfection. As legal instruction, the Hebrew Bible succeeds, but as gnostic instruction—as a teacher of divine knowledge—it fails. This failure is, prima facie, paradoxical. The Old Testament, no less than the New, is authored by the Logos to convey to mankind the divine truths, and gnostic proficiency is attained "by understanding and comprehending it." Why, then, does it fail to communicate these truths? Why, in other words, is a second revelation necessary?

As Clement explains, the failure of the Hebrew Bible is not the result of theological shortcomings, but of hermeneutical ones. As a text, the Hebrew Bible is clear and instructive in matters of behavior and conduct, but it fails to clearly communicate its divine gnosis because it presents its gnostic teaching in enigmas and mysteries. The enigmatic nature of the Hebrew Bible is not extrinsic to its mission, but necessitated by the inner logic of the text: "For many reasons, then, the Scriptures hid the sense. First, that we may become inquisitive. . . . Then it was not suitable for all to understand, so that they might not receive harm in consequence of talking in another sense of things declared for salvation by the Holy Spirit. Wherefore the holy mysteries of the prophecies are veiled in the parables—preserved for chosen men."[76]

Clement goes on to enumerate a long list of reasons for the obscurity of the Old Testament, the details of which are not important for the present discussion.[77] Whatever the merit of these justifications, the key issue is that the obscurity, the hermeneutical opacity, of the Old Testament explains the need for the New Testament. The hermeneutical difficulties make necessary the "New Song of the Logos," in which the Logos that had been an angel now becomes flesh.[78] The Logos's transformation from angel to flesh—paralleling the shift from Old to New Testament— is not one of substance: the Logos is the same in both cases. But the incarnate Logos, now in human form, allows for a new level of intimacy and immediacy with humanity and thus for a more direct educational relationship. To be sure, the new manifestation of the Logos is first and foremost its physical manifestation in the person of Jesus Christ. But alongside this physical transformation, there is also a manifestation—a making manifest—of the previously hidden meaning of the Hebrew Bible. Here is how Clement characterizes the hermeneutical force of Christ's advent: "[John the Baptist] said 'I am not worthy to loose the latchet of the Lord's shoe' (Mark 1:7). . . . Perhaps this signified the final exertion of the Saviour's power toward us—the immediate, I mean—that by His presence, concealed in the enigmas of prophecy, inasmuch as he, by pointing out to sight Him that had been prophesied of, and indicating the Presence which had come, walking forth into the light, <u>loosed the latchet of the oracles of the [old] economy, by unveiling the meaning of the symbols</u>."[79]

Clement further states: "We must know, then, that if Paul is young in respect to time—having flourished immediately after the Lord's ascension—yet his writings depend on the Old Testament, breathing and speaking of them. For faith in Christ and the knowledge of the Gospel are the explanation and fulfillment of the law . . . unless you believe what is prophesied in the law, and oracularly delivered by the law, you will not understand <u>the Old Testament, which He by His coming expounded</u>."[80]

As these texts suggest, the explicative force of the advent of Christ is— on a very basic level—the direct and necessary outcome of the Hebrew Bible's status as a prefigurative text: the Hebrew Bible enigmatically foretells the coming of Christ, so Christ's appearance makes manifest the meaning of these statements. In this respect, the advent of Christ clarifies the Old Testament in the same way that Croesus's defeat at the hands of the Persians clarified the Oracle of Delphi's pronouncement that by attacking Persia, Croesus would "destroy a great empire"—his own, as it turned out. But the New Testament is not only a factual record of Christ's historical appearance; it contains a divine message, a gospel that teaches faith and forgiveness. The Logos did not become flesh for its own sake, but to better teach humanity the gnostic truth hidden in the Hebrew Bible. In this sense, the advent of Christ is a hermeneutical event that reveals not only the fact of Christ's advent but the enigmas and the symbols of the Hebrew Bible.

For Clement, then, the New Testament is a record of the incarnation of the Logos in the person of Christ and, at the same time, the teachings of the incarnate Logos and thus a manifestation of the Logos's divine-educational message. Both Christ and the New Testament manifest the teachings of the Logos, and thus Christ's appearance and Christ's gospel are part of a single divine message—so much so that Clement speaks of the manifestation of the Logos as consisting of both a carnal and a textual aspect: "John, the herald of the Word, besought men to make themselves ready against the coming of the Christ of God. And it was this which was signified by the dumbness of Zacharias, which waited for fruits in the person of the harbinger of Christ, that the Logos, the light of truth, <u>by becoming the Gospel</u>, might break the mystic silence of the prophetic enigmas."[81] The Logos *becomes the gospel*, it becomes Scripture. The New Testament is, for Clement, the Logos "incarnated" textually, come to reveal the mysteries of the Hebrew Bible. When Clement states, "This is the New Song, the manifestation of the Logos . . . for the Logos . . . has appeared as our teacher,"[82] the teacher is both Christ and the gospel itself.

At this point, the fundamental similarity to Rabbi Ishmael becomes apparent: both writers describe Scripture as an instructor that comes to the aid of the reader struggling to understand Scripture. For Rabbi Ishmael, Scripture (as HA-KATUV) comes to clarify the halakhic meaning of Scripture (*torah*); for Clement, Scripture (as the new testament of the Logos) comes to clarify the gnostic meaning of the Hebrew Bible. As phenomenologies of reading Scripture, the two accounts are structurally similar, almost to the point of homology: the reader of Scripture encounters a difficult or enigmatic passage and is unsure how to interpret it; responding to the reader's difficulty, a distinct manifestation of Scripture appears, an instructor that leads the reader to the correct understanding of the biblical text.

There are also significant differences between the two interpretive models. As noted, for Rabbi Ishmael, Scripture elaborates legal issues, while for Clement Scripture clarifies the gnostic content of the Old Testament. Then there is the not-insignificant question of the identity of the instructor. Rabbi Ishmael holds that there is only one divine revelation, the Sinai theophany, and as a result the Torah given at Sinai must play a double role as the content of God's word and its interpretation—thus the dual characterization of the Hebrew Bible as TORAH and HA-KATUV. Clement's Christian hermeneutic posits a second, post-Sinaitic, revelation that provides the reader with the instruction needed to understand Torah. The appearance of a second testament, the extension of Scripture beyond the Hebrew Bible, allows Clement to shift the interpretive agency to the later revelation and avoid bifurcating the Hebrew Bible, as Rabbi Ishmael must.

Note, however, that the difference in teaching agency only emerges after the advent of Christ. When discussing the teaching of the Logos prior to this event, Clement describes the Logos as both the author and the message of the Hebrew Bible. Like Rabbi Ishmael's Scripture and Ben Sira's Wisdom, the Logos is simultaneously the instructor and the content of its instruction. Thus Clement writes: "With the greatest clearness, accordingly, the Logos has spoken respecting Himself by Hosea: 'I am your instructor' (Hos 5:2)."[83] Moreover, it is worth noting that Clement's terminology is also similar to Rabbi Ishmael's. For instance, Clement states that Christ's coming could be known to the reader of the Hebrew Bible prior to the event since ἡ γραφὴ παιδαγωγήσει, "the written [Scripture] will instruct [you]."[84] The use of ἡ γραφὴ (the written) for Scripture is not common among early Christian writers. The singular ἡ˛ γραφὴ usually refers to a verse or phrase while the plural form ἁι γραφαί (or ἁι ἱεραὶ γραφαί, the holy writings) refers to Scripture as a whole. Clement, however, regularly uses ἡ γραφὴ as Scripture.[85] Coupled with the verbal predicate παιδαγωγήσει (will teach, or, will instruct),

the result is strikingly similar to the "Ishmaelian" "HA-KATUV [the writ-
ten] teaches" (הכתוב מלמד). The issue of Christ does, of course, represent
a formidable theological boundary between Rabbi Ishmael and Clement,
but should not obscure the very significant hermeneutical similarities.
Clement's full and consistent identification of the instructor with Christ
marks him as the apogee of the *Christos Didaskalos* tradition; Rabbi Ishmael's identification of the instructor with personified Scripture suggests a structurally similar *Nomos Didaskalos* tradition.

*   *   *

In his important article on Jewish binitarianism, Daniel Boyarin argues
against the venerable idea that the Rabbis rejected divine intermediation
in general and the Logos in particular.[86] More accurately, Boyarin shows
that the eventual rejection is best understood against the backdrop of
earlier shared theological traditions and language, largely excised from
rabbinic literature, but still visible as a palimpsest beneath later editorial
strata, or in rabbinically marginal works such as the Targumim.[87] I would
argue that the parallel between the understanding of Christ in the *Christos Didaskalos* tradition and Rabbi Ishmael's representation of Scripture
as personified teacher—*Nomos Didaskalos*—is part of such a shared reservoir of theological language and imagery.

Clement and Justin Martyr, the outstanding representatives of the
Christos Didaskalos tradition, are also key figures in the eventually discarded Christian tradition that emphasized the role of Nomos as a
medium of revelation.[88] This view is inherent in Clement's positive assessment of the role of Torah as a revelation of the Logos, but also in his dis-
cussion of Christ. For example, Clement approvingly quotes from the
Kerygma Petrou, stating: "Peter in his *Preaching* [*kerygma*] called the Lord
Nomos and Logos," and similarly, "in the *Preaching* of Peter you will
find the Lord called Nomos and Logos."[89] This explicit identification of
Christ as Nomos (Torah) is also found in Clement's predecessor in the
Christos Didaskalos tradition, Justin Martyr, who speaks of Christ as "the
Son of God, who was proclaimed as about to come to all the world to be
the everlasting law and the everlasting covenant."[90] Indeed, in his study
of Justin's Logos theology, M. J. Edwards argues that Justin drew more
from the biblical and Jewish sources than from Plato and the Stoa.[91]
Edwards's concluding remarks are extremely suggestive: "Our conclusion, therefore, is that . . . Christ is the Logos who personifies the Torah
[Nomos, A. Y.]. In Jewish thought the Word was the source of being, the
origin of the Law, the written Torah and a Person next to God. Early
Christianity announced the incarnation of this Person, and Justin makes
the further claims that Scripture is the parent of all truth among the

nations, and that the Lord who is revealed to us in the New Testament is the author and the hermeneutic canon of the Old." [92]

Here we find many of the theological issues underpinning the Rabbi Ishmael midrashim: the personification of Scripture (Nomos), the Wisdom-derived idea of Scripture bringing truth to all the nations, and the hermeneutical contribution of personified Scripture that comes to teach the proper understanding of (for Rabbi Ishmael) Torah.

I am not arguing for outright identity here. There is no question that the Logos plays a much larger role in the theology of Clement and Justin than does the Nomos, and it also appears that the Nomos tradition is limited to Patristic authors with strong Palestinian ties. Justin was a native of Shechem, while Clement, who came to Alexandria from Athens, identifies his greatest teacher as a Palestinian thinker "of Hebrew origins." [93] Nonetheless, the use of Nomos as a category by which to describe Christ's advent, along with the *Nomos Didaskalos* tradition in Rabbi Ishmael, and traces of Logos theology elsewhere, indicates that these categories circulated much more freely among early Christians and rabbis than is usually recognized. Shared theological categories may be viewed as evidence for rabbinic influence on the church fathers, or vice versa, but I suspect that this is not the proper historical model. It is widely recognized that Wisdom theology served as a model for Christ in the early church, and that Logos theology took over many Wisdom motifs. [94] I have already argued (following Hirshman) that Rabbi Ishmael's conception of personified Scripture may be linked to Ben Sira's identification of Torah and Wisdom. In light of their shared genealogy, both the *Logos Didaskalos* and the *Nomos Didaskalos* may plausibly be seen as later developments of the personified Wisdom tradition, with each side adapting it to fit the evolving and still-inchoate needs of their respective communities. [95]

Whether this is the best historical explanation remains to be seen. What has, I hope, been shown is that the Rabbi Ishmael midrashim are connected, albeit in different ways, to different communities and their attendant literary corpora, reflecting a historical reality in which the boundaries between these groups were not as fixed as they would become. The groups in question, rabbis, priests, Christians, did formulate exclusive identities and became separate (or extinct) communities. But the process was long, and even as they worked to establish and then seal their borders, the groups drew upon a shared reservoir of religious motifs and imagery, a broad religious *koine*, within which rabbinic literature is located. And it is in the context of this *koine* that rabbinic literature is best studied.

Notes

Preface

1. David Stern, *Midrash and Theory: Ancient Jewish Exegesis and Contemporary Literary Studies* (Evanston, Ill.: Northwestern University Press, 1996), 1.

2. Stern, *Midrash and Theory*, 95 n. 5.

3. Geoffrey Hartman and Sanford Budick, eds., *Midrash and Literature* (New Haven, Conn.: Yale University Press, 1986); Daniel Boyarin, *Carnal Israel: Reading Sex in Talmudic Culture* (Berkeley and Los Angeles: University of California Press, 1993); Daniel Boyarin, *Intertextuality and the Reading of Midrash* (Bloomington: Indiana University Press, 1990); James L. Kugel, *In Potiphar's House: The Interpretive Life of Biblical Texts* (San Francisco: Harper, 1990); José Faur, *Golden Doves with Silver Dots: Semiotics and Textuality in Rabbinic Tradition* (Bloomington: Indiana University Press, 1986); Steven D. Fraade, *From Tradition to Commentary: Torah and Its Interpretation in the Midrash Sifre to Deuteronomy* (Albany: State University of New York Press, 1991); Michael Fishbane, *The Garments of Torah: Essays in Biblical Hermeneutics* (Bloomington: Indiana University Press, 1990); David Stern, *Parables in Midrash: Narrative and Exegesis in Rabbinic Literature* (Cambridge, Mass.: Harvard University Press, 1991).

4. Menahem Kahana, *The Two Mekhiltot on the Amalek Portion: The Originality of the Version of the Mekhilta d'Rabbi Ishma'el with Respect to the Mekhilta of Rabbi Shim'on ben Yohay* (Jerusalem: Magnes, 1999) (Hebrew); Jay Harris, *How Do We Know This?: Midrash and the Fragmentation of Modern Judaism* (Albany: State University of New York Press 1995); Moshe Halbertal, *Interpretive Revolutions in the Making: Values as Interpretive Considerations in Midreshei Halakhah* (Jerusalem: Magnes, 1997) (Hebrew).

5. On the manuscript history and editions of the Mekhilta of Rabbi Ishmael, see H. L. Strack and Günter Stemberger, *Introduction to Talmud and Midrash*, trans. Markus Bockmuehl (Minneapolis: Fortress, 1996), 255–56; M. Kahana, *Manuscripts of the Halakhic Midrashim: An Annotated Catalogue* (Jerusalem: Yad Ben Zvi, 1995), 37–49 (Hebrew); and Liora Elias, "The Mekhilta of Rabbi Ishmael According to an Excellent Text from the Genizah," (M.A. thesis, Hebrew University, 1997), 1–8 (Hebrew).

6. There is currently no complete critical edition of the Sifra. For a discussion of the available editions, see Strack and Stemberger, *Introduction*, 264; and Kahana, *Manuscripts*, 60–88. A critical edition is currently being published under the editorship of Rabbi Avraham Shoshana (*Sifra on Leviticus* [Jerusalem and

Cleveland: Ofeq, 1991–98] [Hebrew]), of which three volumes have appeared: vol. 1, *Baraita de-R. Ishmael* (The 13 Hermeneutical Rules of R. Ishmael); vol. 2.1, *Vayikra Dibura D'Nedaba*; vol. 3, *Vayikra Dibura D'Hoba*. A partial edition was produced by Louis Finkelstein: *Sifra on Leviticus*, 5 vols. (New York and Jerusalem: Jewish Theological Seminary, 1983–91). The standard reference edition is still I. H. Weiss, *Sifra: Commentar zu Leviticus* (Vienna: Schlossberg, 1862).

7. See Strack and Stemberger, *Introduction*, 267–68; Kahana, *Manuscripts*, 89–96; and, in greater detail, Menahem Kahana, *Prolegomena to a New Edition of the Sifre* (Jerusalem: Hebrew University, 1982) (Hebrew).

8. See Strack and Stemberger, *Introduction*, 271; Kahana, *Manuscripts*, 97–107.

9. J. N. Epstein and E. Z. Melammed, eds., *Mekhilta de-Rabbi Shimon ben Yohai* (Jerusalem: Meqitze Nirdamim, 1959); H. S. Horovitz, ed., *Sifre Zutta*, bound with his edition of Sifre Numbers (Leipzig: Gustav Fock, 1917; repr., Jerusalem: Shalem, 1992); D. Z. Hoffmann, ed., *Midrash Tannaim zum Deuteronomium* (Berlin: H. Itzkowski, 1908; repr. Jerusalem: n.p., 1984); Menahem I. Kahana, *Sifre Zuta on Deuteronomy: Citations for a New Tannaitic Midrash* (Jerusalem: Magnes, 2002) (Hebrew).

10. On the Mekhilta of Rabbi Ishmael see Menahem Kahana, "The Critical Editions of the Mekhilta of Rabbi Ishmael in Light of the Genizah Fragments," *Tarbiz* 55 (1986): 489–524 (Hebrew); and Daniel Boyarin, "From the Hidden Light: Toward the Original Text of the Mekhilta of Rabbi Ishmael," *Sidra* 2 (1986): 5–13 (Hebrew).

11. See the discussion and works cited in Strack and Stemberger, *Introduction*, 247–75.

12. David Hoffmann, *Zur Einleitung in die halachischen Midraschim* (Berlin, 1888), translated into Hebrew as *Le-Ḥeqer Midreshei ha-Tanna'im*, trans. A. S. Rabinowitz, in *Mesilot le-Torat ha-Tanna'im* (Tel Aviv: M. Drisner, 1928).

13. J. N. Epstein, *Prolegomena to Tannaitic Literature* (Tel Aviv: Dvir, 1957) (Hebrew).

14. A. J. Heschel, *Theology of Ancient Judaism*, vol. 1 (London and New York: Soncino, 1962); ibid., vol. 2 (London and New York: Soncino, 1965); ibid., vol. 3 (New York and Jerusalem: Jewish Theological Seminary, 1995) (Hebrew).

15. For a defense of Heschel's approach on existential and hermeneutical grounds see Rebecca Schorsch, "The Hermeneutics of Heschel in *Torah min Hashamayim*," *Judaism* 40 (1991): 301–8.

16. Chanoch Albeck, *Untersuchungen über die halachischen Midraschim* (Berlin: Akademie Verlag, 1927), argues against the attribution of the midrashic corpora to Rabbi Ishmael and Rabbi Aqiva, but his view has not found wide acceptance.

17. See the essays on rabbinic literature as a historical source collected in Jacob Neusner and Alan J. Avery-Peck, eds., *Where We Stand: Issues and Debates in Ancient Judaism* (Leiden: Brill, 1998). On biography, see William Scott Green, "What's in a Name?: The Problematic of Rabbinic 'Biography,'" in *Approaches to Ancient Judaism*, ed. W. S. Green (Missoula, Mont.: Scholars Press, 1978), 77–98, whose work builds on many of Neusner's insights. A recent example of the need for critical, diachronic analysis of rabbinic figures is Goshen-Gottstein's study of the figure of Elisha ben Abuya, the paradigmatic sinner, who only becomes such in amoraic literature—the tannaitic sources represent him as a minor sage of no particular distinction. See Alon Goshen-Gottstein, *The Sinner and the Amnesiac: The Rabbinic Invention of Elisha ben Abuya and Eleazar ben Arach* (Stanford, Calif.: Stanford University Press, 2000).

18. Harris, *How Do We Know This*, 51–72. See also Gary Porton's discussion of Rabbi Ishmael and Rabbi Aqiva debates in the Mishnah, with similar conclusions,

Gary Porton, "The Artificial Dispute: Ishmael and `Aqiva," in *Christianity, Judaism and Other Greco-Roman Cults: Studies for Morton Smith at Sixty*, ed. Jacob Neusner, Studies in Judaism of Late Antiquity 12 (Leiden: Brill, 1975), 18–29.

19. The Mekhilta is first attributed to Rabbi Ishmael by Rav Nissim Gaon and Rav Shmuel ben Hofni Gaon (*floruerunt* late tenth and early eleventh century). See Jacob Lauterbach, "The Name of the Mekhilta," *Jewish Quarterly Review* 11 (1920): 178; and Kahana, *The Two Mekhiltot*, 25. Kahana emphasizes (there, n. 2) that the traditional title *Mekhilta of Rabbi Ishmael* and the modern association of this work with the school of Rabbi Ishmael are unrelated.

20. I follow the terminological conventions suggested by Halivni in *Midrash, Mishnah, and Gemara: The Jewish Predilection for Justified Law* (Cambridge, Mass.: Harvard University Press, 1986), 15–16, where "midrash" refers to an interpretive institution, while "derashah" (plural, "derashot") signifies a single literary unit of midrash. Large midrashic collections such as the Mekhilta or the Sifre Numbers are also called a midrash (plural, midrashim).

21. A full list of the *ḥakhamim* by tractate can be found in Epstein, *Prolegomena*, 572–80.

22. See Epstein, *Prolegomena*, 597–601.

23. See Hoffmann, *Le-Ḥeqer Midreshei ha-Tannaim*, 30; and Epstein, *Prolegomena*, 640–41.

24. Distinct, but not hermetically sealed. It is common for derashot that exhibit the characteristics of one school to appear in the corpora of the other, sometimes changing their terminology to suit the interpretive style of the "host." On this phenomenon see Avraham Goldberg, "The Phrase *Davar 'Aḥer* in the Halakhic Midrashim," in *'Iyyunim be-sifrut ḥazal, ba-mikra uve-toldot yisrael* (E. Z. Melammed *Festschrift*), ed. Y. Gilat et al. (Ramat Gan: Bar Ilan University Press, 1982), 99–107 (Hebrew).

25. This is Menahem Kahana's conclusion in *Prolegomena*.

26. *Sifre Numbers*, ed. H. S. Horovitz (Jerusalem: Shalem, 1992; repr. of Leipzig, 1917); *Mekhilta de-Rabbi Ishmael*, ed. H. S. Horovitz and I. Rabin (Jerusalem: Bamberger and Wahrman, 1960; repr. of Frankfurt, 1931); *Siphre ad Deuteronomium*, ed. Louis Finkelstein (New York: Jewish Theological Seminary, 1993).

27. Jacob Z. Lauterbach, *Mekilta de-Rabbi Ishmael*, 3 vols. (Philadelphia: Jewish Publication Society of America, 1933–36).

28. Herbert Danby, *The Mishnah* (Oxford: Oxford University Press, 1933).

29. Gary Porton, *The Traditions of Rabbi Ishmael*, Studies in Judaism of Late Antiquity 19; 4 vols. (Leiden: Brill, 1976–82).

30. *Tanakh; A New Translation of the Holy Scriptures According to the Traditional Hebrew Text* (Philadelphia and New York: Jewish Publication Society, 1988).

Introduction

1. Moshe Halbertal's *Interpretive Revolutions* is exceptional in this respect.

2. This question is discussed below, p. 167.

3. Epstein, *Prolegomena*, 522.

4. On this spelling, see below, Chapter 4, n. 7.

5. See Epstein, *Prolegomena*, 522. The Rabbi Aqiva–Rabbi Ishmael debates differ in this respect from the debates between the Houses of Hillel and Shammai, where a legal question is always at stake.

6. At this point, MS Oxford 151 contains a scribal error; the remainder of the Hebrew is quoted according to Horovitz-Rabin.

7. See pp. 57–59.

8. David Weiss Halivni, *Peshat and Derash: Plain and Applied Meaning in Rabbinic Exegesis* (New York: Oxford University Press, 1991).

9. Halivini, *Peshat and Derash*, appendix 2, 158–62.

10. Halivni, *Peshat and Derash*, 159.

11. Natalie B. Dohrmann, "Law and Narrative in the Mekilta de-Rabbi Ishmael: The Problem of Midrashic Coherence" (Ph.D. diss., University of Chicago, 1999), 171.

12. Halivni may be rejecting the philosophical and literary criticism leveled at the notion of objective meaning, but, if so, the grounds for rejection ought be articulated.

13. Richard E. Palmer, *Hermeneutics* (Evanston, Ill.: Northwestern University Press, 1969), 84.

14. Jean Grondin, *Introduction to Philosophical Hermeneutics*, trans. Joel Weinsheimer (New Haven, Conn., and London: Yale University Press, 1994), 67.

15. Palmer, *Hermeneutics*, and Grondin, *Introduction to Philosophical Hermeneutics* are both useful surveys. For a discussion of the development of the term "hermeneutics" see Michael Ermarth, "The Transformation of Hermeneutics," *The Monist* 64 (1981): 175–94.

16. Martin Heidegger, *Being and Time*, trans. John Macquarrie and Edward Robinson (New York: Harper, 1962).

17. In fairness, Heidegger was aware of this difficulty but saw it as a necessary outgrowth of his philosophic project. In §7 of *Being and Time* he discusses the need for a new philosophic vocabulary and explains the "inelegance" of his treatise as the result of the need to chart a course that runs contrary to that taken by Western philosophy from Plato on. "[I]t is one thing to give a report in which we tell about entities, but another to grasp entities in their Being. For the latter task we lack not only most of the words but, above all, the 'grammar,'" *Being and Time*, 63.

18. "The phenomenology of Dasein is a *hermeneutic* in the primordial signification of this word, where it designates this business of interpreting," *Being and Time*, 62; italics in original.

19. The translation of *Dasein* as "human being" is taken from Hubert Dreyfus, *Being-in-the-World: A Commentary on Heidegger's* Being and Time, *Division I* (Cambridge, Mass.: MIT Press, 1991); and see the discussion at 13–14, where Dreyfus clarifies that "human being" does not refer to *a* human being but to the being that belongs to humans.

20. "When we are talking ontically we sometimes use the expression 'understanding something' with the signification of 'being able to manage something,' 'being a match for it,' 'being competent to do something.' In understanding as an *existentiale*, that which we have such competence over is not a 'what,' but Being as existing," *Being and Time*, 183.

21. Interestingly, Heidegger here returns to the pre-Schleiermacher view that understanding (albeit in a very different sense of the word) is self-evident, requiring no conscious engagement.

22. "In interpreting, we do not, so to speak, throw a 'signification' on some marked thing . . . . [W]e do not stick a value on it; but when something within the world is encountered as such, the thing in question already has an involvement which is disclosed in our understanding of the world, and this involvement is one which gets laid out by interpretation," *Being and Time*, 190–91.

23. Heidegger suggests that the understanding that underlies interpretation can be divided into three categories: fore-having, fore-sight, and fore-conception (*Being and Time*, 191). For a lucid discussion of the fore-structures of understanding, see Dreyfus, *Being-in-the-World*, 198–202.

24. The translators of *Being and Time* capitalize "interpetation" when it stands for the German *Interpretation*, but write it in lower case for *Auslegung*.

25. Heidegger, *Being and Time*, 192.

26. See Hans-Georg Gadamer, *Truth and Method*, translation revised by Joel Weinsheimer and Donald G. Marshall (New York: Crossroad, 1989). The relevance of Gadamer for the study of legal midrash was discussed in Halbertal, *Interpretive Revolutions*, 193–97.

27. Archaeologists are constantly faced with difficulties of this sort when they debate, e.g., whether a figurine belongs to the realm of ritual, medicine, or perhaps is "merely" decorative.

28. Philo, *Questions and Answers on Genesis*, trans. Ralph Marcus, Loeb Classical Library 380 (Cambridge, Mass.: Harvard University Press, 1953), 178.

29. On Gikatilla, see Moshe Idel's historical introduction to the English translation of *Sha'arei 'Orah (Gates of Light)*, trans. Avi Weinstein (San Francisco: HarperCollins, 1994), xxii–xxxiv; on Gikatilla's writings, see Efraim Gottlieb, *Studies in Kabbalistic Literature*, ed. Yosef Hacker (Tel Aviv: Tel Aviv University Press, 1976), 97–131 (Hebrew). The passage is from the tenth chapter of *Sha'arei Tzedeq*, which was discovered by Gottlieb and published in *Studies in Kabbalistic Literature*, 132–62, here 154–55.

30. This phrase comes from Hubert Dreyfus, "Holism and Hermeneutics," *Review of Metaphysics* 34 (1980): 3–24.

31. Lieve Teugels, "Midrash in the Bible or Midrash on the Bible," in *Bibel und Midrasch: Zur Bedeutung der rabbinischen Exegese für die Bibelwissenschaft*, ed. Gerhard Bodendorfer and Matthias Millard, Forschungen zum Alten Testament 22 (Tübingen: Mohr Siebeck, 1998), 47–48.

32. See Arnold Goldberg, "The Rabbinic View of Scripture," in *A Tribute to Geza Vermes: Essays on Jewish and Christian Literature and History*, ed. Philip Davies and Richard White, Journal for the Study of the Old Testament Supplement Series 100 (Sheffield: Sheffield Academic Press, 1990), 153–66; Alexander Samely, "Scripture's Implicature: The Midrashic Assumptions of Relevance and Consistency," *Journal of Semitic Studies* 37 (1992): 167–205; idem, "Between Scripture and Its Rewording: Towards a Classification of Rabbinic Exegesis," *Journal of Jewish Studies* 42 (1991): 39–67; David Instone Brewer, *Techniques and Assumptions in Jewish Exegesis before 70 CE*, Texte und Studien zum antiken Judentum 30 (Tübingen: J. C. B. Mohr, 1992).

Chapter 1

1. Wilhelm Bacher, *Die bibelexegetische terminologie der Tannaiten*, published as volume 1 of *Die exegetische Terminologie der jüdischen Traditionsliteratur* (1899; repr., Darmstadt: Wissenschaftliche Buchgesellschaft, 1965).

2. Bacher, *Exegetische Terminologie*, 1.197.

3. See M. Mishor, "Tense System in Tannaitic Hebrew" (Ph.D. Dissertation, Hebrew University, 1983), 250–58 (Hebrew).

4. H. B. Rosén, "The Comparative Assignment of Certain Hebrew Tense Forms," in *Proceedings of the International Conference on Semitic Studies* (Jerusalem: The Israel Academy of Sciences and Humanities, 1969), 212.

5. An interesting example from the history of English involves the reception of Germa᾽ c ᾱnd Romance synonyms. When such a couple was accepted into English, ᾽ ᵉre i᷈ a clear tendency to introduce a semantic differentiation, endowing the ᷈ᴧance word with a more abstract sense. Thus "deep" is primarily

applied to physical depth—just like German *tief.* But, unlike Latin *profundus* and French *profonde* (which also refer primarily to physical depth), the English word "profound" refers primarily to an abstract quality. The same is true of the Germanic/Romance pairs gross/grand; small/petite; cold/frigid: in each case, the Romance word took on a more abstract sense. Even when the words entered English as equivalents in their respective languages they did not remain synonyms, but rather a semantic shift occurred.

6. See George Lakoff, *Women, Fire, and Dangerous Things: What Categories Reveal about the Mind* (Chicago: University of Chicago Press, 1987); and George Lakoff and Mark Johnson, *Metaphors We Live By* (New York: Free Press, 1980).

7. Based on Lakoff, *Women, Fire, and Dangerous Things,* 411.

8. Eviatar Zerubavel, *The Fine Line: Making Distinctions in Everyday Life* (New York: Free Press, 1991).

9. This formula appears some twenty times in the Mekhilta and nine times in the Sifre Numbers. It is rare in the Sifra, appearing five times in total. Of these, three occurrences are in the tractate Qedoshim, which generally shows a strong affinity to the language and interpretive techniques of the Rabbi Ishmael midrashim. Of the remaining two occurrences, the first (Sifra Nedava parshata 2.4; Weiss 4b) has a parallel in the Sifre Deuteronomy §306, where the version is אמר הקדוש ברוך הוא (the Holy One Blessed be He said), and the second (Sifra Tzav parshata 5.1; Weiss 34a) opens an argument attributed to Rabbi Ishmael.

10. Absent from MS Oxford 151.

11. For a concise summary of the different calendars, see James C. Vanderkam's article in *The Anchor Bible Dictionary,* ed. David Noel Friedman (New York: Doubleday, 1992), 1.810–20.

12. Not all commentators understand the derashah thus. Rabbi Naftali Zvi Berlin (*Natziv*) suggests that the interpretation is based on the singular "sign" (פירוש 'לאות' אות אחת), *Mekhilta with Birkat ha-Natziv Commentary* (Jerusalem: Volozhin Yeshiva, 1997), 87 (Hebrew).

13. For a review of biblical scholarship on the meaning of this term, see Jeffrey Tigay, "On the Meaning of *T(W)TPT*," *Journal of Biblical Literature* 101 (1982): 321–31. Tigay argues that *ṭ(w)ṭpt* is a singular noun that means "headband."

14. For another example of an interpretation becoming so accepted as to be understood by later readers as the plain meaning of the Torah, see Admiel Kosman, "More on Associative Thought in Midrash," *Tarbiz* 63 (1994): 443–50 (Hebrew), in particular his discussion of the way in which philologically distinct texts are merged in the midrashic process to constitute, phenomenologically, a single text, p. 448 n. 19. See also Halivni's discussion of Rashbam (twelfth century) and his integration of rabbinic midrash into the *peshat* or plain meaning in the case of phylacteries (Halivni, *Peshat and Derash,* 169–70).

15. On the use of א as a *mater lectionis* (as in דיאנין) see Kahana, *Prolegomena,* p. 130 and Moshe Bar-Asher, "Preliminary Investigations of the Rabbinic Hebrew Found in MS Vatican 32 of the Sifre Numbers," *Te'udah* 3 (1983): 139–165, §10 (Hebrew). On the ין- ending for masculine plural nouns, see Kahana, *Prolegomena,* 130.

16. This phrase appears three times in the Sifra (twice in Qedoshim). There are too few occurrences of *dibberah torah* for the distribution to be meaningful, and the phrase does not appear to be typical of any group within the tannaitic corpus.

17. Though this approach is cited (there) in the name of Rabbi Eleazar ha-Kappar, who argues that *yayin* refers to mixed wine (*mazug*) and *shekhar* to unmixed wine (*ḥai*), effectively denying the synonymity of the terms.

18. See Heschel, *Theology of Ancient Judaism*, 1.4.

19. MS Vatican 32 reads "תכרת הנפש ההיא".

20. On the emphatic sense of the infinitive absolute plus finite verb, see Paul Joüon and Takamitsu Muraoka, *A Grammar of Biblical Hebrew* (Rome: Editrice Pontificio Istituto Biblico, 1991), §123, 2.422.

21. The interpretation of the infinitive absolute plus finite verb is one of the classic differences between the approaches of Rabbi Aqiva and Rabbi Ishmael; see Epstein, *Prolegomena*, 521.

22. The same idea may be expressed as follows: not every characteristic that some readers identify as a textual cue is, in fact, one.

23. Nothing in the semantics of *dibber* and *'amar* in Mishnaic Hebrew suggests the distinction. On these terms see Rivkah Shemesh, "About 'Speaking' That Is Not 'Saying': A Survey of Verbs of Speech Production in Mishnaic Hebrew," *Jewish Quarterly Review* 93 (2002): 201–15.

24. The phrase "TORAH designated him a slave" (התורה קראתו עבד) appears in Mekhilta Neziqin 1, p. 247; Lauterbach 3.4, but MS Oxford 151 reads "HA-KATUV designated him a slave" (הכתוב קראו עבד); there is also an additional derashah, Sifre Numbers §107, that combines the terms TORAH and HA-KATUV and will be discussed below.

25. The phrase also occurs in Sifre Numbers §152 (p. 197) and §154 (p. 205).

26. The term *ha-katuv* appears often in the Sifra and the Sifre Deuteronomy as well, though not as part of the contrast *torah–ha-katuv* to be outlined below.

27. This formula is more frequent in the Rabbi Ishmael midrashim, appearing dozens of times in both the Mekhilta and the Sifre Numbers. The Sifra contains some fifteen discrete instances of the phrase; half of them are in tractate Qedoshim.

28. For a discussion of the legal categories generated by different understandings of Numbers 30:17, see Halbertal, *Interpretive Revolutions*, 69–74.

29. Rabbi Ishmael's interpretation is based on the juxtaposition of the father and the husband in a single phrase ("between a man and his wife, and as between a father and his daughter"), which he interprets as referring to the condition in which both the father and the husband have the right to annul the woman's vows, i.e. when she is betrothed but still in her father's custody. This interpretation strictly limits the scope of the biblical law, determining that only the vows of a betrothed woman can be annulled.

30. Note that this midrashic quality is substantively different from, e.g., Mekhilta to Exodus 13:9, in which the TORAH commands that phylacteries be laid. There the Mekhilta's argument rests on a midrashic argument that identifies the biblical *totafot* as phylacteries, but this identification is not the goal of the derashah. The Mekhilta's interpretation of Exodus 21:20, on the other hand, engages HA-KATUV in an explicitly midrashic context.

31. This formula is very common in the Rabbi Ishmael midrashim, appearing over twenty times in the Mekhilta and over fifty times in the Sifre Numbers, but only four times in the Sifra, two of them in tractate Qedoshim.

32. This is a very common phrase, appearing dozens of times in the Rabbi Ishmael midrashim. There are five passages in the Sifra that contain the phrase *ba' ha-katuv* (HA-KATUV comes), none of which designates teaching as the goal.

33. See the discussion above, pp. 12–13.

34. On the tendency of better rabbinic manuscripts to attach prepositions to the following word see Kahana, *Prolegomena*, 133, and the literature cited there.

35. For the translation of *shelamim* as "well-being," see Jacob Milgrom, *Leviticus 1–16*, Anchor Bible 3 (New York: Doubleday, 1991), 220–21.

36. For a fuller discussion of this derashah, see below pp. 88–93.

37. In both instances, MS Oxford 151 quotes Numbers 5:6 as "איש ואישה" where the MT reads "איש או אישה"

38. On this text, see the discussion in Elias, "An Excellent Text," 124–5.

39. On this form, see Kahana, *Prolegomena*, 299.

40. See the full citations and references above, p. 20.

41. See Mishor, "Tense System," 259–71.

42. On this form, see above, n. 34.

43. Stern, *Midrash and Theory*, 32. This argument first appeared in David Stern, "Moses-Cide: Midrash and Contemporary Literary Criticism," *Prooftexts* 4 (1984): 203 n. 5.

44. See m. Avot 5.6 and parallels.

45. It should be clear that these statements are an "inside" description of the argument presented by the Rabbi Ishmael midrashim. From the "outside," the entire argument (especially the distinction between TORAH and HA-KATUV) is a midrashic construct.

Chapter 2

1. On the meaning of this term, and on this *middah* in particular, see below pp. 109–21.

2. The bracketed phrase does not appear in MS Vatican 32.

3. Rabbi Aharon Even Hayyim, *Middot Aharon*, quoted in Ostrovsky, *Ha-Middot*, 27.

4. There are no derashot of this kind in the Sifra.

5. The first part of the derashah is quoted according to the Horovitz-Rabin edition.

6. On these different meanings in biblical Hebrew, see Brown, Driver, and Briggs, *A Hebrew and English Lexicon of the Old Testament* (Oxford: Clarendon Press, 1962), 252 (the disjunctive sense is discussed at section 1, subsection d). On the two senses of *vav* in rabbinic Hebrew see J. N. Epstein, *Introduction to the Text of the Mishnah*, (Jerusalem: Magnes, 1964), 2.1050–64 (Hebrew).

7. See also Sifre Numbers §7, p. 12, the interpretation of "and there is no witness against her" (ועד אין בה) (Num 5:13).

8. This phrase is common in the Rabbi Ishmael midrashim—some fifty occurrences in the Mekhilta and over twenty in the Sifre Numbers. The Sifra is very interesting on this point. The phrase *lo' shama'nu* does appear in the Sifra, but its meaning and distribution are significant. In its three occurrences in Ḥova (pereq 1.8, 9, and 10; Weiss 16a), the phrase refers to an extra-scriptural tradition rather than a biblical verse, and the same is true of Tazria' (pereq 2.10; Weiss 61a). There are also fifteen occurrences in a single parasha of Qedoshim (10), all of which involve the formula "We have heard the punishment but we have not heard the warning" (or vice versa). Eight more occurrences are found in the formula "If two verses do not state this we have not heard." After sifting through all these occurrences, the bottom line is that by my reckoning there are two (!) derashot in the Sifra that employ the phrase "We have not heard" in a way similar to that of the Rabbi Ishmael midrashim: 'Emor pereq 14.9 (Weiss 102a) and 'Emor pereq 17.13 (Weiss 103a).

9. This is an oversimplification. The Sinai narrative contains different views regarding the speaker at Sinai; some sources describe a direct encounter between

God and Israel, and in others, Moses mediates. See Aryeh Toeg, *Lawgiving at Sinai* (Jerusalem: Magnes, 1977) (Hebrew) and, for a discussion that includes later traditions, Benjamin Sommer, "Revelation at Sinai in the Hebrew Bible and in Jewish Theology," *Journal of Religion* 79 (1999): 422–51.

10. This formula appears roughly a dozen times in the Mekhilta and three times in the Sifre Numbers. It appears once in Sifra Qedoshim pereq 9.12 (Weiss 92a), part of the Mekhilta de-'Arayot, an established part of the Rabbi Ishmael corpus. *Ki-shmu'o* is not to be confused with *bemashma'*, which indicates the possibility of one concept falling within the semantic purview of a broader category.

11. See below, 61–68

12. This form, and not כמשמעו, is also found in the Genizah copy of the Mekhilta. See Elias, "An Excellent Text," 68. I will employ this form throughout.

13. This formula occurs some 250 times in the Rabbi Ishmael midrashim, fourteen times in the Sifra.

14. On *talmud lomar*, see Bacher, *Exegetische Terminologie*, 1.199–200, who suggests that *lomar* behaves much like the biblical *le'mor*, introducing a citation. This view has gained widespread acceptance (see Eliyaqim Weissberg, "On *Talmud* and *Talmud Lomar*," *Leshonenu* 39 [1975]: 146–52 (Hebrew), and Boyarin, "From the Hidden Light," 13 n. 26), but it seems to me that the contrast to *shome'a 'ani* endows the phrase with a more dialogic sense than this explanation allows. The reader *hears* a possible interpretation, but Scripture teaches otherwise by *saying* "[verse]."

15. Among the passages that employ both *shome'a 'ani* and *ki-shmu'o* are: Mekhilta Pisha 5, p. 17 (Lauterbach 1.42); Mekhilta Pisha 10, p. 34, following MS Munich (Lauterbach 1.77); Mekhilta Pisha 17, p. 66 (Lauterbach 1.148); Mekhilta, Bahodesh 9, p. 239 (Lauterbach 2.276); Mekhilta Neziqin 7, p. 274 (twice; Lauterbach 3.61).

16. The Horovitz edition contains another example at Sifre Numbers §49, p. 52–3, the derashah to Numbers 7:13. However, Horovitz here follows the testimony of the Yalqut Shimoni. MS Vatican 32, a much better manuscript, does not contain the opposition between *shome'a 'ani* and *talmud lomar*, but rather the rare, non-polemic *shome'a 'ani* (שומע אני בניזחותא), that is, a *shome'a 'ani* whose proposed reading is accepted. On this form, see Kahana, *Prolegomena*, 167.

17. The form אף על פי (without a ש preceding the next word) is attested in the better manuscripts. See Kahana, *Prolegomena*, 147.

18. There is also one derashah in which *shome'a 'ani* is followed by an explanatory note:

"ויקם פרעה" (שמות יב ל): שומע אני בשלש שעות שכן דרך מלכים לעמוד בשלש שעות תלמוד לומר לילה.

"And Pharaoh arose in the night" (Exod 12:30): I could understand that he woke up in the third hour [of the morning] for it is the custom of kings to wake up in the third hour, [Scripture] teaches, saying "at night." (Mekhilta Pisha 13, p. 44; Lauterbach 1.99)

19. See Sifra Nedava pereq 2.10 (Weiss 4a). The Sifra rejects this interpretation but for a different reason than the one given in the Sifre Numbers.

20. Note that the argument of Deuteronomy 5:19 is opposed to the Sifre's argument. The verse follows the account of the Ten Commandments and reads: "The Lord spoke those words to your whole congregation at the mountain— those and no more." The last phrase is polemic, "a Deuteronomistic attempt to divest the Covenant Code of its authority by rejecting its Sinaitic pedigree" (Bernard Levinson, *Deuteronomy and the Hermeneutics of Legal Innovation* [Oxford and New York: Oxford University Press, 1997], 152). Deuteronomy is arguing

against an analogy between' Sinai and later revelations, including the Tent of Meeting, while the Sifre is quoting Deuteronomy in support of such an analogy.

21. See Yigael Yadin, *The Temple Scroll* (Jerusalem: Israel Exploration Society, 1983), 328–29.

22. Halbertal, *Interpretive Revolutions*, 178, and see his comments there, n. 4, where he discusses the evidence of the Dead Sea Scrolls.

23. The two exceptions are discussed above, 39–40.

24. There are significant differences between the Horovitz-Rabin edition (which is here cited) and MS Oxford 151 (particularly toward the end of the derashah), but in both the *shome'a 'ani* reading contrasts a very elaborate midrashic reading—which is the point of the discussion.

25. This is not the only difference. Rabbi Ishmael midrashim present the self-evident reading as untenable because the relevant interpretive context is not the discrete verse but Scripture as a whole, while the Sifra presents two readings of the same verse. That is, in the Mekhilta and Sifre Numbers, the *talmud lomar* introduces a new verse; in the Sifra, it returns to the verse being discussed.

26. On the translation of this passage I have consulted Jacob Neusner, *Sifra: An Analytic Translation* (Atlanta: Scholars Press, 1988), 2.312. The phrase "mountain-palm" is usually understood as a reference to a tree that gives little fruit, with support from m. Bikurim 1.3 ("First fruits may . . . [not] be brought from dates from the mountains").

27. Though the main body of the Sifra is not part of the Rabbi Ishmael corpus, the attribution to Rabbi Ishmael of a statement so fully in accord with the practices of the Mekhilta and the Sifre Numbers fits well with the heuristic principle of reading the tanna Rabbi Ishmael in conjunction with the midrashim. Again, this accord may be understood as a sign of historical fidelity or as consistent cultural representation, a *dramatis persona* that remains "in character" in different texts.

28. For a discussion of the employment and history of *ribbui* interpretation, see Michael Chernick, *Hermeneutical Studies in Talmudic and Midrashic Literatures*, (Lod, Israel: Habermann Institute, 1984), 79–126 (Hebrew).

29. The same logic applies to interpretations generated by the repetition of a root in the absolute construct and finite form (e.g., הכרת תכרת, המול ימול ובשל, מבושל). Since the finite verb suffices to convey the meaning of the sentence, the absolute construct is understood as a *ribbui*.

30. See Epstein, *Prolegomena*, 529.

31. Chernick, *Hermeneutical Studies*, 80–82.

32. Chernick, *Hermeneutical Studies*, 81.

33. See Sifre Numbers §123, p. 154. Chernick also assumes that the term *ribbui* can be applied to any derashah that interprets repetition, as in his discussion of m. Shevu'ot 2.5. This mishnah responds to the repetition of the phrase "and the fact has escaped his notice" in Leviticus 5:2–3: "Rabbi Ishmael says: 'the fact has escaped his notice,' 'the fact has escaped his notice'—[the phrase is] repeated to teach that he becomes liable both because the uncleanness is forgotten of him and because the Temple is forgotten of him" (m. Shevu'ot 2.5; Danby, p. 411). Chernick states that Rabbi Ishmael understands the repetition as a *ribbui*, using the redundancy to expand the scope of the halakhic ruling. However, the term *ribbui* does not appear in this mishnah, and there is no reason to assume that the argument is a *ribbui*, since the Rabbi Ishmael midrashim often interpret redundancies without resorting to the term *ribbui*, as Sifre Numbers §123 itself demonstrates.

Chapter 3

1. Both Trubetzkoy's letter and Jakobson's response quoted in Linda R. Waugh, "Marked and Unmarked: A Choice Between Unequals in Semiotic Structure," *Semiotica* 38 (1982): 300.

2. Boyarin, *Intertextuality and the Reading of Midrash*, 27.

3. See, e.g., Samely, "Between Scripture and Its Rewording," and Brewer, *Techniques and Assumptions.*

4. On this form, see Kahana, *Prolegomena*, p. 129, and Bar-Asher, "Preliminary Investigations," §8.

5. This statement does not imply that the Rabbi Ishmael midrashim do not consider the Torah to be perfect, only that perfection is not what sanctions the interpretation of textual difficulties.

6. This derashah was discussed briefly above, p. 30, and see the textual notes there.

7. On this dispute, see Epstein, *Prolegomena*, 567.

8. With the exception of *shome‘a 'ani* (discussed above, pp. 39–43), these formulas appear in the Sifra as well and cannot be considered unique to the Rabbi Ishmael midrashim. This does not mean that they function in the same way in the Sifra, a matter for separate investigation.

9. See the list of midrashic models in Miguel Pérez Fernández, "Modelos de argumentación en la exégesis de los tannaítas," *Sefarad* 47 (1987): 363–81.

10. This is not the only hermeneutical style of the Sifra, but it figures prominently in that work and other Rabbi Aqiva midrashim.

11. Jacob Milgrom characterizes both "the breast of elevation" and "the thigh of the contribution" as "stock expressions," Milgrom, *Leviticus 1–16*, 432.

12. Following pseudo-Raabad, *ad loc.*

13. The meaning of the last statement may be clarified with an example from linguistics. Suppose a grammarian asserted that all English nouns are masculine in gender and proceeded to describe the morphological and syntactic behavior of masculine English nouns: masculine nouns usually form the plural with an *s* suffix (house: houses) though some plural forms are based on a change in the vowel stem (mouse: mice); masculine nouns take *a* (or *an*) as their indefinite particle in the singular; *the* is the definite particle for both singular and plural forms; masculine nouns follow the adjective that modifies them ("a big boy"), but precede the adjective when joined by a copula ("the boy is big"), and so forth. Our grammarian can, theoretically, write a full and complete grammatical account of masculine nouns in English, except that the designation "masculine" is meaningless without (at minimum) another category of nouns (feminine) that can be distinguished from the male nouns. Without such a category, there can be no markedness and the nouns are, with regard to grammatical gender, nouns "as such." In the same way, it makes no sense to speak of the Sifra considering every word to be hermeneutically marked. This is no marking at all. See also the discussion of biblical omnisignificance below, pp. 54–55.

14. Brewer, *Techniques and Assumptions*, 166–67.

15. Samely, "Scripture's Implicature," 178; emphasis in the original.

16. See Genesis Rabbah 1:14, *Midrash Bereshit Rabbah*, ed. J. Theodor and Ch. Albeck (Jerusalem: Wahrman, 1965), 1.12. Samely cites Mekhilta Neziqin 10, p. 283 (Lauterbach 3.80), but the most critical element, the *'et*, is not found in MS Oxford 151 and the Munich Mekhilta, two of the most important textual witnesses to the passage. The *'et* in question was discussed at some length by

Menahem Kahana in his response to B. Z. Wacholder's argument that the Mekhilta is post-tannaitic. See Wacholder, "The Date of the Mekilta de-Rabbi Ishmael,"
Hebrew Union College Annual 39 (1968): 117–44, and Kahana's decisive rebuttal
in "The Critical Editions of Mekhilta De-Rabbi Ishmael in Light of the Genizah
Fragments," *Tarbiz* 55 (1986): 489–524 (Hebrew), and especially his comments
at the top of p. 517. Aside from the controversial *nota accusativi*, see Samely's
assertion that rabbinic interpretation cannot accept at face value "the mild insin-
cerity of irony or hyperbole" ("Scripture's Implicature," 192). This may be true
in some cases, but cannot be said of "the Rabbis" as such, as the following explicit
attribution of hyperbole to Scripture indicates: "The cities are great and fortified
up to heaven" (Deut 1:28): Rabban Gamliel says, Scripture uses hyperbole (לשון
הבאי) here" (Sifre Deuteronomy §25, p. 35; Hammer, p. 46).

Samely devotes much of his analysis to the textual phenomena I have characterized as hermeneutic markers, to which he applies Paul Grice's theory that, in
conversation, certain maxims are employed that determine the way a speaker's words are understood (Paul Grice, "Logic and Conversation," in *Studies in
the Way of Words* [Cambridge, Mass.: Harvard University Press, 1989], 22–40). I
would question whether Grice's work is a suitable tool of analysis for the midrashic phenomena described by Samely. The power of Grice's argument lies
in our intimate but often unarticulated familiarity with the rules of conversation:
by laying bare the logical and pragmatic presuppositions that underlie conversation, Grice taps our intuitive knowledge of how conversation proceeds and
makes it explicit. Samely, however, applies this procedure to a type of conversation that is profoundly unfamiliar. Neither attaching meaning to the particle *'et*
nor the impossibility of recognizing irony are typical modes of human discourse.
As a result, making explicit the assumptions that underlie these practices does
not produce a Gricean recognition of something intuitively known. Samely uses
the analysis of ordinary language philosophy, when the foreignness of the midrashic texts is better suited for the analytic tools of anthropology. (I would like
to thank Dr. Amichai Kronfeld, who first suggested to me the relevance of Grice's
work to my analysis of midrash. When I subsequently became familiar with
Samely's work, I was able to appreciate it more fully and, I hope, understand it.)

17. James L. Kugel, *The Idea of Biblical Poetry: Parallelism and its History* (New
Haven, Conn. and London: Yale University Press, 1981), 104. For an analysis of
the later career of this concept, see Yaakov Elman, "The Rebirth of Omnisignificant Biblical Exegesis in the Nineteenth and Twentieth Centuries," *Jewish Studies Internet Journal* 2 (2003): 1–40.

18. One such statement, at least in what it implies, has already been encountered, namely, Rabbi Ishmael's assertion that synonymity is not, in and of itself,
grounds for interpretation, rather "TORAH spoke using two expressions" (Sifre
Numbers §23, p. 27).

19. In addition to the derashah discussed here, this formula appears once in
the Mekhilta (Pisḥa 3, p. 10; Lauterbach 1.24) and once more in the Sifre Numbers (§152, p. 197). It does not occur in the Sifra.

20. Discussed above, pp. 49–51.

21. David Weiss Halivni argues that tannaitic literature exhibits a tendency to
see biblical *vav*s as conjunctive, though this derashah indicates that, at least in
some quarters, the difference between the *vav*s was clear (David Weiss Halivni, "The
Bavli's Tendency to See the *Vav* as Conjunctive *Vav*," in *Issues in Mishnaic Hebrew:
Summaries of Papers Presented in the Workshop on the Grammar and Lexicon of Mishnaic
Hebrew* [Jerusalem: Institute for Advanced Studies, 1991], 51–52 [Hebrew]).

22. The only other occurrence of this formula is in Mekhilta Kaspa 20, pp. 335–36 (Lauterbach 3.188). It does not occur in the Sifra.

23. Mentioned briefly above, p. 3, as an example of disputes with no halakhic ramifications, and see also the comments made there regarding the manuscript version.

24. On the meaning of *'elohim* in this context, see Nahum Sarna, *The Jewish Publication Society Torah Commentary: Exodus* (Philadelphia and New York: Jewish Publication Society, 1991), 120 and the literature cited at 252 n. 16.

25. Samely, "Scripture's Implicature," 174. Samely makes the claim in the context of an aggadic passage from Genesis Rabbah, where it may well be accurate.

26. The phrases "from among the Gentiles" and "from among Israel" mean simply Gentiles and Israel, respectively. The language echoes that of Leviticus 25:44: "Such male and female slaves as you may have, it is <u>from</u> the nations round about you <u>from</u> whom you may purchase male and female slaves." The root *l-q-ḥ* in Mishnaic Hebrew is semantically equivalent to *q-n-h* in biblical Hebrew, so the slave who is נלקח מן הנוי refers to a gentile slave, as does מאת הגוים מהם תקנו. On the semantic development from *l-q-ḥ* to *q-n-h*, see Azzan Yadin, "A Greek Witness to the Semantic Shift לקח-Buy," *Hebrew Studies* 43 (2002): 31–37, and the literature cited therein.

27. This phrase reflects the rabbinic understanding of the verse. The Bible refers to slaves from among the aliens residing with the Israelites.

28. Nor to many commentators. See the circuitous arguments of Rabbi Naphtali Zvi Yehudah Berlin (the *Natziv*), *Mekhilta with Birkat ha-Natziv Commentary*, 256.

29. Saul Lieberman, *Hellenism in Jewish Palestine* (New York: Jewish Theological Seminary, 1962), 61.

30. On *mufneh lehaqish* as typical of the Rabbi Ishmael midrashim, see Epstein, *Prolegomena*, 522–23. The formula appears some fourteen times all told in the Mekhilta and Sifre Numbers, and once in the Sifra Qedoshim pereq 10.9 (Weiss 92a), which contains a great deal of Rabbi Ishmael terminology. For a discussion of the types of "displacements" that allow a term to be considered *mufneh* and of the development of the technique in amoraic literature, see Michael Chernick, "The Essence of *Mufneh*: Developments from the tannaitic Period to the End of the Talmudic Period," *Proceedings of the Tenth World Congress of Jewish Studies* (1989): 3.47–53 (Hebrew), and, more fully, Chernick, *Gezerah Shavah: Its Various Forms in Midrashim and Talmudic Sources* (Lod, Israel: Habermann Institute, 1994) (Hebrew), 38–60.

31. G. F. Moore, *Judaism in the First Centuries of the Christian Era: The Age of the Tannaim* (Cambridge, Mass.: Harvard University Press, 1927–30), 1.248.

32. Cited in David Instone Brewer, *Techniques and Assumptions*, 1, a work that deals largely with halakhic midrash. Arnold Goldberg also endorses this view, though most of his studies concern aggadic interpretation.

33. Stern, *Midrash and Hermeneutics*, 18.

34. See above, pp. 38–39.

35. In biblical Hebrew, *'olam* means "eternity" and not "world." It is only in Mishnaic (and later) Hebrew that *'olam* means "world."

36. *Oxford English Dictionary*, 1971, 1638 of compact edition. The terms "symbolic" and "figurative" can mean very different things in contemporary discussions. For the purpose of this chapter, they are (as they were for Philo, Clement, and others) near synonyms and can be used interchangeably. The distinction between literal and figurative has been challenged by thinkers in various philosophical and literary traditions. The present discussion does not suggest that the

literal-figurative distinction is given or even tenable, rather that it was a culturally viable hermeneutical option for Bible interpreters in the eastern Mediterranean in the first centuries of the common era. In other words, the subject at hand is the literal-figurative distinction as a cultural practice that exists in a particular historical context.

37. Clement combines verses from Leviticus 11 and Deuteronomy 14.

38. Clement of Alexandria, *Stromata* V, chap. 8 (Alexander Roberts and James Donaldson, eds., *Ante-Nicene Fathers, Volume 2: Fathers of the Second Century: Hermas, Tatian, Athenagoras, Theophilus, and Clement of Alexandria* [Peabody, Mass.: Hendrickson, 1999], 456. References to patristic texts will be to this edition, cited as ANF, unless otherwise noted).

39. Gerald Bruns, "The Problem of Figuration in Antiquity," in *Hermeneutics: Questions and Prospects*, ed. Gary Shapiro and Alan Sica (Amherst: University of Massachusetts Press, 1984), 149.

40. Written with a lowercase *g*, "gnostic" means only "knower."

41. See, e.g., *Stromata* VI, chap. 16, "The Gnostic Exposition of the Decalogue" (ANF 511–515). For an explicit contrast between plain sense and Clement's gnostic reading, see the comment of Bertrand de Margerie, "la méthode gnostique de Clément n'est pas une méthode critique cherchant à déterminer le sense littéral des textes . . .," *Introduction à l'histoire de l'exégèse* (Paris: Cerf, 1980; volume 1: *Les Pères grecs et orientaux*), 98–99.

42. This derashah is also found in the Mekhilta Neziqin 6, p. 270 (Lauterbach 3.53–54) and Mekhilta Neziqin 13, p. 293 (Lauterbach 3.102), though these passages do not record the contrary view, which is important to the current discussion. See also the discussion of this passage in Elias, "An Excellent Text," 139–40. On the "rabbinization" of this biblical passage, see Halbertal, *Interpretive Revolutions*, 87–90.

43. Following Finkelstein's reading; MS Oxford 151 has conflated two traditions at this point.

44. The odd syntax of the Hebrew phrase אחד מן הדברים שהיה ר' ישמעאל דורש מן התורה במשל (one of the matters that Rabbi Ishmael explicated from the Torah by *mashal*) as opposed to the more natural אחד מן הדברים [בתורה] שהיה ר' ישמעאל דורש במשל (one of the matters in the Torah that Rabbi Ishmael explicated by *mashal*) may emphasize that the *mashal* is מן התורה, "from Torah," an expression of Rabbi Ishmael's reticence to adopt an ungrounded allegorical approach even in these instances.

45. Hammer, p. 471 n. 11.

46. The symmetry is not perfect, since the formula used in the second derashah is *shome'a 'ani* and not *ki-shmu'o*, but the structure of the argument is identical, and the two formulas often appear in tandem.

47. These terms were suggested to me by Daniel Boyarin.

48. The idea that "the Rabbis" were oblivious to context has been challenged by Christine Hayes in "Displaced Self-Perceptions: The Deployment of *Minim* and Romans in *B. Sanhedrin* 90b-91a," in *Religious and Ethnic Communities in Later Roman Palestine*, ed. Hayim Lapin, Studies and Texts in Jewish History and Culture, 5 (Bethesda, Md.: University Press of Maryland, 1998), 249–89. Hayes argues that "rabbis of late antiquity felt a deep ambivalence about non-contextual or midrashic methods of exegesis" (249). Hayes deals primarily with Babylonian amoraim, and so my discussion of *ki-shmu'o* complements her finding (see particularly 252–53). It should be emphasized that my discussion of contextual and non-contextual meaning—like Hayes's—should not be confused with the very different terminology of *peshat* and *derash*, the traditional understanding of which has been challenged by David Halivni in *Peshat and Derash*.

49. This formula appears some thirty times (all told) in the Mekhilta and the Sifre Numbers, but only once in the Sifra, in tractate Qedoshim (pereq 10.2; Weiss 92b), part of the "Ishmaelian" Mekhilta de-'Arayot.

50. Appears as Exodus 20:26 in some Bibles.

51. This argument seems quite forced—does the Bible need to issue separate prohibitions for ascent and descent? The key issue for the current discussion, however, is not the argument itself but the grounds on which Rabbi Ishmael rejects it.

52. For a fuller discussion, see Azzan Yadin, "The Hammer on the Rock: Polysemy and the school of Rabbi Ishmael," *Jewish Studies Quarterly* 10 (2003): 1–17.

53. This passage, and particularly the image of the hammer striking the rock, has become a powerful image of midrash itself. When more than half a century ago Nahum Glatzer published an anthology of aggadic midrash in English, he titled it *Hammer on the Rock* (*Hammer on the Rock: A Short Midrash Reader* [New York: Schocken, 1948]). More recent scholarship has focused on parallels between the polysemic view championed in this pericope and kindred currents in contemporary literary theory. See, in particular, the exchange of David Stern and Susan Handelman: David Stern, "Moses-Cide: Midrash and Contemporary Literary Criticism," *Prooftexts* 4 (1984): 193–204; Susan Handelman, "Fragments of the Rock: Contemporary Literary Theory and the Study of Rabbinic Texts—a Response to David Stern," *Prooftexts* 5 (1985): 73–95; David Stern, "Literary Theory or Literary Homilies? A Response to Susan Handelman," *Prooftexts* 5 (1985): 96–103.

54. For a survey of a number of rabbinic positions regarding this derashah see Daniel Boyarin, "Shattering the Logos; or, the Talmuds and the Genealogy of Indeterminacy," in *The Talmud Yerushalmi and Graeco-Roman Culture III*, ed. Peter Schäfer, Texte und Studien zum antiken Judentum 93 (Tübingen: Mohr Siebeck, 2002), 273–99.

55. First suggested in Stern, "Literary Criticism or Literary Homilies?" 102–3 n. 2. More fully developed in idem, *Midrash and Theory*, 18.

56. Hananel Mack, "Torah Has Seventy Aspects—The Development of a Saying" (Hebrew), in *Rabbi Mordechai Breuer Festschrift: Collected Papers in Jewish Studies*, ed. Moshe Bar-Asher (Jerusalem: Akademon, 1992), 2.449–62. See also Richard Sarason, "Interpreting Rabbinic Biblical Interpretation: the Problem of Midrash, Again," in *Hesed ve-Emet: Studies in Honor of Ernest S. Frerichs*, ed. Jodi Magness and Seymour Gitin, Brown Judaic Studies 320 (Atlanta: Scholars Press, 1998), 133–54.

57. Mack, "Seventy," 450. Mack also mentions the Sifre Numbers §42, p. 47, but this entire section is a late addition, as Horovitz demonstrates in his notes *ad loc.*

58. Horovitz-Rabin's ב is a typographic error.

59. This is the version of Horovitz-Rabin; MS Oxford 151 contrasts God's ability to produce distinct enunciations simultaneously with man's inability to *hear* from two speakers at the same time.

60. The derashah is divided from the one discussed above by a brief gloss of the second half of Exodus 15:11 ("Who is like you, majestic in Holiness"), but obviously continues the motif of God's speech.

61. On the reverberations of this derashah in rabbinic and later medieval literature see Ezra Zion Melammed, "'Observe' and 'Remember' in One Utterance," trans. by Gershon Levi, in *The Ten Commandments in History and Tradition*, ed. Ben-Zion Segal (Jerusalem: Magnes, 1990), 191–218.

62. See Horovitz's notes, *ad loc.*

63. The last of these exceptions is not biblical but a rabbinic interpretation

based on the proximity of the verses prohibiting *sha'aṭnez* and commanding tassels. See b. Yevamot 3b-4a.

64. See Moshe Weinfeld, *Deuteronomy 1–11*, Anchor Bible 5 (New York: Doubleday, 1991), 302–3.

65. The first-person plural form may reflect a communal, Sinaitic understanding of the divine communication. The Mekhilta's reading of שתים זו שמענו instead of the MT שתים זו שמעתי is attested in several biblical MSS.

66. These are admittedly late sources, the *Yalqut Shimoni* and *Editio Princeps* (see Horovitz's critical apparatus to p. 229, line 9).

67. Sifre Deuteronomy §233, pp. 265–66; Hammer, 242–43.

68. This is precisely the function of Psalm 62:12 when cited by Abbaye in b. Sanhedrin.

69. This gloss is at odds with the masoretic pointing of the prooftext, which reads כה דְבָרִי (thus is my word) while the Bavli's glosses "so each and every statement," as though the verse reads כה דְבָרַי (thus are my words) or even כל דְבָרַי (all my words). This discrepancy is noteworthy because the plural reading "my words" is preserved in the LXX (οὕτως οἱ λόγοι μου λέγει Κύριος), and it may be that there are different vocalization traditions underlying the two versions of the derashah. On the biblical traditions reflected in rabbinic glosses, see Menahem Kahana, "The Biblical Text Reflected in MS Vatican 32 to Sifre Numbers and Deuteronomy," in *Meḥqere Talmud I*, ed. David Rosenthal and Yaakov Sussmann (Jerusalem: Magnes, 1990), 1–10 (Hebrew); Yeshayahu Maori, "Rabbinic Midrash as Evidence for Textual Variants in the Hebrew Bible: History and Practice," in *Modern Scholarship in the Study of Torah: Contributions and Limitations*, ed. Shalom Carmy (New York: New York Orthodox Forum, 1991), 101–29.

70. For example, in the Sifre Numbers §23 (p. 27), "'He shall abstain from *yayin* [wine] and *shekhar* [intoxicant]' (Num 6:3): But *yayin* is *shekhar* and *shekhar* is *yayin*, except that the Torah spoke in two expressions (*leshonot*)."

71. See Mack, "Seventy," 452, for additional examples of this formula.

72. Solomon Schechter, "The Mekhilta Deuteronomy, Pericope *Re'eh*," in *Tif'eret Yisra'el: Festschrift zu Israel Lewy's siebzigsten Geburtstag*, ed. M. Brann and J. Elbogen (Breslau: Marcus, 1911), 187–92 (Hebrew).

73. Schechter, "Mekhilta Deuteronomy," 189. The bracketed words are lacking in the manuscript and have been completed following Saul Lieberman's reconstruction in *Tosefta ki-feshutah, Nashim* (New York and Jerusalem: Jewish Theological Seminary, 1993), 700 (to Sotah chap. 8).

74. And see the recent discussion in Menahem (Marc) Hirshman, *Torah for the Entire World* (Tel Aviv: Hakibbutz Hameuḥad, 1999), 108–13 (Hebrew).

75. The terminology reflects the framework discussion of Sanhedrin 34a, which is concerned with the derivation of multiple legal justifications from a single verse (which is permitted) and the derivation of a single legal justification from multiple verses (which is prohibited).

76. See Kugel, *In Potiphar's House*; Jeffrey L. Rubinstein, *Talmudic Stories: Narrative Art, Composition and Culture* (Baltimore and London: Johns Hopkins University Press, 1999), esp. 105–38.

77. How this connection is made cannot be said with certitude, but it may have been motivated by the similarity between the phrase *kol divrei ha-torah* in Deuteronomy 27:8 and *koh (kol?) devarai* in Jeremiah 23:29, if that is indeed the vocalization that underlies the gloss of the passage in Sanhedrin 34a. It is also possible that the school of Rabbi Ishmael held that the *torah* written on the altar

was the Decalogue, in which case the *davar/dibber* similarity may have played a part as well.

78. For a discussion of this transformation, see Boyarin, "Shattering the Logos."

Chapter 4

1. Neziqin 8, p. 277; Lauterbach 3.67.

2. One of the University of Pennsylvania Press readers pointed out to me that Mekhilta Baḥodesh 8, p. 232 (Lauterbach 2.257–58), contains a series of *heqqeshim* involving the honor accorded one's parents and the honor accorded God, *heqqeshim* generated by different verses rather than proximate elements within a verse. This is indeed unusual, but the argument is aggadic—no legal conclusions result, and this may explain the laxer mode of argument.

3. On *gezerah shavah*, its use, and its development from tannaitic to amoraic literature, see Chernick, *Gezerah Shavah*. The formula appears roughly a dozen times in the Rabbi Ishmael midrashim. In the Sifra it appears only once, in tractate Qedoshim pereq 10.9 (Weiss 92b), a section full of Rabbi Ishmael terminology. On the meaning of the term *gezerah shavah*, see Lieberman, *Hellenism in Jewish Palestine*, 58–60.

4. For a discussion of this problem, see Yitzhak Gilat, "The Development of the *Gezerah Shavah*," in *Studies in the Development of Halakhah* (Ramat Gan: Bar Ilan University Press, 1992), 365–73 (Hebrew).

5. See above, pp. 59–60.

6. See the comments of Kosman, "More on Associative Thought," 449.

7. The reading *qol* is to be preferred to *qal* on both philological and linguistic grounds. *Qol* is the reading of the better manuscripts, and makes better linguistic sense since both *qol* and *ḥomer* are abstract nouns designating quality. See Daniel Boyarin's linguistic notes to Avraham Shoshana's edition of the Sifra, 1.1 n. 1.

8. This formula appears roughly a dozen times in Rabbi Ishmael midrashim, but not once in the Sifra.

9. The term "weighty" is meant to reflect the etymological sense of *ḥomer*, whose primary sense is "heaviness," but comes to mean "seriousness" or "importance," much like English "grave."

10. See, e.g., Louis Jacobs, "The Aristotelian Syllogism and the Qal wa-Homer," *Journal of Jewish Studies* 4 (1953): 154–57.

11. On the employment and development of *kelal u-feraṭ*, see Chernick, *Hermeneutical Studies*, especially 15–29, which address the tannaitic sources.

12. For a full discussion of the different formulas, see Moshe Ostrovsky, *Ha-Middot she-Hatorah Nidreshet Bahen* (Jerusalem: Mosad Harav Kook, 1924), 173–83. It is doubtful that the full-blown typology that Ostrovsky outlines was known to the tannaitic interpreters. For a discussion of the historical development of this formula, see Norman Solomon, "Extensive and Restrictive Interpretation of Terms in Rabbinic Hermeneutics," in *Jewish Law Association Studies* (Chico, Calif.: Scholars Press, 1985), 1.125–39.

13. And compare also the need for HA-KATUV to adjust a particular matter before the interpreter can proceed in the Sifre Numbers §37:

"כל דבר שהיה בכלל ויצא לידון בדבר החדש אי אתה יכול להחזירו לכללו עד
שיחזירנו הכתוב לכללות דברי ר' אליעזר"

"Every statement that was part of its general statement and it goes off to discuss a new matter, you cannot return it to its general statement until HA-KATUV returns it to its general statement, the words of Rabbi Eliezer" (Sifre Numbers §37, pp. 40–41).

14. This formula, which also appears in Sifre Numbers §127, p. 165, does not occur in the Sifra.

15. For a textual discussion of this passage, see Ben Zion Rosenfeld, "Rabbi Yose the Galilean and the Rabbinic Leadership at the Outbreak of the Bar Kochba Revolt," *Sidra* 11 (1995): 92–94.

16. The bracketed words are added in superscript.

17. שנית added in superscript.

18. On *ribbui* see above, pp. 45–47.

19. See *Sifre Numbers with the Commentary of Rabbenu Hillel*, ed., Shachne Koleditzky (Jerusalem: n.p., 1983), 73b (Hebrew).

20. The entire passage is polemic, as Rabbi Aqiva and Rabbi Tarfon are unable to provide a justification for their own decisions. Furthermore, the phrase 'קפץ ר עקיבא ואמר—"Rabbi Aqiva jumped up and said"—may well be pejorative, following Lieberman's characterization of *qafatz* as the action of "a scholar who volunteers an opinion in the academy (or makes an ill-considered statement)," Saul Lieberman, *Texts and Studies* (New York: Ktav, 1974), 211–12. The insertion of C may be an attempt to emphasize Rabbi Aqiva's inability to respond to Rabbi Yose's query, sharpening the polemic tone.

21. Note that this is one of the sections (§§134–41) that do not exhibit the terminology, names of sages, and other characteristics typical of the Rabbi Ishmael midrashim.

22. Heschel, *Theology of Ancient Judaism*, 1.12.

23. Susan Handelman, *The Slayers of Moses* (Albany: State University of New York Press, 1982).

24. See the collection of essays in Peter Ochs and Nancy Levene, eds., *Textual Reasonings: Jewish Philosophy and Text Study at the End of the Twentieth Century* (Grand Rapids, Mich.: Eerdmans, 2002).

25. Umberto Eco, *The Role of the Reader: Explorations in the Semiotics of Texts* (Bloomington: Indiana University Press, 1979). My discussion of Eco is indebted to Scott Simpkins, "Reeling in the Signs: Unlimited Semiosis and the Agenda of Literary Semiotics," *VS: Quaderni di Studi Semiotici* 55–56 (1990): 153–57 and idem, lecture 4 of his *Critical Semiotics* series, http://www.chass.utoronto.ca/epc/srb/cyber/sim4.html.

26. Eco, *Role*, 3.

27. Eco, *Role*, 7.

28. Eco, *Role*, 8.

29. Eco, *Role*, 9.

30. Lévi-Strauss in an interview with Paolo Caruso, quoted in Eco, *Role*, 4.

31. Eco, *Role*, 9.

32. Umberto Eco, "Joyce, Semiosis and Semiotics," in *Limits of Interpretation* (Bloomington: Indiana University Press, 1990), 148.

33. It is important to distinguish between infinite and unlimited. The set of whole numbers is infinite but it nonetheless excludes fractions. In the same way, Eco argues that there could be infinite legitimate readings but others that are illegitimate.

34. Eco, *Limits of Interpretation*, 7

Chapter 5

1. Porton, *The Traditions of Rabbi Ishmael*, 2.64.

2. For the Hebrew text, see Avraham Shoshana, Sifra, vol. 1, with linguistic notes by Daniel Boyarin. English translations can be found in Porton, *The Traditions of Rabbi Ishmael*, 2.63–81; W. S. Towner, "Hermeneutical Systems of Hillel and the Tannaim: A Fresh Look," *Hebrew Union College Annual* 53 (1982): 101–35; and Brewer, *Techniques and Assumptions*, 226–28, which I have consulted in my own translation.

3. On the attempts to harmonize the list with its introductory statement, see Ostrovsky, *Ha-Middot*, 20–26, who surveys the solutions offered by classical commentators.

4. On the significance of genre distinctions, see Daniel Boyarin, "On the Status of the Tannaitic Midrashim: A Critique of Jacob Neusner's Latest Contribution to Midrashic Studies," *Journal of the American Oriental Society* 112 (1992): 455–65.

5. Porton, *The Traditions of Rabbi Ishmael*, 4.201–5

6. I have omitted from the list the following (cited according to Ms. Oxford):

זאת היא מדה טובה בתורה כל כלל ופרט שדרך הדין לוקה בו נתקיימו זה וזה אל

תלקה דרך הדין (ספרי במדבר ח, עמ' 15)

It seems to me that מדה טובה is different from מדה.

7. The bracketed phrase does not appear in MS Vatican 32.

8. And see also Mekhilta, Baḥodesh 9, p. 238 (Lauterbach 2.275).

9. MS Oxford reads מיתות.

10. As noted by Friedmann, *Mekhilta*, 70a n. 15.

11. On the superiority of MS Oxford, see Kahana, *Manuscripts of the Halakhic Midrashim*, 38–39. Lauterbach, in a curious compromise, includes "thirteen" in his Hebrew text, but omits it from his translation on the facing page.

12. My analysis is based on Judah Goldin, *The Munich Manuscript of the Mekilta*, Early Hebrew Manuscripts in Facsimile 7 (Copenhagen: Rosenkilde and Bagger, 1980), 19 *recto*.

13. Goldin, *Munich Mekilta*, introduction, p. 16.

14. Jacobs, "The Aristotelian Syllogism and the Qal wa-Homer."

15. Jacobs, "The Talmudic Hermeneutical Rule of 'Binyan 'Abh' and J. S. Mill's 'Method of Agreement,'" *Journal of Jewish Studies* 4 (1953): 59–64.

16. Jacobs, "Binyan 'Abh," 59.

17. Especially Adolf Schwarz, who wrote a series of studies on the *middot*.

18. David Daube, "Rabbinic Methods of Interpretation and Hellenistic Rhetoric," *Hebrew Union College Annual* 22 (1949) 239–64; Lieberman, *Hellenism in Jewish Palestine*, 47–82. The quotation is from Lieberman, *Hellenism in Jewish Palestine*, 54.

19. Lieberman, *Hellenism in Jewish Palestine*, 58; emphasis added. See also Louis Finkelstein, *Sifra on Leviticus*, 5 vols. (New York and Jerusalem: Jewish Theological Seminary, 1983–91), 1.147–153 (Hebrew).

20. Rabbi David Cohen, *Qol ha-Nevua*, (Jerusalem: Mosad Harav Kook, 1979); see also Dov Schwarz, "A Unique Hebrew Logic in the Teachings of *haRav haNazir*," *Higayon* 2 (1993): 9–28 (Hebrew).

21. Some scholars argue that b. Bava Metzia 104a demonstrates that midrashic canons were applied to non-scriptural texts. In this passage, a number of Sages are said to דורש לשון הדיוט, which could be translated as "interpreted secular

contracts using the methods of Torah interpretation." In fact, none of the examples in the Talmud involves the application of hermeneutical argument to a non-scriptural text; rather, the question is whether a legal text containing nonrabbinic formulations can be accepted as authoritative. On this passage, see Halivni, *Peshat and Derash*, 161; and Adiel Schremer, "'[T]he[y] did not Read in the Sealed Book': Qumran Halakhic Revolution and the Emergence of Torah Study in Second Temple Judaism," in *Historical Perspectives: From the Hasmoneans to Bar Kokhba in Light of the Dead Sea Scrolls*, ed. David Goodblatt, Avital Pinnick, and Daniel R. Schwartz, Studies on the Texts of the Desert of Judah 37 (Leiden: Brill, 2000), 105–26, particularly 120–21.

22. Following the numbering of the list above, p. 100.

23. See above, pp. 86–88.

24. Chernick, *Hermeneutical Studies*, 15.

25. This dynamic is also visible in interpretive techniques not designated as *middot*. When the Sifre Numbers §124 states that, "A *ribbui* that follows another *ribbui* indicates a limitation," it is transforming an open-ended interpretive principle into one that limits the freedom of the interpreter. See the discussion of *ribbui* above, pp. 45–47.

26. For fuller discussion of this issue, see Azzan Yadin, "*Shnei Ketuvim* and Rabbinic Intermediation," *Journal for the Study of Judaism* 33 (2002): 386–410.

27. Shoshana, Sifra, 1.2. And compare:

זו מדה בתורה: שני כתובים זה כנגד זה והרי הם סותרים זה על ידי זה יתקיימו
במקומם עד שיבא כתוב אחר ויכריע ביניהם.

This is the version that appears in Zvi Meir Rabinovitz, *Ginze Midrash: The Oldest Forms of Rabbinic Midrashim according to Genizah Manuscripts* (Tel Aviv: Tel Aviv University Press, 1976), 30 (Hebrew).

28. Most commentators understand the contradiction of the verses as revolving aroung the type of sacrifice, but it seems to me the more fundamental difference is the location of the sacrifice. Exodus states explicitly that, "in every place where I cause My name to be mentioned I will come to you and bless you" (Exod 20:24), suggesting that sacrifice can take place anywhere. In Deuteronomy, the sacrifice is part of the centralization of the cult. Whatever the precise meaning of the contradiction, no third verse is adduced to resolve it.

29. The relative ש is omitted, as often in MS Vatican 32. See Kahana, *Prolegomena*, 152–3.

30. My translation mirrors the logic of the rabbinic argument, not the semantics of biblical Hebrew.

31. This admittedly awkward designation for the *middah* is preferable to the common Hebrew shorthand, *shnei ketuvim* (two verses), since the derashot that resolve scriptural contradictions without recourse to a third verse employ this phrase as well.

32. A Genizah text lists derashot that resolve contradictory verses in an ad hoc manner, without reference to a third verse. See *Batei Midrashot*, ed. Shlomo Aharon Wertheimer (Jerusalem: Ketav-yad ve-sefer, 1988), 1.245–59.

33. Mekhilta Pisḥa 4, p. 13 (Lauterbach 1.32); Mekhilta Baḥodesh 9, pp. 238–39 (Lauterbach 2.275); Sifre Numbers §58, pp. 55–56.

34. Mekhilta Pisḥa 4, p. 13 (Lauterbach 1.32). It is common for derashot that exhibit the characteristics of one school to appear in the corpora of the other, sometimes changing their terminology to suit the interpretive style of the "host." See Goldberg, "The Phrase *Davar 'Aḥer* in the Halakhic Midrashim," 99–107.

35. Miguel Pérez Fernández , "Herméneutica de los tannaítas. La exégesis introducida con *Lmmh N'mr*," *Sefarad* 46 (1986): 391–96.

36. Kahana (*Prolegomena*, 153 [§25.10]) cites this passage as an example of MS Vatican 32's tendency to omit the relative ש (מגיד הכת׳ היה משה נכנס ועומד באהל), but the ש is visible and by the same hand as the rest of the passage (p. 97 of the Maqor facsimile edition).

37. Meir Ish-Shalom (Friedmann), *Sifra, der älteste Midrasch zu Levitikus* (Breslau: M. & H. Marcus, 1915; reprint, Jerusalem: n.p., 1967).

38. Friedmann, *Sifra*, 27.

39. David Henshke, "On the Sages' Approach to Scriptural Contradictions," *Sidra* 10 (1994): 39–55 (Hebrew).

40. Henshke, "The Sages' Approach," 45.

41. Henshke (p. 45) mentions this derashah in his article and rightly states that the Sifra "does not see a contradiction between 'Tent of Meeting' and 'above the cover of the Ark,'" but he does not explain the nature of the putative contradiction.

42. Yadin, "*Shnei Ketuvim*," 394–96.

43. See Milgrom, *Leviticus 1–16*, 134–36, with references to classical commentators.

44. Cited in *Torat Hayyim: Exodus*, ed. Mordechai Leyb Katzenellenbogen, 2 vols. (Jerusalem: Mosad Harav Kook, 1988), 2.95.

לא אבין איך יכחיש זה הפסוק, פסוק "וידבר ה' אליו מאהל מועד לאמר"
(ויקרא א א), כי אהל מועד שם כולל את המשכן ואת כל אשר בו, ואין צורך למכריע.

45. Martin Noth, *Numbers: A Commentary*, trans. James D. Martin (Philadelphia: Westminster, 1968) 65. The Septuagint has Moses hearing "τὴν φωνὴν Κυρίου λαλοῦντες"

46. Philip J. Budd, *Numbers*, Word Biblical Commentary 5 (Waco, Tex.: Word Books, 1984), 85.

47. A. H. McNeile, *The Book of Numbers* (Cambridge: Cambridge University Press, 1911), 43.

48. The Sifre's interpretation is plausible, and arguably correct. See Azzan Yadin, "*Qol* as Hypostasis in the Hebrew Bible," *Journal of Biblical Literature* 122 (2003): 601–26.

49. This verse appears in other Bibles as 20:18.

50. The word *middah* does not appear in this derashah, but the terminology—"two verses contradict and a third resolves"—and the deciding third verse mark it as a second instance of the *middah*.

51. See Henshke, "The Sages' Approach," 41, and the literature he cites in n. 12.

52. For an analysis of Deuteronomy's hermeneutics, see Levinson, *Deuteronomy and the Hermeneutics of Legal Innovation*. Levinson emphasizes Deuteronomy's complex dialogue with Exodus, a dialogue that consists of direct quotations alongside legal and theological innovations. This innovative hermeneutic, garbed in the rhetoric of continuity, is very much in evidence in Deuteronomy 4:36.

53. Moshe Weinfeld, *Deuteronomy 1–11*, 213. See also below, n. 56, for a nuancing of Weinfeld's position. On Deuteronomy 4 as a revision of Exodus 19, see also See Moshe Greenberg, "נסה in Exodus 20:20 and the Purpose of the Sinaitic Theophany," *Journal of Biblical Literature* 79 (1960): 273–76. Greenberg claims that the revision is done "without substantial alteration" (274), a view I do not accept, as the following argument makes clear.

54. See also Rashi to Exodus 20:19, the discussion in Heschel, *Theology of Ancient Judaism*, 2.58 n. 1, and *Sefer ha-Bahir*, §§45–47.

55. At first sight, Deuteronomy 4:36c might appear to be in tension with 4:36a, since the former speaks of God's words (*devarav*) coming from the fire, and the latter of God's disciplining voice (*qolo*) being heard from the heavens. But this

tension is more apparent than real, for the discipline "denotes not the instruction of the intellect [למד, הודיע] but the discipline or education of the moral nature" (S. R. Driver, *A Critical and Exegetical Commentary on Deuteronomy*, International Critical Commentary 5 (Edinburgh: T&T Clark, 1906], 76). God's *qol*, voice, does not communicate with the Israelites; rather, it instills in them the reverence befitting a group about to receive God's law.

56. Moshe Weinfeld argues that Deuteronomy "has taken care to shift the centre of gravity of the theophany from the visual to the aural plane" (Moshe Weinfeld, *Deuteronomy and the Deuteronomic School* [Oxford: Oxford University Press, 1972], 206–7). Weinfeld suggests that the Israelites were privy to direct aural revelation, a position that, on my reading, Deuteronomy rejects. This critique also holds for Weinfeld's statement cited above, n. 53.

57. Ian Wilson, to cite a recent discussion of 4:36, adopts a "harmonizing" reading very much in keeping with the understanding that Henshke attributes to the Mekhilta. Wilson argues that, "taking into account the clear parallelism between the two halves of the verse, the consistent application of this approach [by which the second half of the verse qualifies the subject of its main clause] locates YHWH both in heaven *and* on earth," Ian Wilson, *Out of the Midst of the Fire: Divine Presence in Deuteronomy*, Society for Biblical Literature Dissertation Series 151 (Atlanta: Scholars Press, 1995), 68 (emphasis in the original). Wilson (like Henshke) ignores the tripartite division of the verse and blurs the theological differences between Deuteronomy 4 and 5. See Eckart Otto, "Die Pentateuchredaktion im Deuteronomiumsrahmen," in *Das Deuteronomium und Seine Querbeziehungen*, ed. Timo Veijola (Helsinki and Göttingen: Finnische Exegetische Gesselschaft and Vandenhoeck & Ruprecht, 1996), 196–222.

58. R. E. Clements, *God and Temple* (Oxford: Basil Blackwell, 1990), 90. Though Clements appears to have softened the force of this statement in more recent writings, see Clements's statement cited in Wilson, *Out of the Midst of the Fire*, 67 n. 91.

59. Jeffrey H. Tigay, *The Jewish Publication Society Torah Commentary: Deuteronomy* (Philadelphia and New York: Jewish Publication Society, 1996), 56.

60. Though the introduction of intermediaries is often portrayed as foreign to rabbinic sensibilities, see the appendix to Yadin, "*Shnei Ketuvim*," 405–10.

61. In another article ("Two Contradictory Verses," *Proceedings of the Eleventh World Congress in Jewish Studies* [1990]: 3.39–46 [Hebrew]), David Henshke proposes an explanation for the relationship between the *middah* in question and the *shnei ketuvim* (two verses), a formula attributed to Hillel the Elder. Henshke explains the absence of the third, resolving, verse from Hillel's formula by drawing on Eliezer Rosenthal's classic article on *shnei devarim* (two accounts), Eliezer Shimshon Rosenthal, "*Shnei Devarim*," in *The Yitzhak Seligman Memorial Volume*, ed. Y. Zakovitch and A. Rofé (Jerusalem: Magnes, 1983), 3.463–81 (Hebrew). In this article, Rosenthal proves that the phrase *shnei devarim* in p. Bava Qama, 4, 3, 4b is a calque of the sophistic phrase *dissoi logoi*, which refers to two contradictory accounts. As such, *shnei devarim* already contains the notion of contradiction, even though this contradiction is not explicitly stated. Henshke applies Rosenthal's argument to Hillel the Elder's *shnei ketuvim*, suggesting that this pithy formulation already contains the notion of contradiction later made explicit in Rabbi Ishmael's *middah*: "It seems, then, that the original phrasing of the *middah* 'Two Verses that Contradict One Another' was in fact 'Two Verses' and nothing more" (Henshke, "Two Verses," 40). However, the theological force of the Rabbi Ishmael *middah* suggests that there is more at work here than a refinement of logical phraseology. Henshke's use of Rosenthal's argument is also problematic. In the

Palestinian Talmud, it is two Roman generals who make the *dissoi logoi* argument, a fact that Rosenthal considers significant: "Perhaps, then, this is the meaning of the statement made by the two generals—*who were no doubt well versed in eristics and forensics and their respective terminologies*" (Rosenthal, "*Shnei Devarim,*" 480; emphasis added). Rosenthal's statement suggests that the Hellenistic education of high Roman officers is key to understanding the generals' employment of "two accounts." It is hard to attribute such knowledge to Hillel and curious that Hillel (or the Palestinian Talmud) would assume that calques of Greek sophistic terminology would be generally understood and thus employed without explanation.

62. This question has troubled traditional commentators, as evidenced by the medieval attempts to classify them as part of the extra-scriptural tradition handed down at Sinai. See Louis Finkelstein, "On the Notion that the Thirteen *Middot* are *Halakhah le-Moshe mi-Sinai,*" in *Sefer Zikaron le-Rabi Shaul Lieberman*, ed. Shamma Friedman (Jerusalem and New York: Jewish Theological Seminary, 1993), 79–84 (Hebrew).

63. T. Sanhedrin 7.11 (Zuckermandel ed., 427).

64. See, e.g., m. Zevaḥim 9.7.

65. For example, see Mekhilta Beshalaḥ 5, 108–9; Lauterbach 1.241–42.

66. I render *middot* "characters" following R. Travers Herford, *The Ethics of the Talmud: The Sayings of the Fathers* (New York: Jewish Institute of Religion, 1945), 134–35 (Danby translates "types").

67. See: m. Bava Batra 5.6 and m. Avot 5.11, 13, 14, and 15.

68. See Bacher's statement: "Mit dem Ausdrucke מדה בתורה soll wohl gesagt sein, dass die anzuführende Regel als eine dem Texte der heiligen Schrift inhärirende *Eigenschaft* betrachtet wird. Die exegetischen Regeln sind nach dieser Auffassung Feststellungen gewisser Eigenheiten des auszulegende Bibeltextes, aus denen sich die bei der Auslegung zu befolgende Regel ergiebt" (Bacher, *Exegetische Terminologie*, 1.101; emphasis in the original).

Chapter 6

1. Jacob Neusner, *Sifré to Numbers: An American Translation*, 2 vols., Brown Judaic Studies 118–19 (Atlanta: Scholars Press, 1986), 1.1–43, and in particular 11–13, 33–34, and 38.

2. Neusner, *Sifré to Numbers*, 1.38.

3. Jacob Neusner, *Uniting the Dual Torah: Sifra and the Problem of the Mishnah* (Atlanta: Scholars Press, 1988). I hope to address the shortcomings of this view in future studies.

4. On the distribution of phrases containing the word *din* in tannaitic literature see Miguel Pérez Fernández, "*Din* versus *talmud lomar* en los midrashim tannaíticos," *Proceedings of the Eleventh World Congress in Jewish Studies* (1990): 3.9–16, and especially p. 10. The Rabbi Ishmael midrashim appear to distinguish between *din hu'*, which refers to *qol va-ḥomer* arguments, and *harei 'atah dan*, which refer to *gezerah shavah*.

5. See Halbertal's comments: "It is not for nothing that *qol va-ḥomer* is called *middat ha-din*, since the phrase reflects the thinking and logic (*da'ato ve-higgyiono*) of the interpreter as to the manner in which the argument (*din*) is to be applied," *Interpretive Revolutions*, 20 n. 15.

6. This is the conclusion of the Sifre Deuteronomy §207, p. 242; Hammer, pp. 221–22.

7. Aside from four occurrences in the Mekhilta de-'Arayot (tractate Qedoshim), the formula appears three times in the Sifra.

8. Leviticus 14:17 reads: "Some of the oil left in his palm shall be put by the priest on the ridge of <u>the right ear</u> of the one being cleansed."

9. Lauterbach punctuates "But we have not heard where" with a question mark, understanding it as a rhetorical question. I think, however, that this is an indicative sentence to the effect that the specific site is not stated outright in the Torah; thus it must be derived through *din*.

10. This passage presents a *gezerah sharah* argument.

11. The derashah was discussed above, pp. 37–38.

12. See Fernández, "*Din* versus *talmud lomar*," who claims that the purpose of the dialectic arguments involving the terms *din* and *talmud lomar* (representing human reason and scriptural authority, respectively) is to demonstrate "the weakness of empirical logic" but in the very next sentence allows that: "Still, in the Sifre Numbers and the Mekhilta this position is not so clear and in a good number of cases *din* is accepted as valid" ("*Din* versus *talmud lomar*," 16; my translation).

13. Mekhilta Pisḥa 16, p. 57; Lauterbach 1.28.

14. Sifre Numbers §2, pp. 4–5.

15. See above, pp. 121–22.

16. Others derashot of this type appear in Mekhilta Neziqin 6, p. 269 (Lauterbach 3.51): "concerning all the damages in the Torah"; Sifre Numbers §107, p. 106: "concerning all the instances of the word 'enter.'" This formula does not appear in the Sifra.

17. The bracketed phrase does not appear in MS Oxford 151.

18. The phrase "oath of the YHWH" does not appear anywhere else in the Pentateuch, though it is found in 2 Samuel 21:7 and 1 Kings 2:43.

19. On this semantic development, see Daniel Boyarin, "*Doreshei Reshumot* Have Said," *Be'er Sheva'* 3 (1985): 23–35, particularly 30–31 (Hebrew). The overall structure of this derashah, with the interplay between the hermeneutically accessible and the inaccessible, is relevant to the argument of Boyarin's article.

20. The explicit evocation of Scripture may be related to the relatively free hand that the interpreter employs in extending a local conclusion to all instances of the word.

21. Sifre Numbers §118, pp. 140–41, and Mekhilta Neziqin 5, p. 265 (Lauterbach 3.41), respectively.

22. This is a variant form of the participle, on which see Bar-Asher, "Preliminary Investigations," §36.2.

23. This formula appears once in the Mekhilta and eight times in the Sifre Numbers, but not once in the Sifra.

24. Above, pp. 68–69.

25. Harris claims that the same phenomenon occurs in the Sifra, but his reading is not convincing. In the derashah that he cites, it is not Scripture that is rejected but the midrashic reading of the verse (i.e., that the word *min* in Leviticus 1:2 excludes *terefah* as a sacrifice). See Harris, *How Do We Know This?*, 12.

26. The derashah has been discussed above, pp. 85–86.

27. The following paragraph reproduces the analysis offered above, p. 86.

28. To be sure, there is an element of paradox here. If the rhetorical claims of the Rabbi Ishmael midrashim were accepted in full, there would be no reason to limit *din* since it is, according to the hermeneutical ideology of these texts, determined by an integral part of Scripture itself. That *din* is nonetheless delimited

indicates only that the Rabbi Ishmael midrashim recognize the gap between ideology and reality.

29. Though not directly tied to the hermeneutical issues at hand, it is worth noting that this dispute lends itself to a feminist reading. The first reading takes rape and seduction to be comparable offenses because of their taking place while the woman is in the jurisdiction of her father. The second reading argues, in effect, that jurisdiction is not the key issue, but the volition of the woman. In other words, the first position suggests that the decisive point of view is that of the father (in whose care the woman is) and that the pertinent criterion is the woman's status as "care" of her father. The second position posits the woman's consciousness and agency as the determining factors.

30. This passage is discussed above, pp. 52–53.

31. This is another form of the participle, on which, see Bar-Asher, "Preliminary Studies," §36.1.

32. An exception is discussed in chapter 2 n. 16.

33. It should be noted that this assumption is a fixture of Babylonian amoraic biblical interpretation and, indeed, of amoraic assumptions about the Mishnah. As Christine Hayes writes: "The amoraim assume that the Mishnah will not waste words by telling us something that is self-evident (פשיטא, *peshiṭa'*, 'it is obvious'), self-evident either because it is deducible from other teachings of the Mishnah or because it is a known fact of extratextual experience," Christine Hayes, *Between the Babylonian and Palestinian Talmuds: Accounting for Halakhic Difference in Selected Sugyot from Tractate Avodah Zarah* (New York and Oxford: Oxford University Press, 1997), 94.

34. Jorge Luis Borges, "Pierre Menard, Author of the Quixote," trans. James E. Irby, in *Labyrinths: Selected Stories and Other Writings* (New York: New Directions, 1964), 36–44.

35. Unlike, say, the interpretive material in Jubilees, the Targumim, and more.

36. Heschel, *Theology of Ancient Judaism*, 1.3–20 and passim.

37. See the discussion above, pp. 117–20.

38. The numbering of the commandments—the Sifre counts the two statements as part of the First Commandment, and Rav Hamnuna as two distinct commandments—is less important. There were, and are, different views on the division of the Decalogue.

39. The idea that the opening of the Decalogue is to be privileged in relation to the rest of the verses has a long history and figures prominently in Maimonides' *Guide for the Perplexed*, 2.33.

40. This view is also found in b. Sanhedrin 99a, where it is attributed to the school of Rabbi Ishmael. Note also the position of Rabbi Eleazar ha-Modai: "'Because he has spurned the word of the Lord' (Num 15:31), this refers to one who says the Torah is not divine [literally, from the heavens], even if he says the entire Torah is divine except for a single verse that was not said by the Holy One Blessed be He but by Moses." Is this an implicit polemic against Rabbi Ishmael's linking of "the word of the Lord" with "I am the Lord your God" rather than the entire Torah?

41. See the rich discussion of *middot* and their theosophical significance in Michael Fishbane, "The Measures of God's Glory in the Ancient Midrash," in *Messiah and Christos: Studies in the Jewish Origins of Christianity Presented to David Flusser on the Occasion of His Seventy-Fifth Birthday*, ed. Ithamar Gruenwald, Shaul Shaked, and Gedalyah Stroumsa, Texte und Studien zum antiken Judentum 32 (Tübingen: Mohr, 1992), 53–74.

Chapter 7

1. An earlier essay incorporates parts of the present chapter and the discussion of Qumran in Chapter 8; see Azzan Yadin, "4QMMT, Rabbi Ishmael and the Origins of Legal Midrash," *Dead Sea Discoveries* 10 (2003): 130–49.

2. There is some confusion regarding extra-scriptural authorization and orality—confusion largely due to the Hebrew designation of extra-scriptural traditions as *torah she-be'al peh*, "Oral Torah." Historically, this phrase is anachronistic for the present discussion since it does not occur in tannaitic sources, rather emerged along with a broader ideology of Oral Torah. On this development see Martin Jaffee, *Torah in the Mouth: Writing and Oral Tradition in Palestinian Judaism 200 BCE–400 CE* (Oxford and New York: Oxford University Press, 2001), 84–99. More importantly, it is important to distinguish between different modes of authorization (midrash vs. *halakhah*), on the one hand, and the question of transmission, on the other. Orality is a mode of transmission, not (or not necessarily) the source of a teaching's authority: midrashic traditions can be, and were, transmitted orally, while *halakhot* could be, and were, written down. To avoid this confusion, I speak of "extra-scriptural," rather than "oral," *halakhah*.

3. *Halakhah* in italics reproduces the corresponding term in Hebrew and refers to a non-scriptural legal tradition, as opposed to "halakhah" and "halakhic," which refer to Jewish law generally.

4. On this contrast, see Christine Hayes, "*Halakhah le-Moshe mi-Sinai* in Rabbinic Sources: A Methodological Case Study," in *The Synoptic Problem in Rabbinic Literature*, ed. Shaye J. D. Cohen (Providence, R.I.: Brown Judaic Studies, 2000), 61–117, especially 66–77. And see Shmuel Safrai, "*Halakhah le-Moshe mi-Sinai*: History or Theology?" in *Meḥqere Talmud I*, ed. Rosenthal and Sussmann, 11–38 (Hebrew).

5. On the "misplacement" of this Ishmaelian derashah in Sifre Deuteronomy, a compilation not associated with Rabbi Ishmael, see Epstein, *Prolegomena*, 558–59, and Finkelstein's notes *ad loc.*

6. A legal midrash within a largely aggadic tractate of the Mekhilta.

7. David Henshke, "On the Nature of Tannaitic Legal Midrash: Two Issues," *Tarbiz* 65 (1996): 417–38 (Hebrew). Henshke does not cite the fourth and fifth derashot.

8. Henshke, "On the Nature of Tannaitic Legal Midrash," 433.

9. I will argue this point in greater detail elsewhere. See, for now, Halivni's comments on the Mishnaic sayings introduced by *mik'an 'amru*, in Halivni, *Midrash, Mishnah, and Gemara*, 61 and nn. 48–50. A statement is made "in the name of Rabbi Ishmael" (משום רבי ישמעאל) in Mekhilta Pisḥa 16 (pp. 60–61; Lauterbach 1.136–37), but this is probably copied from the Tosefta, as argued by Friedmann, in his edition of the Mekhilta, 19a-b.

10. There are a number of instances in the Tosefta where statements are made in the name of Rabbi Ishmael, but this is not germane since it is clear that Rabbi Ishmael's statements are acceptable within rabbinic circles, while the present inquiry involves the sources of Rabbi Ishmael's views. The Mishnah records Rabbi Ishmael making three halakhic statements before the sages in Yavne (m. Eduyot 2.4) in a tractate devoted to the transmission of extra-scriptural tradition, but the origins of these statements are not discussed. The Sifra (Tazria' pereq 2.10; Weiss 61a) records Rabbi Aqiva asking a *halakhah* of Rabbi Yehoshua and Rabbi Ishmael (their response: "we have not heard"), but pseudo-Raabad in his commentary has Rabbi Aqiva speaking with Rabbi Yehoshua and Rabban Gamliel, as the Gra rightly emends. Even in amoraic literature there are very few instances of Rabbi Ishmael citing the teachings of earlier Sages. Rabbi Ishmael

does cite a teaching in the name of (בשם) Rabbi Yehoshua in p. Pesaḥim 34c, chapter 7 halakhah 5, but it is a midrashic argument, not an extra-scriptural *halakhah.*

11. See Marcus Petuchowski, *Der Tanna Rabbi Ismael* (Frankfurt am Main: Kaufmann, 1894), 11. Aaron Hyman (*Toldoth Tannaim Ve'Amoraim* [Jerusalem: Machon Pri Ha'Aretz, 1987], 1.820) cites a number of cases in which Rabbi Ishmael "learns" *halakhah* from senior sages, but the encounters described are confrontational in nature. The need to cite these passages testifies to the absence of unproblematic evidence of Rabbi Ishmael receiving traditions from teachers.

12. B. Shvu'ot 26a.

13. See Epstein, *Prolegomena,* 71–88.

14. Halivni, *Midrash, Mishnah, and Gemara,* 60–61.

15. See above, pp. 125–26.

16. This passage was discussed above, p. 107.

17. Similar exchanges between Rabbi Aqiva and Rabban Gamliel and Rabbi Yehoshua are recorded in the m. Keritot 3.8–9 and m. Nega'im 7.4.

18. Danby correctly translates: "We have heard no tradition about this." The phrase "we have not heard" in reference to extra-scriptural tradition appears in m. Bekhorot 6.8 and t. Sanhedrin 7.2.

19. A marginal addition.

20. "The Sages" is not attested in MS Kaufmann.

21. This is another instance of "we have not heard" referring to extra-scriptural tradition.

22. The phrase does not appear in the Sifra.

23. The Hebrew does not name the agent who draws the analogy. HA-KATUV is supplied in the translation on the basis of the Mekhilta's propensity for attributing such actions to HA-KATUV.

24. Mekhilta Neziqin 16, p. 303; Lauterbach 3.122–23. Discussed in Chapter 6, pp. 128–29.

25. There are four occurrences of *stam* in the Sifra (excluding two in the Mekhilta de-'Arayot), none of which paves the way for interpretation.

26. The root *q-b-l* could arguably be included in this list. In the Mishnah, it denotes the reception of extra-scriptural tradition, as in m. Avot 1.1. and the phrase מקובלני, which introduces an extra-scriptural tradition received from one's master. In the Rabbi Ishmael midrashim, however, *qabbalah* refers to the prophetic writings and the hagiographa, that is, a word whose literal meaning is "tradition" is applied to Scripture. The term only appears in aggadic contexts and is found in other parts of the rabbinic corpus (e.g., m. Ta'anit 2.1; t. Yoma' 2.4).

27. In this formulation, I differ from Menachem Fisch's suggestion that midrash (and Rabbi Aqiva as its paradigmatic practitioner) is the innovative contrast to the conservative received traditions (*halakhah* [*le-moshe mi-sinai*]). See Menachem Fisch, *Rational Rabbis: Science and Talmudic Culture* (Bloomington: Indiana University Press, 1997), and the discussion of this passage on 104–7. I want to acknowledge Yishai Rosen-Zvi's helpful comments on this point.

28. Other MSS read: שאין לו מקרא מן התורה.

29. Parallel at m. Sotah 5.2.

30. Judging from Rabbi Yehoshua's response, Rabbi Aqiva's reading is bold and unexpected. It is worth noting, nonetheless, that the Bible was not definitively vocalized at the time, and Rabbi Aqiva's reading may represent a different vocalization tradition.

31. Halivni, Midrash, Mishnah, and Gemara, 47.

Chapter 8

1. Steven D. Fraade, "Interpretive Authority in the Studying Community at Qumran," *Journal of Jewish Studies* 44 (1993): 46–69.

2. For Qumran sources and analysis, see Fraade's discussion.

3. Despite the obvious differences in both substance and style, there is a distant family resemblance between the Qumran writings' rejection of Pharisaic extra-scriptural traditions and the marginalization of *halakhot* in the Rabbi Ishmael midrashim.

4. Elisha Qimron and John Strugnell, *Qumran Cave 4 V: Miqṣat* Ma'aśe *Ha-Torah*, Discoveries in the Judaean Desert 10 (Oxford: Clarendon Press, 1994) (cited as *4QMMT*). The text is cited according to this edition.

5. Thus in Finkelstein, MS Oxford (and others) read: התירו חכמים ('the sages permitted').

6. See also Leviticus Rabbah 22:7.

7. See the extended discussion in Esther Eshel, "4QLEV^d: A Possible Source for the Temple Scroll and *Miqṣat Ma'aśe Ha-Torah*," *Dead Seas Discoveries* 2 (1995): 1–13. Eshel's reconstruction of 4QLEV^d is challenged by Menahem Kister, "Studies in 4Q Miqṣat Ma'aśe Ha-Torah and Related Texts: Law, Theology, Language and Calendar," *Tarbiz* 68 (1999) 337 n. 84 (Hebrew), but Kister's critique does not affect the broader issue at hand.

8. Abraham Geiger, *Urschrift und Übersetzungen der Bibel in ihrer Abhängigkeit von der innern Entwicklung des Judenthums* (Breslau: Julius Hainauer, 1857); Hebrew translation *Ha-Miqra ve-Targumav*, trans. Y. L. Baruch (Jerusalem: Mosad Bialik, 1949).

9. See, in particular, *Ha-Miqra' ve-Targumav*, 279–89.

10. Geiger, *Ha-Miqra' ve-Targumav*, 344 (my translation).

11. Qimron and Strugnell, *4QMMT*, 157.

12. Geiger, *Ha-Miqra' ve-Targumav*, 343–44. Geiger's position has been criticized by Z. M. Pineles (*Darkhah Shel Torah* [Vienna: F. Forster, 1861]), and a number of later scholars have referred to Pineles as decisively discrediting Geiger's view, e.g., E. E. Urbach, *The Sages: Their Concepts and Beliefs* (Jerusalem: Magnes, 1983), 214 n. 90 (Hebrew); and Halivni, *Midrash, Mishnah, and Gemara* 134 n. 46. But at least as far as the question of fetal life is concerned (pp. 190–91), Pineles is wrong. Briefly, Pineles's argument hinges on the fact that an explicit statement attributed to Rabbi Ishmael prohibiting the murder of a fetus (b. Sanhedrin 57b) is cited as part of a talmudic discussion of the Noahide laws and thus—Pineles suggests—applies only to non-Jews. But this will not do. As a rule, the context in which the Talmud cites a saying is not necessarily the context in which it was made. And this is indeed the case here since, as Marc Hirshman has recently shown, one of characteristics of the Rabbi Ishmael sources is that they *do not recognize the category of the Noahide* (*bnei Noah*); see Hirshman, *Torah for the Entire World*, 90–104.

13. See the comments of Yaakov Sussmann in Qimron and Strugnell, *4QMMT*, 189, and in greater detail, Sussmann, "The History of *Halakha* and the Dead Sea Scrolls—Preliminary Observations on *Miqṣat Ma'aśe Ha-Torah* (4QMMT)," *Tarbiz* 59 (1990): 33 (Hebrew).

14. Aharon Shemesh, "The Term 'Mizvah Ha-Teluyah Ba-Aretz' Reexamined," *Sidra* 16 (2000): 151–77 (Hebrew).

15. Shemesh, "Mizvah Ha-Teluyah Ba-Aretz," 161–62. Shemesh explains this shift as the result of a particular interpretation of the laws in Deuteronomy 12.

16. In my earlier discussion of this passage, I presented an incorrect argument that I now retract.

17. The following is a summary of Menahem Kister's erudite analysis in "Studies," 330–35.

18. M. Parah 3.7 (Danby, p. 700).

19. Qimron and Strugnell, *4QMMT*, 140.

20. Moshe J. Bernstein, "The Employment and Interpretation of Scripture in 4QMMT: Preliminary Observations," in *Reading 4QMMT: New Perspectives on Qumran Law and History*, ed. John Kampen and Moshe J. Bernstein, Society for Biblical Literature Symposium Series 2 (Atlanta: Scholars Press, 1996), 29–51; here 39 n. 23.

21. George J. Brooke, "The Explicit Presentation of Scripture in 4QMMT," in *Legal Texts and Legal Issues: Proceedings of the Second Meeting of the International Organization for Qumran Studies Cambridge 1995: Published in Honour of Joseph M. Baumgarten*, ed. Moshe Bernstein, Florentino García Martínez, and John Kampen, Studies on the Texts of the Desert of Judah 23 (Leiden: Brill, 1997), 67–88.

22. See the discussion above, Chapter 1.

23. Respectively: Sifre Numbers §156, p. 208; Mekhilta Pisha 15, p. 52 (Lauterbach 1.117); Mekhilta Neziqin 2, p. 253 (Lauterbach 3.15).

24. The absence of *torah* is noted by Miguel Pérez Fernández, "*4QMMT*: Redactional Study," *Revue de Qumran* 18 (1997): 197.

25. Hirshman, *Torah for the Entire World*, and, in shortened form, see his "Rabbinic Universalism in the Second and Third Centuries," *Harvard Theological Review* 93 (2000): 101–15.

26. Or Torah study, depending on the meaning of "עושה תורה." See Hirshman's discussion, *Torah for the Entire World*, 53–54.

27. See the historical analysis in Patrick W. Skehan and Alexander A. Di Lella, *The Wisdom of Ben Sira*, Anchor Bible 39 (New York: Doubleday, 1987), 8–10; translations are from this edition unless otherwise noted.

28. Hirshman, *Torah for the Entire World*, 131–34.

29. M. Bava Batra 10.8.

30. John J. Collins, *Jewish Wisdom in the Hellenistic Age* (Louisville, Ky.: Westminster John Knox, 1997), 52.

31. Skehan and Di Lella, *Wisdom of Ben Sira*, 325.

32. See discussion above, pp. 110–17.

33. For a discussion of biblical Wisdom literature in relation to biblical law, see Joseph Blenkinsopp, *Wisdom and Law in the Old Testament: The Ordering of Life in Israel and Early Judaism* (Oxford and New York: Oxford University Press, 1995). For a helpful survey of Hellenistic Jewish wisdom see Collins, *Jewish Wisdom in the Hellenistic Age*, 1–20.

34. Translation by E. Isaac, in James H. Charlesworth, ed., *The Old Testament Pseudepigrapha*, 2 vols (New York: Doubleday, 1983), 1.33.

35. See Gerhard Kittel, ed., *Theological Dictionary of the New Testament*, 8.507–9, and Bultmann's discussion of the rejected Logos in the prologue of John, "Der religionsgeschichtliche Hintergrund des Prologs zum Johannes-Evangelium," in *Exegetica: Aufsätze zur Erforschung des Neuen Testaments* (Tübingen: J. C. B. Mohr, 1967), 10–35.

36. Ben Sira 24:23 is the only prose verse in the poem, which has caused speculation that it is a late addition. Most scholars do not accept the later dating, but even the later dating places the verse in the first half of the first century B.C.E., where it can count as background for the later developments in the school of Rabbi Ishmael.

37. For a helpful discussion of the Book of Baruch, see David G. Burke, *The Poetry of Baruch: A Reconstruction and Analysis of the Original Hebrew Text of Baruch 3:9–5:9*, Society for Biblical Literature Septuagint and Cognate Studies 10

(Chico, Calif.: Scholars Press, 1982). For a discussion of the role of Wisdom in Baruch, see Walter Harrelson, "Wisdom Hidden and Revealed according to Baruch (Baruch 3.9–4.4)," in *Priests, Prophets and Scribes: Essays in the Formation and Heritage of Second Temple Judaism in Honour of Joseph Blenkinsopp*, ed. Eugene Ulrich, John W. Wright, Robert P. Carroll, and Philip R. Davies, Journal for the Study of the Old Testament Supplement Series 149 (Sheffield: Journal for the Study of the Old Testament Press, 1992), 158–71.

38. For the former position, see Gerald T. Sheppard, "Wisdom and Torah: The Interpretation of Deuteronomy Underlying Sirach 24:23," in *Biblical and Near Eastern Studies: Essays in Honor of William Sanford LaSor*, ed. Gary A. Tuttle rand Rapids, Mich.: Eerdmans, 1978), 166–76; for an interpretation that emphasizes the hostility of the Wisdom and Deuteronomic traditions, see Margaret Barker, *The Great Angel* (Louisville, Ky.: Westminster John Knox, 1992), 60–67. Ben Sira makes a visible effort to combine these traditions in other matters as well. See, e.g., the discussion of life as a motif in Shannon Burkes, "Wisdom and Law: Choosing Life in Ben Sira and Baruch," *Journal for the Study of Judaism* 30 (1999): 263.

39. Translations NRSV. For additional passages and analysis see Eckhard J. Schnabel, *Law and Wisdom from Ben Sira to Paul*, Wissenschaftliche Untersuchungen zum Neuen Testament (2 Reihe) 16 (Tübingen: J. C. B. Mohr, 1985), 69–79.

40. It is worth recalling in this context that *torah* means "instruction."

41. Hirshman, *Torah for the Entire World*, 114–22. The idea that the Rabbi Ishmael legal traditions are priestly is also not new: it was suggested by Abraham Geiger in *Ha-Miqra ve-Targumav* and by Joseph Derenbourg, *Massa Eretz Yisrael*, M.B.Sh.N's [*sic*], Hebrew translation of *Essai sur l'histoire et la geographie de la Palestine* (Saint Petersburg: Behrman and Rabinowitz, 1896), 201–6. Hirshman also refers to a doctoral dissertation by P. Segal that proves that the Rabbi Ishmael sources reflect priestly penal traditions (see Hirshman, *Torah for the Entire World*, 118 n. 212), though I have not seen this work.

42. Helge Stadelmann, *Ben Sira als Schriftgelehrter*, Wissenschaftliche Untersuchungen zum Neuen Testament (2 Reihe) 6 (Tübingen: J. C. B. Mohr, 1980), 40–176; Saul M. Olyan, "Ben Sira's Relationship to the Priesthood," *Harvard Theological Review* 80 (1987): 261–86; Benjamin G. Wright III, "'Fear the Lord and Honor the Priest': Ben Sira as Defender of the Jerusalem Priesthood," in *The Book of Ben Sira in Modern Research*, ed. Pancratius C. Beentjes, Beihefte zur Zeitschrift für die alttestamentliche Wissenschaft 255 (Berlin and New York: Walter de Gruyter, 1997), 189–222.

43. Collins, *Jewish Wisdom in the Hellenistic Age*, 37. Collins's arguments are mostly negative, focusing on what Ben Sira does not mention—e.g., dietary laws—but should have were he a priest.

44. The emphasis here is on shared traditions, not direct lineage. The Qumran community was far from universalism of any type.

45. Robert A. Kugler, "Priesthood at Qumran," *The Dead Sea Scrolls After Fifty Years: A Comprehensive Assessment*, 2 vols., Peter W. Flint and James C. Vanderkam eds. (Leiden: Brill, 1999), 2.93–116, here p. 93.

46. Ephraim Itzchaky, "Jerusalem Targum 'A' and the school of Rabbi Ishmael," *Sidra* 1 (1985): 45–57 (Hebrew). Itzchaky emphasizes that Pseudo-Jonathan is made up of different layers and does not lend itself to a single dating.

47. Beverly Mortensen, "Pseudo Jonathan and the Economics for Priests," *Journal for the Study of Pseudepigrapha* 20 (1999): 41. V. M. Flesher kindly sent me a copy of a conference paper, from which I learned of Mortensen's article. Mortensen dates Pseudo-Jonathan to the mid-fourth century, with the awakened

hope that the Temple would be rebuilt by Julian, though there is no question that the traditions preserved in the work are significantly earlier.

48. T. Hallah, 1.10.

49. B. Hullin 49a.

50. For a summary and bibliography of the various positions, see Porton, *The Traditions of Rabbi Ishmael*, 4.213 n. 2.

51. See Reuven Kimmelman, "The Priestly Oligarchy and the Sages in the Talmudic Period," *Zion* 48 (1983): 135–48 (Hebrew); Stuart A. Cohen, *The Three Crowns: Structures of Communal Politics in Early Rabbinic Jewry* (Cambridge: Cambridge University Press, 1990), 147–78.

52. Rachel Elior, *Temple and Chariot, Priests and Angels, Sanctuary and Heavenly Sanctuaries in Early Jewish Mysticism* (Jerusalem: Magnes, 2002) (Hebrew).

53. For a survey of the shifts in scholarly consensus, see Halivni, *Midrash, Mishnah, and Gemara*, 18–21; and Moshe Halbertal, *Interpretive Revolutions*, 13–15.

54. See Epstein, *Prolegomena*, 501.

55. Chanoch Albeck, "The *Halakhot* and the *Derashot*," in *The Alexander Marx Jubilee Volume* (New York: Jewish Theological Seminary, 1950), 1–8 of the Hebrew section (Hebrew).

56. E. E. Urbach, "The Derashah as the Basis for Halakhah and the Problem of the *Soferim*," *Tarbiz* 27 (1958): 166–82 (Hebrew).

57. Josephus, *Antiquities of the Jews*, 13.10.6, trans. William Whiston, in *The Works of Josephus* (Peabody, Mass.: Hendrickson, 1987), 355.

58. See A. I. Baumgarten, "The Pharisaic *Paradosis*," *Harvard Theological Review* 80 (1987): 63–77.

59. Urbach, "The Derashah as the Basis for Halakhah," 174.

60. Even Hillel the Elder, who famously used scriptural exegesis as the basis for his argument with Bnei Batira (p. Pesahim 6.1, 33) and formulated a list of seven exegetic *middot* was not wont to use this mode of argument as Daniel Schwartz has shown in "Hillel and Scripture: From Authority to Exegesis," in *Hillel and Jesus: Comparative Studies of Two Major Religious Leaders*, ed. James Charlesworth and Lorn Johns (Minneapolis: Fortress, 1997), 335–62. I plan to discuss this matter more fully in a future study.

61. On the biblical priest as interpreter, see Joseph Blenkinsopp, *Sage, Priest, Prophet: Religious and Intellectual Leadership in Ancient Israel* (Louisville, Ky: Westminster John Knox, 1995), 82–83. On priests as interpreters in the Second Temple period, see Michael Stone, "Three Transformations in Judaism: Scripture, History, and Redemption," *Numen* 32 (1985): 218–35, esp. 219–23.

62. Friedrich Normann, *Christos Didaskalos: Die Vorstellung von Christus als Lehrer in der christlichen Literatur des ersten und zweiten Jahrhunderts*, Münsterische Beiträge zur Theologie 32 (Münster: Aschendorff, 1967).

63. *The Ante-Nicene Fathers*, 1.11 (hereafter ANF).

64. Normann, *Christos Didaskalos*, 80.

65. For an overview of the place of the Logos in Clement's thought, see John Egan, "Logos and Emanation in the Writings of Clement of Alexandria," in *Trinification of the World: A Festschrift in Honor of Frederick E. Crowe*, ed. Thomas T. Dunne and Jean-Marc Laporte (Toronto: Regis College Press, 1978), 176–209. The Greek philosophical context of the Logos is discussed in Salvatore R. C. Lilla, *Clement of Alexandria: A Study in Christian Platonism and Gnosticism* (Oxford and New York: Oxford University Press, 1971). On the place of gnosis in Clement's religious thought see Walther Völker, *Der wahre Gnostiker nach Clemens Alexandrinus*, Texte und Untersuchungen 57 (Berlin: Akademie Verlag, 1952), 301–445.

66. But see Lilla, *Clement of Alexandria*, 9–59.

67. On the role of the Logos as instructor, see Erich Fascher, "Der Logos-Christus als göttlicher Lehrer bei Clemens von Alexandrien," in *Studien zum neuen Testament und zur Patristik*, ed. Otto Eissfeldt, Texte und Untersuchungen 77 (Berlin: Akademie Verlag, 1961), 193–207.

68. *Instructor*, book 1, chap. 1 (ANF 209).

69. *Instructor*, book 1, chap. 2 (ANF 210). Here, and throughout, I have substituted "Logos" for ANF's "word," where appropriate.

70. *Instructor*, book 1, chap. 8 (ANF 224); emphasis added.

71. *Instructor* book 1, chap. 7 (ANF 222–225). And see Einar Molland, *The Conception of the Gospel in Alexandrian Theology* (Oslo: I Kommisjon Hos Jacob Dybwad, 1938), esp. 16–33 and 69–71.

72. *Stromata*, book 4, chap. 1 (ANF 409).

73. *Stromata*, book 3, chap. 12 (ANF 394).

74. *Stromata*, book 2, chap. 9 (ANF 356) and see also *Instructor* book 1, chap. 11 (ANF 234).

75. *Stromata*, book 4, chap. 21 (ANF 433).

76. *Stromata*, book 6, chap. 15 (ANF 509).

77. For a compelling analysis of the theological role of scriptural obscurity, see Marguerite Harl, "Origène et les interprétations patristiques grecques de l'«obscurité» biblique," *Vigiliae Christianae* 36 (1982): 334–71.

78. *Protreptikos*, chap. 1 (ANF 173). For a rich analysis of the transformation of the Logos, see David Dawson, *Allegorical Readers and Cultural Revision in Ancient Alexandria* (Berkeley and Los Angeles: University of California Press, 1992), 183–234.

79. *Stromata*, book 5, chap. 9 (ANF 457).

80. *Stromata*, book 4, chap. 22 (ANF 434).

81. *Protreptikos*, chap. 1 (ANF 174; emphasis added).

82. *Protreptikos*, chap. 1 (ANF 173).

83. *Instructor*, book 1, chap. 7 (ANF 223; emphasis added).

84. *Protreptikos* chap. 9 (ANF 196).

85. For a list of Clement's employment of ἡ γραφή for Scripture, see Otto Stählin, *Clemens Alexandrinus Wortregister* (Griechischen christlichen Schriftsteller der ersten Jahrhunderte 39 (Leipzig: J. C. Hinrichs, 1936), 319; and also Gottlob Schrenk's article in *TDNT* 1.754–55, which suggests that the employment of the singular γραφή "may well have developed out of the Rabbinic הַכָּתוּב " (p. 754). Neither Philo nor Josephus employs the term in this fashion, so there is no reason to think that it came from Jewish-Greek authors.

86. Daniel, Boyarin, "The Gospel of the Memra: Jewish Binitariansim and the Prologue to John," *Harvard Theological Review* 94 (2001): 243–84.

87. Hans Bietenhard ("Logos-Theologie im Rabbinat: Ein Beitrag zur Lehre vom Worte Gottes im rabbinischen Schrifttum," *Principat* 19 [1979]: 580–618) argues that a number of rabbinic passages contain traces of a Logos theology, though a good number of the passages he cites refer to all the *dibburim* (statements) of the Torah rather than to a single mediator.

88. See Edwin Luther Copeland, "Nomos as a Medium of Revelation, Paralleling Logos, in Ante-Nicene Christianity," *Studia Theologica* 27 (1973): 51–61, whose discussion I follow.

89. *Stromata* book 2, chap. 15 (ANF 362–63), *Stromata* book 1, chap. 29 (ANF 341), respectively, and see Willy Rordorf, "Christus als Logos und Nomos: Das Kerygma Petrou un seinem Verhältnis zu Justin," in *Kerygma und Logos: Festschrift*

für Carl Andresen zum 70. Geburtstag, ed. Carl Andresen and Adolf Martin Ritter (Göttingen: Vandenhoeck & Ruprecht, 1979), 424–34.

90. Justin Martyr, *Dialogue of Justin, Philosopher and Martyr, with Trypho the Jew* XLIII, quoted in Copeland, "Nomos as a Medium of Revelation," 57.

91. M. J. Edwards, "Justin's Logos and the Word of God," *Journal of Early Christian Studies* 3 (1995): 261–80.

92. Edwards, "Justin's Logos and the Word of God," 279; also quoted in Boyarin, "The Gospel of the Memra."

93. This testimony is found in a fragment preserved in Eusebius, *Ecclesiastical History,* v, xi, trans. Kirsopp Lake, Loeb Classical Library 153 (Cambridge, Mass.: Harvard University Press, 1965), 465. Eusebius suggests that this Palestinian Jew is Pantanaeus, Clement's teacher of Scripture.

94. A very accessible discussion of Jesus as Sophia is Karen Jo Torjesen, "'You Are the Christ': Five Portraits of Jesus from the Early Church," in *Jesus at 2000,* ed. Marcus J. Borg (New York: Westview, 2000), 73–88, esp. 75–78. A more technical discussion with copious references to secondary literature is Hermann von Lipps, "Christus als Sophia? Weisheitliche Traditionen in der urchristlichen Christologie," in *Anfänge der Christologie: Festschrift für Ferdinand Hahn zum 65 Geburtstag,* ed. Cilliers Breytenbach and Henning Paulsen (Göttingen: Vandenhoeck & Ruprecht, 1991), 75–95. This connection is also evident in Philo. Indeed, the similarities between Logos and Sophia are so great in Philo's writings that Harry Wolfson estimates: "Wisdom, then, is only another word for Logos, and it is used in all the senses of the term Logos" (quoted in Ronald H. Nash, "The Notion of Mediator in Alexandrian Judaism and the Epistle to the Hebrews," *Westminster Theological Journal* 40 [1977]: 89–115, quoted on p. 94).

95. See Gianantonio Borgonovo, "Incarnazione del Logos: Il Logos giovanneo alla luce della tradizione giudaica," *Scuola Cattolica* 130 (2002): 43–75, which charts the evolution of the Wisdom motifs in Proverbs and Job into the prologue of John and rabbinic literature.

Bibliography

Rabbinic Texts and Editions

MEKHILTA

MS Oxford 150, microfiche copy (courtesy of the library of the Jewish Theological Seminary).

Mekhilta de-Rabbi Ishmael. Edited and annotated by Meir Friedmann (Ish-Shalom). Vienna, 1870. Reprint, Jerusalem: n.p., 1967.

Mekhilta de-Rabbi Ishmael. Edited by Haim Shaul Horovitz and Israel Rabin. Jerusalem: Bamberger and Wahrman, 1960.

Mekilta de-Rabbi Ishmael. Translated by Jacob Z. Lauterbach. 3 vols. Philadelphia: Jewish Publication Society of America, 1933–36.

Mekhilta with Birkat ha-Natziv Commentary. Jerusalem: Volozhin Yeshiva, 1997.

The Munich Manuscript of the Mekilta. Edited by Judah Goldin. Copenhagen: Rosenkilde and Bagger, 1980.

SIFRA

MS Vatican Ebr. (Assemani) 66, facsimile edition. *Sifra or Torah Kohanim According to Codex Assemani LXVI,* edited by Louis Finkelstein. New York: Jewish Theological Seminary, 1956.

Sifra on Leviticus. Edited by Rabbi Avraham Shoshana. Jerusalem and Cleveland: Ofeq, 1991–98.

Sifra with the Commentary of Rabbenu Hillel. Edited by Shachne Koleditzky. Jerusalem: n.p., 1992.

Sifra with the Commentary of Rabbi Avraham ben David. Jerusalem: Sifra, 1959.

Sifra, der älteste Midrasch zu Levitikus. Edited by Meir Friedmann (Ish-Shalom). Breslau: M. & H. Marcus, 1915. Reprint. Jerusalem: n.p., 1967.

Sifra: An Analytic Translation. Translated by Jacob Neusner. 3 vols. Atlanta: Scholars, 1988.

Sifra: Commentar zu Leviticus. Edited by I. H. Weiss. Vienna: Schlossberg, 1862.

Sifra on Leviticus. Edited by Louis Finkelstein. 5 vols. New York and Jerusalem: Jewish Theological Seminary, 1983–91.

SIFRE NUMBERS

MS Vatican Ebr. 32, facsimile edition. *Midrash Vayiqra Rabba, Sifre Bamidbar u-Devarim.* Jerusalem: Maqor, 1972.
Sifre de-Be Rav. Edited by Meir Friedmann (Ish-Shalom). Vienna: J. Holzwarth, 1864. Reprint, Jerusalem: n.p., 1978.
Sifre Numbers. Edited by Haim Shaul Horovitz. Leipzig, 1917. Reprint, Jerusalem: Shalem, 1992.
Sifre Numbers with the Commentary of Rabbenu Hillel. Edited by Shachne Koleditzky. Jerusalem: n.p., 1983.
Sifré to Numbers: An American Translation. Translated by Jacob Neusner. 2 vols. Atlanta: Scholars Press, 1986.

SIFRE DEUTERONOMY

MS Vatican Ebr. 32, facsimile edition. *Midrash Vayiqra Rabba, Sifre Bamidbar u-Devarim.* Jerusalem: Maqor, 1972.
Siphre ad Deuteronomium. Edited by Louis Finkelstein. New York: Jewish Theological Seminary of America, 1993.
Sifre: A Tannaitic Commentary on the Book of Deuteronomy. Translated by Reuven Hammer. New Haven, Conn.: Yale University Press, 1986.

OTHER RABBINIC WORKS

Mishnah MS Kaufmann, facsimile edition. *Faksimile-Ausgabe des Mischnacodex Kaufmann A 50, mit Genehmigung der Ungarischen Akademie der Wissenschaften in Budapest.* Edited by Georg Beer. N.p.: Jerusalem, 1967.
Shisha Sidrei Mishnah. Edited by Chanoch Albeck. Jerusalem and Tel Aviv: Mosad Bialik and Dvir, 1952–59.
The Mishnah. Translated by Herbert Danby. Oxford: Oxford University Press, 1933.
Mekhilta de-Rabbi Shimon ben Yohai. Edited by Jacob Nahum Epstein and Ezra Zion Melammed. Jerusalem: Meqitze Nirdamim, 1959.
The Ethics of the Talmud: The Sayings of the Fathers. Translated by R. Travers Herford. New York: Jewish Institute of Religion, 1945.
Midrash Tannaim zum Deuteronomium. Edited by David Zvi Hoffmann. Berlin: H. Itzkowski, 1908. Reprint, Jerusalem, n.p., 1984.
Sifre Zutta. Edited by H. S. Horovitz. Leipzig: Gustav Fock, 1917. Reprint, Jerusalem: Shalem, 1992 (bound with Sifre Numbers).
Tosefta ki-feshutah: be'ur arokh la-Tosefta. Edited and annotated by Saul Lieberman. Jerusalem: Jewish Theological Seminary, 1992.
Tosefta: 'Al pi ketav yad Vinah ve-shinuye nusha'ot mi-ketav yad 'Erfurt, Keta'im min ha-genizah u-defus Venetsiyah . . . be-tseruf masoret ha-Tosefta. Edited by Saul Lieberman. New York: Jewish Theological Seminary, 1955–73.
Midrash Bereshit Rabba. Edited by Judah Theodor and Chanoch Albeck. Jerusalem: Wahrman, 1965.

Non-Rabbinic Ancient Sources

Ante-Nicene Fathers. Edited by Alexander Roberts and James Donaldson. New York, 1885. Reprint, Peabody, Mass.: Hendrickson, 1999.
Eusebius. *Ecclesiastical History.* Translated by Kirsopp Lake. Loeb Classical Library 153. Cambridge, Mass.: Harvard University Press, 1965.
Philo. *Questions and Answers on Genesis.* Translated by Ralph Marcus. Loeb Classical Library 380. Cambridge, Mass.: Harvard University Press, 1953.
Qimron, Elisha, and John Strugnell. *Qumran Cave 4 V: Miqṣat Ma'ase Ha-Torah.* Discoveries in the Judaean Desert 10. Oxford: Clarendon Press, 1994.
Josephus Flavius. *Antiquities of the Jews.* Translated by William Whiston. In *The Works of Josephus.* Peabody, Mass.: Hendrickson, 1987.

Secondary Sources

Albeck, Chanoch. *Untersuchungen über die halachischen Midraschim.* Berlin: Akademie Verlag, 1927.
———. "The *Halakhot* and the *Derashot.*" In *The Alexander Marx Jubilee Volume* (Hebrew section), 1–8. New York: Jewish Theological Seminary, 1950 [Hebrew].
Bacher, Wilhelm. *Die exegetische Terminologie der jüdischen Traditionsliteratur.* Leipzig: J. C. Hinrichs, 1899. Reprint, Darmstadt: Wissenschaftliche Buchgesellschaft, 1965.
Bar-Asher, Moshe. "Preliminary Investigations of the Rabbinic Hebrew Found in MS Vatican 32 of the Sifre Numbers." *Te'udah* 3 (1983): 139–65 [Hebrew].
Barker, Margaret. *The Great Angel.* Louisville: Westminster John Knox Press, 1992.
Baumgarten, A. I. "The Pharisaic *Paradosis.*" *Harvard Theological Review* 80 (1987): 63–77.
Benjamin Sommer. "Revelation at Sinai in the Hebrew Bible and in Jewish Theology." *Journal of Religion* 79 (1999): 422–51.
Bernstein, Moshe J. "The Employment and Interpretation of Scripture in 4QMMT: Preliminary Observations." In *Reading 4QMMT: New Perspectives on Qumran Law and History.* Edited by John Kampen and Moshe J. Bernstein, 29–51. Society for Biblical Literature Symposium Series 2. Atlanta: Scholars Press, 1996.
Bietenhard, Hans. "Logos-Theologie im Rabbinat: Ein Beitrag zur Lehre vom Worte Gottes im rabbinischen Schrifttum." *Principat* 19 (1979): 580–618.
Blenkinsopp, Joseph. *Sage, Priest, Prophet: Religious and Intellectual Leadership in Ancient Israel.* Louisville, Ky.: Westminster John Knox, 1995.
———. *Wisdom and Law in the Old Testament: The Ordering of Life in Israel and Early Judaism.* Oxford and New York: Oxford University Press, 1995.
Borges, Jorge Luis. "Pierre Menard, Author of the Quixote." Translated by James E. Irby. In *Labyrinths: Selected Stories and Other Writings,* 36–44. New York: New Directions, 1964.
Borgonovo, Gianantonio. "Incarnazione del Logos: Il Logos giovanneo alla luce della tradizione giudaica." *Scuola Cattolica* 130 (2002): 43–75.
Boyarin, Daniel. *Carnal Israel: Reading Sex in Talmudic Culture.* Berkeley and Los Angeles: University of California Press, 1993.

————. "*Doreshei Reshumot* Have Said." *Be'er Sheva* 3 (1985): 23–35 [Hebrew].

————. "From the Hidden Light: Toward the Original Text of the Mekhilta of Rabbi Ishmael." *Sidra* 2 (1986): 5–13 [Hebrew].

————. "The Gospel of the Memra: Jewish Binitarianism and the Prologue to John." *Harvard Theological Review* 94 (2001): 243–84.

————. *Intertextuality and the Reading of Midrash.* Bloomington: Indiana University Press, 1990.

————. "On the Status of the Tannaitic Midrashim: A Critique of Jacob Neusner's Latest Contribution to Midrashic Studies." *Journal of the American Oriental Society* 112 (1992): 455–65.

————. "Shattering the Logos; or, the Talmuds and the Genealogy of Indeterminacy." In *The Talmud Yerushalmi and Graeco-Roman Culture III.* Edited by Peter Schäfer, 273–99. Texte und Studien zum antiken Judentum 93. Tübingen: Mohr Siebeck, 2002.

Brewer, David Instone. *Techniques and Assumptions in Jewish Exegesis before 70 CE.* Texte und Studien zum antiken Judentum 30. Tübingen: J. C. B. Mohr, 1992.

Brooke, George J. "The Explicit Presentation of Scripture in 4QMMT." In *Legal Texts and Legal Issues: Proceedings of the Second Meeting of the International Organization for Qumran Studies Cambridge 1995: Published in Honour of Joseph M. Baumgarten.* Edited by Moshe Bernstein, Florentino García Martínez, John Kampen, 67–88. Studies on the Texts of the Desert of Judah 23. Leiden: Brill, 1997.

Brown, Francis, S. R. Driver, and Charles Briggs. *A Hebrew and English Lexicon of the Old Testament with an Appendix Containing the Biblical Aramaic.* Oxford: Clarendon Press, 1962.

Bruns, Gerald. "The Problem of Figuration in Antiquity." In *Hermeneutics: Questions and Prospects.* Edited by Gary Shapiro and Alan Sica, 147–64. Amherst: University of Massachusetts Press, 1984.

Budd, Philip J. *Numbers.* Word Biblical Commentary 5. Waco, Tex.: Word Books, 1984.

Bultmann, Rudolf. "Der religionsgeschichtliche Hintergrund des Prologs zum Johannes-Evangelium." In *Exegetica: Aufsätze zur Erforschung des Neuen Testaments,* 10–35. Tübingen: J. C. B. Mohr, 1967.

Burke, David G. *The Poetry of Baruch: A Reconstruction and Analysis of the Original Hebrew Text of Baruch 3:9–5:9.* Society for Biblical Literature Septuagint and Cognate Studies 10. Chico, Calif.: Scholars Press, 1982.

Burkes, Shannon. "Wisdom and Law: Choosing Life in Ben Sira and Baruch." *Journal for the Study of Judaism* 30 (1999): 253–76.

Capozzi, Rocco. "*Interpretation and Overinterpretation*: The Rights of Texts, Readers and Implied Authors." In *Reading Eco: An Anthology.* Edited by Rocco Capozzi, 217–34. Bloomington and Indianapolis: Indiana University Press, 1997.

Charlesworth, James H., ed., *The Old Testament Pseudepigrapha.* 2 vols. New York: Doubleday, 1983.

Chernick, Michael. *Hermeneutical Studies in Talmudic and Midrashic Literatures.* Lod, Israel: Habermann Institute, 1984 [Hebrew].

————. "The Essence of *Mufneh*: Developments from the Tannaitic Period to the End of the Talmudic Period." In *Proceedings of the Tenth World Congress of Jewish Studies* (1989): 3.47–53 [Hebrew].

————. *Gezerah Shavah: Its Various Forms in Midrashim and Talmudic Sources.* Lod, Israel: Habermann Institute, 1994 [Hebrew].

Clements, R. E. *God and Temple.* Oxford: Basil Blackwell, 1990.

Cohen, David (*ha-Rav ha-Nazir*). *Qol ha-Nevua.* Jerusalem: Mosad Harav Kook, 1979.
Cohen, Stuart A. *The Three Crowns: Structures of Communal Politics in Early Rabbinic Jewry.* Cambridge: Cambridge University Press, 1990.
Collins, John J. *Jewish Wisdom in the Hellenistic Age.* Louisville, Ky.: Westminster John Knox, 1997.
Copeland, Edwin Luther. "Nomos as a Medium of Revelation, Paralleling Logos, in Ante-Nicene Christianity." *Studia Theologica* 27 (1973): 51–61.
Daube, David. "Rabbinic Methods of Interpretation and Hellenistic Rhetoric." *Hebrew Union College Annual* 22 (1949): 239–64.
Dawson, David. *Allegorical Readers and Cultural Revision in Ancient Alexandria.* Berkeley and Los Angeles: University of California Press, 1992.
Derenbourg, Joseph. *Massa Eretz Yisrael.* Translated by M. B. Sh. N. [*sic*]. Saint. Petersburg: Behrman and Rabinowitz, 1896.
Dohrmann, Natalie B. "Law and Narrative in the Mekilta de-Rabbi Ishmael: The Problem of Midrashic Coherence." Ph.D. diss., University of Chicago, 1999.
Dreyfus, Hubert. *Being-in-the-World: A Commentary on Heidegger's Being and Time, Division I.* Cambridge, Mass.: MIT Press, 1991.
———. "Holism and Hermeneutics." *Review of Metaphysics* 34 (1980): 3–24.
Driver, S. R. *A Critical and Exegetical Commentary on Deuteronomy.* International Critical Commentary 5. Edinburgh: T&T Clark, 1906.
Eco, Umberto. "Joyce, Semiosis and Semiotics." In *Limits of Interpretation.* Bloomington: Indiana University Press, 1990.
———. *The Role of the Reader: Explorations in the Semiotics of Texts.* Bloomington and Indianapolis: Indiana University Press, 1979.
Edwards, M. J. "Justin's Logos and the Word of God." *Journal of Early Christian Studies* 3 (1995): 261–80.
Egan, John. "Logos and Emanation in the Writings of Clement of Alexandria." In *Trinification of the World: A Festschrift in Honor of Frederick E. Crowe.* Edited by Thomas T. Dunne and Jean-Marc Laporte. Toronto: Regis College Press, 1978.
Elias, Liora, "The Mekhilta of Rabbi Ishmael According to an Excellent Text from the Genizah." M.A. thesis, Hebrew University, 1997 [Hebrew].
Elior, Rachel. *Temple and Chariot, Priests and Angels, Sanctuary and Heavenly Sanctuaries in Early Jewish Mysticism.* Jerusalem: Magnes, 2002 [Hebrew].
Elman, Yaakov. "The Rebirth of Omnisignificant Biblical Exegesis in the Nineteenth and Twentieth Centuries." *Jewish Studies Internet Journal* 2 (2003): 1–40.
Epstein, Jacob Nahum. *Introduction to the Text of the Mishnah.* Jerusalem: Magnes, 1964 [Hebrew].
———. *Prolegomena to Tannaitic Literature.* Tel Aviv: Dvir, 1957 [Hebrew].
Ermarth, Michael. "The Transformation of Hermeneutics." *The Monist* 64 (1981): 175–94.
Eshel, Esther. "4QLEV^d: A Possible Source for the Temple Scroll and *Miqsat Ma'ase Ha-Torah.*" *Dead Sea Discoveries* 2 (1995): 1–13.
Fascher, Erich. "Der Logos-Christus als göttlicher Lehrer bei Clemens von Alexandrien." In *Studien zum Neuen Testament und zur Patristik: Erich Klostermann zum 90 Geburtstag dargebracht.* Texte und Untersuchungen 77. Edited by Otto Eissfeldt, 193–207. Berlin: Akademie Verlag, 1961.
Faur, José. *Golden Doves with Silver Dots: Semiotics and Textuality in Rabbinic Tradition.* Bloomington: Indiana University Press, 1986.
Fernández, Miguel Pérez. "*4QMMT*: Redactional Study." *Revue de Qumran* 18 (1997): 191–205.

———. *"Din* versus *talmud lomar* en los midrashim tannaíticos." *Proceedings of the Eleventh World Congress in Jewish Studies* (1990): 3.9–16.

———. "Herméneutica de los tannaítas. La exégesis introducida con *Lmmh N'mr." Sefarad* 46 (1986): 391–96.

———. "Modelos de argumentación en la exégesis de los tannaítas." *Sefarad* 47 (1987): 363–81.

———. "Tipología exegética en los tannaítas." *Micelánea de Estudios Árabes y Hebraicos* 41 (1992): 53–62.

Finkelstein, Louis. "On the Notion that the Thirteen *Middot* Are *Halakhah le-Moshe Mi-sinai."* In *Sefer Zikaron le-Rabi Shaul Lieberman.* Edited by Shamma Friedman, 79–84. Jerusalem and New York: Jewish Theological Seminary, 1993 [Hebrew].

Fisch, Menachem. *Rational Rabbis: Science and Talmudic Culture.* Bloomington and Indianapolis: Indiana University Press, 1997.

Fishbane, Michael. *The Garments of Torah: Essays in Biblical Hermeneutics.* Bloomington: Indiana University Press, 1990.

———. "The Measures of God's Glory in the Ancient Midrash." In *Messiah and Christos: Studies in the Jewish Origins of Christianity Presented to David Flusser on the Occasion of His Seventy-Fifth Birthday.* Edited by Ithamar Gruenwald, Shaul Shaked, and Gedalyah Stroumsa, 53–74. Texte und Studien zum antiken Judentum 32. Tübingen: Mohr, 1992.

Fraade, Steven. *From Tradition to Commentary: Torah and Its Interpretation in the Midrash Sifre to Deuteronomy.* Albany: State University of New York Press, 1991.

———. "Interpretive Authority in the Studying Community at Qumran." *Journal of Jewish Studies* 44 (1993): 46–69.

Friedman, David Noel, ed. *The Anchor Bible Dictionary.* New York: Doubleday, 1992.

Gadamer, Hans-Georg. *Truth and Method.* Translation revised by Joel Weinsheimer and Donald G. Marshall. New York: Crossroad, 1989.

Geiger, Abraham. *Ha-Miqra ve-Targumav.* Translated by Y. L. Baruch. Jerusalem: Mosad Bialik, 1949.

Gikatilla, Yosef. *Sha'arei 'Orah (Gates of Light).* Translated by Avi Weinstein. San Francisco: HarperCollins, 1994.

Gilat, Yitzhak. *Studies in the Development of Halakhah.* Ramat Gan: Bar Ilan University Press, 1992 [Hebrew].

Glatzer, Nahum. *Hammer on the Rock: A Short Midrash Reader.* New York: Schocken, 1948.

Goldberg, Arnold. "The Rabbinic View of Scripture." In *A Tribute to Geza Vermes: Essays on Jewish and Christian Literature and History.* Edited by Philip Davies and Richard White, 153–66. Journal for the Study of the Old Testament Supplement Series 100. Sheffield: Sheffield Academic Press, 1990.

Goldberg, Avraham. "The Phrase *Davar 'Aher* in the Halakhic Midrashim." In *'Iyyunim be-sifrut hazal, ba-mikra uve-toldot yisrael* (E. Z. Melammed *Festschrift*). Edited by Y. Gilat et al., 99–107. Ramat Gan: Bar Ilan University Press, 1982 [Hebrew].

———. "The school of Rabbi Aqiva and the school of Rabbi Ishmael in Sifre Deuteronomy §§1–54." *Te'udah* 3 (1983): 9–16 [Hebrew].

Goshen-Gottstein, Alon. *The Sinner and the Amnesiac: The Rabbinic Invention of Elisha ben Abuya and Eleazar ben Arach.* Stanford, Calif.: Stanford University Press, 2000.

Gottlieb, Efraim. *Studies in Kabbalistic Literature.* Edited by Yosef Hacker. Tel Aviv: Tel Aviv University Press, 1976 [Hebrew].

Green, William Scott. "What's in a Name?: The Problematic of Rabbinic 'Biography.'" In *Approaches to Ancient Judaism*. Edited by W. S. Green, 6–17. Brown Judaic Studies 1. Missoula, Mont.: Scholars Press, 1978.

Greenberg, Moshe. "נסה in Exodus 20:20 and the Purpose of the Sinaitic Theophany." *Journal of Biblical Literature* 79 (1960): 273–76.

Grice, Paul. "Logic and Conversation." In *Studies in the Way of Words*, 22–40. Cambridge, Mass.: Harvard University Press, 1989.

Grondin, Jean. *Introduction to Philosophical Hermeneutics*. Translated by Joel Weinsheimer. New Haven, Conn. and London: Yale University Press, 1994.

Halbertal, Moshe. *Interpretive Revolutions in the Making: Values as Interpretive Considerations in Midreshei Halakhah*. Jerusalem: Magnes, 1997 [Hebrew].

Halivni, David Weiss. "The Bavli's Tendency to See the *vav* as Conjunctive *vav*." In *Issues in Mishnaic Hebrew: Summaries of Papers Presented in the Workshop on the Grammar and Lexicon of Mishnaic Hebrew*, 51–52. Jerusalem: Institute for Advanced Studies of the Hebrew University, 1991 [Hebrew].

———. *Midrash, Mishnah, and Gemara: The Jewish Predilection for Justified Law*. Cambridge, Mass.: Harvard University Press, 1986.

———. *Peshat and Derash: Plain and Applied Meaning in Rabbinic Exegesis*. New York: Oxford University Press, 1991.

Handelman, Susan. "Fragments of the Rock: Contemporary Literary Theory and the Study of Rabbinic Texts—a Response to David Stern." *Prooftexts* 5 (1985): 73–95.

———. *The Slayers of Moses*. Albany: State University of New York Press, 1982.

Harl, Marguerite. "Origène et les interprétations patristiques grecques de l'«obscurité» biblique." *Vigiliae Christianae* 36 (1982): 334–71.

Harrelson, Walter. "Wisdom Hidden and Revealed according to Baruch (Baruch 3.9–4.4)." In *Priests, Prophets and Scribes: Essays in the Formation and Heritage of Second Temple Judaism in Honour of Joseph Blenkinsopp*. Edited by Eugene Ulrich et al., 158–171. Journal for the Study of the Old Testament Supplement Series 149. Sheffield: Journal for the Study of the Old Testament Press, 1992.

Harris, Jay. *How Do We Know This? Midrash and the Fragmentation of Modern Judaism*. Albany: State University of New York Press, 1995.

Hartman, Geoffrey, and Sanford Budick, eds. *Midrash and Literature*. New Haven, Conn.: Yale University Press, 1986.

Hayes, Christine. *Between the Babylonian and Palestinian Talmuds: Accounting for Halakhic Difference in Selected Sugyot from Tractate Avodah Zarah*. New York and Oxford: Oxford University Press, 1997.

———. "Displaced Self-Perceptions: The Deployment of *Minim* and Romans in *B. Sanhedrin* 90b-91a." In *Religious and Ethnic Communities in Later Roman Palestine*. Edited by Hayim Lapin, 249–89. Studies and Texts in Jewish History and Culture 5. Bethesda, Md.: University Press of Maryland, 1998.

———. "*Halakhah le-Moshe mi-Sinai* in Rabbinic Sources: A Methodological Case Study." In *The Synoptic Problem in Rabbinic Literature*. Edited by Shaye J. D. Cohen, 61–117. Brown Judaic Studies 326. Providence, R.I.: Brown Judaic Studies, 2000.

Heidegger, Martin. *Being and Time*. Translated by John Macquarrie and Edward Robinson. New York: Harper, 1962.

Henshke, David. "On the Nature of Tannaitic Legal Midrash: Two Issues." *Tarbiz* 65 (1996): 417–38 [Hebrew].

———. "On the Sages' Approach to Scriptural Contradictions." *Sidra* 10 (1994): 39–55 [Hebrew].

———. "Two Contradictory Verses." *Proceedings of the Eleventh World Congress in Jewish Studies* (1990): 3.39–46 [Hebrew].

Heschel, Abraham Joshua. *Theology of Ancient Judaism.* 3 vols. Vol. 1, London and New York: Soncino, 1962; vol. 2, London and New York: Soncino, 1965; vol. 3, New York and Jerusalem: Jewish Theological Seminary, 1995 [Hebrew].

Hirshman, Marc. "Rabbinic Universalism in the Second and Third Centuries." *Harvard Theological Review* 93 (2000): 101–15.

Hirshman, Menahem (Marc). *Torah for the Entire World.* Tel Aviv: Hakibbutz Hameuchad, 1999 [Hebrew].

Hoffmann, David. *Le-Ḥeqer Midreshei ha-Tanna'im.* Translated by A. S. Rabinowitz. In *Mesilot le-Torat ha-Tanna'im.* Tel Aviv: A. S. Rabinowitz, 1928.

Hyman, Aaron. *Toldoth Tannaim Ve'Amoraim.* Jerusalem: Machon Pri Ha'Aretz, 1987.

Itzchaky, Ephraim. "Jerusalem Targum 'A' and the school of Rabbi Ishmael." *Sidra* 1 (1985): 45–57 [Hebrew].

Jacobs, Louis. "The Aristotelian Syllogism and the Qal wa-Homer." *Journal of Jewish Studies* 4 (1953): 154–57.

———. "The Talmudic Hermeneutical Rule of 'Binyan 'Abh'' and J. S. Mill's 'Method of Agreement.'" *Journal of Jewish Studies* 4 (1953): 59–64.

Jaffe, Martin. *Torah in the Mouth: Writing and Oral Tradition in Palestinian Judaism 200 BCE–400 CE.* Oxford and New York: Oxford University Press, 2001.

Joüon, Paul, and Takamitsu Muraoka. *A Grammar of Biblical Hebrew.* Rome: Editrice Pontificio Istituto Biblico, 1991.

Kahana, Menahem. *Manuscripts of the Halakhic Midrashim: An Annotated Catalogue.* Jerusalem: Yad Ben Zvi, 1995 [Hebrew].

———. "The Biblical Text Reflected in MS Vatican 32 to Sifre Numbers and Deuteronomy." In *Meḥqere Talmud I.* Edited by David Rosenthal and Yaakov Sussmann, 1–10. Jerusalem: Magnes, 1990 [Hebrew].

———. "The Critical Editions of Mekhilta De-Rabbi Ishmael in Light of the Genizah Fragments." *Tarbiz* 55 (1985): 489–524 [Hebrew].

———. "New Fragments from the Mekhilta Deuteronomy." *Tarbiz* 54 (1985): 485–551 [Hebrew].

———. *Prolegomena to a New Edition of the Sifre.* Jerusalem: The Hebrew University, 1982 [Hebrew].

———. *The Two Mekhiltot on the Amalek Portion: The Originality of the Version of the Mekhilta d'Rabbi Ishma'el with Respect to the Mekhilta of Rabbi Shim'on ben Yohay.* Jerusalem: Magnes, 1999 [Hebrew].

Katzenelenbogen, Mordechai Leyb, ed. *Torat Hayyim.* Jerusalem: Mosad Harav Kook, 1986.

Kimmelman, Reuven. "The Priestly Oligarchy and the Sages in the Talmudic Period." *Zion* 48 (1983): 135–48 [Hebrew].

Kister, Menahem. "Studies in 4Q Miqṣat Ma'aśe Ha-Torah and Related Texts: Law, Theology, Language and Calendar." *Tarbiz* 68 (1999): 317–71 [Hebrew].

Kittel, Gerhard, ed. *Theological Dictionary of the New Testament.* English edition translated and edited by Geoffrey W. Bromiley. Grand Rapids, Mich.: Eerdmans, 1967.

Kosman, Admiel. "More on Associative Thought in Midrash." *Tarbiz* 63 (1994): 443–50 [Hebrew].

Kugel, James L. *The Idea of Biblical Poetry: Parallelism and Its History.* New Haven, Conn. and London: Yale University Press, 1981.

———. *In Potiphar's House: The Interpretive Life of Biblical Texts.* San Francisco: Harper, 1990.

Kugler, Robert A. "Priesthood at Qumran." In *The Dead Sea Scrolls After Fifty Years:*

A Comprehensive Assessment. 2 vols. 2.93–116. Edited by Peter W. Flint and James C. Vanderkam. Leiden: Brill, 1999.

Lakoff, George, and Mark Johnson. *Metaphors We Live By.* New York: Free Press, 1980.

Lakoff, George. *Women, Fire, and Dangerous Things: What Categories Reveal about the Mind.* Chicago: University of Chicago Press, 1987.

Lauterbach, Jacob. "The Name of the Mekhilta." *Jewish Quarterly Review* 11 (1920): 169–98.

Levinson, Bernard. *Deuteronomy and the Hermeneutics of Legal Innovation.* Oxford and New York: Oxford University Press, 1997.

Lieberman, Saul. *Hellenism in Jewish Palestine.* New York: Jewish Theological Seminary, 1962.

———. *Texts and Studies.* New York: Ktav, 1974.

Lilla, Salvatore R. C. *Clement of Alexandria: A Study in Christian Platonism and Gnosticism.* Oxford and New York: Oxford University Press, 1971.

Mack, Hananel. "Torah Has Seventy Aspects—The Development of a Saying." In *Rabbi Mordechai Breuer Festschrift: Collected Papers in Jewish Studies.* 2 volumes. Edited by Moshe Bar-Asher, 2.449–62. Jerusalem: Akademon, 1992 [Hebrew].

Maori, Yeshayahu. "Rabbinic Midrash as Evidence for Textual Variants in the Hebrew Bible: History and Practice." In *Modern Scholarship in the Study of Torah: Contributions and Limitations.* Edited by Shalom Carmy, 101–29. New York: New York Orthodox Forum, 1991.

Margerie, Bertrand de. *Les Pères grecs et orientaux.* Volume 1 of idem, *Introduction à l'histoire de l'exégèse.* Paris: Cerf, 1980.

McNeile, A. H. *The Book of Numbers.* Cambridge: Cambridge University Press, 1911.

Melammed, Ezra Zion. "'Observe' and 'Remember' in One Utterance." Translated by Gershon Levi. In *The Ten Commandments in History and Tradition.* Edited by Ben-Zion Segal, 191–218. Jerusalem: Magnes, 1990.

Milgrom, Jacob. *The JPS Torah Commentary: Numbers.* Philadelphia and New York: Jewish Publication Society, 1990.

———. *Leviticus 1–16.* Anchor Bible 3. New York: Doubleday, 1991.

Mishor, Mordechai, "Tense System in Tannaitic Hebrew." Ph.D. diss., Hebrew University, 1983 [Hebrew].

Molland, Einar. *The Conception of the Gospel in Alexandrian Theology.* Oslo: I Kommisjon Hos Jacob Dybwad, 1938.

Moore, G. F. *Judaism in the First Centuries of the Christian Era: The Age of the Tannaim.* 3 vols. Cambridge, Mass.: Harvard University Press, 1927–30.

Mortensen, Beverly. "Pseudo Jonathan and the Economics for Priests." *Journal for the Study of Pseudepigrapha* 20 (1999): 39–71.

Nash, Ronald H. "The Notion of Mediator in Alexandrian Judaism and the Epistle to the Hebrews." *Westminster Theological Journal* 40 (1977): 89–115.

Neusner, Jacob, and Alan J. Avery-Peck, eds. *Where We Stand: Issues and Debates in Ancient Judaism.* Leiden: Brill, 1998.

Neusner, Jacob. *Uniting the Dual Torah: Sifra and the Problem of the Mishnah.* Atlanta: Scholars Press, 1988.

Normann, Friedrich. *Christos Didaskalos: Die Vorstellung von Christus als Lehrer in der christlichen Literatur des ersten und zweiten Jahrhunderts.* Münsterische Beiträge zur Theologie 32. Münster: Aschendorff, 1967.

Noth, Martin. *Numbers: A Commentary.* Translated by James D. Martin. Philadelphia: Westminster, 1968.

Ochs, Peter, and Nancy Levene, eds. *Textual Reasonings: Jewish Philosophy and Text Study at the End of the Twentieth Century.* Grand Rapids, Mich.: Eerdmans, 2002.

Olyan, Saul M. "Ben Sira's Relationship to the Priesthood." *Harvard Theological Review* 80 (1987): 261–86.

Ostrovsky, Moshe. *Ha-Middot she-Hatorah Nidreshet Bahen.* Jerusalem: Mosad Harav Kook, 1924.

Otto, Eckart. "Die Pentateuchredaktion im Deuteronomiumsrahmen." In *Das Deuteronomium und seine Querbeziehungen.* Edited by Timo Veijola, 196–222. Helsinki and Göttingen: Finnische Exegetische Gesselschaft and Vandenhoeck & Ruprecht, 1996.

Palmer, Richard E. *Hermeneutics.* Evanston, Ill.: Northwestern University Press, 1969.

Petuchowski, Marcus. *Der Tanna Rabbi Ishmael.* Frankfurt am Main: Kaufmann, 1894.

Pineles, Z. M. *Darkhah shel Torah.* Vienna: F. Forster, 1861.

Porton, Gary. "The Artificial Dispute: Ishmael and `Aqiva." In *Christianity, Judaism and Other Greco-Roman Cults: Studies for Morton Smith at Sixty.* Edited by Jacob Neusner, 18–29. Studies in Judaism of Late Antiquity 12. Leiden: Brill, 1975.

———. *The Traditions of Rabbi Ishmael.* Studies in Judaism of Late Antiquity 19. Leiden: Brill, 1976–82.

Rabinovitz, Zvi Meir. *Ginze Midrash: The Oldest Forms of Rabbinic Midrashim according to Genizah Manuscripts.* Tel Aviv: Tel Aviv University Press, 1976 [Hebrew].

Rordorf, Willy. "Christus als Logos und Nomos: Das Kerygma Petrou un seinem Verhältnis zu Justin." In *Kerygma und Logos: Festschrift für Carl Andresen zum 70. Geburtstag.* Edited by Carl Andresen and Adolf Martin Ritter, 424–34. Göttingen: Vandenhoeck & Ruprecht, 1979.

Rosén, Haiim. "The Comparative Assignment of Certain Hebrew Tense Forms." In *Proceedings of the International Conference on Semitic Studies,* 212–34. Jerusalem: Israel Academy of Sciences and Humanities, 1969.

Rosenfeld, Ben Zion. "Rabbi Yose the Galilean and the Rabbinic Leadership at the Outbreak of the Bar Kochba Revolt." *Sidra* 11 (1995): 89–111 [Hebrew].

Rosenthal, Eliezer Shimshon. "*Shnei Devarim.*" In *The Yitzhak Seligman Memorial Volume.* Edited by Y. Zakovitch and A. Rofé. 3 vols., 3.463–81. Jerusalem: Magnes, 1983 [Hebrew].

Safrai, Shmuel. "*Halakhah le-Moshe mi-Sinai*: History or Theology?" In *Meḥqere Talmud I.* Edited by David Rosenthal and Yaakov Sussmann, 11–38. Jerusalem: Magnes, 1990 [Hebrew].

Samely, Alexander. "Scripture's Implicature: The Midrashic Assumptions of Relevance and Consistency." *Journal of Semitic Studies* 37 (1992): 167–205.

———. "Between Scripture and Its Rewording: Towards a Classification of Rabbinic Exegesis." *Journal of Jewish Studies* 42 (1991): 39–67.

Sarason, Richard. "Interpreting Rabbinic Biblical Interpretation: The Problem of Midrash, Again." In *Hesed ve-Emet: Studies in Honor of Ernest S. Frerichs.* Edited by Jodi Magness and Seymour Gitin, 133–54. Brown Judaic Studies 320. Atlanta: Scholars Press, 1998.

Sarna, Nahum. *The JPS Torah Commentary: Exodus.* Philadelphia and New York: Jewish Publication Society, 1991.

Schechter, Solomon. "The Mekhilta Deuteronomy, Pericope *Re'eh.*" In *Tif'eret Yisra'el: Festschrift zu Israel Lewys siebzigsten Geburtstag.* Edited by M. Brann and J. Elbogen, 187–92. Breslau: M. & H. Marcus, 1911 [Hebrew].

Schnabel, Eckhard J. *Law and Wisdom from Ben Sira to Paul.* Wissenschaftliche Untersuchungen zum Neuen Testament 16 (2 Reihe). Tübingen: J. C. B. Mohr, 1985.

Schorsch, Rebecca. "The Hermeneutics of Heschel in *Torah min Hashamayim.*" *Judaism* 40 (1991): 301–8.

Schremer, Adiel. "'[T]he[y] Did Not Read in the Sealed Book': Qumran Halakhic Revolution and the Emergence of Torah Study in Second Temple Judaism." In *Historical Perspectives: From the Hasmoneans to Bar Kokhba in Light of the Dead Sea Scrolls.* Studies on the Texts of the Desert of Judah 37. Edited by David Goodblatt, Avital Pinnick, and Daniel R. Schwartz, 105–26. Leiden: Brill, 2000.

Schwartz, Daniel. "Hillel and Scripture: From Authority to Exegesis." In *Hillel and Jesus: Comparative Studies of Two Major Religious Leaders.* Edited by James Charlesworth and Lorn Johns, 335–62. Minneapolis: Fortress, 1997.

Schwarz, Dov. "A Unique Hebrew Logic in the Teachings of *haRav haNazir.*" *Higayon* 2 (1993): 9–28 [Hebrew].

Shemesh, Aharon. "The Term 'Mizvah Ha-Teluyah Ba-Aretz' Reexamined." *Sidra* 16 (2000): 151–77 [Hebrew].

Shemesh, Rivkah. "About 'Speaking' That Is Not 'Saying': A Survey of Verbs of Speech Production in Mishnaic Hebrew." *Jewish Quarterly Review* 93 (2002): 201–15.

Sheppard, Gerald T. "Wisdom and Torah: The Interpretation of Deuteronomy Underlying Sirach 24:23." In *Biblical and Near Eastern Studies: Essays in Honor of William Sanford LaSor.* Edited by Gary A. Tuttle, 166–76. Grand Rapids, Mich.: Eerdmans, 1978.

Simpkins, Scott. "Reeling in the Signs: Unlimited Semiosis and the Agenda of Literary Semiotics." *VS: Quaderni di Studi Semiotici* 55–56 (1990): 153–73.

Skehan, Patrick, and Alexander Di Lella. *The Wisdom of Ben Sira.* Anchor Bible 39. New York: Doubleday, 1987.

Solomon, Norman. "Extensive and Restrictive Interpretation of Terms in Rabbinic Hermeneutics." In *Jewish Law Association Studies I*, 125–39. Chico, Calif.: Scholars Press, 1985.

Stadelmann, Helge. *Ben Sira als Schriftgelehrter.* Wissenschaftliche Untersuchungen zum Neuen Testament 6 (2 Reihe). Tübingen: J. C. B. Mohr, 1980.

Stählin, Otto. *Clemens Alexandrinus Wortregister.* Griechischen christlichen Schriftsteller der ersten Jahrhunderte 39. Leipzig: J. C. Hinrichs, 1936.

Stern, David. "Literary Theory or Literary Homilies? A Response to Susan Handelman." *Prooftexts* 5 (1985): 96–103.

———. *Midrash and Theory: Ancient Jewish Exegesis and Contemporary Literary Studies.* Evanston, Ill.: Northwestern University Press, 1996.

———. "Moses-Cide: Midrash and Contemporary Literary Criticism." *Prooftexts* 4 (1984): 193–204.

———. *Parables in Midrash: Narrative and Exegesis in Rabbinic Literature.* Cambridge, Mass.: Harvard University Press, 1991.

Stone, Michael. "Three Transformations in Judaism: Scripture, History, and Redemption." *Numen* 32 (1985): 218–35.

Strack, H. L., and Günter Stemberger. *Introduction to Talmud and Midrash.* Translated by Markus Bockmuehl. Minneapolis: Fortress, 1996.

Sussmann, Yaakov. "The History of *Halakha* and the Dead Sea Scrolls: Preliminary Observations on *Miqṣat Ma'aśe Ha-Torah* (4QMMT)." *Tarbiz* 59 (1990): 11–76 [Hebrew].

Teugels, Lieve. "Midrash in the Bible or Midrash on the Bible." In *Bibel und Midrasch: Zur Bedeutung der rabbinischen Exegese für die Bibelwissenschaft.* Forschungen zum Alten Testament 22. Edited by Gerhard Bodendorfer and Matthias Millard, 43–63. Tübingen: Mohr Siebeck, 1998.

Tigay, Jeffrey. *The JPS Torah Commentary: Deuteronomy.* Philadelphia and New York: Jewish Publication Society, 1996.

———. "On the Meaning of *Ṭ(W)ṬPT**." *Journal of Biblical Literature* 101 (1982): 321–31.

Toeg, Aryeh. *Matan Torah be-Sinai.* Jerusalem: Magnes, 1977.

Torjesen, Karen Jo. "'You Are the Christ': Five Portraits of Jesus from the Early Church." In *Jesus at 2000.* Edited by Marcus J. Borg, 73–88. New York: Westview, 2000.

Towner, W. S. "Hermeneutical Systems of Hillel and the Tannaim: A Fresh Look." *Hebrew Union College Annual* 53 (1982): 101–35.

Urbach, E. E. "The Derashah as the Basis for Halakhah and the Problem of the *Soferim.*" *Tarbiz* 27 (1958): 166–82 [Hebrew].

———. *The Sages: Their Concepts and Beliefs.* Jerusalem: Magnes, 1983 [Hebrew].

Völker, Walther. *Der wahre Gnostiker nach Clemens Alexandrinus.* Texte und Untersuchungen 57. Berlin: Akademie Verlag, 1952.

Von Lipps, Hermann. "Christus als Sophia? Weisheitliche Traditionen in der urchristlichen Christologie." In *Anfänge der Christologie: Festschrift für Ferdinand Hahn zum 65 Geburtstag.* Edited by Cilliers Breytenbach and Henning Paulsen, 75–95. Göttingen: Vandenhoeck & Ruprecht, 1991.

Wacholder, Ben Zion. "The Date of the Mekilta de-Rabbi Ishmael." *Hebrew Union College Annual* 39 (1968): 117–44.

Waugh, Linda R. "Marked and Unmarked: A Choice Between Unequals in Semiotic Structure." *Semiotica* 38 (1982): 299–318.

Weinfeld, Moshe. *Deuteronomy 1–11.* Anchor Bible 5. New York: Doubleday, 1991.

———. *Deuteronomy and the Deuteronomic School.* Oxford: Oxford University Press, 1972.

Weissberg, Eliyaqim. "On *Talmud* and *Talmud Lomar.*" *Leshonenu* 39 (1975): 146–52 [Hebrew].

Wertheimer, Shlomo Aharon. *Batei Midrashot.* Jerusalem: Ketav-Yad ve-Sefer, 1988.

Wilson, Ian. *Out of the Midst of the Fire: Divine Presence in Deuteronomy.* Society for Biblical Literature Dissertation Series 151. Atlanta: Scholars Press, 1995.

Wright, Benjamin G. III. "'Fear the Lord and Honor the Priest': Ben Sira as Defender of the Jerusalem Priesthood." In *The Book of Ben Sira in Modern Research.* Edited by Pancratius C. Beentjes, 189–222. Berlin and New York: Walter de Gruyter, 1997.

Yadin, Azzan. "4QMMT, Rabbi Ishmael and the Origins of Legal Midrash." *Dead Sea Discoveries* 10 (2003): 130–49.

———. "A Greek Witness to the Semantic Shift לקח-Buy." *Hebrew Studies* 43 (2002): 31–37

———. "The Hammer on the Rock: Polysemy and the school of Rabbi Ishmael." *Jewish Studies Quarterly* 10 (2003): 1–17.

———. "*Qol* as Hypostasis in the Hebrew Bible." *Journal of Biblical Literature* 122 (2003): 601–26.

———. "*Shnei Ketuvim* and Rabbinic Intermediation." *Journal for the Study of Judaism* 33 (2002): 386–410.

Yadin, Yigael. *The Temple Scroll.* Jerusalem: Israel Exploration Society, 1983 [Hebrew].

Zerubavel, Eviatar. *The Fine Line: Making Distinctions in Everyday Life.* New York: Free Press, 1991.

Index

GENERAL INDEX

Acknowledgments

I wish to acknowledge the assistance and support of individuals and institutions at different stages of this work's (and my own) development. Since this is my first book, I must start at the beginning, thanking my teachers at the Hebrew University in the departments of Philosophy and Jewish Thought, in particular, Moshe Idel, a kind and generous teacher, and Shlomit Rimon-Keinan, who continued to read with me during the big strike. Shlomo Naeh and Aharon Shemesh, my teachers at the Hartman Institute, introduced me to rabbinic literature. Moshe Halbertal allowed me to audit his class on legal midrash, which taught me how exciting the encounter between *midreshei halakhah* and critical inquiry could be.

At the University of California, Berkeley, Hubert Dreyfus provided a steady hand in matters of hermeneutics and philosophy, as well as unbounded enthusiasm for the rabbinic material. Chana Kronfeld was a great support and a steadfast friend, and I have benefited greatly from her analysis and discussion of literary matters. David Biale, in particular, contributed on many different levels. It was David who pushed me to explore more fully the relationship between the terms *torah* and *hakatuv*, which proved to be a turning point in my understanding of the Rabbi Ishmael midrashim. Many other scholars gave freely of their time and talent: Uri Alter, in later discussions of biblical narrative; G. R. F. Ferrari, with whom I read neoplatonic commentaries; Naomi Seidman offered insightful comments and exciting ideas; David Winston shared with me his tremendous knowledge of Philo. I take this opportunity to mention the late Amos Funkenstein. Many years ago, I used to go AWOL from my army base every Wednesday evening to hear his lectures at Tel Aviv University. His absence is still felt.

I spent 1997–98 in Jerusalem, a trip I could not have made without the assistance of the Interuniversity Fellowship, which I gratefully acknowledge. While in Israel I had the opportunity to work with Menahem

Kahana, the foremost expert on the manuscript traditions of the legal midrashim, and with Haiim Rosén, a wonderful philologist, who died a few years later. I learned much from both. Special thanks also to Almog Likwornik.

In 1999, I joined the Department of Classical and Near Eastern Studies at the University of Minnesota. Eva von Dassow, Nita Krevans, Barbara Lehnhoff, Bill Malandra, Renana Schneller, Phil Sellew, George Sheets, and Judy Scullin provided friendship and companionship. Jonathan Paradise was always willing to discuss all things Hebrew; Doug Olson, who served as my senior mentor, read drafts of every article I wrote, always offering helpful comments. (Doug did heroic battle with my excessive use of adverbs—for which I am truly grateful.) Bernard Levinson provided much-appreciated scholarly guidance and, on more than one occasion, a lift home on frozen Minnesota nights. Andrea Berlin was just great—period. Thanks also to the broader group of scholars with whom I worked and from whom I learned: Riv-Ellen Prell, Leslie Morris, and Michael Wise. Emily Glodek helped with research. Fred (Trinh) Carpenter, a gourmet ghetto refugee, provided tremendous assistance with the early drafts of this work, and much laughter.

The final work on this book was done at Rutgers University, where I have been a member of the Department of Jewish Studies since 2002. The Jewish Studies faculty has made me feel very much at home. This is particularly true of my department colleagues, Jeffrey Shandler and Nancy Sinkoff, with whom I look forward to future collaboration, and Chaim Waxman of Sociology and Jewish Studies. Thanks to Simone Fisch, Arlene Goldstein, and the rest of the Bildner Center staff who keep the department running. Special thanks to Yael Zerubavel, who created Rutgers's Jewish Studies in its current form; she is a great boss and a great friend.

Earlier versions of parts of the book were published in the *Journal for the Study of Judaism*, *Dead Sea Discoveries*, and the *Jewish Studies Quarterly*. My thanks to the editors of these journals, Florentino García Martínez, Hindy Najman (guest editor), and Peter Schäfer, respectively, for their permission to use these materials.

A number of scholars read the manuscript at different stages and offered helpful comments. Thanks to Virginia Burrus, Charlotte Fonrobert, Michal Govrin, Marc Hirshman, Yishai Rosen-Zvi, Jeffrey Rubinstein, and an anonymous reader at the University of Pennsylvania Press. I have engaged in countless conversations with fellow scholars. I thank Hindy Najman, Yishai (again), Jonathan Schofer, Adi Schremer, and Benjamin Sommer. Steve Zipperstein offered helpful and much-appreciated advice on a number of occasions. Sincere apologies to anyone whose name I have omitted. Since coming to Rutgers, I have benefited from the proximity of other scholarly institutions. Richard Kalmin has made me feel welcome at the Jewish Theological Seminary; Froma Zeitlin, John Gager, and Peter Schäfer did the same at Princeton; and Clifton Black at Princeton Theological Seminary.

I have learned much with, and still more from, Sam Moyn, a years-long study partner. I have derived particular joy from the companionship, intellectual and otherwise, of Abe Socher.

My grandmother, Evelyn Meyerson, has read everything I have written over the past half-decade and has often offered helpful comments and advice. My mother-in-law, Noa Yadin, said this was the right path for me and I am beginning to think she was right. My parents, David and Honey Meir-Levi, have provided unstinting love and support (and some timely proofreading).

It was from Daniel Boyarin that I learned to see how culturally rich the interaction between text and interpreter could be, how—like Philippe de Champaigne's seventeenth-century painting of Moses presenting the Israelites a French Decalogue—each generation employs its own language in appropriating Scripture. Daniel's deep erudition, abiding curiosity, and commitment to serious thinking have profoundly influenced this book; his generosity, humor, and heart have had the same effect on its author.

This work is the culmination of a period in my life that saw dramatic personal changes: marriage to Nirit and the birth of Hallel, Daniel, and Kerem. I thank them for that for which I cannot give enough thanks.